The Franklin Report

The Insider's Guide to Home Services

- Et Veritas Liberabit Vos -

www.franklinreport.com

Chicago

Allgood Press
New York

AN ALLGOOD PRESS PUBLICATION

MANAGING EDITOR Elizabeth Franklin

PROJECT MANAGER Melissa Foster

MAIN CONTRIBUTORS
Emily Max Bodine, Liza Bulos, Jason Carpenter, Barbara Glatt,
Michelle Habash, Deborah Horn, Bridgette Miller,
Chase Palmer, Paige Sutherland, Emily Wolahan

DIRECTOR OF TECHNOLOGY Rebecca Fisher

TECHNOLOGY TEAM
Michael Brennan, Christya Izett,
Charles "Skip" Schloss, Laura Wahl

GRAPHIC DESIGNER Sarah Heffez

PROJECT EDITOR Marita Thomas

SPECIAL THANKS TO
Leah Becker, Paula Crown, Kathy Kaplan, Pete Mueller

ISBN 0-9705780-1-6

Printed in the United States of America

First Edition

1 2 3 4 5 6 7 8 9 10

For information about permission to reproduce
selections from this book, write to Permissions at
permissions@allgoodcompany.com

To purchase books directly from The Franklin Report,
call our toll free number, 1-866-990-9100

Library of Congress Cataloging-in-Publication Data
Please check directly with the Library of Congress for
The Franklin Report cataloging data, which was
not available at the time of initial publication.

This book compiles consumer opinions and comments. Ratings and comments published do not convey any recommendation or endorsement of any specific providers by The Franklin Report. The Franklin Report is not responsible for any services performed by the companies listed in this book.

While the comments compiled in this book become the property of The Franklin Report, they still represent the opinions of consumers; The Franklin Report does not take responsibility for their accuracy and completeness. It is the responsibility of the end user to evaluate the accuracy, completeness and/or usefulness of any information, opinion, advice or other content found through this book.

All information is provided "as is" with no warranties of any kind, expressed or implied. The Franklin Report disclaims all warranties including, but not limited to, warranties of title, fitness for a particular purpose, merchantability and non-infringement or proprietary or third-party rights. Names, phone numbers, addresses and other factual information were correct to the best of our knowledge upon publication of this book; nonetheless The Franklin Report makes no warranties about the accuracy, reliability, completeness, timeliness or statistical significance of the content.

Please forward any corrections to editor@franklinreport.com

Allgood Press
New York

Table of Contents

THE FRANKLIN REPORT™
The Insider's Guide to Home Services

INTRODUCTION

Welcome to the first print edition of *The Franklin Report™* (*Chicago*). The Franklin Report has created a comprehensive survey, based on client reviews, of the city's top home service providers. Some of these companies and individuals have been profiled in national magazines, and others are well-kept secrets or rising stars, but all reportedly excel in their fields.

In this guide, you will find factual information and opinions about service providers from architects and interior designers to electricians and pest control specialists. The Chicago book is our second in a national series of publications, and we invite you to use this guide and participate in our project. To submit reports on providers you have used, please visit our website at www.franklinreport.com or use the postcard or reference forms provided at the end of this book. We are committed to keeping all reviews anonymous.

Our mission is to simplify the task of choosing a home service provider by codifying the "word-of-mouth" approach. We do the homework for you with detailed fact checking, research and extensive interviews of both vendors and clients. We then give you and the community a chance to contribute to this ongoing dialogue. We hope you will join us.

Understanding The Franklin Report

The evaluations and reports on the service providers in *The Franklin Report* are based on factual information from the providers themselves, publicly available information, industry experts and thousands of in-depth customer interviews and surveys submitted through our website and by email, fax, telephone and in person. The Summary, Specific Comments and Ratings that make up each entry are based on these sources and do not reflect the opinion of The Franklin Report.

We have gone to great lengths to ensure that our information originates from verifiable and reliable sources, and conducted follow-up interviews when any questions arose. In addition, it is our policy to disregard any unsubstantiated information or surveys that differ markedly from the consensus view.

Each service category opens with a brief, informative introduction to the specific home service industry. These summaries provide facts and valuable insights on how to choose a service provider, including realistic expectations and cost considerations. Armed with this information, you'll be well prepared to speak to service providers listed in *The Franklin Report* and make your best choice. In addition, the following section, "What You Should Know About Hiring a Service Provider," covers general issues that apply to all the home service categories, from interior design to appliance repair.

Each listing contains the following components:

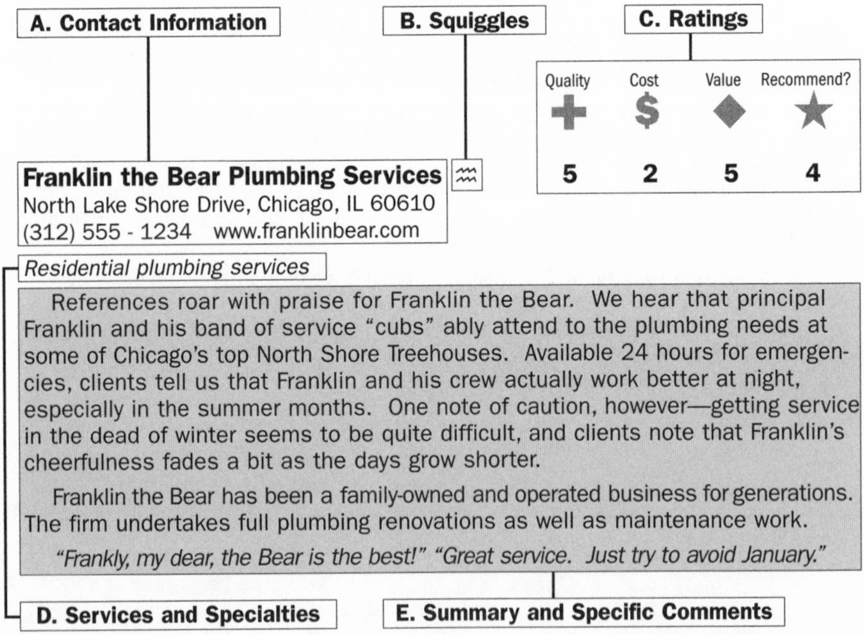
A. Contact Information
B. Squiggles
C. Ratings
Quality
Cost
Value
Recommend?
5
2
5
4
Franklin the Bear Plumbing Services
North Lake Shore Drive, Chicago, IL 60610
(312) 555 - 1234 www.franklinbear.com
Residential plumbing services
References roar with praise for Franklin the Bear. We hear that principal Franklin and his band of service "cubs" ably attend to the plumbing needs at some of Chicago's top North Shore Treehouses. Available 24 hours for emergencies, clients tell us that Franklin and his crew actually work better at night, especially in the summer months. One note of caution, however—getting service in the dead of winter seems to be quite difficult, and clients note that Franklin's cheerfulness fades a bit as the days grow shorter.
Franklin the Bear has been a family-owned and operated business for generations. The firm undertakes full plumbing renovations as well as maintenance work.
"Frankly, my dear, the Bear is the best!" "Great service. Just try to avoid January."
D. Services and Specialties
E. Summary and Specific Comments

A. Contact Information: Vendors are listed alphabetically by the first word in the name of the company (Alexander Zed Designs comes before Elizabeth Anderson Designs). Some vendors provide multiple home services and are listed in more than one category.

B. Squiggles: The graphic of two squiggly lines indicates a significant number of mixed reviews about a provider.

C. Ratings: Providers are rated in four columns—Quality, Cost, Value and Recommend?—on a 5-point scale, with 5 as the highest rating. Keep in mind that because we only include the firms that received the most positive reviews, a 3 in Quality is still an excellent score: the ratings differentiate the top providers.

Note also that while a high rating is generally better, a higher Cost rating means that vendor is more expensive. Reading the introductory section of each home service category will help you understand the specific pricing structure in each profession. Value is determined by the relationship between Quality and Cost. Recommend? indicates whether the customer would use the provider again or recommend the firm to a friend.

Quality
- 5 – Highest Imaginable
- 4 – Outstanding
- 3 – High End
- 2 – Good
- 1 – Adequate

Cost
- 5 – Over the Top
- 4 – Very Expensive
- 3 – High End
- 2 – Moderate
- 1 – Inexpensive

Value
- 5 – Worth Every Penny
- 4 – Good Value
- 3 – Fair Deal
- 2 – Not Great
- 1 – Poor Value

Recommend?
- 5 – My First and Only Choice
- 4 – On My Short List, Would Recommend to a Friend
- 3 – Very Satisfied, Might Hire Again
- 2 – Have Reservations
- 1 – Not Pleased, Would Not Hire Again

Open folders indicate that we did not feel we had enough information to issue a rating. If you have worked with any of the firms with open folders, please fill out reference reports on these providers on our website or on the forms provided in this book.

D. Services and Specialties: This describes the main services the company provides.

E. Summary and Specific Comments: The Franklin Report editors distilled information from all sources to write a summary profiling each service provider that reflects the consensus view. In select categories, where appropriate, we use several abbreviations to indicate certain special recognitions the firm has received:

KB 2000: featured in a Kips Bay Showhouse in that year
AD 100, 2000: listed in *Architectural Digest*'s top 100 in that year
HB Top Designers, 2000: listed in *House Beautiful*'s annual compendium
ID Hall of Fame, 1999: Interior Design's Hall of Fame Award

A number of schools, well-known firms and associations are mentioned throughout this section, with the indicated abbreviations: American Society of Interior Designers ("ASID"), Foundation for Interior Design Education Research ("FIDER"), Harrington Institute of Interior Design ("Harrington"), Illinois Institute of Technology ("IIT"), International Furnishing and Design Association ("IFDA"), International Interior Design Association ("IIDA"), The Merchandise Mart ("the Mart"), Parsons School of Design ("Parsons"), Rhode Island School of Design ("RISD") and Skidmore, Owings & Merrill LLP ("SOM").

In Specific Comments, clients describe the process of working with the service provider—and the end results—in their own words.

What You Should Know About Hiring a Service Provider

Hiring a service provider to work in your home is not a task to be undertaken lightly. In addition to issues of quality, cost and scheduling, keep in mind that these professionals and their team may become an integral, albeit temporary, part of your life. The following nine-step process will help you make the best choice.

1. Determine Your Needs

First, you need to think about the nature and scope of your project. The service firm that may be perfect for a full-scale renovation may be unresponsive and unnecessarily costly for repair or maintenance work. Are you looking for simple built-in bookcases or an integrated, elaborate library? Do you want an heirloom-quality sofa or a playroom sleeper? Next, weigh your priorities. Is it crucial that the project is done by the holidays? Or is it more important to get a particular style? Is budget a driving factor? Evaluating your requirements will make it easier to decide upon a vendor, because you will know where you can compromise and where you can't. Your requirements may evolve as you learn more about what is in the marketplace, but it's a good idea not to stray too far from your original intent.

2. Identify Possible Candidates

To find the best professional for the job, start by asking for recommendations from friends, colleagues, neighbors, your building superintendent or related service providers you trust. *The Franklin Report* will help you evaluate those candidates and identify others by offering insight into their competitive strengths and weaknesses.

3. Check Public Records

To make most efficient use of your time, first do quick background checks of the candidates to eliminate those with questionable records. For all categories you should check with the Better Business Bureau (312-832-0500 or www.bbb.org) to see if any complaints have been filed against the vendor. In addition, for each specific category, licenses may be required or professional associations may offer additional information (check *The Franklin Report* overviews for each category for specifics). If you are investigating *Franklin Report* service providers, you will be informed of past client satisfaction in this book and on our regularly updated website, www.franklinreport.com.

4. Interview Service Providers

While it may not be necessary to conduct a face-to-face interview with a provider who is going to do a one- or two-day project, phone interviews are recommended before they show up. For larger projects, it is wise to meet with the potential providers to learn all you possibly can about process, expectations, quality and price and to judge your potential compatibility. Don't be shy. Personality and style "fit" are extremely important for longer-term projects that will involve design decisions or complicated ongoing dialogues, but are less critical when seeking a professional steam cleaner.

The following are general interview questions that will help you make the most of discussions with potential vendors. More specific questions that apply to each specific profession may be found in the category overviews.

- How long have you been in the business?
- What are your areas of expertise?
- Have you recently completed similar jobs?
  Can I speak with these clients for a reference?
- Who will be my primary day-to-day contact? What percentage of time will they spend on site?
- What sections of the job will be done by your employees and what sections will be subcontracted?
- Are you licensed, registered and insured? What about the subcontractors? (It is crucial to verify that all workers are covered by worker's compensation; otherwise, you may be liable for any worksite injuries.)
- How long will the project take? Any concerns or qualifications?
- Do you offer warranties? Do you provide written contracts? Will the contract have an arbitration clause?
- Are you a member of any national or local professional associations? (While not essential, this can show dedication to the profession.)
- How will we communicate? Will we have regular meetings?

Other things to consider:

- How long it took them to return your initial phone call.
- Whether or not the firm's principal attended the meeting.
- How receptive they were to your ideas.
- How thoughtful and flexible they were in pricing, budgeting and scheduling.
- Personality/fit and how interested they were in your project.

Licenses, registrations, insurance, bonding and permits are key parts of the equation, but are category dependent (again, check the overviews). Any suspicious activity on this front, like a contractor who asks you to get the permits yourself or can't seem to find his proof of insurance, is a red-flag event. Similarly, anyone who refuses to give you references, asks for all the money up front or who tells you what a great deal you can have if you sign today should be eliminated from your list.

5. Speak With Past Clients

In discussions with references provided by the potential candidates, be aware that these clients should be their greatest fans. For a more balanced view, review their Franklin Report write-up.

Suggested questions for client references:

- What was the scope of your project?
- Were you happy with both the process and quality of the result?
- How involved were you in the process?
- Were they responsive to your concerns?
- Were work crews timely and courteous, and did they leave the worksite clean?
- Did they stick to schedule and budget?
- Were they worth the cost?
- Were they communicative and professional about any issues or changes?
- Were they available for any necessary post-mortem follow up?
- **Would you use this firm again?**

6. ASK ABOUT COST

Each service category works differently in terms of pricing structure. Projects may be priced on a flat fee, estimated or actual time, a percentage over materials, a percent of the total job (if other contractors are involved) and a host of other variations. What appears difficult and costly to some providers may be routine for others. Many providers will be responsive to working with you on price (and it is always worth a try). However, under strong economic conditions, the service provider may only be pushed so far; they may actually be interviewing *you* during your call. For more specific details and recommendations, see the pricing discussions in each of *The Franklin Report* category overviews.

7. EVALUATE THE BIDS AND MAKE YOUR CHOICE

Narrow your list and ask for at least three bids for substantial jobs. Describe your project clearly and thoroughly, including any timing constraints. Once received, do your best to compare the bids on an "apples to apples" basis. Ask each provider to break down their bids so you can see whether some include more services or higher quality specifications (processes and materials) than others. Don't be afraid to keep asking questions until you fully understand the differences between the bids.

Cheaper is not always better, as a bid might be lower because the workers are less skilled or the materials are of lower quality. Compare samples where possible. If speed is important, you may be willing to pay more for the person who can start next week instead of six months from now and who checked out to be more reliable on timing.

8. NEGOTIATE A CONTRACT

Just as with pricing, you will need to understand what the acceptable business practices are within each industry and negotiate a contract, if appropriate. Most service professionals have standard contracts that they prefer.

SMALLER JOBS: For one-time-only situations that you will be supervising (rug cleaning, window washing, etc.) a full-blown contract approved by your lawyer hardly seems necessary. Just ask for a written estimate after you thoroughly discuss the job with the provider.

LARGER JOBS: For larger projects, like a general contracting job that will cost multiple thousands of dollars and will involve many people and lots of materials, a detailed contract is essential. Don't be afraid to ask about anything that is unclear to you. This is all part of the communication process, and you don't want to be working with a service provider who intimidates you into accepting anything that you don't understand.

The contract should clearly spell out, in plain English, the following:

- ✧ The scope of the project in specific, sequential stages.
- ✧ A detailed list of all required building materials, including quality specifications. Assume that they are just meeting minimum code standards unless otherwise specified.
- ✧ Timing expectations. Don't be too harsh here, since much may be contingent upon building conditions or supply deliveries. Some, but very few providers are open to a bonus/penalty system in meeting specific timing deadlines.
- ✧ A payment schedule, which is usually triggered by completion of the stages above, offering incentives to move on to the next stage.
- ✧ Permit issues and responsibilities if applicable.
- ✧ A description of how any design changes ("change orders") will be processed and priced.
- ✧ The specific tasks and accountability of the service provider, noting exactly what they will and will not do.

Once the contract is written, you may want an attorney to review and identify any potential issues. While most homeowners do not take this step, it could save you from costly and frustrating complications further down the road.

9. OVERSEEING THE JOB

No matter how professional your team of service providers may be, they need your input and direction to satisfactorily complete the job. Be specific as to who will be the overall project manager (responsible for the interaction between service providers and, ultimately, the dreaded punch lists). This task will fall to you unless you assign it away.

On larger projects, generally the architect (usually within their standard fee contract) or the interior designer (usually for an additional fee) will fulfill the project manager role. You should be available and encourage periodic meetings to ensure that there are no surprises in design, timing or budget. Whether or not you are project manager, stay on top of the process (but do not get in the way), as this will be your home long after the dust settles and these professionals move on to the next project.

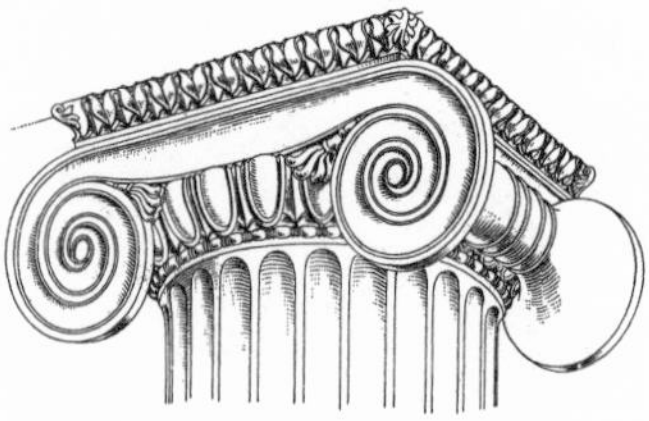

The Franklin Report website—a virtual companion to this reference book—is updated regularly with new vendor commentaries and other helpful material about home repairs, maintenance and renovations. With expert, accessible information guiding you through the process and dedicated professionals on the job, every stage of your home project will move smoothly towards completion. Knowledge is power, regardless of whether you're engaging a plumber for a contained upgrade or a general contractor for a complete renovation. *The Franklin Report* is your companion in this process, with current, insightful home service information.

Hiring an Air Conditioning & Heating Service Provider

Known in the trades as Heating, Ventilation and Air Conditioning (HVAC), this home service industry keeps your climate controlled and family comfortable. It is also often responsible for custom sheet metal work, such as kitchen hoods and copper window dressing. An HVAC unit means central air, central heat, central convenience. To keep your home fit for human habitation throughout Chicago's stifling summers and icy winters, an HVAC system—expertly installed and maintained—will keep you smiling smugly at whatever Mother Nature throws your way.

An HVAC Primer

All air conditioning (A/C) systems operate under the same principle: a fan sucks in your home's warm air across coils that contain a refrigerant (freon), and the cooled air is then blown into the room. Central A/C operates with two principle components: a condensing unit and evaporator coil. The condenser pressurizes the refrigerant to cool it. Heat is released in the process, so the condenser must be located outside of the home or with an opening to the outside. The cooled refrigerant is then pushed to the evaporator coil, where it cools and dehumidifies the warm air collected from your plenum (the dead space above the ceiling). Finally, this cool air is directed via ductwork back into the rooms. (And you thought an air conditioner just contained a fan and a block of dry ice!)

Heating is supplied in one of three ways: forced air, hydronic or steam. In the forced air system, air is heated by your furnace or a heat pump and a blower pushes air through the heat source, then into your home. While a furnace heats the air through burning natural gas, oil, wood or coal, a heat pump functions like an air conditioner with the refrigerant cycle reversed. Chill is captured by the condenser and warm air is produced with the evaporator coil. The air is further heated through electric heating coils at the blower. In the hydronic system, water is heated via gas or electricity in a boiler and distributed to radiators. The steam system works similarly to a boiler, with steam, rather than water, distributed directly to radiators.

How Much Do You Need

Believe it or not, it's not the air that makes your room a delightful temperature. It's math. By understanding the following, your eyes will not glaze over when your mechanical man starts spouting acronyms such as BTU, EER and CFM. All of this has to do with the efficiency of your system. Heating is measured in BTUs (British Thermal Units). Cooling is measured in tons. The capacities of furnaces, boilers, heat pumps and air conditioners are determined by how many tons or BTUs they carry. The standard for an 800-square-foot area is 30,000 BTUs of heat and one ton of air conditioning. Obviously, the bigger the space, the more capacity you will need.

The EER, or Energy Efficiency Rating, measures the relationship between space and the energy needed to properly condition its climate. Equipment with higher EERs will properly condition more space with less capacity. The higher the EER, the higher the quality (and cost) of the equipment and the lower your energy bills. Ducts are a significant aspect of HVAC system efficiency. Obviously, you want to have as direct a path as possible between the heat/cool source and the space it's to condition. If the ductwork is too small; the distance from the source too far, or if there are too many bends and jogs, the airflow will suffer. Designers specify the amount of CFMs (the measurement of the airflow through your ductwork) necessary to properly condition a space. If this isn't met, the efficiency of your system is compromised because your equipment has to work harder than it should for a given space.

On Cost and Contracts

As in any other trade, you'll be charged for labor, materials and a 10- to 20-percent mark-up for overhead and profit, plus tax. Demand a flat fee for equipment and installation of new systems. Make sure the estimate specifies any other associated work—electrical, plumbing, plaster—that may be necessary for the installation if you expect someone to do it. All makes and models of equipment should be spelled out on the bid proposal. It's okay to sign off on the bid proposal to execute the work, but it should refer to drawings (best generated by an engineer as opposed to a sketch on the back of a napkin) and they should be attached. Clean-up, transportation, commencement and completion dates, payment schedule, change order procedure, licensing and insurance information should all be included in the contract, if not on the bid proposal. The technician should be responsible for the cost and time of obtaining permits. If your HVAC professional is fishing for a service agreement to cover the gaps in the warranty, see if you can get him to discount his price if you accept.

On Service

There are a lot of variables in HVAC, so warranties count. One year for parts and labor is typical. You should get your mechanical contractor to do a check-up once a year. Service calls often include a travel or truck fee just to show up for the diagnostic, and hourly rates in the Chicagoland area run around $85 an hour, union or not. Treat him like a dentist—you wouldn't neglect to brush your teeth between check-ups, and you shouldn't neglect your filters between visits from the HVAC guy. Change them once a month in the summer; dirty filters will degrade the system's efficiency. It's easy to do; just get a lesson before the installer leaves. Also know where the gauges and valves are and how to read them. And try to maintain a good relationship with your mechanical man after the job. You don't want to have to pay someone else to become familiar with your custom-designed, intricate home system.

What Should I Look for in an HVAC Professional?

Your HVAC service provider is essentially putting the lungs into your house, and you don't pick your surgeon based on a nudge and a wink. Talk to general contractors and ask who they recommend. Know that HVAC invariably involves plumbing and electrical work. You want to know whether the person you hire can handle the work necessary to make the system function, or if you'll have to bring in other trades to assist. If there is going to be work in and around your existing space, find out how clean and careful he is.

Choose the service provider and system best suited to your project. For renovations in tight spaces like apartments, where ceiling height is precious, high-pressure air conditioning systems that utilize small-diameter ducts permit retrofitting with little disruption to the surrounding structure. When renovating around steam, many HVAC professionals will recommend switching to hydronic. Your research into a good HVAC person will be more effective if you learn a few things about how these systems work. There's more to HVAC than thermostats. Learn the language so that when the installer asks if he can cut ducts in your apartment, you won't immediately report him to People for the Ethical Treatment of Animals.

CREDENTIALS, PLEASE

HVAC is a complicated field. With all the inter-trade coordination, mechanical speak and math involved, your mechanical contractor's civility and credibility should be backed up with the required licensing and insurance. This includes coverage for general liability, worker's comp and property damage. Licensing in Illinois extends only to the city and county business license required to pull permits there. Manufacturers and distributors—a great source of recommendations—will allow only licensed mechanical contractors to purchase certain HVAC equipment.

HVAC Excellence, headquartered in Mount Prospect, IL, is a national organization that certifies HVAC engineers. It can provide you with a list of qualified HVAC engineers in your area. Call (800) 394-5268 or visit www.hvacexcellence.org.

QUESTIONS YOUR HVAC CONTRACTOR WILL ASK

- Where is the interior unit going to go? Large utility room? A closet?
- Do you have permission to place a condenser outside? From the co-op? The city?
- Is there enough ceiling height to add ductwork?
- Where do you want the controls? How many zones?

Air Conditioning & Heating

	Quality	Cost	Value	Recommend?
Beck's Heating & AC Co.	3	3	3	3

111 Washington Avenue, Highwood, IL 60040
(847) 433 - 5242 www.amstd-dealer.com/becks

Heating, ventilation and air conditioning service and repair

Regardless of the type of HVAC system in a residence, this small, family-owned business with eight employees knows how to create comfort. It has been caring for residential heating, ventilation and air conditioning systems on the North Shore for the past decade. The staff has experience with radiators, boilers, steam, forced air and Unico high-pressure air conditioning systems, and will also handle maintenance, such as duct cleaning and chimney sweeping. It offers 24-hour emergency service, and we are told that, no matter how busy, principal Dominick Ugolini returns customer calls the day they are placed.

	Quality	Cost	Value	Recommend?
Bishop Heating	4	3.5	4	4.5

1495 Old Deerfield Road, Highland Park, IL 60035
(847) 541 - 6408

Heating, ventilation and air conditioning sales, installation and service

Under the stewardship of principal Bill Clark and his father before him, Bishop's dedication to getting the job done right has made it a top choice among demanding architects. A specialist in custom replacements, retrofits and additions to heating, ventilation and air conditioning systems in the grandest of North Shore homes since World War II, Bishop Heating has experience with all makes and models of HVAC equipment. It also handles commercial installations and provides complete maintenance service for homes and businesses. Estimates are free and there is always a voice at the other end of its 24-hour emergency service line.

	Quality	Cost	Value	Recommend?
Blue Dot Services Co. - Northbrook	3.5	3.5	3.5	3.5

550 Anthony Trail, Northbrook, IL 60062
(847) 729 - 7889 www.bluedot.com

Heating, ventilation and air conditioning sales, installation and service

Merger mania brings this Northbrook HVAC service provider (formerly AA Service) under the banner of a growing regional chain. It is one of three in the Chicago area to be recently franchised by Blue Dot, which has assembled a chain of top tier local HVAC contractors in 27 states. The Northbrook and Skokie (see review below) companies took the Blue Dot family name, while Wiegold & Sons & Grandsons in Lake Forest (see review) keeps its original moniker for now. As Blue Dot franchisees, all three retain their original, local management and staff while benefiting from the national company's training, performance standards and resources, which includes a large custom sheet-metal shop. All Blue Dot mechanics are uniformed and bonded, receive training in HVAC technology and customer relations, and are "trust-certified," which is a Blue Dot program of reference checks and drug testing. Blue Dot specializes in residential and light commercial service and replacement throughout greater Chicago, including the Gold Coast and North Shore. An estimate is provided before work begins. Maintenance programs and financing options are available, and 24-hour emergency service operates seven days a week.

Quality	Cost	Value	Recommend?
	+	$	◆	★

Blue Dot Services Co. - Skokie 3.5 3.5 3.5 3.5
8245 North Kimball, Skokie, IL 60062
(847) 674 - 8252
Heating, ventilation and air conditioning sales, installation and service

Formerly E. Shavitz & Sons Heating, a long-time Chicago-area HVAC service provider, this firm recently joined the Blue Dot network of HVAC companies in 27 states. The company retains its existing management and staff, which is now supplemented by Blue Dot training, performance standards and resources (see review of Blue Dot - Northbrook).

Bob Amaro 3 2.5 3 3
Brookfield, IL
(312) 571 - 8488
Heating, ventilation and air conditioning installation and service

On the strength of referrals alone, Bob Amaro emerged as a one-man HVAC problem-solver for residents of the North Shore and other Chicago neighborhoods. Although he specializes in small-scale jobs, he'll tackle everything from the removal of an outdated furnace to the repair or replacement of existing heating and cooling systems. For large, complex jobs, he enlists qualified subcontractors who work under his direction. He performs all diagnostics and provides a per-job, rather than a per-hour, estimate, which clients consider a plus. Amaro can be reached by page and generally returns calls within 24 hours.

Carefree Comfort Heating 4.5 3 4.5 5
2068 First Street, Suite 102, Highland Park, IL 60035
(847) 433 - 7377 www.carefreecomfort.com
High-end residential heating, ventilation and air conditioning design and service

A seasoned company, Carefree Comfort is a reflection of its owner, Joe Sciarrone, who founded it in 1984 at the age of 21. Customers give the 12-person staff high marks for knowledge, neatness, personal service and congeniality. The company provides custom design and construction of high-end heating, ventilation and air conditioning systems and will also add to or replace existing systems for residential and light commercial clients. It also handles seasonal maintenance contracts and boasts a client roster of 4,000 active accounts. Though small, it is capable of handling complex, five- and six-furnace residences. While Sciarrone stresses the value of high-end equipment, such as variable-speed furnaces and "Puron" air conditioners, and recommends the best, his customers, who include respected contractors and architects, report that Carefree's design solutions can shave dollars from energy costs. Carefree is always accessible through its 24-hour emergency answering service.

"So good we use them for our business, too." "Been contracting for 18 years, and I've used them exclusively since day one." "Explained the problem in a way that made sense. Then came up with a less costly solution." "Very conscious of surroundings."

Carlson Heating Cooling & Electric Company 🗁 🗁 🗁 🗁
3340 West Lake Avenue, Glenview, IL 60025
(847) 729 - 0123
Heating, ventilation and air conditioning installation, repair and service

Convenient Heating & Cooling Company 🗁 🗁 🗁 🗁
546 Zenith Drive, Glenview, IL 60025
(847) 292 - 2665
Residential heating, ventilation and air conditioning replacement and service

Custom Environment

Waukegan, IL
(847) 623 - 9899

Heating, ventilation and air conditioning installation and service

Deljo Heating & Cooling

Quality	Cost	Value	Recommend?
4	3	4	4.5

2700 North Campbell Avenue, Chicago, IL 60647
(773) 248 - 1144 www.deljoheating.com

Heating, ventilation and air conditioning installation and service

Since 1922, Deljo has kept the finest Gold Coast and North Shore homes comfy, beginning with coal delivery by horse-drawn carriage. Today, under the management of brothers Bill and Bob Clemment, more than 80 percent of Deljo's business is directed to trade-only, design/build clients for residential and commercial rehab and new construction, with the remaining portion devoted to serving residential customers at the upper end of the market. It offers design, installation, repair, replacement and maintenance service by a trained staff, experienced in systems ranging from in-floor radiant heat to natural gas furnaces and Unico high-pressure air conditioning systems. Its costs are said to be competitive with other high-end service providers in this field, and it has gained a strong reputation for quality among its demanding professional clientele. Estimates are free and 24-hour emergency service is available.

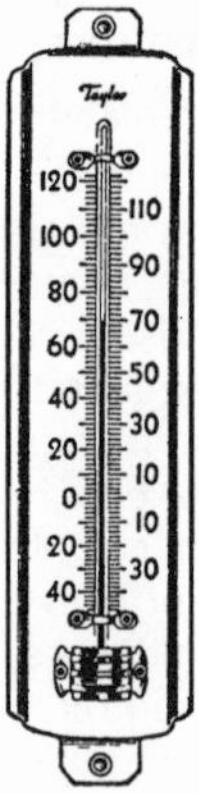

Effective Air Inc.

1238 Waukegan Road, Glenview, IL 60025
(847) 729 - 1820

Residential heating, ventilation and air conditioning installation, replacement and service

Small but, as the name claims, effective, according to references, this company operates along the North Shore to Rogers Park.

Ireland Heating & A/C Co.

28290 North Ballard Drive, Lake Forest, IL 60045
(847) 362 - 4548

Heating, ventilation and air conditioning installation, repair and service

John J. Cahill III, Inc.
1515 Church Street, Evanston, IL 60201
(847) 491 - 1890 www.cahillinc.com

Residential plumbing, HVAC, kitchen and bath remodeling

See John J. Cahill III, Inc.'s full report under the heading Plumbers

Midwesco Services, Inc. — 4 | 4 | 4 | 4
6153 West Mulford Street, Niles, IL 60714
(847) 966 - 2150 www.midwesco-services.com

High-end heating, ventilation and air conditioning design, installation and repair

The best addresses in Chicago take comfort from Midwesco. As the installer and HVAC engineer of record for top architects and contractors, this company has made its way to many of the North Shore's most prestigious addresses and developed such specialties as 24-hour remote monitoring of temperature controls while homeowners are out of town, and a dispatch service to correct problems as they occur. Its expertise in home automation also extends to the integration of temperature control, lighting and stereo sound equipment with built-in energy conservation features. Midwesco has 70 years of experience in designing and installing custom heating, ventilation and air conditioning systems for new construction as well as the renovation of existing systems. Its reach extends to Chicago's northern suburbs, and its emergency service line is staffed 24 hours a day by its own employees.

Northstar Heating and Air — 4.5 | 3.5 | 4.5 | 4.5
2200 Greenbay Road, Evanston, IL 60201-3073
(847) 869 - 9600

High-end heating, ventilation and air conditioning installation and rehab

Treasured interiors are in good hands with Northstar. The staff of 30, under the direction of Tom Tausche, wins praise for its sensitivity to interior architecture when updating the heating, ventilation and air conditioning systems in older, North Shore residences. The installation of cooling systems, forced air furnaces, in-floor radiant heat and other new HVAC equipment in these vintage townhouses and high-rise co-ops, with minimum disturbance, has been Northstar's specialty for 30 years. It has its own custom sheet metal shop and offers full-coverage maintenance contracts. Although it gained its reputation along the North Shore, Northstar operates throughout metropolitan Chicago. References, which include some of the city's most respected architects, say Northstar is the responsible, knowledgeable choice for quality HVAC rehab and renovation.

Pasquesi Plumbing
3218 Skokie Valley Road, Highland Park, IL 60035
(847) 433 - 3426

High-end plumbing, heating, ventilation and air conditioning installation and service

See Pasquesi Plumbing's full report under the heading Plumbers

Ravinia Plumbing & Heating
595 Roger Williams Avenue, Highland Park, IL 60035
(847) 432 - 5561

High-end remodeling, plumbing and HVAC repair, installation and service

See Ravinia Plumbing & Heating's full report under the heading Plumbers

RH Witt Heating — 4.5 | 3 | 4.5 | 4.5
2049 Johns Drive, Glenview, IL 60025
(847) 724 - 1690 www.rhwitt.com

High-end heating, ventilation and air conditioning installation and service

This second-generation family business has been installing and servicing heating and cooling systems for the upper end of the residential market since 1966. Now run by brothers Rick and Mike Witt, it has a staff of 36, experienced in "quiet" geothermal air conditioning, forced air furnaces, radiant and hydronic heat and other up-to-date HVAC equipment and technology. This crew also provides metal work, such as copper chimney dressing, window trim and trellis caps. Its pride in prompt, efficient service is confirmed by builders and clients alike who say only the witt-less don't know this company is among the best out there. The majority of RH Witt's work is concentrated on the North Shore, and 24-hour emergency service is limited to existing customers. Pricing, we hear, is based on national standards.

Superior Sheet Metal and Heating **4.5 4 4.5 5**
28814 North Nagel Court, Lake Bluff, IL 60044
(847) 234 - 4020

High-end heating, ventilation and air conditioning design, installation and service

Superior is just that, say its loyal customers. This company takes custom work seriously, often introducing commercial solutions to the engineering of residential HVAC systems, indoor pool dehumidification, and multifaceted applications of architectural sheet metal work, including inlaid gutters, chimney liners, ornamental conductor heads and radiused gutters. It will even repair and maintain a slate roof. Superior was established as a custom exterior sheet metal shop by the current owner's father and mother in 1969. Jeff Soprani and his wife, Karen, maintain the tradition of hands-on, personal service and high quality standards that now extend to designing, installing and servicing all types of heating and cooling systems, primarily along the North Shore and in other choice downtown neighborhoods. All first contacts and 24-hour emergency calls are handled by a Soprani. The staff's talent and the owners' attention to service have won Superior high praise among its clients and the most sought after Chicago-area contractors and architects.

"Johnny-on-the-spot." "Absolutely first rate!" "They truly spoil me!" "I wouldn't use anyone else." "I don't think you can do better." "We wish all service companies could be half as professional and capable." "Besides doing exceptional work, the people at this company are reliable, pleasant and very immaculate."

The V.J. Killian Company
939 Greenbay Road, Winnetka, IL 60093
(847) 446 - 0908

Residential plumbing and HVAC remodeling and repair

See The V.J. Killian Company's full report under the heading Plumbers

Unique Indoor Comfort - Elmhurst **4 3.5 4 4.5**
551 South Route 83, Elmhurst, IL 60126
(630) 833 - 4400
Heating, ventilation and air conditioning renovation and service

Old architecture gets respect from Unique's work crews. The four Chicago-area franchises (see reviews) of this national company are specialists in the installation of air conditioning systems in existing, often older, homes. The specialty arises from the national company's pioneering development of the Unico high-pressure air conditioning system that utilizes small-diameter ducts that permit retrofitting with little disruption to the surrounding structure. That system is now manufactured separately and its use is widespread. In addition to its historic experience with Unico systems, the Chicago Unique Indoor Comfort companies also provide a variety of heating as well as cooling options to residents of the North Shore and western suburbs. References praise the company's neat, courteous and efficient staff. Unique has a 24-hour emergency answering service.

"The whole process took five days to complete in our 1873 house." "Friendly, polite, cleaned-up. What more could we ask for?" "One of the best jobs ever done in my house." "Every claim made was followed through!"

Unique Indoor Comfort - Libertyville
624 North Second Street, Libertyville, IL 60048
(847) 362 - 1910

Heating, ventilation and air conditioning renovation and service

See review above

Unique Indoor Comfort - Northbrook
667 Academy Drive, Northbrook, IL 60062
(847) 559 - 9777

Heating, ventilation and air conditioning renovation and service

See review above

Unique Indoor Comfort - Palatine
653 South Vermont Street, Palatine, IL 60067
(847) 359 - 5100

Heating, ventilation and air conditioning renovation and service

See review above

Wiegold & Sons & Grandsons **3.5 3.5 3.5 4**
100 North Skokie Highway, Lake Bluff, IL 60044
(847) 234 - 2660 www.bluedotservices.com

Heating, ventilation and air conditioning installation, repair and service

Long-time clients of Wiegold, a family firm established in 1940, will be happy to know that the company's recent alliance with Blue Dot Services Co., a national franchise, will not alter the existing management and staff. Why would it? With what we hear is the "best boiler boy" in the business, Wiegold services the North Shore's oldest stokers and boilers. The Blue Dot alliance will, however, give Wiegold expanded support, such as ongoing training and additional resources (see review of Blue Dot Services). In addition to repairing and updating existing systems, Wiegold installs HVAC systems in new construction and renovations. Its expertise ranges from high-pressure air conditioning to steam and hot water heating to custom sheet metal work. The shop is said to be clean and orderly. It is the Weigold policy to respond to 24-hour emergency service calls within 20 minutes.

"A lot of contractors disappoint, Wiegold is different." "Just fine all around." "Matters a lot whether people are agreeable to work with. Wiegold's are."

Hiring an Architect

Creating a home will be one of the largest investments in your lifetime. An excellent architect may bring your dreams to life and furthermore, may avoid potential construction nightmares. He's your ally in ensuring that the construction process delivers exactly what you have envisioned and protects your investment. Famous architects have made history through their brilliant work as well as their eccentricities, such as Frank Lloyd Wright's demands to control every inch of design in the home, right down to the table settings, and Stanford White's headline-making personal life (and death). But don't get your heart set on achieving fame through an architect who brings celebrity to your address. The best matches are usually with talented, hard-working and experienced professionals who commit themselves to your project. The work of architects lives on indefinitely making their mark on people's lives and on the community itself.

The architect is your guide through the entire building process—from refining your vision and defining your needs to documenting them in plans and specifications; from suggesting contractors to counseling on budget; from monitoring progress and quality of construction to certifying payment to the contractor; and from answering questions to settling disputes. He is the point man working on behalf of your interests. The clarity and thoroughness of the drawings and the extensiveness of the involvement in the process are keystones to a successful job. If the architect misses a beam, the whole job could come crashing down—or more likely, you'll have to pay a little extra to get that beam retrofitted.

Where Do I Start?

Choosing an architect isn't easy. Each professional has his or her own design philosophy, style and way of doing business. Talk to friends, realtors and contractors. You should interview three to five firms to get a sense of what you're looking for. Make sure to meet with the individual who will be designing the project, not just a principal selling you the firm. If you and the architect don't click, move on. The most important thing to look for is stylistic understanding and good chemistry. You're going to be working closely for a long time, bouncing ideas and problems off each other with a lot at stake. You want somebody with whom you'll enjoy the ride. Not surprisingly, architects consider the same thing when choosing which clients to take on.

Get a sense of the quality of the architect's past designs. Ask to see not only the portfolio, but the blueprints of those past jobs. The architect's clarity and thoroughness will be evident in the detailing and the notes. Not all blueprints are created equal, and the same goes for the people who draft them. Another important step is to get feedback from past clients. You want to know if a prospect was accessible and collaborative, if he was expedient in turning drawings around, responsive to questions and revisions and if he visited the site and met with the contractor regularly.

If an architect makes his living doing leading edge homes and you have a historic brownstone, it's clear that this collaboration isn't going to work. Go with somebody who is well versed in the style you're looking for. Also keep in mind that the specific task to be designed is as important as the style. An architect who has never designed a rooftop addition in Chicago is bound to be ignorant of certain details and codes that will inevitably become major factors in the job. This may also be the case if you are renovating an old house on the North Shore and are subject to historic preservation restrictions. Your architect should relate to your personality and preferences, vision, logistical constraints and lifestyle.

SPECIFIC CONSIDERATIONS

It's very important you have a realistic sense of constraints and possibilities regarding budget and code. It's the architect's job to define these things for you. Identify how familiar a candidate is with the local codes, and whether he is sensitive to cost. He needs to be able to help you navigate the permitting and inspection process and massage the budget by substituting materials and methods or modifying the design. Also, be vocal about any special stylistic interests and timing specifications you have from the outset. If using a particular contractor is important to you, or building an environmentally considerate and efficient home, speak up. Remember, certain architects only dabble their toes in certain ponds.

ON COST AND CONTRACTS

If you think you've found a partner, it's time to start thinking about the fee. There are no set fees for architectural services. The scale of the job, the level of quality and detail, the pace and length of schedule and the amount of other clients the firm has already taken on all factor into how an architect calculates his service. An architect will typically charge an hourly rate or percentage of construction, but many do a combination of the two. For example, many architects may charge hourly through skematics stage, and then charge a percentage of construction cost for the remainder of the project. Alternatively, there may be a fixed fee based on hourly or an hourly rate not to exceed a certain percent for construction. Regardless of the method of calculation, fees will typically range from 12 to 15 percent of the total cost of construction. Larger projects generally have smaller fee percentages.

This fee, the responsibilities associated with it (revisions through permitting, frequency of on-site visits, payment certifications, punch list review) and the compensation procedure for any extra work should be spelled out in a contract. This can be an Architect's Letter of Agreement or a standard AIA contract as issued by The American Institute of Architects.

LICENSES AND PERMITS

To earn his title, an architect must have a state license. He does not have to be a member of the AIA (Frank Lloyd Wright never joined). The typical qualifications for licensing are: 1.) a degree from an accredited school of architecture, requiring three or more years of study, 2) three years of apprenticeship under the supervision of a licensed architect and 3) passage of a five-day exam. Exact requirements vary from state to state. Remember, if using a Chicago firm for say, your Michigan summer home, verify they have an architect around to sign and seal (a signature and certifying stamp) the drawings in the state of the job. Cities require that drawings submitted for permit review be certified by a state-licensed architect.

It is also essential your architect be quite familiar with the local code requirements and regulations. Local codes vary widely, and a small misunderstanding can lead to a big inflation of budget and schedule after everyone's committed. In Chicago, as in most places, any alteration that does not fit the building code's definition of a minor repair requires an architect's application and certification of plans for approval and issuance of a building permit. The City Building Department also requires the architect to certify completion of the construction before anyone can occupy the space. If you live in a landmark building, you will also have to consider the approval of your plans by the Landmarks Commission. Your architect should be responsible for filing all the appropriate paperwork and addressing any code concerns during the permitting process.

THE ARCHITECTURAL DESIGN PROCESS

Whether you're courting your architect or have already made the plunge, communication is critical. You're choosing someone to translate an epic fantasy only you have in your imagination. For an architect to develop an idea of what's in your head, you need to be able to convey in detail what it is you are looking for. Bring sketches, pictures, notes, clippings, Rorschach tests—anything that will tune him in to the same frequency. And take your turn to listen. Your architect will invariably come up with design ideas offering inventive solutions and innovative alternatives to your rough-hewn proposal. Also, you want an architect who can deliver options.

Once you've made your architect the designer of record, your first big discussion should begin to flesh out your nebulous dreams into cold hard details. The number of rooms, how and when you will use them and the flow of space are questions he will need answered in order to come up with a first round of schematic designs. Don't panic at their incompleteness. These rough sketches and drawings will be revised and refined as you review them until you are satisfied. The architect may produce a model to help you visualize the layout of your future residence.

HOW LONG WILL IT TAKE TO DRAW UP A PLAN?

The easy answer: as long as you keep changing your mind. Even though you're the one spending the pretty penny and the design plan is for your home, you'll be astounded by the number of people who get to throw their two cents into your architectural plan. After you and your architect have come to terms, your drawings may pass through the hands of co-op boards; various historical, design or landmark review boards; planning and zoning, structural, mechanical, electrical, plumbing, fire life/safety, and Americans with Disabilities Act (ADA) reviewers; and your kids. You'll know how a writer feels when he tries to get his screenplay through the Hollywood system unscathed. When it comes to architectural plans, it's design by committee. Depending on the complexity of the job and profile of the location, expect the process to take from two to six months, or much longer if you make a hobby of it.

Once basic layout is approved, the architect can strike forward to prepare more detailed drawings to define the scale and scope of the project. The devil, never more true than in construction, is in the details. You must communicate absolutely everything you little heart desires. Finishes, brands, models, installation methods, notations on code, fixture selection, materials to be used— it all needs to be documented in plans and specs by the architect. At this point the estimate for cost gets a whole lot clearer.

The Architect Through the Process

It is only with thorough and clear documents that you should approach a contractor to bid. Your architect will manage (or assist you in) the process of hiring a contractor to coordinate construction. He should have a selective stable of reliable and friendly contractors with whom he has had good experiences and can recommend, or you may have your own ideas. As it is typical for several contractors to bid a job, he can help you sift through the proposals to make sure everything is included and you are comparing the same bang for the buck. Ultimately, however, the decision to hire the contractor is yours.

Throughout construction it is your architect's responsibility to make frequent appearances on site in order to monitor job progress, troubleshoot, answer questions and verify that all details and code requirements are being met per his plans and specs. It is becoming increasingly common for banks to require the architect of record to certify pay applications in order to release a funding to the contractor. Again this requires the architect to visit the site to assess whether or not the work completed is commensurate with the request for payment. As construction draws to a close, he must lead "punch list process" of those missing, incomplete, unpolished and mishandled loose ends. Working with an architect who is the perfect match for your personality, ideas and particular project will make this one of the most memorable adventures of your life. You may enjoy it so much that, like Thomas Jefferson, you'll immediately start to eye another project: "Architecture is my delight," wrote Jefferson, "and putting up and pulling down one of my favorite amusements."

Drawing Is Just the Beginning. You Hire an Architect To:

- Interpret code.
- Estimate budget and schedule.
- Offer options for materials and methods.
- Recommend contractors and review bids.
- Document contractual obligations.
- Sign and seal plans for permitting.
- Review and certify pay applications.
- Monitor progress and quality.

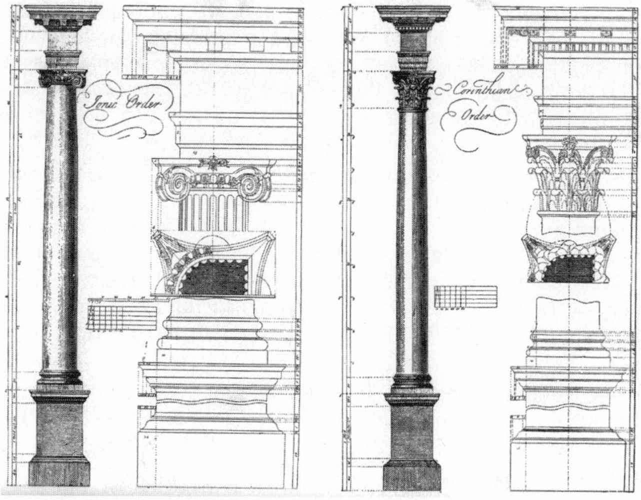

ARCHITECTS

Bauhs Dring Main Architects **3.5** **3** **4** **4**
One East Delaware Street, Suite 500, Chicago, IL 60611
(312) 649 - 9484

Residential architecture with historical references

Best known by industry insiders for its historical remodeling and modern contemporary styles, Bauhs Dring Main Architects has a diverse practice and taking on projects ranging from low-income residences to multi-million dollar homes. One notable project includes a simple barn residence anchored by two silos to which the firm added an unusual modern twist of silver galvanized aluminum sheathing. We are told the firm is dedicated to providing personalized service and creating lasting bonds with its clients.

Approximately 80 percent of the firm's work is residential with the vast majority centered in the city. The 10-person firm is lead by Todd Main, who, in 1974, founded the company with the late Bill Bauhs and Bill Dring, who retired in the 1980s. The firm charges standard architectural percentage rates or a fixed fee.

BGD&C Corp.
875 North Michigan Avenue, Suite 1414, Chicago, IL 60611
(312) 255 - 8300

High-end new residential construction

See BGD&C Corporation's full report under the heading Contractors & Builders

Becker Architects, Ltd. **4** **4** **4.5** **4.5**
595 Elm Place, Suite 225, Highland Park, IL 60035
(847) 433 - 6600 www.beckerarchitects.com

Historically accurate, yet comfortable residential architecture

Known by clients as excellent problem solvers with a heightened awareness of budgetary concerns, Becker Architects is especially noted for its expertise in home rehabilitation and additions. We hear the firm also does numerous historical preservation projects, but is not a group of strict preservationists. Clients applaud the firm's ability to meld the old with the new, matching scale and style in projects where historical residences must remain true to form, yet receive updated amenities.

Becker's supporters say the firm's style is "rational, straightforward and classic." Clients say they choose Becker for the firm's expertise in making improvements or additions to historically significant homes, essentially allowing the aesthetic history "to repeat itself" while adding tasteful and functional touches. Approximately 60 percent of the firm's work is residential, with most projects on the North Shore. Led by principals Richard and Nancy Becker, the firm has been in business for 19 years and employs eight. Both principals were educated at Syracuse University.

Becker Architects charges standard architectural percentage rates or a fixed fee, and its services come highly recommended. The firm's work has been featured in such magazines as *Traditional Home* and *Better Homes and Gardens.*

"Budgets were easy to discuss and he paid good attention to those budgets." "The work is so impressive." "Whenever there was an issue, they found someone to fix it quickly and efficiently."

Booth Hansen & Associates 5 4 5 4.5
555 South Dearborn Street, Chicago, IL 60605
(312) 427 - 0300 www.boothhansen.com

Innovative residential architecture and interiors

This mid-sized firm has been a pillar of the Chicago architectural community for more than two decades. While Larry Booth approaches each project with the same guiding principles, he carries no preconception of style, believing that a structure's design should blend into, rather than impose upon the surrounding community. Booth and Sandy Stevenson lead the firm, along with William Massey and Rick Nelson in residential design. The firm's designs evolve from Booth's philosophy, which is based on "stewardship, connectivity and spirit."

Clients praise Booth's attention to detail in every aspect of the project, from selection of materials to execution of construction, and say he lives up to everything that "stewardship" implies. They remark he's always very receptive to their ideas, and proves a good collaborator. One delighted client goes on to tell us her project architect was still responsive "after three years." Booth's clients comment he creates spaces that resonate with a sense of peace and calm through his faithfulness to "connectivity"—connecting past to future, building to surroundings. They are also impressed by Booth's efforts to capture the "spirit" of each individual project—the excitement of the client's personal and creative experience along with the energy and history of the site. In the end, even those intimidated by Booth's reputation, experience and intellectual approach to building ended up loving the experience and felt that he was extremely down to earth.

Booth Hansen focuses on new construction or major gut renovations in and outside the city. About one quarter of its projects are residential and start in the $300,000 range at between $120 and $500 per square foot. Booth considers the practice of charging a percentage of the total construction cost unfair and believes it penalizes clients for using specialty materials. Instead he works on an upset/hourly fee. If billable hours fall below the maximum coverage fee, clients are charged the lesser amount. We hear this saves not only dollars, but also time and grief.

"Very, very good. Innovative, creative and easy to work with. Always has a fresh idea." "Gutted an old factory in the city. Booth managed to keep the feel but added warmth and serenity." "One of the best in Chicago." "Sense of calm and peace due to symmetry laid out by the architect." "In part, it was an intellectual process for us all."

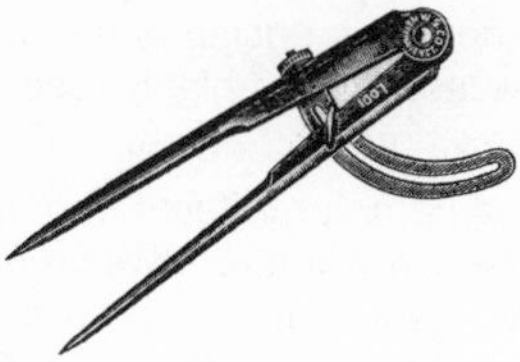

Brininstool + Lynch, Ltd. 4.5 3.5 5 5
230 West Superior Street, 3rd Floor, Chicago, IL 60610
(312) 640 - 0505 www.brininstool-lynch.com

Tailored, minimalist residential architecture

The team approach at Brininstool + Lynch has won this firm high accolades from clients who rely on it primarily for carefully edited, minimalist, contemporary interiors that are simultaneously warm and comfortable. One speciality that clients praise is the firm's attention to natural light and the movement of light throughout a space. The company is also commended for incomparable attention to detail, which can include custom hardware and furniture, designed especially to complement the firm's architectural design and clients' needs. The firm's standards of quality are unparalleled, we are told, which accounts for much repeat business among its loyal clientele.

After meeting at Pappageorge Haymes (see review), David Brininstool and Brad Lynch formed their own firm in 1989. Since then, they have assembled a small, select team of skilled professionals who create architecture that has not only met the demands of some of Chicago's most discriminating "contemporary" devotees, but also won numerous design awards and gained widespread publicity in prestigious magazines. The firm charges standard architectural percentage rates or a fixed fee.

"His strength is his design sensibility." "I really liked working with Brad—it is rare to work with the same man three times and still say you would hire him again." "Always delivered the optimum value." "He transformed my condo on the Lake (that was covered in gold and mirrors when I purchased it) into a minimalistic, simplistic, warm and contemporary home."

Burns & Beyerl Architects, Inc. **4 3.5 5 4.5**
1010 South Wabash Avenue, Chicago, IL 60605
(312) 663 - 0222 www.bba1.com

Warm intimate residential architecture

Clients praise Burns & Beyerl for its uncanny ability to maximize space within a home while making rooms feel warm and intimate. References tell us that the firm is extremely respectful of and sensitive to clients' input, no matter how detailed, and is religious about incorporating it into the result. And, as much as Burns & Beyerl is known for accommodating its clients, it also has a reputation for being assertive and commanding in managing general contractors' budgets and timelines—a combination of qualities that has gained the firm enormous trust with clients. The vast majority of Burns & Beyerl's projects are single-family residences, including approximately three new residences a year along with numerous renovations and additions, most of which are on the North Shore.

We are told the firm values versatility more than a particular style of architecture. Clients confirm Burns' mantra, "It's all about the client," and say he ensures that the firm remains dexterous and flexible enough to turn visions into reality, regardless of style. Steven Burns received his Master of Architecture degree from Harvard University; his partner, Gary Beyerl received his degree from Syracuse University. The pair created this eight-person firm, which has been in business since 1993, after working separately at SOM, Krueck Olsen and Booth Hansen (see reviews).

Some clients report that the firm's pricing is below what they expect to pay for the superb quality of its services. Clients highly recommend the firm and many seek Burns & Beyerl's services time and again.

"We interviewed several big-name architects and in the end, we felt Steve Burns would give us the house we wanted." "We've built several houses and this is by far our best experience." "Not a hammer, but not passive." "We asked to pay him more that what was in the contract!"

Charles Page, Architect **3 3.5 3 3.5**
100 Evergreen Lane, Winnetka, IL 60093
(847) 441 - 7860

Residential architecture

For more than 30 years, Charles Page has devoted his energies to providing architectural services for residential new home construction. Both he and his son now run this small firm that conducts most of its business on the North Shore. Sources say Page is best known for his large traditional homes with a signature steep, high pitched roof. The firm charges a standard fee that translates into an overall percentage of total construction costs.

✚	$	◆	★

Chicago Workshop Architects
2068 First Street, Suite 101, Highland Park, IL 60035
(847) 266 - 1125
Residential design/build

See Chicago Workshop Architects's full report under the heading Contractors, & Builders

Cordogan, Clark & Associates 3.5 3 3.5 4
716 North Wells Street, Chicago, IL 60610
(312) 943 - 7300 www.architects-cca.com
Residential and commercial architecture, planning and engineering

Clients know Cordogan, Clark & Associates as a full-service architectural, planning and engineering firm that is highly regarded for executing projects within budget and on schedule. We are told the firm prides itself in creating spaces of functional efficiency while keeping an eye on the bottom line to contain costs. Insiders say a core philosophy of the firm is the importance of customer involvement. The firm engages clients in all decisions and throughout every phase of the project to ensure the client's vision is realized in the final product. Cordogan Clark devotes 40 percent of its business to residential projects and will take on a variety of projects from new construction to renovations.

This 50-person architectural firm, in business since 1984, serves Chicago and its suburbs with offices in Chicago and Aurora. Principal of the Chicago office, John Clark, earned both his undergraduate architecture degree in 1977 and his Master of Urban Planning and Policy Curriculum in 1979 from the University of Illinois. He also studied under Felix Candela at École des Beaux Arts, of Versailles in 1976. Principals John Codogan and John Clark guide each project personally. The firm charges standard architectural percentage rates or a fixed fee.

Darcy Bonner & Associates
205 West Wacker Drive, Suite 307, Chicago, IL 60606
(312) 853 - 3470
Graceful, transitional interior design and architecture

See Darcy Bonner & Associates's full report under the heading Interior Designers & Decorators

David Woodhouse Architects 🗁 🗁 🗁 🗁
811 West Evergreen, Suite 203, Chicago, IL 60622
(312) 943 - 3120
Residential architecture

Dirk Denison Architects 4.5 4.5 5 4.5
754 North Milwaukee Avenue, Suite 2F, Chicago, IL 60622
(312) 455 - 1388
Integrated, clean, residential architecture and interiors

Admired for his ability to tie all elements of a project together, this highly-respected architect not only creates the architectural designs for his clients, but also does the furnishings and interiors for most projects. Typically, he handles everything from hardware to landscaping in order to create a consistent vision throughout. Dirk Denison's pared-down interiors are said to reflect a Miësian approach to materials, space and light, while also incorporating the client's lifestyle and interests. This practitioner is also known for his ability to gracefully integrate artwork—which he considers very important to interiors—into his designs.

Clients, decorators and contractors agree that Denison is among the best architects in Chicago, and some say they would never look elsewhere for architectural needs. Others love Denison because he makes them feel that their needs and desires are of the utmost importance to him. We're told that, because Denison is such a wonderful communicator, he is able to "transform those needs into clean, creative, architecturally intelligent designs." With clients that have recommended him to their mothers-in-law, parents and friends, this architect is also favored by contractors who say his designs are flawless, and his drawings are so complete from the start that "nothing is left to guesswork."

A graduate of the Harvard Graduate School of Design, Denison is now a professor at the Illinois Institute of Technology, where he has served as the Associate Dean and Director of Graduate Programs. His research and teaching now focuses on socially-conscious housing and urban development. With fees that are right in line with the rest of the top architects, clients feel that Denison and his small firm are well worth every penny.

"Working with Dirk is a pleasure, and the results were even more special than we anticipated." "He was always open to our ideas and wishes, but was the first to lead us in a different direction if he thought our concepts were not feasible, too costly, or would not fit in with the overall design." "Mr. Denison does meticulous work and was able to work harmoniously with us, the contractor and the interior designer. He is a real pleasure."

Durrett Design
3343 South Halstead, Suite 201, Chicago, IL 60608
(773) 581 - 2107

Residential new construction and remodeling

See Durrett Design's full report under the heading Contractors & Builders

Eifler & Associates **4.5 4.5 4 5**
223 West Jackson Street, Suite 1000, Chicago, IL 60606
(312) 362 - 0180

Historic preservation architecture as well as forward thinking, modernist design

John Eifler is known by clients, the media and his contemporaries as one of the most respected preservation architects in the Chicago area—and beyond. Clients tell us his esteemed reputation as a preservationist cannot dilute the fact that Eifler & Associates is a versatile firm that delivers exquisite, forward-thinking, modernist design in addition to elegant historic restoration. Eifler, the sole principal of the firm, remains humble in light of the many awards he has received for his preservation work, according to clients. In fact, insiders say Eifler actually cringes at being labeled a preservation architect. They say he believes that historic preservation should be a normal and highly regarded practice, rather than a niche of architecture.

Although Eifler is extremely receptive to clients' input, clients say they trust his design and impeccable understanding of the prairie style, particularly with regard to historic renovations, and leave all planning in his hands. Eifler, FAIA, has been in business since 1990. With a staff of seven architects, the firm undertakes projects of all kinds including new single and multi-family home construction as well as commercial construction. The firm also takes on smaller projects. The bulk of the firm's business is spilt evenly between the city of Chicago and its suburbs.

Eifler's fees are on par with other leaders in the industry, and recent projects include a 5,500-square-foot new single-family home in Oak Brook and a large restoration project in Rhode Island. Clients highly recommend the firm and praise Eifler and his firm's services as worth every penny of its high-end price tag.

"Eifler is the only choice for authentic prairie architectural restoration." "The work and service was simply outstanding." "John and his staff can easily assimilate a complex problem and produce a very clear and comprehensive report." "Is his work quality the highest imaginable? I can imagine a lot—and he came close."

Environ Inc.
401 West Superior Street, 5th Floor, Chicago, IL 60610
(312) 951 - 8863 www.environ-inc.com
Commercial, residential and institutional architecture, design & planning

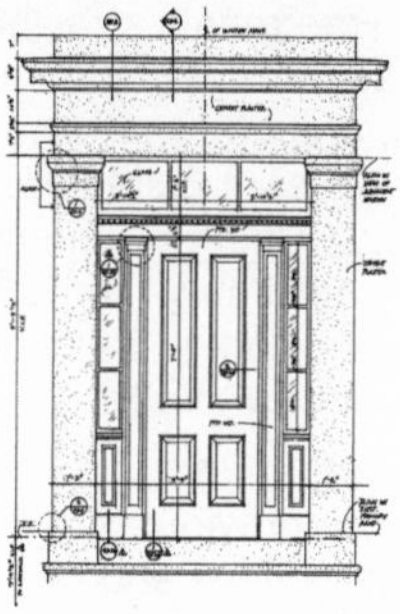

Florian Architects **4** **3.5** **4.5** **5**
432 North Clark Street, Suite 200, Chicago, IL 60610
(312) 670 - 2220 www.florianarchitects.com
Detailed contemporary residential architecture

Incredible attention to detail and superb communication skills are highlights of the praise that is bestowed upon Florian Architects by former and current clients. While the firm's design style is highly contemporary, it adapts a sensitivity to contemporary with other styles. Principal Paul Florian is pegged as a confident and assertive architect who possesses superior communications skills. He was named one of the World's Foremost Architects by Architectural Digest in 1991. While Florian designs many large spaces, he continues to delight clients by "expressing more with less" in both large and small environments.

Florian, one of three principals of the firm, holds degrees from Washington University, the Architectural Association School of Architecture in London and a M.A. from the University of Illinois at Chicago. Florian created his own firm 15 years ago, and previously served as president of Florian Wierzbowski. Chris Manfre and Gary Hodonicky are also principals of this 10-person firm, which is highly sought for large single-family new home construction. The firm will not hesitate to become involved with smaller projects, especially interesting and challenging endeavors. Clients applaud the principals' accessibility and their respect for communications and budgetary issues.

Florian's fees fall in line with those of other high-end architectural firms. The scope of a project is laid out at its inception, and a fixed fee is calculated, based on the services required to see it to completion. Clients say that while Florian is sensitive to budgetary needs, the firm remains committed to the highest quality end-product. The firm comes highly recommended and can boast of many happy repeat clients who cite an appreciation for Florian's candor and responsiveness to their feedback.

"Their strength is that they're able to accommodate different styles." "Very good at listening to my ideas and incorporating what was important." "If there were problems, they would let it be known." "They pay extraordinary attention to detail." "Budgets increased, but it was easy to talk to them about it." "Paul's strength is his creativity."

Fraerman Associates Architecture, Inc — 4.5 | 3.5 | 4.5 | 5

508 Central Avenue, Suite 200, Highland Park, IL 60035
(847) 266 - 0648 www.fraermanarch.com

Collaborative, disciplined residential architecture

Jim Fraerman is hailed by clients as an extremely accommodating architect with a natural instinct for the "art of his craft." His firm boasts a devoted client base that repeatedly speaks of Fraerman's straightforward communication, personable manner and well-grounded advice regarding the projects he undertakes. They also say he is soft-spoken, and many refer to his penchant for discipline and precision. Fraerman is known as a collaborative firm that works well and coordinates easily with designers. Clients appreciate his flexibility and project management skills. The firm is not known for just one architectural style—Fraerman is highly respected for its work in traditional and contemporary interiors and also noted for the ability to work within the context of an existing structure.

Fraerman holds both an undergraduate and M.A. in architecture from Yale. On his own since 1995, Fraerman previously served as senior vice president of Booth Hansen Architects (see review) and has more than 20 years experience in the industry. Fraerman himself works closely with clients. He and his three-person firm handle new home construction, additions and remodeling, primarily on the North Shore, where many clients admire the architect's incorporation of natural materials.

The firm charges an hourly rate, and its fees parallel those of other architects of similar reputation and quality. Clients tell us they wouldn't hesitate to call on Fraerman again or recommend it to others. They say the architectural team's work represents high value, both in relation to cost and to the peace of mind they enjoy for the duration of the project.

"His attention to detail and his sensitivity to the homeowner was A-1 fabulous." "I wouldn't hesitate to use him again." "He had the consideration to arrange to move the piano so my husband could play in the basement where we were living for four months while the rest of the house was being remodeled." "He's so good, I'm not sure our project was the best use of his ability." "He's an extremely disciplined and precise person." "He has the right combination of respect, aptitude and instinct." "If it took six different versions of a design, he gave me six different versions." "He didn't have an overabundance of ego."

Frederick Phillips & Associates — 4 | 4.5 | 4 | 4.5

1456 West Dayton, Suite 200, Chicago, IL 60622
(312) 255 - 0415 www.frederickphillipsassociates.com

High-end, imaginative residential architecture

Frederick Phillips, FAIA, is known by clients for highly intelligent contemporary design that is appealing to a wide range of tastes. Phillips applied his skills to a collection of homes known as Prairie Crossing, located about an hour's drive north of the city. Phillips holds six distinguished building awards from the Chicago chapter of the American Institute of Architects along with three "Record Houses" awards from Architectural Record. We hear that Phillips has a keen ability to define and solve unusual architectural puzzles with creative and appropriate alternatives.

Phillips received his B.A. from Lake Forest College and earned his M.A. in architecture from the University of Pennsylvania. Prior to opening his own practice in 1976, Phillips was an architect on staff at Harry Weese and Associates (see review). Approximately half of Phillips' projects are residential, split equally between the city and the suburbs. Of its residential work, about half is new construction and half substantial renovations and additions, although, on occasion, the firm will take on a smaller project.

Phillips generally charges hourly rates with a fee cap based on a percentage of construction. Percentages tend to be higher on smaller projects, and some say the firm's fees tend to be somewhat higher in general.

"I'm convinced he's the finest I could have found." "His creative abilities and use of light and space are tremendous." "A thoughtful and imaginative solution to a complex design problem."

Garofalo Architects **4 4 4 4.5**

3752 North Ashland Avenue, Chicago, IL 60613
(773) 975 - 2069

High-end progressive residential architecture

Undulating surfaces, extraordinary shapes and angles along with other variations on what is considered conventional architecture dominate the work of Doug Garofalo. This highly sought architect actively redefines not only the contemporary design aesthetic, but also the method by which it is achieved. Garofalo collaborates with other architects, consultants and specialists in various locations through cutting-edge computer software and networks. His firm's highly contemporary work results in notable—even unique—structures that his clients and many "modern" fans see as representations of forward-thinking design.

This four-person firm was founded in 1992 by Garofalo following his work at William Graham Associates of Seattle and Kessler Merci Architects and Solomon Cordwell Buenz, both of Chicago. Garofalo holds a B.A. in architecture from Notre Dame and an M.A. from Yale.

Gary Lee Partners **4.5 3.5 4.5 5**

360 West Superior, Chicago, IL 60610
(312) 640 - 8300 www.garyleepartners.com

High-end, clean, contemporary interior architecture and design

Gary Lee Partners has long been known for its clean, highly contemporary style. Industry insiders and clients agree that Gary Lee is a disciplined and innovative architect that pushes the envelope of contemporary and classic contemporary design. Clients also praise Lee's budgetary sensibility in planning and spending funds wisely.

The firm boasts a staff of 45, with eight AIA architects on staff. Gary Lee associates focuses mainly on designing commercial interior properties, but about ten percent of its projects are residential renovations of existing buildings. The vast majority of those take place in the city for repeat clients and range anywhere from 1,000 to 9,000 square feet.

In addition to Chicago, Gary Lee's firm has done work across the globe including London, New York, L.A. and Paris. Lee is described by clients as a pleasure to work with and someone who builds a great deal of trust with clients. The firm creates a great deal of custom design work and has its own line of furniture. ID Hall of Fame.

"Great to work with." "Our ongoing relationship with Gary Lee is something that is very important to us." "They were really great at 'knowing me' and what I would like and want." "Pretty phenomenal." "Flawless and results-oriented." "Beautiful work and a nice guy." "Project management was excellent and they were always accessible."

Gastinger Walker Harden Architects

20 North Wacker Drive, Chicago, IL 60606
(312) 236 - 3993 www.gwhm.com

Residential, commercial and industrial architecture

	Quality	Cost	Value	Recommend?
Geudtner & Melichar Architects	3.5	3.5	4	4

711 North McKinley Road, Lake Forest, IL 60045
(847) 295 - 2440

Residential architecture

Specializing in high-end custom residential new home construction and historical preservations, Diana Melichar is the sole principal of the firm she created eight years ago. The firm has six architects and sources say the firm is often approached for its expertise in traditional design and historic preservation. Residential projects account for approximately 70 percent of Geudtner & Melichar's annual projects, nearly all of which are located in the suburbs, primarily in Lake Forest.

Melichar holds a B.A. from Tulane and an M.A. from Columbia. The firm takes on moderate to very large-size residential projects and charges either a standard architectural percentage rate of total job cost or a fixed fee.

"Added a huge amount of discipline to the project." "They're super nice people." "Extreme integrity. I very much trusted Diana with her design sense." "The attention to detail and the finishes on the outside of the house are spectacular." "They've got the feel down perfect. If you didn't know any better, you'd think everything in the house was a hundred years old and kept perfectly preserved."

	Quality	Cost	Value	Recommend?
Gibbons, Fortman & Weber Ltd.	4	3.5	4	4.5

900 North Franklin Street, Chicago, IL 60610
(312) 482 - 8040 www.gfwarchitects.com

Versatile residential architecture

Clients say the Gibbons Fortman & Weber, Ltd. firm is exceptional at communicating with clients and supervising the construction process in addition to providing sensible architectural design. The firm is known for superlative attention to detail in its designs that range in style from strictly traditional to cutting-edge modern. Clients tell us they can rely on these architects for intelligent design that is both creative and sensible in its choice of materials.

The firm has operated under its current name since last year, but has been in business since 1984. It consists of six architects, with Richard Gibbons, Scott Fortman and Edward Weber as principals. The firm focuses overwhelmingly on residential architecture, which accounts for 90 percent of all projects, and more than half of those take place on Chicago's Gold Coast. Although the firm specializes in large renovations, clients say Gibbons Fortman & Weber is equally skilled with new home projects.

The firm charges standard architectural percentage rates or a fixed fee and enjoys a loyal client base that employs it time and again for additional projects.

"The design was creative and wonderful, but I was also impressed by the day-to-day supervision of the builders—and the ability to get results from them." "They are strong on overall scope conception, field communication, customer relations and professionalism." "Each project is beautiful, evocative, highly intelligent and finished down to the last exquisite detail."

Gregory Maire Architects, Ltd.	**4.5**	**4**	**5**	**5**

2635 Poplar Avenue, Evanston, IL 60201
(847) 492 - 1776 www.maire.com

High-end contemporary and arts and crafts residential architecture

Described by clients as a soft-spoken gentlemen, Gregory Maire lets his design do the talking. He is known primarily for contemporary and Arts and Crafts style, although Maire himself is not limited to working in any particular architectural "school." All designs are said to be seamless and unobtrusive. With additions, for example, clients say Maire's work blends in so well with existing structures that it goes completely unnoticed. Clients commend Maire for incredible detail and diligence in creating designs that translate their abstract visions into reality in a single introductory sketch. He is also lauded for his mastery of lighting, used creatively to make homes warm and inviting.

Maire is the sole principal of this five-person firm, which has been in business since 1996. More than half of his projects are residential, primarily new home construction on the North Shore and apartment renovations on the Gold Coast. Maire has 20 years experience in the industry and holds an undergraduate degree from Wesleyan University in Connecticut and an M.A. in architecture from Harvard. References often speak of Maire's integrity and excellent execution.

Maire's fees are comparable to other high-end architects in the area. His firm charges a flat fee that is equivalent to a percentage of total construction costs. Remodeling or renovation projects command a slightly higher percentage than new home construction. Clients recommend Maire as an architect of great integrity and vision and refer to him as a genius and an artist. Their positive and lasting impressions derive from both his design and his demeanor.

"Very detail-oriented; he even provided us with monthly spending spreadsheets." "He really is a genius." "The detail he put into the home was phenomenal." "People are stunned by the design. It really speaks to his artistic talents." "He's such a gentleman and a pleasure to work with." "We can't recommend him enough." "He came back with a first design that was exactly what we wanted." "From an execution standpoint, it was about as flawless as you could get." "When we finished, we were like, 'Wow, this is exactly what I had envisioned'."

Grunsfeld & Associates	**5**	**4.5**	**5**	**5**

211 East Ontario, Suite 1390, Chicago, IL 60611
(312) 202 - 1800

High-end residential architecture with modernist approach

A Chicago native, Tony Grunsfeld has been a prominent voice and major influence in architecture for over four decades. This "perfectionist" has achieved iconic stature among the area's most discerning and well-heeled clients, creating what are widely called, "contemporary, yet livable masterpieces." The Grunsfeld aesthetic is based on the modernist principles of symmetry, geometry and integrity of materials and is not willingly compromised to clients who don't share his vision. With a style that has been described as sleek, this firm produces residences with modern lines and modern textures. The result is a refined space that incorporates unique wood and stone into a seamless and luxurious design.

After four successful decades that included commercial projects, this practitioner now focuses on residential work. A great deal of these homes are constructed on the bluffs overlooking Lake Michigan, a Grunsfeld specialty, having even employed the Army Corps of Engineers for a project. He is reputed by those who work with him to produce the most meticulously detailed blueprints in the city, and is known to visit each of his worksites every morning and even on weekends to check the progress of the construction. We hear the most technically complex jobs are run with precision. As a result of Grunsfield's very hands-on approach, clients end up becoming life long friends, and peers become life long fans.

With an education from MIT, Grunsfeld started his own practice in 1956. His staff is purposefully small, reflecting his personal investment in each project. Fees are charged by the hour on renovation work, and as a percentage of new construction. The higher expense is worth it, client's report, adding "You always end up with more than you could ever have imagined." Like a piece of Chicago history.

"He doesn't design other people's homes, he lets them move in to his." "As a contractor, you get spoiled working with Tony. Everything's perfectly mapped out."

Hammond Beeby Rupert & Ainge
440 North Wells, Chicago, IL 60610
(312) 527 - 3200
Residential architecture

Hartshorne + Plunkard, Ltd. **3.5** **3.5** **3** **4**
232 North Carpenter Street, Chicago, IL 60607
(312) 226 - 4488 www.hparchitecture.com
Contemporary residential architecture with wit

Contemporary design with a touch of humor is seen as a hallmark of projects by Hartshorne + Plunkard, Ltd. The firm is also adept at traditional and modern architecture. Approximately 70 percent of its work is residential, and the company's practice encompasses new luxury homes, condos and townhouses in Chicago and throughout the suburbs.

Raymond Hartshorne holds a B.A. in architecture from Iowa State University and an M.A. from the University of Illinois at Chicago. Partner James M. Plunkard has a B.A. in architecture from the University of Detroit and a M.A. from the University of Illinois at Chicago. This 25-person firm began 15 years ago doing primarily home rehabilitations and smaller projects and has since become a thriving organization that takes on mostly large custom home construction projects.

Hartshorne + Plunkard's fees are comparable to those of other high-end architects in the area and are usually based on a percentage of total construction costs.

Hasbrouck Peterson Zimoch Sirirattumrong Ltd.
104 South Michigan Avenue, Chicago, IL 60603
(312) 553 - 9600 www.hpzs.com
Historically sensitive, residential and commercial architecture and design

J. Stoneberg Architects — 3 | 3 | 3.5 | 4
3320 North Ravenswood, Chicago, IL 60657
(773) 281 - 1878

Residential architecture, specializing in over-sized downtown lofts

New homes in Chicago's over-sized downtown lots account for a significant number of projects designed by Jack Stoneberg and Julie Gross, the principals of this small firm that has been in business since 1992. The firm also takes on smaller downtown renovations and does both new home and renovation work in the suburbs. On occasion, clients call on the firm for out-of-town projects, such as a current mountainside home in Vail. While 60 percent of Stoneberg's projects are residential, he also does commercial work. Stoneberg has degrees from New York's Cooper Union and the University of Illinois at Chicago. The percentage of total construction cost, charged by this firm, is typically on the lower side.

Jaffe Pruchno Architects — 4.5 | 3 | 4.5 | 4.5
811 West Evergreen, Loft 400 A, Chicago, IL 60622
(312) 475 - 1800

Innovative, contemporary residential architecture and design

This firm, led by Lisa Jaffe and Marcia Pruchno Lawrence, is finding its way onto many people's short lists because of its tireless pursuit of intelligent residential design that marries functionality, practicality and aesthetics. While its design philosophy is based in contemporary style, the firm's work leans more toward the warm, contextual side of contemporary rather than to minimalism. Because these practitioners are committed to serving every client's needs, however, they excel in a range of styles. Commended for their passion for architecture, Jaffe and Pruchno create projects that are "architecturally significant" in design and style while also making budgetary sense. Whether the firm is working for a young couple with a limited budget, or for a large, established family on the North Shore where the sky's the limit, we hear it translates its clients' visions into reality through careful selection of materials and finishes. Many clients acknowledged that once they got to know this team of "remarkable" and "incredibly devoted professionals," they wanted the architects involved in every decision for the rest of the project, from custom hardware to landscape, furnishings, audio/video equipment and lighting design.

This progressive, firm has been seeking to elevate the everyday living of its residential clients since 1997. Jaffe received her M.A. from the University of Pennsylvania where she concentrated on the theoretical aspects of design. Lawrence received her M.A. from the University of Michigan. With no real minimum, the firm charges standard architectural fees for its services. Some clients say they feel that the high level of attention they received from this firm actually merited more than the company charged.

"Lisa and Marcia will go the extra mile every time." "You do not see architects on the site measuring to the nth detail like these two." "Their strength is being able to design and envision." "My new home is warm and inviting. It just flows beautifully—you feel good when you walk in the space."

Jerome Cerny Architects, Inc.
234 West Northwest Highway, Barrington, IL 60010
(847) 382 - 4433 www.jeromecerny.com

Residential architecture

John A. Hagenah, Architect
512 Green Bay Road, Kenilworth, IL
(847) 256 - 5575

Residential architecture

	Quality	Cost	Value	Recommend?
Kathryn Quinn Architects, Ltd.	4	4	4	4.5

363 West Erie Street, Chicago, IL 60610
(312) 337 - 4977

Residential architecture of varying styles

Adept in styles ranging from contemporary to traditional, Kathryn Quinn Architects is a 10-person firm with eight full-time staff architects, including its namesake and sole partner, Kathryn Quinn. Approximately 80 percent of the firm's work is residential, which includes new homes as well as remodeling projects and additions. The firm handles projects in downtown Chicago, throughout the suburbs and vacation homes in neighboring states. The firm's fees are based on a combination of standard hourly charges with a maximum based on a percentage of total construction costs.

"Kathryn is extremely responsive to ideas—and phone calls." "She really helped to rationalize a confusing layout and flow." "Was soothing to me as an anxious client." "Was always there to gently push us away from silly choices."

Konstant Architecture, Planning

5300 Golf Road, Skokie, IL 60077
(847) 967 - 6115

Residential architecture and planning

	Quality	Cost	Value	Recommend?
Krueck & Sexton	5	4	4.5	4.5

221 West Erie Street, Chicago, IL 60610
(312) 787 - 0056 www.ksarch.com

Contemporary, residential and commercial architecture

The sharp, staccato name of this firm perfectly captures the arresting aesthetic of its architecture. Krueck & Sexton's innovative work has been internationally acclaimed, and it remains one of Chicago's most respected architectural firms. The company engages in a broad array of architectural challenges, from commercial to institutional, and residential "urban work" that consists of both new construction and renovation. It is also a noted designer of furniture.

The firm was founded in 1979 by Ronald Krueck, and Mark Sexton came aboard the following year. Krueck and Sexton's aesthetic is uniquely modern, cultivated by a tradition of challenging assumptions and rethinking conventional methods, all the while focusing exclusively on client aspirations and values, we're told. Rigorous design research is always part of the process. Krueck & Sexton works in complex state-of-the-art building components such as metals and glass, producing a collage of solids and transparencies, color and light, form and texture, all in dizzying layers of clean and simple planes that clients say is truly inspired.

Clients report good chemistry with the practitioners, which they describe as having great attention to detail. With a diverse and talented staff of 14, they find the firm just the right size. Even the most discriminating "loved every minute of" the experience.

Fees vary based on the scope of the project. For large projects clients will typically pay a standard percentage of the total cost of construction. If the scope is small or unclear, hourly rates apply. While Krueck & Sexton's projects and costs are definitely high end, clients say they eliminate excessive fee structures, and are worth every penny. HB Top Designers, 1999, 2000. ID Hall of Fame.

"Loved the home-building process so much with Krueck & Sexton I put my new house on the market so that I could build another one with them." "I'm very picky, and for me to be extremely satisfied with them means a lot." "Some say they're minimalist. I say less is more. They make every last detail count beautifully."

Landahl Design Studio, PC
213 West Institute Place, Suite 301, Chicago, IL 60610
(312) 642 - 4999
Residential architecture

Larson Associates
542 South Dearborn, Suite 610, Chicago, IL 60605
(312) 786 - 2255
Classic contemporary architecture and interior design

See Larson Associates's full report under the heading Interior Designers & Decorators

Liederbach & Graham Architects
500 Northwells, Suite 2, Chicago, IL 60610
(312) 828 - 0900
Residential architecture

The majority of this 10-person firm's annual portfolio consists of sizeable new homes in the suburbs. It is capable of developing plans for any style of home and is known for balancing quality with a "stylistic impulse." The firm has been in business for a decade and charges either a standard percentage of the construction costs or a fixed fee.

Linda F. Grubb & Associates, Architects **4** **3** **4.5** **4.5**
102 North Cook Street, Suite 23, Barrington, IL 60010
(847) 381 - 6939
Understated, true-to-form period architecture

The scope of work by this small, 27-year-old firm extends from historic residential rehabilitation and remodeling projects to large, new, high-end custom homes. Linda Grubb, sole principal, takes particular pride in creating what is said to be "honest and clean traditional design," although she is comfortable working in any style and has a number of noteworthy contemporary projects to her credit. Clients say Grubb's keen eye for proportion and her intimate knowledge of period homes is her greatest asset. We understand that Grubb is passionate about intricate detail and reproducing historical architecture "to a T."

Barrington is this firm's main trading ground, and approximately 70 percent of all projects are there or in the nearby Chicago suburbs, where they typically encompass smaller renovations and new multi-million-dollar homes. Grubb holds a degree from Kansas State University. The firm charges standard hourly rates or an architectural percentage rate.

"Her eye for proportion and exemplary attention to quiet details makes a big difference." "Nobody can bring the amount of knowledge and professionalism to the project that Linda brings." "We're still using her nine years later." "If you're doing a period home, she's the woman to do it." "Very understated, magnificent detail." "She was very vested in the project; she took as much pride in it as we did."

Lucien Lagrange **4.5** **3.5** **4** **4.5**
605 North Michigan Avenue, Suite 301, Chicago, IL 60611
(312) 751 - 7400
Elegant, continentally influenced residential architecture

Lucien Lagrange earns praise from clients and industry leaders alike for his sophisticated blend of influences—from his native France and the rich architectural legacy of Chicago. His vision of classic Continental design is appreciated in much of his work, creating an elegant feel, particularly to the many luxury high-rise condominiums the firm has designed. Lagrange is conversant in multiple schools of design and clients say his diverse portfolio—ranging from old-world traditional to cutting-edge modernism—is his greatest strength.

Lagrange came to the United States in 1968 to work for the renowned architecture firm of Skidmore Owings & Merill, where he stayed until creating his own practice in 1985. Since then, his firm has grown steadily and now employs 70, providing architecture, master planning and interior design services. Lagrange's work is 60 percent residential, most of which involves multi-family condominium buildings and individual units. The firm does, however, design certain high-end single-family homes in the area. Recently recognized by several regional groups for its innovative design of the 67-story Park Tower hotel and condominium building, Lagrange is doing the interior architecture for several of these owners.

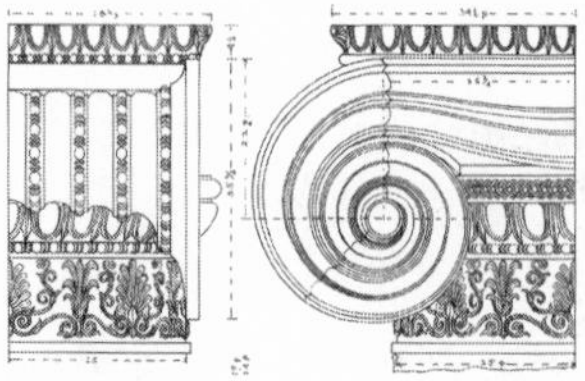

Mark Johnson and Associates **4 4 4.5 5**
23810 Woodward Avenue, Pleasant Ridge, MI 48069
(248) 543 - 5411

Collaborative residential architecture

Clients say Mark Johnson's greatest attribute is his collaborative, team approach to projects. We understand that Johnson goes out of his way to integrate the ideas of clients, while working closely with interior designers and landscape architects. As a result, clients say projects tend to run smoothly, with all parties involved working as a cohesive unit with a shared vision. References appreciate Johnson's ability to create eclectic takes on historical traditional styles, yet the firm also takes on historically accurate endeavors and is currently working on five turn-of-the-century projects. Clients applaud Johnson's midwestern interpretations of French architectural styles.

The majority of Johnson's work takes place on the North Shore and is mostly residential. Many of his clients are well-established or celebrity figures whose homes tend to be large in scope, ranging from 7,000 to 17,000 square feet. Mark Johnson and Associates is an eight-person firm that was established in 1997 by it's sole principal and namesake. The firm charges a standard fee, based on an overall percentage of construction.

"He creates fabulously designed French architecture." "Johnson is extremely talented, professional and a wonderful coordinator." "Without a doubt, I will hire him again for any future projects."

Marvin Herman & Associates **4.5 5 4 4**
1203 North State Parkway, Chicago, IL 60610
(312) 787 - 0347

High-end, highly detailed residential architecture

For the carriage trade and established professionals looking for refined, acclaimed architecture, Marvin Herman & Associates is an obvious choice. Principal Marvin Herman has been practicing independently for two decades. He heads a small firm, consisting of seven architects, three draftsmen and two interior designers. Most of its commissions are in the penthouses and landmark homes of the Gold Coast, with others along the North Shore and at Chicagoans' second homes in Palm Springs, L.A. and the Napa Valley.

Clients have high praise for Herman's talent, saying he is equally accomplished at working in a range of periods from traditional to Art Deco to contemporary. A finished Marvin Herman project almost always includes exceptionally detailed millwork and stone, and even custom-designed furniture and accessories. Supporters call his taste "exquisite," and mindful of the context.

Herman attracts the top general contracting and interior design talent for projects, ensuring clients are surrounded by competent, interesting people. Described as "a prince of a guy," Herman is praised by clients for his professionalism. Clients also compliment his staff, citing their artistic prowess and attentiveness. We hear he's so popular and busy, however, that occasionally things fall through the cracks.

We're told many of Herman's clients give him carte blanche resulting in a wonderful, if pricey, experience. A new-client minimum for Herman's architectural services is generally a $150,000 project. Typical project costs range upward to $400,000, and can top $10 million. Fees are standard, based on the estimated project cost. The experience, clients insist, is anything but standard.

"Marvin's an artist. Such vision." "He is obsessed by detail, and makes everything work. Got after people if they got it wrong." "Completely attuned to the nuances and problems of city apartments." "He's a very masterful eye, but the firm can drop the ball on occasion." "Without question, he's the number one person I go to." "The people working for him are just wonderful." "As good as it gets."

Metzler/Hull Development Corp.
1103 West Webster Avenue, Chicago, IL 60614
(773) 871 - 2258

High-end design/build

See Metzler/Hull Development Corporation's full report under the heading Contractors & Builders

Michael E. Breseman Architects, Ltd. **5 4 5 5**
2911 Fawn Trail Court, Prairie Grove, IL 60012
(847) 845 - 4000

High-end residential and period architecture

Michael Breseman is highly regarded for his ability to remain true to style in designing large, high-end homes in the French eclectic, French Country and Tudor styles. We are told he is so passionate about maintaining the highest architectural integrity that Breseman will turn down clients who are unwilling to meet this criteria for period-based new homes or additions and renovations to historic ones. Breseman is highly regarded for designing additions that seamlessly maintain the original structure's historic reference. Clients tell us that Breseman has been sighted driving through North Shore neighborhoods, taking photos of historic homes to catalog them and study their details for his work, which, we are told, is characterized by meticulous attention to detail.

While disciplined in his focus on authenticity, Breseman is credited with a friendly and personable manner. He has a reputation for working with clients' ideas while sticking to his own principles and the dictates of his knowledge of period design. He was educated at the Illinois Institute of Technology and is the sole principal of this four-person firm that has been in existence for the past eight years.

Breseman himself works very closely with all of his clients, and they say he is an excellent communicator who is always accessible and returns calls promptly. The firm's clientele tends to come from among the circle of well-established North Shore residents who share his respect and intellectual pursuit of design. Breseman charges by the hour and has a reputation for estimating budgets with pinpoint precision. Clients suggest that his superb skills and agreeable demeanor are under-reflected in the firm's overall pricing.

"The amount of research he did was tremendous. He went up and down the neighborhood scoping out the other houses to make sure ours would fit in." "His only weakness is that he's too nice." "We've recommended him to friends and they're so impressed, they wonder where this guy came from." "I think he can get more money for his services, but I didn't tell him that until we were done with our project." "His interest in really being true to an architectural style is why we chose him." "Our house burned down, so we weren't planning on building a new one, but he was so sensitive to our situation that we built our new home with Michael."

Michael Hershenson Architects 3 3 4 4

935 West Chestnut Street, Chicago, IL 60622
(312) 226 - 3252

Single and multi-family residential architecture of numerous styles and periods

An aptitude for creating thoughtful and inviting spaces across the full spectrum of architectural styles is Michael Hershenson's greatest strength, we are told. An architect of true versatility, Hershenson is conversant in contemporary, traditional, Tudor, Prairie, French and Georgian styles of design.

Hershenson is the sole principal of this firm which has been in business for seven years. Nearly all the firm's work is residential, divided equally between city and suburban projects. The firm's scope of projects ranges from smaller additions and rehabilitation projects to the construction of 12,000-square-foot single and multi-family residences. The firm charges standard architectural percentage rates or a fixed fee.

Michael Pado

161 East Erie Street, Suite 101, Chicago, IL 60611
(312) 440 - 1474

Contemporary residential architecture

Michael Pado's more than two decades of experience in architecture can be witnessed in Utah, Wisconsin and Michigan as well as at his many projects in the Chicago area. Pado started his four-person firm 22 years ago, following experience at SOM. His signature style is contemporary, although he also works on historic renovations. The scope of his work encompasses small additions, renovations, large new homes and commercial installations, and more than half of it is residential. Insiders tell us the apartment he designed for himself is a marvel of contemporary design and he carries that vision to his clients.

Nagle Hartray Danker Kagan McKay 4.5 3.5 4 4.5

One IBM Plaza, Chicago, IL 60611
(312) 832 - 6900 www.nhdkm.com

Collaborative contemporary residential architecture with wit

From 100,000-square-foot recording studios in the city to historic renovations in the suburbs, Nagle Hartray Danker Kagan McKay has delighted clients with versatility and strong design concepts for 35 years. A true full-service firm, NHDKM has extensive experience in virtually all styles, but contemporary, in both residential and commercial endeavors, is the jewel in the company's crown. Insiders point to the firm's generous use of natural lighting as its greatest strength in creating inviting environments. The creation of spaces that are at once sophisticated, yet livable, is its indelible signature.

Principal Jim Nagle founded the firm in 1966, and insiders tell us the man loves to have fun with his work and encourages his clients to have fun in the process. Nagle and his associates are well known for their collaborative approach to incorporating clients' ideas and input in projects. Nagle holds an M.A. in architecture from Harvard and undergraduate degrees from MIT and Stanford.

There are four other principals of the firm: John Hartray, who managed the design of the Washington D.C. Metro Subway; and Dirk Danker, Howard Kagan and Donald McKay, each of whom holds a B.A. in architecture from the University of Illinois at Chicago. The NHDKM staff of 32 includes 19 architects registered in 12 states. Clients that enlist the firm's services typically work with two or three of the principals throughout a project's duration.

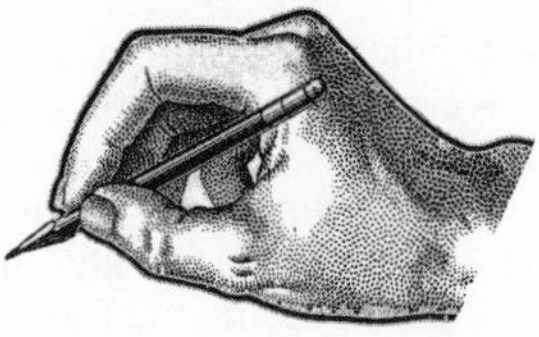

Orren Pickell Designers & Builders
2201 Waukegan Road, Suite W-285, Bannockburn, IL 60015
(847) 914 - 9629 www.pickellbuilders.com

Residential design/build and general contracting

See Orren Pickell Designers & Builders's full report under the heading Contractors & Builders

Pappageorge Haymes, Ltd.
814 North Franklin, Suite 400, Chicago, IL 60610
(312) 337 - 3344

Residential architecture with a specialty in high rises

Pappageorge Haymes is most recognized for its designs of high-rise apartment buildings in addition to new, custom single-family homes. While the firm is conversant in many styles of architectural design, its contemporary endeavors are most mentioned by industry insiders. Recent Chicago projects range from a 5,500-square-foot city row house to a 29-story high-rise apartment building.

George Pappageorge, who was educated at the University of Illinois at Chicago, and partner David Haymes, run this 40-person firm. Approximately 75 percent of its work is residential.

Paul Berger & Associates **4 4 4 4.5**
1255 North State Parkway, Suite 1S, Chicago, IL 60611
(312) 664 - 0640

Elegant, classical, residential and commercial architecture

Paul Berger's reputation for elegant, classical design has developed over the two decades he has offered his services to the Chicago area. The firm's projects range from small residential rehabilitations to gut renovations of some of Chicago's larger penthouse condos. The vast majority of the firm's projects take place within Chicago city limits, although the firm does occasionally take on projects in the surrounding area. Clients applaud Berger's approach to customer service, saying he is very responsive to clients' ideas—and phone calls. Berger is also said to be very accurate in estimating budgets.

Intimate, and some say "exquisite," contemporary or traditional style are the forte of Berger and his 10-person firm. Berger also does historic preservation work and occasionally designs new, single-family development and custom homes in the surrounding suburbs. Berger holds degrees from the University of Illinois and Harvard. The firm charges standard architectural percentage rates or a fixed fee.

"He returned phone calls and he followed through, and that's important." "His budgets were right on." "Design is his major strength, along with practicality." "He's personable and easy to talk to." "He shows an incredible level of competency and interest."

Powell/Kleinschmidt Inc. **4.5** **4** **4.5** **5**
645 North Michigan Avenue, Suite 810, Chicago, IL 60611
(312) 642 - 450 www.powellkleinschmidt.com

Modern high-end interior architecture and design

For modern, minimalist, sophisticated styles in both interior architecture and design, Powell/Kleinschmidt is considered high among the top firms in the area, as well as around the world. The firm splits work evenly between residential and commercial endeavors, and, in both cases, the modern classics it creates are seen by clients and the public as timeless designs, firmly rooted in Chicago's rich architectural heritage for early modernism. The firm is best known for its interior architecture for corporations and high-end residential clients.

This 18-person firm includes 10 architects and six interior designers, most of whom have more than ten years of experience. It was formed in 1976 and generally takes on between 20 to 25 projects each year. We hear the firm is excellent at minding subtle details, such as a generous use of fabric to absorb sound while also adding the warmth that makes an environment inviting. We are also told Powell/Kleinschmidt is extremely skilled at incorporating fine art and antiques into its interiors. The firm accepts a wide range of projects, from 500,000 square-foot office spaces to 2,000-square-foot residential apartments. A high level of quality and style is consistent with the firm, regardless of a project's size.

Not surprisingly, it enjoys a large percentage of repeat customers. It charges an hourly rate up to a pre-set maximum and establishes the budget prior to taking on a project. Insiders say Powell/Klienschmidt is conscientious in its provision of customer service, includes clients in frequent project meetings and returns phone calls promptly. HB 1998, 1999, 2000. ID Hall of Fame. Contract Magazine, 20 Best Internationally 1975-1999.

"Bob has an encyclopediatic knowledge of fine art and architecture." "You will never meet anyone more acutely aware of particular details than Bob." "They remain on the leading edge of forward modernism." "Their presentations are more professional than the ones for board meetings at IBM." "They are as professional as they are creative."

Ray Basso & Associates **3.5** **3** **4** **4**
1 South 105 Summit Avenue, Oakbrook Terrace, IL 60181
(630) 629 - 3400

Personalized, service-oriented residential architecture

For nearly 50 years, two generations of the Basso family have provided architectural services to the Chicago area. Ray Basso now carries on the family tradition that began in 1953, recently adding a construction company to the mix, allowing an integrated approach appreciated by clients.

Insiders say the father-son duo prides itself on responsive customer service, creating a strong, friendly bond with clients. The personal, responsive relationship Basso cultivates with customers brings it much return business and strong referrals. Basso is said to be capable of designing in all architectural styles, from the 1800s to the recent variations of the 1950s through the 1970s.

This father-son duo's projects range from small renovations to massive new homes, and approximately 60 percent of all work is residential. A majority of Basso's projects are split evenly between downtown Chicago and the suburbs, but the firm has also done work in Wisconsin, Indiana, Utah and Florida.

"His work is painstakingly detailed." "We were thrilled with the level of excitement, enthusiasm and creativity." "Above and beyond the other architects we interviewed." "Our house looks like none other—Ray is so unique in styling."

Robyn Shapiro Design, Inc.
220 West Kinzie Street, 5th Floor, Chicago, IL 60610
(312) 396 - 0400

Minimalist, architecturally-inspired interior design with heart

See Robyn Shapiro Design, Inc.'s full report under the heading Interior Designers & Decorators

Rugo-Raff — Quality 4, Cost 3, Value 4.5, Recommend? 5
20 West Hubbard, Chicago, IL 60610
(312) 464 - 0222

Versatile, service oriented residential architecture

Steve Rugo pays meticulous attention to detail and personally oversees every large project his firm takes on, earning praise from clients and interior designers alike. Moreover, Rugo is said to readily embrace the input and ideas of clients on the belief that the style of a building and its spaces should reflect the personality and personal taste of its inhabitants. The firm is not devoted to any particular architectural style. Industry insiders tell us that Rugo is a friendly, yet confident architect who pursues high and consistent quality and who has earned the loyalty and respect of his clients.

Rugo is the senior architect of this 10-person firm, which handles predominantly residential projects. Its services are split equally among some of the most prestigious neighborhoods in the city, as well as the suburbs and out-of-state locations. The types of projects in the firm's portfolio strike a balance between new construction of homes in the 10,000-square-foot range, residential rehabs of similar size, and apartment and townhouse renovations. Each year, the firm typically takes on from 10 to 15 active projects, each of which lasts for up to three years.

Rugo-Raff charges hourly fees that are a little less pricey than those of other big-name architects in the area. Yet we are told the lower pricing comes at no sacrifice to quality, which many say is top-notch, and personalized service, considered first-rate. The firm has a devoted following with many return customers, including one client that enlisted Rugo's services for three homes.

"Steve is a true gentleman and understands the meaning of a classic, timeless, multi-generational design." "He is the guy to use for those in the know to achieve that 'just so' look of gentility." "Not an innovator, but a really decent guy who delivers a consistent product." "Not only would I love to use him again, but I'd love for him to be my dinner partner."

Schroeder Murchie Laya & Associates — Quality 4, Cost 3, Value 4, Recommend? 4.5
936 West Huron Street, Chicago, IL 60622
(312) 829 - 3355

Residential and commercial architecture

Industry insiders say Schroeder Murchie Laya & Associates is best known for its expertise in architecture that incorporates adaptive-use designs. This comes from the firm's skill and 15 years of experience in adaptive use design that range from high-rise developments to municipal buildings and industrial lofts, and turning them into residential or mixed-use buildings and spaces.

Principal Kenneth Schroeder founded the firm in 1982. He is the director of the architecture department at the University of Illinois at Chicago and holds a B.A. in architecture from the University of Illinois and an M.A. in architecture from the University of Toronto. Jack Murchie and Richard Laya are also principals. Murchie holds a B.A. in architecture from the University of Michigan, and Laya has a B.A. from the University of Illinois.

Searl and Associates, Architects, PC 4 3 4 4.5
500 North Dearborn Street, 9th Floor, Chicago, IL 60610
(312) 251 - 9200 www.searlarch.com

Texture rich, highly creative residential architecture

With liberal use of rich texture and color, Linda Searl has created a unique modern style that, according to industry insiders, has propelled her to the upper echelon of Chicago architects. We are told that Searl has a keen ear for clients' needs and for developing spaces that are rooted in practical design, yet creative.

Led by Searl, the firm has served the Chicago area since 1990, following a philosophy that meshes clients' needs within the context of a building's existing environment. Searl's firm provides planning, feasibility, master planning, programming and architectural services. The firm will take on any kind of project, including new construction, restoration and high-end additions as well as interior design.

Shafer Architects, PC 4 3.5 4 4
417 South Dearborn Street, Suite 910, Chicago, IL 60605
(312) 360 - 9969 www.shaferarchitects.com

High-end, modern residential architecture

Modernist style that professionals describe as "highly intellectual," is the aesthetic hallmark of Shafer Architects. Clients say the firm provides them with exceptional personal service, particularly from Tom Shafer, sole principal of the firm. Shafer is also lauded by insiders for his ability to take control of a project to ensure that budgets and deadlines are closely met. Together, these qualities make Shafer a highly sought-after firm. The firm specializes in large renovations and additions, with nearly all of it's work residential. Clients say Shafer has "impeccable taste" and a keen eye for detail.

The six-member team splits its portfolio between the city and the suburbs and occasionally takes on out-of-state projects. Its pricing is said to be standard. Fees for new construction are based on a percentage of total costs, and renovations and additions are billed on an hourly rate. Insiders tell us that Shafer's own home is the quintessential example of the firm's expertise in modernist design.

"Tom has great imagination and foresight." "His use of materials is really quite innovative." "Very knowledgeable on specialty products." "Tom has the highest integrity." "We are satisfied clients in every possible aspect." "Very accurate timing and delivered exactly on budget."

Stuart Cohen & Julie Hacker Architects 4.5 4 4.5 5
1322 Sherman Avenue, Evanston, IL 60201
(847) 328 - 2500

Custom residential architecture, interior architecture

A husband-and-wife team, Stuart Cohen and Julie Hacker are said to appreciate not only the aesthetic of building, but also the ergonomics of living. Clients applaud the modern, dramatic play of space and light punctuated by traditional forms and design that incorporates the best of both styles. The firm is also credited with designs that are extensions of their surroundings, whether they are built from the ground up in a natural environment, a major addition to a historic home, or an interior remodeling project. Clients say that instead of eliminating the elements of an existing space, Cohen & Hacker works with the space to improve its aesthetic and function.

Cohen, a professor of architecture at the University of Illinois, Chicago, has been in practice here for more than 25 years and joined by Hacker for 15 of them. Together they head this small firm that specializes in residential architecture on the North Shore with the occasional commission in the city. Prior to opening this firm in 1973, Cohen worked in the offices of such notables as Richard Meier, Phillip Johnson and John Burgee. In keeping with this company of stellar architects, his own firm has gained wide recognition and its work has been published nationally.

Interior designers as well as clients laud the firm for what they call "extraordinary" talent, and enjoy the collaboration. We're told the firm keeps contractors in control with strong direction and brings a sense of proportion to projects while maintaining good working relationships with everyone on the job. Its communication skills are considered excellent, whether talking budget or schedule. Problems, we hear, are resolved quickly and well.

The typical 5,000- to 6,000-square-foot Cohen & Hacker home costs between $200 and $250 per square foot. Fees are based on a sliding scale, dropping after the first $1 million in total job cost. Smaller projects command a more hefty fee, and the smallest are billed on an hourly rate.

"Stuart loves what he does. I want him on my team." "Whenever there was a glitch, there was always a good resolution." "Budget always becomes an issue, but they were very realistic about it up front. . . and they were right on the mark." "One of only two architects I'd ever recommend. Stuart is an unmistakable talent—and a good guy to boot." "Stuart has wonderful design sense."

Stuart D. Shayman & Associates **3.5 3.5 4 4**

1780 Ash Street, Northfield, IL 60093
(847) 441 - 7555

Clean, practical residential architecture

Highly respected for his design instinct, Stuart Shayman is also said to bring rational, practical solutions to this firm's projects. We're told Shayman's design judgement is intelligent and carefully suited to each client's style of living. He is particularly known for his exquisite remodeling and historic renovation projects. Clients say the firm's fees are very reasonable in relation to the quality of both its design and service. Shayman's architectural style ranges from conservative contemporary to traditional.

Shayman, the sole principal, created this three-person firm 25 years ago after working at Grunsfeld and Associates. The vast majority of this firm's work is residential, with approximately 80 percent taking place in the suburbs, remaining in the city. About half of the firm's yearly projects are single-family new home construction and the other half are additions. Shayman tends to attract well-established empty nesters on the North Shore and charges standard hourly fee.

"Good judgement, like not spending too much on fixtures in the children's bathroom." "Good sense of home." "Some of his ideas are just marvelous." "Smart in his approach to creating sensible, livable spaces."

Susan Grant Architectural Design **3.5 3 4 4**

4800 South Chicago Beach Road, Suite 1405 North, Chicago, IL 60615
(773) 548 - 3322 www.sgrantdesign.com

Residential architecture

Susan Grant began her career at the San Francisco Housing Authority, developing uplifting designs for depressed urban areas and that city's disadvantaged populations. Insiders say these influences contributed, no doubt, to her humanistic approach to the design of spaces of all size. Sources say Grant has now taken her skills to serve a well-heeled clientele within Chicago's city limits, with a small percentage of projects in the suburbs. We hear Grant goes to great lengths to create intimate, highly personal environments.

As the sole principal of this three-person firm, Grant offers clients personalized service in a friendly, collaborative atmosphere. While her style leans toward modern, she will take on others, including Victorian and Georgian. While approximately three-quarters of the firm's work is residential, Grant has created some of the city's high-profile commercial properties.

Grant has operated the firm since 1994 and holds a B.A. in architecture from Dartmouth and an M.A. from the University of California at Berkeley. The firm charges standard architectural percentage rates or a fixed fee.

Susan Regan Architect **4** **4** **4** **4.5**

1124 Florence Avenue, Evanston, IL 60202
(847) 864 - 0999

True-to-form residential architecture

According to clients, Susan Regan brings an intelligent, well-researched knowledge of historic preservation and traditional architectural style. From knowing the complicated building codes of historic districts and buildings to creating virtually seamless additions, clients say Regan is always aware of the nuances of such projects. In addition to thoughtful intelligent design, clients say they appreciate Regan's personalized service and prompt response to questions and phone calls.

Regan is the sole practitioner of the firm she created in 1989 and works exclusively in residential architecture. The vast majority of her work takes place in the Winnetka/Evanston area, but she also takes on an occasional project in Chicago proper. Regan works with a diverse clientele whose needs range from the renovation of a single bathroom to the design of multi-million-dollar single-family homes.

"Great follow-through." "Meticulous drawings that are incredibly original." "She creates design that ultimately reflects client input." "Her work on the major renovation of my 1883 residence was sympathetic to the original structure, yet creative and innovative."

Sutherland Architectural Associates **4.5** **4.5** **4** **4.5**

548 West Fullerton, Chicago, IL 60045
(847) 234 - 1996

Architectural historic preservation

Preserving the rich architecture of Lake Forest is what sources say is Dan Sutherland's passion. He is the sole practitioner of this firm that has been steeped in architectural history for more than 20 years. Sutherland concentrates overwhelmingly on the renovation of historic estates, working with a clientele that wants to remain faithful to the original style of their homes. All of Sutherland's work is residential. His passion for preserving the past extends to philanthropy as well as architecture. He sits on the board of several organizations devoted to historic preservation, including The Open Land Architect Review Committee and the Preservation Foundation of Lake Forest.

Sutherland was educated at the University of Kentucky, and prior to starting his own firm, worked for Stanley Tigerman (see review). He charges standard hourly rates through skematic drawings and then a percentage of overall cost of construction.

The Poulton Group, Ltd. **4.5** **3.5** **4** **4.5**
268 Market Square, Lake Forest, IL 60045
(847) 615 - 1178

High-end, intricately detailed residential architecture and interior design

The Poulton Group takes the phrase "attention to detail" to its highest level, according to clients and industry insiders. We are told if a client wants five different hand crafted hardwood flooring designs, Poulton will happily oblige. If another longs for cabinetry and quarry stone from Italy, David Poulton hops on a plane. Industry insiders say old-world authenticity, craftsmanship and detail account for the superb quality of projects mastered by Poulton and his partner, Sharon Harvey.

The two principals and their firm practice both architecture and interior design. Nearly all of The Poulton Group's projects are in Lake Forest, and approximately 80 percent are new construction, with the firm assuming the general contracting function. The remainder of work is in renovations of significant, top-tier historic estates in the area, an expertise that this duo has also mastered. The firm undertakes just a few projects a year in order to give full attention to each. Its client-base consists primarily of well-heeled people with architectural and design savvy.

By living up to these clients' demanding expectations for 15 years, The Poulton Group has succeeded solely on referrals and a clientele that not only passes its name along to friends and acquaintances, but also uses the firm time and again. The firm charges standard architectural percentage rates or a fixed fee.

"Brilliant understanding of working within the context of the historical parameters." "Examined every detail, right down to the grain of the wood." "Very hands-on kind of person with a tremendous amount of respect for the style—and a nice guy too." "Fabulous, wouldn't think twice about hiring again." "Great at handling problems and honest." "More than patient, he knew what he was doing and was a great listener."

Tigerman McCurry Architects **5** **5** **4** **5**
444 North Wells Street, Suite 206, Chicago, IL 60610
(312) 644 - 5880

High-end intelligently designed residential and institutional architecture

With more than 59 years combined experience in the field, Stanley Tigerman and Margaret McCurry operate one of the most respected and lauded architecture firms in the country. Praised by clients for its consummate professionalism and gift of designing cutting-edge spaces, the firm takes on 15 projects a year. Most are residential, although the firm also puts its stamp on some notable Chicago-area institutional projects. The scope of Tigerman McCurry residential projects ranges from high-end, one-room renovations to large single-family homes. Although the pair rarely works together on projects, clients hail each principal's individual philosophy of design and highly intellectual approach to the craft. The duo is not bound to a specific style, but a number of its projects lean toward contemporary design. Twenty years ago this firm was founded as a merger of each partner's respective practices that date back as far as 1961.

McCurry concentrates primarily on the firm's high-end residential projects, where she has acquired a devoted client-base that repeatedly seeks her services to build another home, or, in one client's case, to renovate a new room every year for the past 13 years. Clients say McCurry is creative, yet realistic, and is especially talented at selecting unique materials that meet—or beat—initial budgetary requirements. She is especially praised for symmetry that is neither trite nor boring. Clients also cite her use of natural light and creative juxtaposition of rooms to one another.

Tigerman focuses much attention to the firm's institutional projects. He is a co-founder of Archeworks, a multi-disciplined school of design, based on the belief that creative people have an obligation to support design in the context of social cause. Clients say Tigerman has a penchant for intricate detail. Some describe him as an architectural "bad boy," extremely confident of his skills and rather rigid and methodical in his approach to design. ASID. AD 100, 2000. HB Top Designers, 1999, 2000. ID Hall of Fame.

"I'm happy to recommend them." "Particularly good at selecting materials." "The amount of detail is extraordinary." "We hit it off intellectually." "Stanley's strengths are creativity and imagination as well as his philosophy and intellectual approach to solving the architectural conundrum." "Stanley likes to do jewels." "Margaret is thoughtful, dependable and lovely to work with."

Ullman & Fill, Architects

230 West Huron Street, Suite 4W, Chicago, IL 60610
(312) 944 - 0004

Collaborative residential architecture

Client-involvement is among the core strengths references attribute to Marvin Ullman and Charles Fill, this firm's principals. We hear this collaborative approach results in unique and challenging projects that are distinctive, meet their owners' needs and meet expectations. Clients say the firm's modern design are exceptional in both concept and aesthetic. Clients' deep involvement, we are told, also accounts for the firm's noteworthy detailing in designs. The majority of Ullman & Fill projects are residential, primarily in downtown Chicago and the nearby suburbs, although it has accepted projects as far away as London and Martha's Vineyard.

The five-person firm handles a fairly even split of new home construction and renovations. It often handles small projects and occasionally also provides clients with interior design services. The firm charges standard architectural percentage rates or a fixed fee.

Vinci-Hamp Architects Inc. **4.5 4.5 4 5**

1147 West Ohio Street, 6th Floor, Chicago, IL 60622
(312) 733 - 7744

Institutional architecture and historic preservation

This firm's practice is known largely for its restoration, museum and remodeling projects, including the restoration of the Frank Lloyd Wright home and studio, for which principal, John Vinci, FAIA, received a National Honor Award from the American Institute of Architects in 1987. Vinci holds historical style and preservation in high regard and sits on the board of directors of the Society of Architectural Historians. He also serves on several advisory committees for the preservation of historic landmarks and is an accomplished lecturer and writer on this subject.

Industry insiders, ranging from high-end interior designers to top-notch general contractors, tell us Vinci-Hamp is among the best for creating and remodeling projects that are true to historic references in style and form. The firm's clientele leans toward classic modernism of the early 20th century and say they appreciate Vinci-Hamp's keen sense of that era's historical context.

	Quality	Cost	Value	Recommend?
Wheeler Kearns Architects	5	4.5	5	5

343 South Dearborn Street, Chicago, IL 60604
(312) 939 - 7787 www.wkarch.com

Residential architecture

Clients, decorators, and even competitors seem to agree that Wheeler Kearns is at the top of its game. A collective practice of architects, the firm gains accolades for its superb residential architecture. Work also includes everything from designing furniture to children's museums, elementary schools and dental clinics. Whatever the project, clients say, the firm is aesthetically, technically, and professionally devoted to the pursuit and practice of architecture.

We hear WKA creates spaces that depict and enhance a full, rich and dignified way of life. Its style is described as simple and adaptable. Simple, direct solutions are favored on the firm's belief that an architect's task is to improve the world with enlightened problem-solving and that each project begins with an "emotional center." Clients find Wheeler Kearns wonderfully innovative and especially commend its selection and use of materials.

Dan Wheeler established his private practice in 1987. Since then, his work has been widely published, and he's become a highly respected figure in the community. He is chairman of the Architectural Alliance at the Chicago Historical Society and teaches graduate-level design studies at the University of Illinois, Chicago. Larry Kearns joined the firm in 1988 and has been a partner since 1990. Technical skills accompany his architectural accomplishments, developing the firm's proprietary computer-aided design programs.

The firm is deliberately limited to a staff of 10 architects. A project architect is assigned to each job, managing it from schematic design through final construction. All of the firm's architects, however, have input on all jobs. This collaboration and free exchange of ideas is at the heart of the firm's true "studio" philosophy and, no doubt, the reason why many of its project architects have devoted followers.

Wheeler Kearns also wins accolades for its pricing structure, with clients mentioning that "they deserve to be paid three times more than I paid them." ID Hall of Fame.

"Great firm and Dan is such a good person." "They spec'd the job down to the last nut." "The firm wins the clients by my friends just seeing my apartment!" "Budgets were easy to discuss and never an issue." "Very responsive. Met every Tuesday at site for three years." "My project architect was absolutely tremendous."

	Quality	Cost	Value	Recommend?
Wilkinson Blender Architecture Inc.	4	3	4	4

2041 West Roscoe Street, Chicago, IL 60618
(773) 665 - 8377

Residential architecture

The small group of architects at Wilkinson Blender receives outstanding reviews from clients and top decorators for its highly intelligent designs. It is especially credited with an ability to listen to clients' needs, respect their tastes and incorporate individual and often imaginative solutions into clients' projects. Formed in January 1999, the firm has already won praise for its innovative use of materials. While it is equally adept at designing in the full range of architectural styles, its attention to the use of natural light is said to be common to all projects.

Led by Michael Wilkinson and Richard Blender, the six architects at Wilkinson Blender handle projects as diverse as a screened-in porch pavilion in Michigan and a 7,000-square-foot, updated shingle-style house on the North Shore. The majority of the firm's work is residential, and we're told it actively seeks clients who are concerned about and interested in design as sources for especially interesting projects. The firm charges standard architectural percentage rates for its services.

"These young guys are totally professional and very smart."

Hiring an Audio/Video Design & Installation Service Provider

These days, one doesn't have to crave global domination to enjoy a room that can, at the punch of a button, transform itself into a ground control headquarters that rivals any James Bond movie scene. Home theaters, multi-zone entertainment systems, home-automation and lighting controls, online capability —if you can dream it, they can hook it up. Just make sure you ask for the remote, or you may never be able to use what you paid for.

Audio/video (A/V) home service providers can seamlessly integrate almost anything—media walls, touch screen panels, speakers, structured cabling—into your existing components or into the architectural integrity of any room. If this isn't possible, they will build new cabinets to accommodate the equipment. Custom installation is the name of the game.

What to Expect From an A/V Specialist

A/V providers can be contracted through general contractors, designers or directly by you. Whomever they bill, communication with the homeowner is essential. When courting your A/V guru, remember that they may specialize only a few of the following areas: audio, video, telephone, Internet, security, lighting and climate control. A service provider who excels in home theater installation may not be as well versed in, or even deal with, security. You should also know whether the service provider can perform all the functions of integration. Determine your needs, get references, ask questions. Will the A/V specialist both design and engineer your project, or will he or she be coordinating with other trades?

Even when working through a designer, a good A/V contractor will want to meet with you one-on-one to assess your needs. Make the time. You don't want your system to outreach your ability or desire to operate it. Don't get swept up in your tech-happy A/V provider's enthusiasm for all the cool things available to you. Stand fast. Are you really looking for a movie palace complete with stadium seating, and does it really need to be tied into the landscape lighting and the air conditioner in the kitchen? Remember, the latest may not be the greatest if the newest innovation hasn't been around long enough to be tested. Some A/V contractors prefer a lag time of six months after the introduction of a product so that they can follow its performance before recommending it to their customers. If you're the first one in on a new gizmo, know that you may be the first one out of luck.

The means of customization and the materials used differ widely from shop to shop. Some contractors only work in certain brands. Others will install anything you want. Request that the bid proposal be itemized and a sketch attached if you want the finished product to perfectly match your dreams.

Who Will Install My New System?

Although you'll first talk with either a principal or a representative of the A/V firm, traditionally a crew of field-techies will be dispatched to perform the installation and service. Don't fret: this crew is likely to be as well informed and passionate about its business as any front man, so you should feel you're in good hands. It's invaluable to be able to speak to the same person from the beginning to the end of the project.

Miscommunication commonly surrounds the role of the electrician in an A/V installation. Some A/V providers want your electrician to pull the low voltage cable if he's already on site and already holds a permit, eliminating a coordination headache. Many prefer to do it themselves, knowing that some electricians treat delicate cables with the care of baggage handlers at O'Hare. Just check that someone's on it before the walls close up. Also, know that A/V contractors are not going to install or relocate the electrical receptacles that will power up your system and provide the jolt for the sub-woofers.

PRICING AND SERVICE WARRANTEES

The cost of your A/V project will be a reflection of the design work involved, the degree of customization, the type and number of devices and pieces of equipment to be installed, the length of cable to be pulled and the anticipated man hours, plus overhead and profit. Many jobs require a deposit of up to 50 percent, with progress payments to be made when materials and equipment arrive on site, and again upon job completion. The warranty guarantees should appear on the bid proposal. A year of free service is standard.

LICENSE CONSIDERATIONS

Because this is a new field, there is currently no licensing requirement for A/V services in the Chicago metro area. Fortunately, this also means that no permit is required. Check your municipality, however, because where it's mandated, these service providers should be licensed and insured. If you're still confused, the Custom Electronic Design and Installation Association (CEDIA at www.cedia.org) is an excellent resource.

THE HOTTEST NEW TRENDS

When it comes to home theater, blockbuster breakthroughs include Digital Video Disc (DVD) players, which offer much higher sound and visual quality than videos or laser discs. A movie on a DVD comes through at 500 lines of resolution, double the clarity of a 250-line videocassette. DVD players also offer lush Dolby Digital Surround Sound (DDSS). The quality of television output has advanced, too, with the advent of High Definition Television (HDTV) and Plasma TVs (those sleek, thin TVs, only four inches in depth that can be hung on the wall). Cutting-edge, multi-zone entertainment systems allow you to play CDs jukebox-style or listen to the radio or TV in any room of the house. For example, programming the system to air your favorite classical radio station through the bathroom speakers while you relax in the jacuzzi is simply a matter of pressing a touch screen.

Some A/V companies also provide a full line of home automation services, including wireless lighting controls that you can run from your phone (to turn the lights on if you'll be working late) or from a pad clipped onto your car visor. Home automation also applies to climate control, with wireless systems that let you turn on the heat, air conditioning or lawn sprinklers from any room in the house—or virtually anywhere, via telephone. Thanks to the latest user-friendly A/V programming systems, the days of not being able to program your VCR are over.

HOW TO GET THE MOST OUT OF YOUR SYSTEM

- Sit down with the installer to discuss your wants and needs in detail.
- Don't rush for the newest technology.
- Only install gear you'll actually use.
- Don't fall asleep during the technician's instructions on how to program each device.

Quality	Cost	Value	Recommend?
✚	$	◆	★

AUDIO/VIDEO DESIGN & INSTALLATION

ABT Electronics
| 3.5 | 2.5 | 3.5 | 4 |

9000 Waukegan Road, Morton Grove, IL 60053
(847) 967 - 8830 www.abtelectronics.com
Audio/video and appliance sales and installation

In testimony to both the importance of electronics and this company's expertise, ABT has grown from a tiny, three-person, storefront shop in 1936 to a company of truly enormous scope. Today ABT occupies nine acres in Morton Grove and has more than 800 employees, 50 trucks and a fleet of 38 installer vans and 46 service vans. Its current 130,000-square-foot showroom displays and demonstrates a full array of products, and, if that's not enough—and, apparently it isn't—ABT will move this year to a new 350,000-square-foot show-room and headquarters in nearby Glenview.

We're told that it has been satisfying consumers' electronic needs through-out the midwest since its inception. Clients say its inventory is extensive and includes nearly every upper-end brand of electronic equipment and appliance. Our sources tell us the ABT appliance installation and repair centers are efficient and that its delivery of products and services is timely, even though it makes approximately 6,000 delivery and repair calls each week. References also applaud ABT Electronic's customer service and reasonable prices.

"Knowledgeable technicians with customer-friendly attitudes." "Great prices!" "These guys do wonderful installation work which surprised and delighted me."

Audio Consultants
| 4 | 3 | 4 | 4 |

1014 Davis Street, Evanston, IL 60201
(847) 864 - 9565 www.audioconsultants.com
Audio/video sales, service and installation

Whether you want a couple of new speakers or every A/V bell and whistle, Audio Consultants delivers. For more than 33 years, this full-service audio/video retailer has been selling, designing and installing high-performance products in the Chicago area. We are told it has the tools and expertise to provide quality, professional installation to customers who are building a new home, remodeling, or adding to an existing system. Clients who've used Audio Consultants for everything from a simple enhancement to a multi-zone, multi-source system with remote sensors and speakers in many rooms, report that Audio Consultants' work has made them happy listeners and viewers. They also rank this company's service departments among the best in the city.

Barretts, The Home Theater Store
| 3 | 3 | 3 | 4 |

744 Industrial Drive, Elmhurst, IL 60126
(630) 941 - 0070 www.barrettshometheater.com
Audio/video and home theater sales, installation and service

This company has a reputation for providing the latest in home entertainment technology. This family owned and operated company has been designing and installing home theater and audio systems in Chicago and the surrounding area for more than 30 years. Its technicians get high marks from clients who also say Barretts' customer service makes the Hit Parade.

"We love our state-of-the-art custom home theater system they designed and installed for us." "Great customer service!" "I am and continue to be impressed with the level of service before and after the installation of the system."

Baumeister Audio Video Interiors **4.5** **3.5** **4.5** **4.5**
5342 North Northwest Highway, Chicago, IL 60630
(773) 774 - 9080 www.bavi.net

Audio/video integration and custom home theater design

Chicago A/V aficionados love the guys at Baumeister, whom some characterize as media-savvy aging rock stars. That's a compliment. For 12 years Baumeister has kept abreast of audio visual trends and technology and incorporated them into its designs, which extend to highly complex systems with multiple-room controls and diverse capabilities. The firm's top-of-the-line equipment and professional expertise have made it a favorite resource for interior designers and demanding clients. The 12-person staff has a loyal following and is credited with a high level of customer satisfaction and strict attention to the different needs of individual clients.

"Two aging rock stars that really know their stuff." "They were able to put an incredibly complicated system in our house where you can choose the CD from any room. My husband is very particular in this area and he just loves these guys." "Their installers left our house cleaner than when they arrived." "Great follow-up service."

Cinematronix **4.5** **3.5** **4.5** **4.5**
424 North Oakley Boulevard, Chicago, IL 60612
(312) 243 - 2009 www.cinematronix.com

Trade only—Custom upholstery and design of home theaters

For those who want true theater ambiance, this is a firm that specializes in the design of residential theaters that often include upholstered wall systems and custom-built theater seating, but it doesn't make popcorn. The Cinematronix in-house staff of theater designers has expertise in fine woodworking, theatrical carpentry and the restoration and reproduction of art objects and antiques. It is a contracted service that charges a retainer for design, which includes provision of an initial floor plan, room elevations and a cost estimate. The company does not handle audio/video installation, but has joined forces with Baumeister Audio Video Interiors (see review above) to complete projects.

"Great people to work with." "Craftsmen are excellent." "They really take pride in their work." "We have the most beautiful theater we will enjoy for years."

Columbia Audio/Video **5** **4** **5** **5**
1741 Second Street, Highland Park, IL 60035
(847) 433 - 6010 www.columbiaaudiovideo.com

Audio/video integration and custom home theater design

Columbia is in that top tier of audio/video specialists that works with many of Chicago's best interior designers, architects and builders. It has secured a reputation for designing and installing very high-end, complex audio visual systems, including home theaters, and its clients enjoy the support of continuing service. References agree that the staff's work is very high quality and the firm's products and technology are state-of-the-art. Columbia is credited with providing individual attention to the design, supply and installation of each system it develops. What's more, the service is said to be timely and hassle-free.

"They're amazing. They made our home system so user-friendly and easy to use." "They presented valuable input to our contractor and architect that saved us from costly structural changes later."

Quality	Cost $	Value ◆	Recommend? ★

Custom Electronic Systems
956 West Bartlett Road, Bartlett, IL 60103
(630) 837 - 6254

Audio/video installation and service

Custom Home Theaters, Ltd.

| 4.5 | 3 | 4 | 4 |

514 Regan Drive, East Dundee, IL 60118
(847) 836 - 8197

Audio/video integration and custom home theater design

Since opening its doors in 1998, Custom Home Theaters has been giving Chicago-area residents the classic theater experience at home, we're told. The company serves the upper-end market and specializes in the design and installation of private theater systems along with the complex integration of audio and video equipment and home automation. One client said he was so pleased with the company's work that he had Custom Home Theaters also oversee the design and installation of a theater system, done by local installers, at his second, out-of-state residence. He said he was particularly impressed to see principal Ray Finato show up there for a final inspection to ensure complete satisfaction. Despite Custom Home's attention to detail and service, the total ticket, according to clients, is relatively moderate.

"Their professionalism and attention to detail and budget is wonderful." "A very pleasurable team." "Ray gets to know his clients and their needs. He didn't try to sell us more than we needed. In fact, he helped us stay within our budget, and everything was installed on schedule."

Father & Sons Home Services, Inc.

| 3.5 | 3.5 | 4 | 3.5 |

22 West 421 Oldwoods Drive, Naperville, IL 60565
(630) 985 - 3600

Audio/video, security, telephone and home theater design and installation

Think of all the mind-boggling technology that could make life simpler and then call Father & Sons. This company supplies and skillfully integrates the full range of automated residential electronics systems. These encompass audio/video, security, telephone and communications, lighting and acoustical design, and satellite installation along with closed circuit TV. Father & Sons will not only combine all these capabilities into an easy-to-use system, but also provide monitoring of the system's integrated burglar and fire alarms. It has served the Chicago area for 27 years and wins praise for its talent in making the complex simple.

"They're great at systems integration."

Gill Custom House, Inc.
8813 West 95th Street, Palos Hills, IL 60465
(708) 598 - 2400

Custom home theater design

	Quality	Cost	Value	Recommend?
Good Vibes Sound Inc.	3.5	3	3.5	3

1807 South Neil Street, Champaign, IL 61820
(217) 351 - 0909 www.gvibes.com

Audio/video and home theater design, installation and service

Good Vibes has just what its name implies, and it spreads them generously among homeowners, architects and builders in both new homes and existing ones. The company designs, installs and services custom audio visual systems, home theaters, and integrated home automation. It also installs data distribution systems that require digital satellite phone and computer wiring. Its vibes have been picked up by a leading electronics trade magazine, Audio/Video International, which consistently names Good Vibes a Retailer of The Year. References agree that the firm's staff is knowledgeable and gives friendly, personal service, and they praise the technicians' level of professional service and attention to detail.

"Very meticulous." "Great in-home service repair."

	Quality	Cost	Value	Recommend?
Holm Audio	4	3.5	4	4

2050 West 75th Street, Woodridge, IL 60517
(630) 663 - 1298 www.holmaudio.com

Audio/video and home theater installation and service

References tell us Holm Audio's installations are high end and that its 10-person staff is very knowledgeable, gives excellent advice on audio and video systems and equipment, and also provides quick and efficient service. The company has been in business for 10 years. Its services include structured wiring, home automation and home theater systems integration. References appreciate the company's ability to stick to a budget. Holm does not handle security or telephone systems.

"I'm extremely happy with Holm Audio from purchase to final installation." "I received very helpful training on the system they installed in my home." "They were responsible and provided excellent advice regarding my home audio needs."

	Quality	Cost	Value	Recommend?
ISR Inc.	5	4	5	5

1997 Ohio Street, Lisle, IL 60532
(630) 515 - 9100 www.isr-usa.com

Home management systems

ISR rates "platinum" for its record of achievement in custom-tailored, unified systems solutions that enable clients to easily manage their luxury homes and commercial facilities. Its 50-year history and third-generation management has taken it to the top of the charts with builders, interior designers, consultants and contractors. ISR offers comprehensive, one-stop solutions that unify climate, lighting, security, phone/data, audio/video, water management and aroma systems. The majority of ISR's projects are large and complex. Its roster of clients and installations is impressive with projects ranging from 10,000- and 70,000-square-foot residences and estates to a million-square-foot public transportation facility for Amtrak. Small wonder it has gained a reputation for leadership in home management systems.

Among its many honors are two awards for Home of the Year at the 2000 Consumer Electronics Show, ranking as top installer in the country by the Custom Electronic Design & Installation Association (CEDIA), and a place on *Audio Video International* magazine's list of top 10 custom installers in the country. This year, the trade magazine, CE PRO, includes ISR in its ranking of top 50 consumer electronic retail revenue producers nationwide, and, for the second year in a row, ISR received the Robb Report's "Best of the Best" award for home convenience technology. It has also won two gold key awards from the Chicago Home Builders Association.

"This is a company of professionals from the top to the bottom, and I would not hesitate to recommend them to anyone who is looking for an automation or audio/video contractor." "They are total professionals and very service-oriented." "Being a national organization allows them to service my needs in two states."

Kass Electronics **3.5** **3** **4** **4**

26W515 Saint Charles Road, Carol Stream, IL 60188
(630) 221 - 8480 www.kasselectronics.com

Audio/video, telephone, home theater, lighting and automation design and installation

Since 1987, Kass Electronics has been offering a variety of custom home entertainment and electronic systems to Chicago-area clients. Its specialties encompass home theater design, computer networking and high-speed Internet access networks, full integration of multi-room audio and video systems and equipment, lighting control, climate control, automated window treatments and the design and installation of telephone systems. It works on both new construction and existing homes with individual clients and/or with their architects, interior designers and contractors. Home Theater Interiors Magazine ranked a Kass project among its top 20 home theater installations in the United States.

"Responsive to my needs." "Listened to my questions and answered with good clear explanation." "Bill Dwyer is a top-notch designer and salesman. He knows what he's talking about—no tap dancing."

Media Designers and Installation **4.5** **5** **4.5** **5**

By appointment only, Kildeer, IL
(847) 550 - 9040 www.media-designers.com

Audio/video sales, design, installation and integration

Known in the industry as a leader in low voltage systems, Media Designers' workmanship has been exceeding expectations since its doors opened in 1990, according to our references. This company specializes in high-end residential control-system integration and designs, sells, installs and services a complete range of electronic solutions for the home or office. Media Designers' expertise encompasses integration of audio and video, lighting, HVAC (heating, ventilation and air conditioning), spa and pool temperature-control and motorized covers, security systems and surveillance cameras, and motorized window-screens. When it comes to audio/video, principal Lou Santello has been referred to as a "Professor Emeritus." Clients are uniformly pleased with the company's quality of work, and we are told that top Chicago decorators readily recommend Media Designers to their clients. The firm's work has been featured in *Better Homes and Gardens*, *Remodeled Homes* magazine and *USA Today*.

"Solid designs, quality installation and personal service." "We are so pleased with their trouble-free, simple-to-use home theater system." "No false promises."

Metronet Safe & Sound **4** **3.5** **4** **4**

67 East Madison Street, Suite 265, Chicago, IL 60603
(312) 781 - 0051 www.safesound.com

Audio/video, security, telephone and home theater design and installation

Gillian and Jack Schultz, the husband-and-wife owners of Metronet, have been making futuristic technology safe, sound and easy for residents of the Chicago metro area since 1981. The company designs, installs, services and maintains sophisticated, high-end home systems that integrate entertainment and security. Audio/video, home theater, whole-house automation, Internet-ready home networks, security, telephone communications and climate and lighting control are within Metronet's capabilities. While clients appreciate the convenience of putting all their high tech needs in the capable hands of electronics engineer, Jack Schultz, and his company, they are even more grateful that these custom systems are so easy to use after installation. "User-friendly" applies here.

"Great state-of-the-art products." "They worked well with our architect and builder in the planning and implementation of our system." "They know their electronics inside and out." "A highly impressive company."

Mills Custom Audio/Video **4.5** **4** **4.5** **5**
358 Lexington Drive, Buffalo Grove, IL 60089
(847) 419 - 9990

Audio/video and telephone system design, installation and integration

Demand for Mills' eight great technicians is so high that while some clients would like to see the company grow, others fear expansion might jeopardize its personal service and attention to detail. Led by a second generation, Mills brings more than 60 years of experience to the design and installation of custom audio/video systems, home theaters and other electronic capabilities. Its expertise also includes lighting-control, phone systems and computer networking. Clients praise its wide-ranging technical know-how and user-friendly integration of multi-room controls and systems. The company works on new construction, renovations and on smaller consolidations of existing home entertainment systems. We are told, regardless of a project's size or complexity, Mills delivers all the right stuff. It works with individual clients as well as architects, interior designers and contractors.

"Their ability to take highly technical equipment and make it simple to use is very much appreciated." "Fred Thomas is the man." "Great at being able to network." "They don't abandon you when the project's complete."

Paul Heath Audio, Ltd. **4** **4** **4** **4**
2036 North Clark Street, Chicago, IL 60614
(773) 549 - 8100

Audio/video design and integrated home automation

Paul Heath Audio has a reputation for staying in tune with industry innovations and orchestrating complex and diverse technologies into systems that are easy to use. It employs 15 technicians that create home automation that integrates audio/video with a full range of electronic capabilities. The company has 25 years of experience in this evolving specialty, and we are told it has a track record for tailoring its repertoire to the specific needs of different clients and budgets. References also cite the firm's professionalism and friendly service.

"Techno geniuses." "They set up our entire low voltage system. And I couldn't be happier with the results." "The staff is very knowledgeable, courteous and conscientious. I'm looking forward to working with them again."

Pechlife **3** **3** **3** **3**
2114 North Milwaukee Avenue, Chicago, IL 60647
(773) 486 - 5433

Audio/video integration and custom home theater design

This small firm of four translates tech talk into ordinary English. It specializes in the conceptual design, installation, service and maintenance of high-end home electronics systems, including whole-house audio, structured wiring, networking, automation and, when required, the integration of home theater systems. Clients are at no loss for words in praising the ease of operation and control in Pechlife's custom-designed packages.

"Their willingness to explain technical details is refreshing." "Excellent service." "Very professional."

ProLine Integrated Systems **4.5** **4** **5** **4.5**
3160 Skokie Valley Road, Highland Park, IL 60035
(847) 681 - 1500 www.prolineintegrated.com

Audio/video and home theater sales, design, installation and home automation

Those who fear tech wrecks from the invasion of electronic equipment turn to ProLine, which is recognized for its ability to discreetly merge integrated technology into architectural surroundings and interior design. In its 12 years as a specialist in home electronics, ProLine has branched beyond its original offering of only home theater and audio/video systems to become a full-service electronic systems resource for homeowners, architects, interior designers and builders. Its services encompass consulting, complete custom design, engineering, product sales, installation, home automation, project management, and, following installation, future refinements of systems as technology evolves.

"They have enhanced our lifestyle and made our home more comfortable, safe and efficient." "Whether conventional or extremely eccentric, they deliver."

R-2 Electronics **4 3 4 4.5**

139 Heather Lane, Wilmette, IL 60091
(312) 807 - 5400

Audio/video, telephone and computer installation and integration

We're told that R-2 Electronics can make your home future-proof by wiring it with cabling systems that enable you to take advantage of future technologies from the computer telecommunications, and entertainment industries. Customers willingly priase R-2 Electronics as attentive and up-to-date on the latest technology. We hear that this small two-person team aims to please and will work closely with clients, architects and designers to build and install the system that best suits the customer needs.

Sound & Vision **4.5 4 5 5**

14474 La Grange Road, Orland Park, IL 60462
(708) 403 - 2500 www.soundandvisionusa.com

Audio/video and home theater sales, design, installation and home automation

Be dazzled by the sights and sounds that can be previewed in operation at this showroom, one of Chicago's best one-stop sources for state-of-the-art audio/video, home theater, and home automation. In addition to offering products retail, Sound & Vision also designs and installs systems, including complex ones that call for integration of multi-room controls, lighting, satellite television and telephone communications. It does not handle home security systems. For a decade, interior designers as well as retail customers have been putting their complete audio/video needs in the capable hands of Sound & Vision's skilled and responsive staff. One designer source won't entrust his clients' structural wiring and audio visual work to anyone else.

Sound & Vision recently received The John Bowers Quest for Perfection award from Bowers & Wilkens, the premier maker of high-end speakers. According to the industry trade magazine, CE PRO, Sound & Vision ranked 27th in 2000 sales revenues among consumer electronics retailers nationwide.

"Excellent design, installation and upgrades—state-of-the-art systems." Quality work." "Their installation services are well-organized, skilled and responsive."

	Quality	Cost	Value	Recommend?

Superior Satellite & Home Theater
96 West Northwest Highway, Palatine, IL 60067
(847) 358 - 9283
Audio/video design and integration

The Audio Video Consultant Neil Morganstein — 4 | 3 | 4 | 4.5
2930 North Sheridan Road, Suite 1912, Chicago, IL 60657
(773) 528 - 5017
Audio/video, satellite, telephone, computer network and automation design, installation and maintenance

We were asked to keep this firm under wraps. Its three technicians, including the company's namesake, are an "insider's find," capable of providing complete design, installation and maintenance of audio, video, satellite, telephone, automation and computer network systems for new construction or renovations. Whether adapting available wiring to new technology or customizing a system around the client's existing componentry this company delivers. When it comes to anything electronic, Chicago-area building and design professionals say The Audio Video Consultant Neil Morganstein is music to their ears.

"A marvel." "Does everything." "Great at getting work done in a timely fashion."

The Little Guys — 4 | 3.5 | 4 | 4
18305 South Halsted Street, Glenwood, IL 60425
(708) 754 - 8844 www.thelittleguys.com
Audio/video and home theater design, installation and integration

Don't be deceived, The Little Guys is a big place with big capabilities and a big-time reputation for service as well as product. It counts Chicago celebrities among its clientele, which also includes architects, interior designers and high-end builders as well as homeowners. The 13,000-square-foot showroom previews the lastest in A/V exotica. Professionals appreciate that the operation is "non-retail" in nature. The company is run by four members of the same family with a staff of 30. Designing and installating whole-home, custom audio/video systems, often integrated with home theater, is The Little Guys' specialty, and it will also design and install advanced wiring structures for computer and telephone connections. It does not handle home security.

"These guys are anything but little."

Tweeter (formerly United Audio) — 5 | 4 | 5 | 5
900 North Michigan Avenue, Chicago, IL 60611
(312) 664 - 3100 www.tweeter.com
Audio/video installation and service

Tweeter just feathered its nest with the acquisition of seven United Audio and four Douglas TV stores. United in particular built a great reputation among Chicago's top interior designers, architects, builders and upper-end residents over the past 37 years. They rank it among the top 10 A/V suppliers and installers in all of Chicago. Some are concerned that its merger into a larger family of A/V providers will erode the care and attention they've come to expect from United's skilled and knowledgeable technicians. Rest assured, although the name changed, many of those technicians will still be on hand. On its own, Tweeter has won accolades as Consumer Electronics Retailer of the Year from *AudioVideo International*, an insider trade publication, in four of the past five years.

"They deliver the goods." "High quality systems." "Masters at orchestrating the installation process."

	Quality	Cost	Value	Recommend?
Village Audio/Video	**4**	**3.5**	**4**	**4**

809 Ridge Road, 1st Floor, Wilmette, IL 60091
(847) 251 - 0250

Audio/video, telephone, computer and home theater installation and service

Custom applies to both the systems and the service clients have come to expect from Village Audio/Video since 1960. Its stellar reputation stands on the service that accompanies its design and installation of complex custom audio/video, telephone, computer network and home theater systems. We're told that its 11-person staff is as attentive to small-job customers as it is to its higher-profile architect and contractor clientele. Customers at all levels say Village Audio/Video doesn't miss details. More recently, the company added future-ready wiring systems for new and existing homes to its roster of capabilities.

"Great in-house service center." "These professionals are very thorough."

Hiring a Closet Designer

Are you embarrassed to take your guest's coat because you're not sure what's going to come crashing down as soon as you open the closet door? Are you tired of being late to dinner because you can't remember in which dark corner of your closet you last crammed your shoes? If you want to get maximum use out of minimum space, it's time to call a closet professional.

Where Do I Start?

There are many options to consider in designing custom closets. For example, for your bedroom closet you can choose to have more hanging space and fewer shelves, or vice versa, depending on your particular wardrobe. Hanging double rods (one above another) for short items such as jackets and shirts will maximize the hanging space. You can also incorporate drawers, shoe cubbies, sectioned jewelry drawers, and slide-out tie and belt racks, among numerous accessories. Custom closets are just that—customized for your particular needs and space. Familiarize yourself with the options. If you can't visualize what you want or just need some ideas, start by visiting the closet companies. Many stores have showrooms that display their work. Some companies will come to your home to give a free consultation and estimate. Closet professionals can help you determine the exact configuration of shelving, hanging space and accessories to best organize your closets.

Material Choices

Most closet professionals use similar materials. One of the most popular is pressed wood covered with either a wood veneer or melamine (also called laminate). Wood veneer is a thin layer of wood; melamine is a thin layer of vinyl. Pressed wood with a wood veneer gives the appearance of being solid wood. Melamine is durable and comes in numerous color choices, making it a favorite among customers.

Another popular material is vinyl-covered steel wire. It produces a clean and contemporary look. Because this surface is a wire grid and not solid, it allows good air circulation throughout the closet. However, the grids can leave an imprint on soft clothing, so a piece of cardboard or plexiglass may be needed to cover shelves or the bottoms of baskets. Vinyl-covered steel wire sliding baskets allows you to see what is in the drawers without opening them, which can be a great benefit in the case of unreachable or hard-to-access spots. It is generally difficult to find closet companies that use solid wood because it is so expensive and can warp and change over time, however, it is very attractive, and generally used in the highest quality applications with a wood veneer.

On Cost

The cost of custom closets depends on the size and scope of the specific job. There may be a retainer fee and/or a minimum installation fee. After the size of the job, which affects the amount of labor and materials involved, the most important influence on the price is the choice of material. Other details such as the condition of the existing walls will also influence the price. The more prep work a company has to do, the more expensive the job will be.

By far the most expensive material is solid wood. However, if it is important to you that your closet looks like a room in a mansion, with architectural details, inset panels and artistic moldings, you might consider talking to a millworker instead of a closet company.

Pressed wood is much more stable as well as less expensive. The cost of pressed wood with a veneer depends on what kind of wood veneer you choose. Cherry is more expensive than maple, for example. A wood veneer finish will be two to three times the price of melamine. Vinyl-covered steel wire is the cheapest closet system and the easiest to install.

What Should I Expect From a Closet Designer?

Do not underestimate the professionalism needed for maximizing and organizing your home's storage spaces. Closet companies should be licensed, insured and bonded. You should also inquire about each company's warranty, which can range in duration anywhere from one year to a lifetime.

While some companies do everything themselves, from design to installation, others consult and design and then subcontract the actual installation to someone else. Ask exactly how much of the project is kept in house. You also want to find out how long the process takes. For example, if the company has to order your favorite brass doorknobs from Italy, it is going to take longer than using materials that are readily available. Consider your time constraints; are you willing to wait months for the perfect fittings? Also, note that a company might not be able to immediately install your closet due to demand, and it could take a few weeks to begin the job.

Be a Closet Maven

- For the kids, install adjustable shelves that can accommodate a wardrobe that grows with them. If space allows, consider pull-out bins for toys.
- Wire shelves (vinyl-covered or bare) and louvered doors offer better ventilation than pressed wood shelves. Towels or damp items will dry faster and the air will stay fresher. Consider using wire shelves for mudroom and bathroom closets, attics and basements.
- A cedar closet helps to protect off-season clothes from moths.
- Adding a drop-down ironing board in your walk-in closet allows you to quickly press out wrinkles.
- Install a light in your closet so you can see better. You can even wire it so that the light goes on and off automatically when you open and close the door.

CLOSET DESIGNERS

	Quality	Cost	Value	Recommend?
California Closets	**3.5**	**3.5**	**3**	**3**

123 Eisenhower Lane South, Lombard, IL 60148
(630) 916 - 7393 www.calclosets.com

Closet design and installation—laminate

Established in 1978, California Closets continues to be a popular choice for homeowners and is used frequently by designers and builders for closet design and organization. With Chicago-area showrooms in Highland Park, Hinsdale, Naperville and at the Merchandise Mart, California Closets offers designs ranging from the merely simple and functional to the elegant and even chic. While resources praise the company's service, they tell us that it's hard to establish relationships with sales personnel because of high turnover. Some references also tell us this company's prices are disproportionately higher than competitors prices for comparable quality. Nevertheless, many customers keep going back, and last November California Closets passed all the requirements necessary to gain the Good Housekeeping Seal of Approval.

"It is what it is." "I appreciate their standardized methodology." "Excellent service."

	Quality	Cost	Value	Recommend?
Closet Builders	**4.5**	**2.5**	**4.5**	**5**

506 South Elmwood Avenue, Oak Park, IL 60304
(708) 848 - 2510

Closet design and installation—laminate, wire

For 12 years this one-man operation has gained stature through Frank Megyery's undivided attention to clients' needs. Customers say he is not only dedicated, but also pleasant and patient. Closet Builders uses laminate and wire material for its custom designs and works primarily for individual homeowners. The company has also occasionally designed and supplied real estate management companies and high-end condominium builders. In addition to praising Megyery's personal attention, clients tell us he is as thorough in measuring as he is in designing. While closets, including walk-in dressing rooms, are the company's specialty, it is known to also design and install wall units at a client's request.

"A true find!" "I couldn't be happier with his work." "Frank is incredible; professional, meticulous and attentive." "A responsive company delivering excellent work." "I would never use anyone else." "I didn't know what I wanted, but Frank helped me through every phase and designed my dream closet."

	Quality	Cost	Value	Recommend?
Closet Creator	**4.5**	**2.5**	**5**	**5**

856 Cambridge Place, Wheeling, IL 60090
(847) 541 - 5449

Closet design and installation—laminate, wire

Self-proclaimed storage specialist Joseph Galow is the creator of closets in this one-man operation that has been practicing throughout the Chicago suburbs for the past 14 years. He takes pride in his ability to organize closets anywhere in a home, and his confidence is confirmed by a base of satisfied residential customers. This closet organizer is a genuine "find," who came to our attention through several widely respected leading Chicago interior designers. Galow does all measuring, design and installation and offers product in laminate and wood. Prices are based on the linear feet of material used on the job.

"Extremely up-beat and ready to serve." "Highly dependable and very nice—Joseph's truly a great guy." "A helpful company with a good attitude." "Job was done quickly, quietly and efficiently."

Closet Depot **4** **3** **4.5** **4.5**

1441 Elmhurst Road, Elk Grove Village, IL 60007
(847) 718 - 0620

Closet design and installation—laminate, wire

Clients who want to study closet systems before they buy can go to this depot's showroom for a display of its wares, which include custom configured closets, cabinetry and countertops. Owner Fausto Ortiz and his personable, 12-member staff have been serving the Chicago area with for the past six years. While much of its business is with private homeowners, it is also said to be a top choice among many builders and also often works with interior designers. Closet Depot offers free in-home estimates. References say staff members are meticulous in scrutinizing the company's factory-built components for defects, prior to installation. We're told that during installation, the teams are responsible, efficient and tidy. Customers also say the prices are reasonable.

"Their quality is excellent, their pricing is reasonable and their service is professional." "Outstanding and timely installation."

Closet Doctor **3.5** **3.5** **4** **3.5**

Clinic located in Park Ridge, IL 60068
(847) 696 - 0783

Closet design and installation

People choked for storage in many of Chicago's older homes have been calling this doctor for more than 13 years. The prescriptions provided by Kevin Peth, who works from his home, are universally regarded as a reliable cure. His specialty is organization, where he works primarily with owners. Homeowners, including a client with a house based on Frank Lloyd Wright's architectural style, credit Peth for sensitivity to the design. Peth also occasionally develops solutions for select commercial clients. Because he keeps overhead low, the cost, we're told, is lower than that of many competitors. References say they appreciate Peth's personal service.

"Kevin Peth handles projects with ease." "Just what the doctor ordered (to cure my clutter)!"

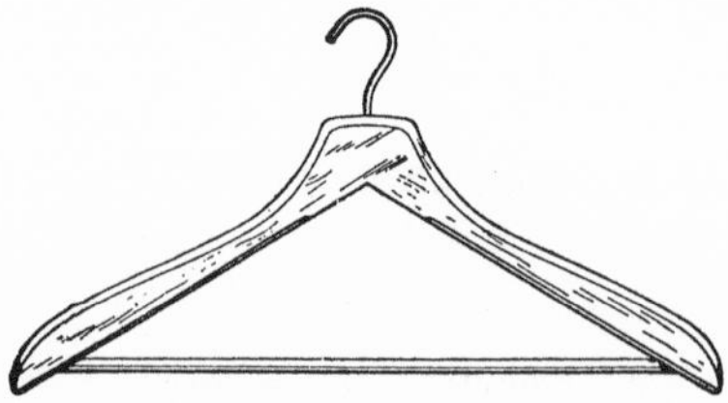

Quality	Cost	Value	Recommend?

Closet Pros

3	3	3	3

555 West Madison Street, Chicago, IL 60661
(888) 310 - 7791

Closet design and installation—laminate

By all accounts, Closet Pros is professional in more than name. Well-regarded by private clients and design professionals alike, the five-year old firm will provide a custom plan and an estimate within 24 to 48 hours and complete installation within 72 hours. Closet Pros' website serves as a virtual showroom of the four-person staff's ability to custom configure solutions from the factory-built components. One client raved that principal George Newman delivered closet plans at his home's closing, so the closets were installed before the family moved in. Efficiency and design capability, we're told, come at a very reasonable price.

Closet Works

4.5	3	4.5	4

953 North Larch Street, Elmhurst, IL 60126
(630) 832 - 3322 www.closetworks.com

Closet design and installation—laminate

Independently-owned since it opened its own doors in 1987, Closet Works organizes behind-door storage for many top area architects, interior designers and builders. This company is top-drawer and totally custom, from planning the space to dressing it in furniture-quality fittings. The staff of 50 are all trained professionals, we're told, and lends its expertise to any area of a home, developing custom storage solutions for laundry rooms, kids' playrooms, bedrooms, bathrooms, pantries, garages and offices. Clients praise the company's courteous, attentive service as much as they appreciate the advice and the beauty of the resulting product and design.

"Service and product are A-1—a top notch company." "I was happy and impressed with the installers' quality and thoroughness in cleaning up after they finished the job."

Closets By Design

3.5	3.5	4	4

10711 West 165th Street, Orland Park, IL 60462
(708) 364 - 0700 www.closets-by-design.com

Closet design and installation

In business since 1982, this 27-unit franchise company was started by European Rafael Feig, a residential developer with a keen understanding of the importance of space planning in a home. The company provides in-home consultation at no obligation. Clients with measurements at hand can even obtain a closet plan by return fax. All Closets By Design systems are manufactured locally and carry a lifetime warranty. References tell us they are pleased with the company's product and say the staff is knowledgeable, friendly and eager to help.

"Good customer service." "They stack up to the rest."

Closets Unlimited

4	2.5	4.5	4

1901 Landmeier Road, Elk Grove, IL 60007
(847) 228 - 1000 www.closetsunlimited.com

Closet design and installation—laminate, wire

Since 1978, this family-owned business has been going to the limit in developing closet systems for master suites, children's rooms, pantries, garages and home offices for top designers and homebuilders. The firm practices throughout the Chicago metro area, and the owner, Scott Chaikin, oversees every job. Closet Unlimited designs systems in either laminate or wire. Clients praise its design expertise as well as its fabrication work and especially applaud the adjustability of shelving and rods. The systems come with a well-received lifetime guarantee.

"They are devoted to their art." "Cost-effective products." "Yes, on schedule and within budget!"

Convert-a-Closet 4 3.5 4.5 4.5

401 South Milwaukee Avenue, Suite 190, Wheeling, IL 60090
(847) 419 - 9696

Closet design and installation—laminate

An excellent resource, this company is a husband-and-wife team that is said to be not only expert at creating clutter-free closet storage, but also equally adept with custom cabinet solutions, wall units, entertainment centers, pantries, home offices and garage storage. Favored by builders and interior designers as well as homeowners, Marsha and Michael Freedenberg are personally responsible for all initial consultations, measurements and final designs. The company has been in operation since 1977, and professional and private clients alike applaud its personal service as well as its workmanship and design capabilities. Laminate is the company's primary material, and it offers clients a choice of 15 to 20 different color and style options.

"This is a company to brag about."

Mosaiko 4 5 4 3.5

2150 North Clybourn, Chicago, IL 60614
(773) 929 - 9209 www.mosaikofurniture.com

Custom closets and manufacturer of high-quality Italian-style furniture

In addition to custom furnishings for bedrooms, dining rooms and living rooms, Mosaiko also creates custom closets for customers' full range of storage requirements. Components come in three standard heights, one depth and infinite length, allowing Mosaiko designers to adapt a system to most measurements. The company also offers a choice of 15 door styles and many variations on interior closet fittings.

Perfection

7183 North Austin Avenue, Niles, IL 60714
(847) 647 - 6461

Closet design and installation—laminate, wire

Poliform Chicago 4.5 4.5 4 4

Merchandise Mart, Suite 1379, Chicago, IL 60654
(312) 321 - 9600 www.poliformusa.com

Closet design and installation; kitchen and door sales

Founded 50 years ago in Italy, Poliform commands a prominent position as a manufacturer of wardrobe systems, wall units and walk-in closets that are self-supporting structures from floor to ceiling. This very high-end firm provides sophisticated closet solutions with a clean and luxurious look. Its designs include everything from clothes hangers and leather-tabbed storage boxes to shelving units and dresser drawers. The firm also handles gut renovations and complete remodeling of kitchens, providing design expertise and a wide selection of cabinetry, countertops and Miele brand, high-end appliances. Each job is customized to meet the client's individual needs. Poliform uses its superbly crafted line of Italian cabinet doors, drawers and furniture-quality accessories. Be advised that, because pieces are milled in Italy, there is a six- to eight-week wait for delivery.

Poliform has been featured in the Robb Report, the luxury media publication, as "a dream closet" and "a study in style and organization with pull-out trouser racks and compartments for shirts, ties and other accessories."

Space Options
509 Wrightwood Avenue, Elmhurst, IL 60126
(630) 279 - 4700
Closet design and installation

Space Organization 4 4.5 4 4
1155 North Howe Street, Chicago, IL 60610
(312) 654 - 1400
Closet design and installation—solid wood, laminate, wire

Having 15 years experience, this company can organize almost any closet, office, garage or kitchen space. Using wire, laminate or solid wood material, Space Organization works directly with homeowners, contractors and architects. They are strong on specialty items—storage islands, computer and entertainment centers, corner shelving, racks for storing bicycles and portable pools. They have two showrooms in Chicago, including one at the Merchandise Mart.

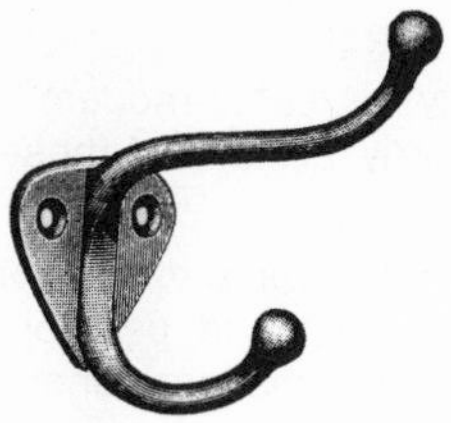

The Closet Factory 3.5 2.5 3.5 4
9551 West Berwyn Street, Rosemont, IL 60018
(847) 928 - 2100 www.closet-factory.com
Closet design and installation—laminate

Storage solutions by The Closet Factory are custom designed and configured using components that are made of fine materials and engineered and produced in its factories around the world. The company offers free consultation in its office, at clients' homes or at the jobsites of its interior designer and contractor clientele. In addition to closet systems, The Closet Factory also develops entertainment centers and storage for offices, garages and pantries.

"Design was excellent; installation was fast and efficient." "Prompt service."

Hiring a Computer Installation & Maintenance Service Provider

Maybe you'd like to connect the computer in your home office to the one in your teenager's room in order to share Internet access. You're worried, however, that if you do it yourself your "network" will turn on the ceiling fans and trip the security system. Fortunately there are plenty of computer service providers who install networks and software, set up new computer systems and do other tasks that would take a lot of your precious time. Today's world requires a new approach to home computer needs, and computer technician professionals have up-to-the-minute knowledge. Though home networks aren't yet that common, they are fast becoming essential in a high speed world of connectivity. Your computer set-up needs to be as custom fit as a tailored suit for you to get the full benefit. While common sense dictates that you should leave the nitty-gritty details to a skilled technician, knowing what to expect will streamline the process.

Do I Need a Computer Network?

What is a network, exactly? A cable modem? DSL? A wireless network? A firewall? And, most importantly, are any of these relevant to your needs or current system?

The most basic network is two computers hooked up to each other so that they can share files, Internet access and, perhaps, printers. If you have to save something to a disk, then put that disk into another computer to open a file in the second machine, you are not in a network. The size of networks is almost limitless and the largest corporations and government offices have a mind-boggling number of computers exchanging information. A common home network can consist of three computers: the home office computer, the kid's computer and maybe a laptop. In a network, computers are linked to an Ethernet hub, which is then linked to a printer and a modem. This usually requires running wire throughout the house, drilling and coordinating phone/cable jacks.

Why should you consider a home network? Quite simply, convenience. With a home network files can be transferred easily, printers and Internet access shared and the phone lines freed up for those important incoming calls from your mother-in-law. While this may seem like a sophisticated situation for a home, times are changing. More kids do their homework on the computer, more people work from home and everyone in the house wants to be on the Internet—at the same time. Home networks can save money because they avoid the added expense of multiple printers and Internet hookups. You'll need to buy a hub, the connection point for all elements of a network, which starts at about $50. Though most new computers already have network software installed, you may need to buy network cards which cost from $20 to $50.

High-Speed Internet Connections

Internet access through a conventional phone line severely limits your online speed and efficiency. Both a Digital Subscriber Line (DSL) and a cable modem are as much as 100 times faster than a standard analog (telephone) hook-up. A DSL line uses the same cabling as regular telephone lines, but it operates on a higher, idle frequency, allowing the user to be on the Internet and the phone at the same time. Also, DSL service is always connected, so the user never has to dial up and wait for a connection. Cable is a broadband connection, which means that lots of information can travel simultaneously (that's how all those cable channels can be available at the same time). A cable modem is also always "on," but it runs on TV cable lines. The speed is comparable to DSL with one difference: cable modems use a shared bandwidth. This means that speed depends on how many users are using that cable service: the more users, the more traffic, the slower the connection. Because DSL runs on single telephone lines, this isn't an issue. In both cases, find out whether the telephone lines and cable connections in your area are equipped with this service. There are various providers, and promotions offering free installation are common. Computer technician companies will install the DSL connection, but generally are not providers themselves. Monthly service for your connection will cost between $30 and $60. The monthly charge for superfast connections (usually for businesses) can be as high as $190.

Most broadband service packages and home network packages come with a firewall installed. This indispensable part of any Internet-ready computer protects the user from hackers and includes options such as the parental control feature, which allows parents to block inappropriate sites.

The Wireless Alternative

Wireless networking is newly available and can be a practical choice in some cases. It saves having to drill holes through your walls and makes the layout of a home office or computer network more flexible. If the network needs to be expanded or rearranged, wireless networking makes the change easy and inexpensive. A wireless network consists of an Ethernet hub and PC cards inserted into the computers. These cards extend slightly from the machine with a small antenna from which information is sent and received. Wireless networks can operate as quickly as a standard network. The hub can cost anywhere from $300 to $900, and the PC cards are approximately $150. A computer technician can advise you whether or not a wireless system is best for your situation.

Buying a New Computer: Where Do I Start?

If your experience lies specifically with PCs (IBM compatible) or Macintoshes, you may want to stick with the type of computer already familiar to you. (Some technicians focus on one type or the other, which can narrow your search for a good techie, too). If there are children in the house, consider what computers their schools use. One computer technician suggests starting with an issue of *PC Magazine* or *Macworld* to see what's available and use it as a reference when you speak to a technician about models, memory sizes and accessories. This way you can get a clear idea of what appeals to you and have a more productive conversation with your computer consultant.

On Cost

Computer technicians charge an hourly service fee, generally in the $60 to $120 per hour range. Before you hire one, ask whether the fee is calculated only in hourly increments. If you go 15 minutes into the next hour, are you charged for a full additional hour? In addition to the fee, you will be charged for whatever hardware or software you purchase. Discuss exactly what will be installed to avoid hidden costs. The key to any home service is the quality of the time spent, not the quantity. A good service provider will not squander the hours they are billing you for, but will arrive prepared and solve your problem as quickly as possible. Ask whether the technician charges for advice on the phone after he's made the house call. Often he will not charge for more time if you just need clarification on the service he recently provided. Once you're a customer, some technicians will even respond to a new question if it doesn't take too long, but others will want the clock to start running again. Find out your techie's policy and how flexible he is. Some consultants offer a package of a given number of hours of help, which can be a combination of an initial house call, follow-up help at home and time on the phone. This might be good for someone just starting out. It's comforting to know that someone is there to help when you panic.

INSURANCE AND CONTRACTS

Most computer maintenance technicians carry some sort of business insurance which protects them from the repercussions of crashing your computer or network. This insurance is for everyone's benefit. Any service that handles office networks as well will carry this insurance. If you chose a smaller operation, ask them how and if they are covered. Computer service providers may have contracts with business accounts, but it is rare with home service. Ask your technician about the firm's policy.

WHAT TO EXPECT FROM A TECHIE

Depending on the scope of the service, the principal of the company may perform the work personally or send out technicians. The key is to find someone who responds quickly and whose service is reliable. Also, the computer industry moves at such a fast speed that it's infinitely helpful to work with someone who knows where it is going and shares that knowledge.

Steer clear of computer service professionals who act as if everyone should have been born with a computer gene. In truth, a lot of people just nod when they are told they need an updated USB port in order to handle the increased amount of EDI coming in over the DSL lines. You want someone who will listen to you, set up exactly what you need and ensure that you fully understand it. Try to quickly get a sense of whether the techie helping you only speaks in technobabble. Believe it or not, there are technicians out there who can make computers understandable to even you, and you should not have to put up with someone who does not patiently explain things in plain English.

Keep in mind that chimps in university labs can learn how to play computer games. If Cheeta can do it, so can you.

INTERNET JARGON
(AT LEAST YOU CAN SOUND LIKE YOU KNOW WHAT YOU'RE TALKING ABOUT.)

- **Bandwidth:** Measured in bits per second (bps), bandwidth is the amount of data that can be both sent and received through a connection.
- **Bozo Filter:** An email feature that allows the user to block messages from specific individuals. Can help reduce spam by creating a list of unwanted addresses affectionately named a "bozo list."
- **Cookie:** A message a Web server sends to your browser when certain Web pages are visited. The cookie is stored and a message is sent back every time the user requests that page. This allows the page to come up customized. For example, after you purchase something on Amazon.com, your user name will appear to welcome you every time you log on from the same computer.
- **Cyberspace:** The inter-connected non-physical space created by the Internet and the World Wide Web, where information is transferred and people communicate electronically through computer networks. Using this word shows how hip you are.
- **DSL (Digital Subscriber Line):** A method for sending data over regular phone lines. A DSL circuit is much faster than a regular phone connection. It uses the same wires already in place for regular phone service, but since it uses an unused frequency you can talk on the phone while connected to the Internet with only one line.
- **ISP (Internet Service Provider):** A company that provides access to the Internet, usually for a monthly fee. Most homes use an ISP to connect to the Internet.
- **LAN (Local Area Network):** A computer network limited to the immediate area, for example, a private residence. Ethernet is the most common type of connection used for LANs.
- **Modem:** A communication device that allows a computer to talk to other computers. Modems vary in speed from slower telephone modems to significantly faster DSL and cable modems.
- **Netiquette:** The accepted rules of conduct that define polite behavior in Cyberspace. If you breach the rules of netiquette, you can be sure your fellow users will let you know.
- **Network:** Any two or more computers connected together to share resources such as files, a printer or Internet access.
- **Newbie**: Term for someone who is new to computers or the Internet. It is not an insult but just a description. If you are reading this, you could be a Newbie.
- **Snail Mail:** Regular paper mail delivered by the U.S. Postal Service. Why use the Postal Service when you can shoot a letter over in seconds via email?
- **Spam**: Junk mail over your email, which wastes your time and the network's bandwidth. Ways of combating spam include filters and private service providers like AOL.
- **T-1:** A wide bandwidth Internet connection that can carry data at 1.544 megabits per second. This is the fastest speed generally used to connect networks to the Internet.
- **URL (Uniform Resource Locator):** Represents the address used to locate a certain file, directory or page on the World Wide Web.
- **Web Browser:** Software such as Netscape Navigator or Internet Explorer that allows the user to access the World Wide Web by translating the language used to build web pages. Short term: "browser."

Quality	Cost	Value	Recommend?
	✚	$	◆	★

COMPUTER INSTALLATION & MAINTENANCE
SERVICE PROVIDERS

Business & Home Computing Solutions
4	3	4	4.5

2232 Grand Avenue, Lindenhurst, IL 60046
(847) 356 - 6666 www.bhcsol.com
Computer maintenance, consulting and networking

In business since 1981, Business & Home Computing Solutions spans the spectrum with technicians certified for Macs and PCs, with Macs being its specialty. We're told that Bill Graham and his technicians are the ultimate computer gurus for at-home service. Count on them for assistance with purchases and upgrades, consulting and maintenance. The company reports installing an increasing number of wireless systems in recent months. It also sells a full complement of replacement and upgrade hardware to boost your memory and streamline productivity and rents equipment. Business & Home Computing Solutions serves commercial and residential customers from Chicago to Milwaukee.

We hear that the company's customer service is excellent. One customer was just about to buy a new Mac when Graham was able to fix not one but two of that customer's computers quickly following a referral. Clients appreciate that the company makes house calls for a small premium charge.

"You can count on the finest equipment and service from Bill Graham." "I've never had a problem that couldn't be fixed quickly by a courteous, knowledgeable technician." "They're so nice! They never talk down to me." "Bill is great!"

Bytes & PC's
4	2	5	5

P. O. Box 409220, Chicago, IL 60640
(773) 955 - 0100 www.bytesandpcs.net
Computer maintenance, consulting, networking and training

Bytes & PC's is fluent in computer. The company sells, installs, networks, programs, upgrades, repairs, troubleshoots and trains. If you're lost in the Internet, they can help you there too. Technicians work with all brands of computers and handle projects from the simple to the complex throughout Chicago and the suburbs. The company prefers to work on-site at the customer's home, finding that things just go smoother that way. They will also provide help over the phone. Clients have reported calling in from across the country for assistance. Bytes & PC's also offers 24-hour service for those late night data recovery emergencies.

All work is guaranteed. If these technicians can't fix whatever problem you can throw their way, you don't pay. Customers describe the company's staff in general, and principal Don Richardson in particular, as "fast, reliable and educational." A high level of repeat business and referrals to friends attest to the quality of this company's work.

"I tell my friends about Don all the time." "They're superb and the cost is reasonable." "Gets the job done."

Computer Services & Consulting Inc. (CSC)
4	3.5	3.5	4

1613 South Michigan Avenue, Chicago, IL 60616
(312) 360 - 1100
Computer maintenance, consulting and networking

This computer company sells, installs and repairs both Macintosh and PC systems. It also does networking installation and consultation. Computer Services & Consulting has been responding to technology needs throughout the greater Chicago area for nearly two decades. Customers benefit from both home and phone service. Don't wait until the last minute to call for service, however, as we hear the firm can be quite busy. The company will conduct basic training for customers to get them started but does not offer intensive training for the truly computer-impaired.

Dean Kletter Consulting **4 3 4 4.5**
1146 South Euclid, Oak Park, IL 60304
(708) 660 - 8010

Computer maintenance, consulting, networking and training

Dean Kletter Consulting offers advice on everything from selecting the right computer to configuring systems and networks for maximum utility. Once your world is hooked up, the firm can also help with training and maintenance. Dean Kletter focuses on the Chicago metropolitan area but will go out to the northern and western suburbs, helping both small businesses and individuals with Macs and PCs.

Principal Al Cantu established this firm at the urging of satisfied former clients after leaving another consulting firm to take a break. Leading decorators appreciate his expertise and suggest his services to their clients. We hear clients are pleased with his quick and attentive service as well as the breadth of knowledge he brings to each encounter.

"I recommend Dean Kletter to my clients all the time." "I can count on Al Cantu." "Very friendly guy."

GH Technologies
3146 West Montrose Avenue, Chicago, IL 60618
(773) 463 - 2907 www.ghtechnologies.com

Computer maintenance and networking

GH Technologies sells, services and networks, computers, and will come to your home for an hourly fee. The firm's technicians will diagnose your problem for free, if you bring the equipment into their shop. This small operation has been in business since 1997.

Hyde Park Computers **3.5 3 3.5 4**
2850 North Clark Street, Chicago, IL 60657
(773) 248 - 6200 www.hydeparkcomputers.net

Computer maintenance, consulting, networking and training

On-site installation and training keeps Hyde Park technicians in demand and on the run. We hear they specialize in PCs and make house calls for everything from installing basic software to configuring a LAN (local area network). The company works with customers to choose the appropriate hardware and custom system set-ups, then will install the equipment, configure the network and provide training on how to use all the new toys. Its technicians can also fix the toys if they break! Hyde Park will repair equipment on a carry-in basis or come to your home for a higher rate. If you're pressed for time, they will pick up and deliver for a small charge. The firm has been serving both individual and business clients since 1983. A second location in Evanston extends the company's reach.

Customers tell us the technicians are courteous and honest. Many of them are in their 20s, about the same age as the PC itself, and so have grown up with technology.

✚	$	◆	★

Karry's Computing

3241 North Ravenswood Avenue, Chicago, IL 60657
(773) 248 - 9278

Computer maintenance

Kennedy Electric

1956 Raymond Drive, Northbrook, IL 60062
(847) 564 - 9863

Electrical installation and service, computer networking and telephone systems

See Kennedy Electric's full report under the heading Electricians

Lapin Systems

4 3.5 3.5 4

832 Dempster Street, Evanston, IL 60202
(847) 328 - 9945 www.lapin.com

Computer maintenance, consulting, networking and training

With the speed of the hare and the wisdom of the turtle, this medium-sized consulting firm can address most computer user's needs. Nicknamed "The Mac Man," Lapin Systems was founded in 1995 as a Mac specialist and today supports PC systems as well. The company offers troubleshooting, repairs and maintenance of both hardware and software as well as one-on-one training in computer basics and applications. Staffers also install and maintain Ethernet networks and Internet systems. We are told that the firm has particular expertise with cross-platform applications. Lapin works with professional, home office and individual computer users throughout the Chicago area and will make house calls.

The company stresses customer satisfaction. Technicians make a concerted effort to speak in layman's tongue and offer tailored customer service. They are adept at providing support for creative and design professionals.

"They do repairs and system upgrades at competitive rates and are very convenient." "Fast, responsive service."

Micro Computer Center (MCC)

4 3.5 4 4

660 South Randall Road, Saint Charles, IL 60510
(630) 584 - 9505 www.mccnow.com

Computer maintenance, consulting and networking

In business since 1979, Micro Computer Center (MCC) (also known as MCC Technology) primarily works on small- and medium-sized business networks but will also do home projects. We hear the well-trained staff provides hardware, software and technical services with an emphasis on quality service and support. They work on PC and Macintosh systems in northern Illinois from Lake Michigan to as far west as Rockford and Dixon.

✚	$	◆	★

MicroAge Computer Center 3.5 3 4 4
9240 West 159th Street, Orland Park, IL 60462
(708) 349 - 8080 www.maop.com
Computer maintenance, consulting, networking and training

This company sells, repairs and supports both Mac- and PC-based computer equipment and systems. MicroAge does a brisk carry-in repair trade but will also dispatch technicians on house calls for equipment and network installation and repair (with a three hour minimum). They also do wiring and business telephone systems. Staffers are trained as problem-solvers and include certified technicians, networking specialists and cabling/wiring engineers. Computer gurus hold training classes in MicroAge offices and will accommodate custom training in clients' homes. MicroAge has been serving the technology needs of Chicago and northwest Indiana since 1981.

Clients appreciate straight talk from MicroAge technicians who don't confuse or intimidate them with computer jargon.

"Very reliable!" "Courteous service." "Repairs are prompt and a full explanation is always provided." "They fixed my printer right away when I needed it the most—that's what I call service!"

Nabih's Inc. 📁 📁 📁 📁
515 Davis Street, Evanston, IL 60201
(847) 869 - 6140
Computer maintenance, consulting and networking

Nabih's has been helping customers make the transition to the information age for the last 28 years. The firm sells and services both Mac- and PC-based systems and equipment and can assist with networking systems. Consulting and basic training are available to customers, and staffers will try to help over the phone. The company will do some on-site service for products they have sold but charges for travel time and limits house calls to a 45-minute drive from the store. We're told that the firm's technicians are friendly and reliable.

PC Doc Computers Inc. 3 2 3.5 4
623-61 North Broadway Street, Chicago, IL 60660
(773) 338 - 2202
Computer maintenance, networking and training

Like the old family physician, PC Doc offers comprehensive services—sales, installation, networking, repairs and training classes in computer basics. The company's web page development service can help you make your mark on the Internet. Technicians willingly make house calls and will also try to assist customers over the phone. PC Doc has been hooking up clients on the North Shore and in Chicago since 1993 but, as the name implies, its prescriptions do not encompass Macs.

We're told that PC Doc is very user-friendly and highly dependable. Customers especially love the pick-up and delivery service.

Rane Tech Enterprises 3.5 3 4 3.5
4911 West Bell Plaine Avenue, Chicago, IL 60641
(773) 202 - 1667
Computer maintenance, consulting and networking

Rane Tech makes all the right connections. Originally known as "the memory guys," Rane Tech has progressed from computer memory upgrades to fully certified network creation and maintenance. The company's business encompasses Macintosh, IBM and PC-clone equipment. Rane professionals build custom computer and system configurations for homes and small offices and have experience networking homes on the North Shore. We're told their customizing capabilities are unparalleled. The company emphasizes service over sales and makes house calls. Following a network installation, technicians provide basic training and help in the necessary "ABCs."

Rane Tech's principal Dan Abrams gets special praise for his knowledge and competent, friendly customer service.

RescueCom **3.5** **3** **3.5** **3.5**

(312) 565 - 2300

Computer maintenance and networking

RescueCom technicians offer speedy service to rescue Chicago-area computer users whenever problems arise. They are certified on Macs and PCs and are facile with both hardware and software. When called in for an emergency, they strive to respond in one hour and charge accordingly—almost double their regular rate for scheduled calls. Technicians do much of their work at the customer's home or business and will come to your aid as late as midnight. RescueCom can also assist with networking and Internet issues.

System Solutions Inc. (SSI)

3630 Commercial Avenue, Northbrook, IL 60062

(847) 272 - 6160

Computer maintenance

This computer company will work on PCs and clones, fixing hardware problems on equipment that you bring in to them. They may go to your home for an extra charge but that is not their primary business. System Solutions is not authorized to work on Macs, so look elsewhere for those solutions.

Windy City Computer People Co.

244 West 31st Street, Chicago, IL 60616

(312) 225 - 0300

Computer maintenance, consulting, networking and training

Like its namesake, Windy City Computer People will come blowing in at any time—the company offers 24/7 service for emergencies. Technicians make house calls to service and repair your Mac or PC system and can also help with other technology needs including networking and the Internet.

Hiring a Contractor or Builder

Understanding a big repair or renovation can be intimidating, especially the thought of selecting the top person in charge, the commander-in-chief—the contractor. That's why an excellent contractor is vital to any major household work. This professional, like a general, takes in the big picture as well as the details, is seasoned through experience, knows his troops and the system, gets the job done well and on time and wins your admiration in the process. Here's a field guide to enlisting a five-star contractor:

Job Description

A traditional general contractor (GC) bids and builds from an architect's, or designer's plans and specifications (the contract documents). The GC's duties are to interpret the drawings, execute the contracts, secure the permits, supervise the trades, manage the budget, make the schedule, deliver the quality and call it a day. There are design/build contracting firms that will draw up the contract documents, eliminating the need for an architect. Be aware, however, many firms which call themselves design/build really only offer conceptual assistance. They do not have practicing architects in-house, and must farm out design services to certified professionals. Some comment this one-stop shop approach more often than not results in uninspired design and cookie-cutter "McMansions," while others believe that nobody is more qualified to see a set of plans realized than its designer. This route is less costly than hiring an outside architect. However, an outside architect serves as a check and balance to the GC. Construction management offers an alternative to hiring the traditional GC. Clients themselves contract with individual trades and the construction manager handles all payments and project administration for a fee based on total job cost. Some clients laud this "open book" approach, while others say it lacks an incentive to save and can result in a less coordinated approach.

What to Look for in a Contractor

Picking the right general contractor is all about communication. A homeowner needs to know as much about the GC's capabilities as the GC needs to know about a homeowner's expectations. With stakes this high—mortgages, reputations, living another day at your in-laws—it's time for everyone to feel completely secure in the leadership on the job and the direction of the project. You should feel comfortable stating your wishes to the contractor and have confidence in his ability to listen, explain, cooperate and delegate.

Before you approach a GC, make sure your contract documents are clear and thorough. If you choose to go design/build, look for a firm sympathetic and attuned to your sense of style, and make sure the company does indeed produce quality detailed drawings. Your candidate should be experienced in jobs of a similar type: restoration, renovation or new construction. Do you want a versatile GC or one that specializes? The GC should be well versed on the architectural features, building applications, specialty installations, customization and level of quality you expect. Consider the scale of the GC's past jobs, including cost and total square footage. You don't want to be the job stuck below the radar screen of a commercial-minded contractor, or hook your wagon to a little guy who can't muster the horsepower.

You want the GC to be fluent in the code requirements and logistical considerations of your locale. Negotiating the elevators, union regulations, and neighbors of Gold Coast high rises is very different from negotiating environmental restrictions on lake front lots. The city permitting and inspection processes, co-op boards, and building management companies are notorious instruments of delay. Also, nail down your GC's availability. If he can't commit to a target start date, you cannot depend on his ability to stick to a completion date, and chances are you'll be living in a construction battle-zone for an indefinite time.

Finally, you wouldn't let a stranger in your door, so before you invite a platoon of workers brandishing power tools and sack lunches, get references. The GC's listed in this section are certainly among the most reputable, but talk to clients and inspect jobs in progress yourself to get a feel for a GC's abilities and current slate of jobs. Also talk to those clients with jobs completed to get a reading on how a GC maintains his word and work. No license is required by the state of Illinois to be a General Contractor. Some municipalities require that one obtain a General Contracting or Business License as a matter of course in order to pull permits there. This usually requires proof of adequate insurance.

ON COST

Typically, three bids should suffice for a clear and fair comparison of estimates of project cost. The market may be cooling down, but it still may mean approaching twice that number just to get a telephone call returned. The more established GC's may bid only for architects with whom they have a relationship, or referrals, or on particularly plum projects. In some cases, you may need to pull strings in order to approach them to consider the project and negotiate a fee.

Cost is a reflection of material and labor (as provided directly or through subcontractors), bonding and insurance, the general conditions (overhead to keep the job running) and the fee. General conditions and the fee are calculated as percentages of the total hard-construction costs, approximately 13 percent in Chicagoland these days, though the percentage will vary depending on the cost, size and location of the job. Bonding offers insurance against a GC's failure to perform or pay subcontractors. It's a protection against negligence and liens—claims of debt that can be attached to the title of your property and prevent it from being sold until all liens are settled. Insurance covers full liability and workman's compensation. Any and all associated permit fees (calculated archaically by the city as a percentage of total job cost), deposits or taxes also figure into the cost.

For the most part GC's come close with their overhead and profit costs, and the degree to which prices vary depends on the quality and cost of their subcontractors, internal resources, their ability to interpret plans accurately and honestly, their ability to meet the schedule, how conservative they wish to estimate, and of course, you. At the end of the day your choice of materials and methods of construction, as well as change orders, determine where the chips are likely to fall.

NEGOTIATING THE BIDS

Jumping on the low bid may be tempting, but don't take the bait. If a bid is enticingly low, it almost assuredly signals that the GC doesn't fully grasp the scope or has value-engineered (cut-corners) without your consent.

A good GC doesn't lowball, he negotiates. Don't be shy about requesting a thorough cost breakdown. If the GC's numbers come from subcontractors, you may ask for the subs' bid sheets. Remember, the more subcontractors are employed, the more overhead and fee mark-ups will inflate the bottom line. In-house carpenters, for example, are a plus, giving the GC direct control over a trade many consider the engine that drives the job. Any top GC draws from a small, consistent stable of subcontractors. These prices tend to be higher due to lack of competition and constant demand for the subs' service. While loyalty speaks for standards of quality, it's always your prerogative to ask the GC for an alternative sub. Just don't be surprised if he refuses.

You may be able to shave a few dollars off the bid by entertaining the possibility of service contracts. These are typically maintenance agreements that plug the gaps in the basic warranties. Many subs will try to snare you into buying one at the end of the job, but beat them to the punch and inquire about them at the outset. Use the prospect of your entering into a service contract as a tool to negotiate for a reduction in the cost of a bid. It offers contractors the incentive to forego dollars today for the chance of a service contract deal in the future.

COMMISSIONING YOUR GENERAL

Cost is always a factor, but at the end of the day personality is at least as important. Can you work together? Don't settle for anything less than a principal of a contracting firm who expresses interest in the status of your job both at the outset and throughout. The tone is set from the top. You should feel like you can trust not only your GC with the keys to your house, but also enjoy having him around. Goodness knows he'll be spending enough time there.

Once the job begins, he should dispatch an on-site supervisor and assign a project manager. In some cases a working foreman will super on-site, in others it may be the company owner. In any case, these on-site managers will be the ones coordinating with your architect or designer. Weekly site meetings are a must. As with picking the right GC, running a smooth and successful job is all about communication.

GET IT IN WRITING

About the only thing that doesn't need to be detailed in your contract documents are the middle names of the contractor's children. Otherwise every detail should be recorded on paper. The plans and specs furnished by your designer provide the fundamental outline of the job. This means noting every raw material and product—including brand, model number, color and installation method. Be meticulous. If it's not on the drawings, it's not going to show up in your home, unless of course you're willing to sign the change order.

The change order, you ask? If you make a request that deviates from the project's scope as defined by the contract documents, expect to pay. Some changes may be inevitable, if you are unfortunate enough not to have x-ray vision or if you fall prey to your own whimsical inclinations halfway through the job. But be sure that any charges passed under your nose weren't already in the original contract. Ask your architect or construction manager to investigate each submission to make sure everything's on the level, otherwise its up to you. Spell out in the contract how change orders will be handled. A smart idea is to fix the unit costs for labor and material that were established with the original contract so there are no surprises about price of extras.

Be warned, a GC's obligation to meet code does not shield you from a city's permitting and inspection schizophrenia. Your contract documents must refer to the applicable codes. Because many are open to interpretation, a city official on a bad day can be a major source of change orders. The rub: if it's not on the drawings, the GC will not claim responsibility. Remember, however, that the GC should be absolutely responsible for obtaining the necessary permits for the job. This includes filing your plans and specs with the city for review and approval.

DECIDE UPON A PAYMENT SCHEDULE

If your partnership with a GC is a waltz, and contract documents the choreography, then payment provides the music. Your contract should specify the schedule of payment. Nothing will undermine a job more than misunderstandings about money. If payment is expected on a certain date, don't expect workers to show up if you miss it. Commit to what you can do. The most desirable arrangement is progressive payment on a phase-completion basis. Use benchmarks, like pouring the foundation or rocking up the walls, to close the end of a phase. Agree on the amount of each payment beforehand. It's a great incentive to push the GC through each phase.

Monthly payments are an alternative, but this setup commands more attention to accounting and is less of an incentive. A request for bi-weekly payments does not bode well—it may indicate that the GC doesn't have the capital to run the job properly. In any case, if you don't want to be dropped, keep the music going. Be sure to hold on to retention—10 percent of the money owed on the job—until all punch list items have been completed and all warranties, manuals, etc. have been handed over.

With many mortgage agreements mandating higher interest charges during construction, penalties charged for not making move-in deadlines and the cost of renting space elsewhere, you might find a bust schedule more painful than a bust budget. Use incentives to motivate the GC to keep costs low and to make schedule. Bonuses go over much better than "damages clauses" that threaten penalties for blowing a deadline. Most GCs won't go for them, and anyway, they're almost impossible to enforce.

TIE UP LOOSE ENDS

Punch list items are loose ends such as missing fixtures, polishing finishes and fine-tuning systems. Left hanging, the punch list and warranties are things that will keep your GC in your life much longer than either of you care for. Spell out the procedure and schedule for generating, attacking and revisiting punch list issues. A good GC doesn't need to be hand held through the process, but it should be clear from the outset who's doing what. And give him a break if not everything is perfect at first. Be patient.

Most of the warranties passed on by the GC are from the subs and manufacturers. Many GCs will offer an umbrella warranty. Ideally you want to have one contact person if things go wrong. Some firms have a computerized database for tracking customer warranties. Warranties can range from one year on parts and labor for equipment to ten years on workmanship items. Any decent GC will be attentive to past clients long into the future. No warranty should kick in until the day the certificate of occupation or completion is issued by the city or municipality.

COVER YOUR BACK

Remember, success is as much about being thorough in your research and preparation as it is about personal chemistry and communication. All this can be wrapped up in a tidy little standard AIA (American Institute of Architects) contract with the usual qualifications attached: plans and specs, the GC's bid proposal, terms and conditions, co-op regulations and anything else you want to include.

TIPS FOR A PAINLESS JOB

- Make contract documents as detailed, clear and complete as possible.
- Establish good chemistry and communication between yourself, the GC and the architect.
- Have GC hold weekly site meetings with subcontractors.
- Make payments on schedule.
- Trust the contractor and keep a sense of humor.

Contractors & Builders

Berliant Builders
101 Ambrogio Drive, Gurnee, IL 60031
(847) 249 - 8990

Residential general contracting

Client's say principal Larry Berliant is a hands-on can-do guy. There's no cause to fret with this North Shore builder, we hear, because he will work everything out.

BGD&C Corp. 4.5 4.5 4 4
875 North Michigan Avenue, Suite 1414, Chicago, IL 60611
(312) 255 - 8300

High-end new residential construction

One-of-a-kind, top-tier, custom single-family homes, primarily in Lincoln Park, is the BGD&C specialty. We are told it is very special. Principals Rodger Owen and Charles Grode expanded to this business on the basis of accolades the firm received for its earlier work on historic renovations and ultra high-end remodeling. Today, it returns to rehab for only projects the partners describe as "exceptionally unique." A design/build firm, BGD&C does complete design, engineering and management of its new-home projects, most of which are traditional in style, although it will develop any style a client desires. Clients turn to BGD&C for homes that complement the architectural integrity of the neighborhood.

Design is what sets BGD&C apart, clients say, while also praising the company's on-the-job workmanship and attention to detail. Owen masterminds the design concepts and is the hands-on manager, while Grode oversees the administrative and business tasks. Both are students of art, classical architecture and design, and they travel to Europe regularly in search of ideas, especially those rendered in the old-world craftsmanship they admire and put into practice.

The BGD&C partners enjoy a reputation as "belt-and-suspender guys" who engineer buildings of unparalleled solidity while also giving each distinctive characteristics. Small details, they believe, add big benefits to the overall value of a home. Their clients agree. References say BGD&C is realistic and honest in its estimates of time and costs. The management is flexible, and keeps clients informed of the job's progress. This firm is considered expensive, but competitive with other area design/build firms that serve this market level.

"Excellent follow-up." "Easy to talk with. We had a good dialogue." "Recommended to a lot of people."

Canada & Klein Ltd. 4.5 4.5 4 5
1028 Cherry Street, Winnetka, IL 60093
(847) 501 - 4884

High-end residential general contracting

When clients say adding a room or having their home remodeled was "a great experience" and that their contractor was "fun to have around," they've either gone over the edge or, possibly, used Canada & Klein for the work. The comments are real and typical of the raves we hear about this firm and its principal, Jeff Cohen. Cited again and again for outstanding quality and attention to detail, Canada & Klein earns its stripes from the Gold Coast to Lake Forest, revitalizing grand Victorians, tailoring smart penthouse interiors and giving growing families more breathing room.

Architects tell us Canada & Klein is on their permanent bidding list, primarily, but not just because the firm's work is of such high quality. They say Cohen and crew exhibit an eye for architecture and creativity with carpentry and are also punctual, trustworthy and easy to work with. Cohen himself visits job sites every day and always returns calls promptly. While Canada & Klein isn't the least expensive of contracting companies, its pricing is said to be realistic and fair—another good reason why many people who have used the firm once, call on it again when the need arises.

"I've used Jeff four times. Gets the job done." "Old-fashioned work ethic." "Only contractor I've dealt with who cleans up everything, down to the dust." "Still keep in contact for referral or advice." "Great sense of humor, not all business."

Carlo Carani & Sons Inc. **5** **5** **4.5** **4**

28841 Nagel Court, Unit 6, Lake Bluff, IL 60044
(847) 295 - 6640

High-end residential remodeling and additions

Since 1945, the name, Carani, has been passed along among select North Shore residents who want to remodel or add to their estates. We are told you cannot find better. This small firm accepts just two or three significant jobs a year, allowing the current owner of the firm, John Carani, to give each client personal attention and to remain personally involved in every aspect of the process. He and clients are in constant collaboration, we're told.

Clients also say Carani doesn't like allowances and demands that the architect's plans reflect every detail of a job and then ensures that the Carani workmen carry out those details to perfection, from framing to final fit and finish. The Carani carpenters' work is praised as "exquisite," and we're told they can accommodate any client's wish or whim, including even the creation of custom furniture.

The degree of detail in projects by Carlo Carani & Sons sometimes keeps the firm on a project for as long as three years. This patience is not for a lack of efficiency, we're told, but a commitment to perfectionism. Work like this does not come cheap. But people who want their residences handled with the greatest of care continue to stand in line for the Carani crew.

Chicago Workshop Architects

2068 First Street, Suite 101, Highland Park, IL 60035
(847) 266 - 1125

Residential design/build

First established in 1985 as an architectural firm, Chicago Workshop Architects incorporated construction management into its operation three years later. As a result, it provides complete design/build capabilities for high-end new residential construction—whole homes or significant additions—along the North Shore. Projects range from $250,000-additions to houses at the six-million-dollar level. Chicago Workshop builds only what it draws.

All projects are designed in collaboration with clients, then supervised and managed by brothers Hernando Moreno, a certified architect, and Alfredo Moreno, a civil engineer. We're told that their professionalism and multi-disciplined approach to projects adds to the service and value clients enjoy from this firm, beginning with design and continuing through construction to final follow-up. Each home is one of a kind.

For an initial fixed fee, Chicago Workshop follows AIA (American Institute of Architects) guidelines in drawing up an agreement covering beginning specifications and budget. Once the scope of the project is finalized, the company lets work out to competitive bidding by qualified subcontractors. Bids are evaluated and negotiated by clients in consultation with Chicago Workshop, which then acts as general contractor.

Chris Carey & Company, Inc. 5 4 5 5

1131 North Winchester Avenue, Chicago, IL 60622
(773) 342 - 2424

High-end renovation and remodeling

The buzz swirling around Carey & Company comes not just from the saw-blades in action at the contractor's beautiful custom renovations and additions, but also from doting architects and clients who say Carey is "a model for how to handle a client." Carey works from Hyde Park to the Gold Coast and all the way up to Lake Forest. Principal Chris Carey started the company a dozen years ago and built it to high-end prominence through condo remodels and gut renovations. Today Carey may be in a class by himself, quickly emerging as one of Chicago's best. Carey looks to old buildings, landmark and otherwise, that represent projects that are interesting and offer what he calls "a process of discovery."

Carey, himself, is intimately involved in projects and adamant that his company be represented on site at all times. He delegates foreman responsibilities to a lead carpenter. The carpentry team controls the flow of the job, and Carey fills in whenever and wherever gaps may occur, from purchasing to typing up the agenda for a weekly meeting or, most importantly, maintaining the relationship with the client. It's this relationship clients unanimously praise. Respect for the customer is innate to Carey, they say, and instilled in his conscientious crew and subs. One client was so inspired by the effort, she gave them all bonuses. Carey & Company even gets the endorsement of building staffs and managers.

Communication, honesty and customer service is said to be the backbone of the company's success. Although $200,000 is the minimum for a new project, once a client always a client. We're told Carey is very proactive in anticipating potential problems and possesses an artistic sensibility that often leaves architects in awe. He likes to work with owners on an open-book basis so there are never questions regarding upcharges or changes and their consequent cost. The company plans to expand into custom home-building.

"I've worked with some established contractors. I thought they were good until I met Chris!" "Absolutely phenomenal. Chris is hands-on, laid back and friendly." "Very business-like. As old executives, we appreciated that." "Honest. Ethical. Good businessman. An absolute pleasure to work with." "I'm buying an expensive apartment so I can work with him again." "Quality a 12 out of 10." "Fabulous. Did everything right." "Workers responsible, on time."

David Smith 4 3 4.5 4.5

3007 West Logan Boulevard, Chicago, IL 60647
(773) 489 - 3961

High-end remodeling, custom kitchen and bath installation and additions

Clients tell us they love to let their "creative juices flow" with David Smith, who often incorporates salvaged materials in his projects, such as brick from the original Chicago water tower or antique sconces and fixtures, cabinets, or old stained glass windows. This makes Smith a prime choice for those clients who want a refined eclectic look in their kitchen and bath remodels for those embarking on a historic renovation. Clients often shop with Smith and tell us he's a great source of interesting options. Although Smith isn't keen on leaving the city's boundaries, we're told he'll go anywhere for past clients. This company takes on loft build-outs, adds second stories to structures and also handles other major additions. Architects tell us the firm is especially sensitive in working in homes that are occupied during remodeling and interfaces well with the residents, including their children. Clients also applaud Smith's mix of workmen, including creative types, such as artists and musicians, who work alongside craftsmen talented in carpentry, tile work and painting. Customers also say the workers keep sites clean and picked up.

"He makes you happy to make him coffee." "Immerses himself in every project. Comes back in the morning with a new idea." "A real gentle way about him. My kids just jump on his lap." "Outstanding problem-solver. Knows his materials." "I can't imagine working with anyone else." "For the money, they have it down."

Dennis Smalley Builders 4 4 4 4.5

1212 Pine, Glenview, IL 60025
(847) 729 - 6212

High-end residential new construction and additions

Smalley's general contracting is hugely appreciated by a select group of North Shore residents who have experienced this firm's expertise in the creation of their new luxury homes and significant add-ons. Principal Dennis Smalley, they say, teams well with architects at the top tier of their profession and is, himself, knowledgeable about architecture. In addition, these clients say they enjoy Smalley's pleasant and unflappable disposition on the job.

Dennis Smalley Builders has a reputation for working with only the best subcontractors and getting their best work out of them. Projects progress smoothly and are consistently on schedule, we are told. To accomplish this, Smalley uses a combination of up-to-date technology and old-world craftsmanship. Work schedules are computerized, drawings are detailed, and the workmanship, clients tell us, can reach "museum quality." Results like this, they understand, come at a price.

"Phenomenal." "Did a magnificent job." "Can't say enough about him." "Done seven homes, this is by far the most intricate. I credit Dennis."

Design Construction Concepts 4 4 4 4

No 425 Huehl Road, Unit 15B Northbrook, IL 60062
(847) 498 - 1676 www.DCC-LTD.com

Design/build custom homes and upper-end remodeling

A provider of all-encompassing design/build service, this company was formed by architects Andy Poticha and Michael Menn who, they say, got fed up with underachieving general contractors and developed an approach they christened "constructures." Clients call it "terrific," and they are not alone. DCC garnered six Key Awards from the Home Builder's Association of Greater Chicago and a spot on *Remodeling* magazine's *Big 50*, where it was cited as one of the nation's top remodeling firms.

From the remodeling of Gold Coast penthouses to the erection of custom new homes on the North Shore, architects and interior designers appreciate DCC's respectful execution of their often elaborate plans, and gratified residents laud the firm's attention to detail and hands-on involvement. Poticha and Menn, they say, hustle to complete jobs on time with no sacrifice to quality and also are respectful of the well-being of clients' neighbors and surroundings.

"A wonderful job." "Good eye for detail. So easy to communicate." "We did an apartment in one of the most beautiful buildings in Chicago and their work lives up to the surroundings." "They'll take care of punch lists 'til the cows come home." "Success is not always measured on how far you go, but where you came from, and, if this is true, then our home speaks for itself—and DCC."

DeWindt Corp.				

1949 Cornell Avenue, Melrose Park, IL 60160
(708) 450 - 9400

High-end residential remodeling

This self-described "boutique" general contracting firm specializes in custom remodeling of historic townhouses and luxury penthouse apartments at the top of the city's residential market. Founded in 1984 by Geoffrey Roger Senior and Terrence O'Shaughessy, DeWindt subs out all construction, makes sure all become part of a coordinated team, and then hovers over projects until—and sometimes even after—the punch list, that final check and review, is completed. DeWindt also offers continuing maintenance on some clients' properties. Look to this firm, we're told, for high quality at a commensurate cost.

	Quality	Cost	Value	Recommend?
DNA Contracting	**4.5**	**4.5**	**4.5**	**4.5**

939 Forest Avenue, River Forest, IL 60035
(708) 366 - 7683

High-end residential general contracting and period restoration

DNA is said to be a perfect match for period restorations and the renovation of historic lake-front residences in Chicago's Gold Coast and along the North Shore. In confirmation of its ranking as a top general contractor for such specialty projects, a year ago, a DNA-restored home brought in one of the highest price tags ever paid in Chicago's history. DNA is now also involved in co-op build-outs and Greystone Development, a company which is building high-end new homes on spec.

Clients say principal Tony Aiello is honest and flexible, but demanding of workers. They also appreciate the design sensibility that partner Alex Demeter, a licensed architect, brings to the mix. The company is as articulate in communication as it is meticulous in craftsmanship and attention to detail, we're told. On-site supervision by a principal ensures that problems are addressed immediately, and foremen are praised for their quick response to clients' concerns.

The DNA stable of carpenters is considered first class, and its subcontractors are lauded for their pleasant, cooperative manner as well as their expertise. In the final analysis, clients say, DNA has the genetic code to improve on the heritage of Chicago's best-bred properties.

"Fantastic. Did more a year later. Only person we put out to bid." "Everything done by them was excellent." "Still in our lives." "A great and expensive project." "We even had the guys over for dinner." "Always told the truth. Didn't try to put anything over on us."

	Quality	Cost	Value	Recommend?
Doomis Custom Builders Inc.	**3.5**	**2.5**	**4**	**4**

79 Watergate Drive, Barrington, IL 60010
(847) 381 - 4644

Custom home builder, residential general contracting and remodeling

Custom is more than a word in this company's name. Both its new-home and remodeling clients marvel at the ideas and recommendations made by the company's owners and workmen. The ideas, we're told, make both economic and architectural sense and give interiors a stamp of individuality. Brothers Mike and Tom Doomis are carpenters by trade and are not just following in their father's footsteps, but also are now remodeling some of the homes built by their Dad over the past quarter-century.

Doomis limits its market to within a 20-mile radius of Barrington, apparently finding plenty of work there, all based on recommendations from happy previous clients, who say Doomis is reliable, honest and fair in pricing. Clients also appreciate that one of the principals is on-site daily and always available for emergencies. Doomis will provide prospects with a CD showing examples of its work.

"Made great recommendations." "Couldn't be more honest. Loads of integrity." "Very nice people. Became like family." "Goes above and beyond." "Stuck to their word."

Durrett Design 3.5 4 4.5 3

3343 South Halstead, Suite 201, Chicago, IL 60608
(773) 581 - 2107

Residential new construction and remodeling

According to clients, Michael Durrett can capture and interpret their design ideas quickly and comprehensively—sometimes before their very eyes—and then infuse them with a degree of creativity that stamps the project with individuality and makes it truly their own. His feel for light in relation to space is given particular note by these clients. Durrett's company engages in residential renovations, significant additions and design/development of custom single-family homes and large, multi-family buildings. On the job, references say Durrett watches over every detail and the crew attends quickly to any of their concerns.

Prospective clients pay an initial fee for conceptual drawings. When the final fit is struck, they pay a retainer before work commences. While clients credit the company with perfectionism, Michael Durrett says the personality of the client and the soul of the property inspire the design while his firm provides the management.

"Great guy—fun, nice, interesting and smart." "Able to replicate everything in the house. Blended our funky gothic home with an Italian country kitchen." "Incredible designer, really an artist." "A great crisis manager. Very good at bringing it down to workable solutions."

Eiesland Builders 4 3 5 5

2041 Johns Drive, Glenview, IL 60025
(847) 998 - 1731

High-end custom home building and remodeling

Eiesland earns solid praise for its new custom homes and cellar-to-attic remodeling jobs. It is, for example, currently gutting and adding to a 14,000-square-foot Lake Forest estate. Owner Arvid Eiesland, clients say, is as beloved for his sense of humor as for his openness to ideas. Others commend the "perfectly beautiful" craftsmanship of his work crew. One reference compares Eiesland's carpentry and millwork to the old-school craftsmanship of great Norwegian shipbuilders. Millwork is an Eiesland specialty, handled at the Eiesland Woodwork shop (see review), where clients are invited to come and see their cabinets being produced.

A remodeling customer says the company's work progressed on time and without trauma. He especially appreciates the crew's concern for clean-up and his family's comfort and safety. During the project, workmen built a temporary kitchen for the family in the basement.

Once a client, always a client. Eiesland encourages past customers to call any time with any problem. Whenever they do, as long as five years after completion of a job and for something as simple as an askew cabinet door, Eiesland calls them right back and fixes it the same day. For all of its crafstmanship and attention, this general contractor is considered reasonably priced by people who now live within its work.

"Everyone we've recommended him to has called and thanked us." "I had a question at the end of the day; he had answers by 7:30 the next morning." "Came in two months early. Did not do one thing wrong." "Stood behind everything." "It's been two years and it's as if I was a current customer." "The customer is always number-one."

Esposito Construction

1755 East 170th Place, South Holland, IL 60473
(708) 474 - 3660

High-end residential remodeling and additions, solariums

Esposito Construction is a family affair, run by Dick Esposito, his two sons and a nephew. Known for hands-on general contracting at a high level of quality, it also offers specialties, mastered by Esposito's sons. One is a carpenter, the other a glazier. It is also known for building solariums, a specialty niche that it now supplies for both residential and commercial clients within a 100-mile radius of Chicago.

Aside from solariums, the company devotes itself to residential remodeling and additions, working primarily in the Hyde Park area and, on occasion, on the near North Shore. We are told it handles any degree of remodeling, from a simple door repair to a kitchen renovation or construction of an addition that runs to high six figures. Yet, we are also told it will not bite off more than it can chew, retaining its care and personal attention, an attribute that has grown the business for a quarter of a century by referrals alone.

Frank H. Stowell & Sons Inc. **4 4 4 4**

8150 Central Park Avenue, Skokie, IL 60076
(847) 329 - 9200 www.fhstowell.com

High-end residential, commercial and institutional remodeling

Despite, and possibly because of, Stowell's mix of general contracting for institutions and commercial properties as well as high-end residential remodels, clients credit the company with bringing high standards of quality to their home work. High-rise clients, in particular, say the company's knowledge of commercial procedures smooths the overall process. While residential clients appreciate Stowell's commercial expertise, however, they are most praiseworthy of its old-school carpentry skills and ability to faithfully replicate the original craftsmanship of an Astor Street townhouse.

Sam Stowell, grandson of the founder who established the company in 1912, agrees that the demands of installing sensitive hospital equipment have impact on the company's exacting standards in home remodeling. Clients say the Stowell crews are highly competent and always attentive to their concerns. They especially appreciate their opening experience, they tell us, in which they talk one-on-one with Sam Stowell about what they envision. A vehicle that has roots in commercial work, Stowell's "Exceptional Expectations" program, they say, leads to frank and easy communication throughout the remodeling process. From the start, clients tell us, Stowell tailors work to their expectations and also comforts them with regular updates all along the way.

While this firm may not occupy the very highest rung on Chicago's ladder of top-tier remodeling contractors, references say it belongs in the company of the best.

"A wonderful experience, terrific people." "I've dealt with contractors in my work over the years and never dealt with anyone so good." "Very attuned to bringing people who know how to work in a high-end environment." "Absolutely, totally and unequivocally thrilled with him and the job he did."

	Quality	Cost	Value	Recommend?
Fraser Construction	4.5	4	4.5	5

8109 Ogden Avenue, Lyons, IL 60534
(708) 447 - 3262

High-end residential remodeling

Fraser is seen as the "old pro" of general contracting at the top of the residential market. For more than a generation, it has been tapped by designers and architects for every style of residential work, from Krueck & Sexton's sleek angles and glass to the aged refinement of historic dwellings, and in buildings ranging from stratospheric high rises to quaint or stately townhouses. The average Fraser job exceeds the million-dollar mark.

Its workmanship is not the only thing that puts Fraser on top of the referral list among Chicago's design cognizanti. Gale Fraser's own low-key demeanor, patience, and calming effect on designers and clients alike, combine with his keen eye for reading plans and demand for quality, we're told, to play a large part in the firm's enduring excellent reputation. Described as "a gentleman of the old school," he succeeds his father in giving clients hands-on—and often hand-holding—attention. The firm's in-house carpenters are said to be top-notch. Pricing is commensurate with the firm's quality, experience and attention, but worth it, we're told, for the best that money can buy.

"Been around forever." "Extremely gentle when the decorator throws a hissy fit." "Everything achieved comes within budget." "Don't know how he makes money" "Very much a midwesterner." "Made every last detail count." "Gale is a man of his word." "So completely outstanding. Delivered the most impeccable quality. Everything was taken care of before I could open my mouth."

	Quality	Cost	Value	Recommend?
G. Wood Construction, Inc.	4	4	4	4

13530 West 167th Street, Lockport, IL 60441
(708) 301 - 5207

High-end residential remodeling, renovations and additions

Clients say Gary Wood is the "ultimate gentleman," and his small firm does a marvelous job with technically difficult high-end renovation, remodeling and room additions. For the past 24 years, we hear Wood has met the challenge of taking apart century old buildings and, like all the kings men, putting them back together again. The firm wins praise for its communication and hands-on management, and clients say they are made to feel as though they are Wood's only priority. Wood is accessible seven days a week. All of the company's business, from the Gold Coast to North Shore, is repeat customers and referrals.

Wood uses his own carpenters and workmen along with an assemblage of subcontractors. Clients say he keeps them all in line and performing at their best. The workmanship is said to be a "magnitude" above norm, and clients say the firm lives up to every promise.

"First-rate guy. First-rate work." "Magnificent job." "Good value." "Had a cabinet guy who was a renegade. It took skill on Gary's part to bring him together with electricians and others." "Important stuff, he'll do right. Doesn't do short-cuts." "Listen to him. When he says it's not going to work, it won't."

	Quality	Cost	Value	Recommend?
Goldberg General Contracting Inc.	4.5	4	4	4.5

3510 North Elston Avenue, Chicago, IL 60618
(773) 279 - 9600

High- end residential remodeling

Clients think they've struck gold when wunderkind Jacob Goldberg applies his sense of design along with his company's diligent and talented crew, to their remodeling project or addition. Goldberg, an accomplished carpenter and the son of an architect, is especially good at interpreting and improving initial designs, we're told. Despite his own artistic bent, however, he is said to be down to earth and work well with interior designers. In addition, clients say he's adept at marshalling plans past co-op boards, and dealing with management companies and special insurance situations.

Goldberg works exclusively on renovations in Gold Coast high-rises and townhouses. The company has in-house carpenters and tile and stone installers, and their work, according to clients, is of superior quality. Some clients tell us they fear that word of the Goldberg standards will spread, making the firm too busy to handle their next project. However, Goldberg already does a lot of repeat business, so much so one client quips, "I'm dating my contractor."

"Top guys, top notch." "I could not imagine anyone else doing it for me. If friends don't use Goldberg, I feel sorry for them." "Much to our delight it was the best decision of our life." "Could have left home for a year and gotten the same product." "Jake could be a designer himself. Heck, he could build a home himself!"

Harold O. Schulz Co., Inc. **5** **5** **4.5** **5**
2124 Ashland Avenue, Evanston, IL 60201
(847) 869 - 4949 www.hoschulz.com

High-end residential general contracting

Known for complex, exquisitely detailed remodeling in high-end residential estates and condominiums, Harold O. Schulz Co. has a loyal following of design professionals and clients who say it sets the bar in its field. One adds, it is "unquestionably the best." In addition to the company's workmanship, clients say its commitment to service sets it apart.

One of the two brothers, Eric and David Schulz, actively oversees each project. They learned the business from the company's namesake, their father. Weekly jobsite meetings are held among subcontractors and the Schulz crew to address potential problems before they occur and keep everyone informed, on time and in step. Crews are praised for their reliability and rigorous, everyday clean-ups. A foreman is assigned as point person on a job, and he stays with the project from beginning to end and can even be reached years afterwards, should any problem arise.

David Schulz sees the company's projects as lifetime commitments, he reasons, "because, through our work, we're with clients for the rest of their lives and their children's lives."

"On a scale of one to five, I give him a six!" "Not cheap but worth it." "Hire in a heartbeat." "Foreman was the nicest guy. Knew what to do." "Ten years later, I called up for something they came the next day."

Harris Builders, LLC **3.5** **2.5** **4** **4.5**
325 East Palatine Road, Barrington, IL 60010
(847) 382 - 2210 www.harriscustomhomes.com

Custom home builder

Harris is an experienced builder of custom and semi-custom homes, including those in planned communities in and around Barrington. Clients generally begin with the Harris databank of home plans, which can be reproduced as shown, modified or re-worked entirely. Squarely in the luxury level, the homes start at 4,200 square feet and typically cost a million or more. Evan Harris, owner, is involved in every project, and we're told he develops a collaborative relationship with clients, takes their special considerations to heart, solves problems easily and delivers a top-quality house.

People also report that Harris chooses excellent subcontractors and that crews are not only efficient, but also nice to work with. Every project has an on-site supervisor, and project manager, Dean Snow, to oversee progress. Design is charged at a fixed fee, and construction is charged on a cost-plus-fee basis.

"Quality blew us away." "Terrific builders." "Top notch." "If not best—one of the top." "We wanted a ranch. Most builders weren't interested, but Harris said, 'Yeah, I can do that'."

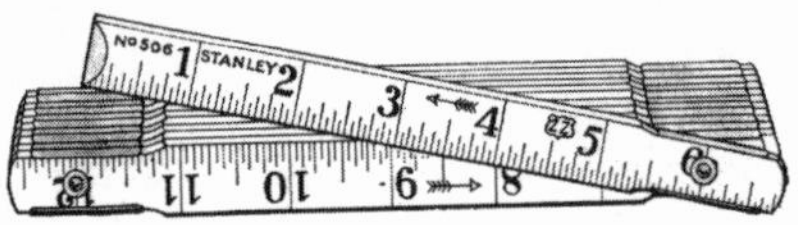

Quality	Cost	Value	Recommend?
			◆	

Horcher Brothers Construction Co. Inc. 3.5 3 4.5 4.5
115 Wedgewood Drive, Barrington, IL 60010
(847) 381 - 6011
High-end residential remodeling and additions

Many North Shore and Barrington area residents have come to rely on Horcher Brothers for larger remodeling and addition projects. An established general contractor since 1959, this firm is run by father-and-son team John Horcher, founder, and Paul Horcher. It divides its time between commercial and residential work. Residential projects typically average $400,000 and top out at the $1.5-million mark. Despite its usual price tags, Horcher returns to past clients to handle their smaller jobs. On occasion the firm also builds new homes.

The company can and will facilitate design service, when required, or work with a client's preferred architect. It has in-house carpenters that are said to be top quality. Clients appreciate Horcher Brothers' long-time experience, hands-on management, quick response and the very reliable quality of workmanship, we're told. While the pricing is upper-end, it is seen as competitive with other high-caliber contractors on the North Shore.

"Very reliable, honest, timely. The actual cost was the bid estimate." "We are using them for the second time and are very satisfied." "Subcontractors were excellent and friendly."

James A. Blackmore Construction 4.5 5 4 4
15020 Cicero Avenue, Oak Forest, IL 60452
(708) 535 - 1000
High-end residential general contracting

An established, widely respected general contractor, Blackmore is said to be on the short list among marquee architects and designers, and the steward of many of Chicago's most exclusive projects. We hear, however, the firm's hot demand isn't lost in it's pricing. Blackmore works throughout the greater metropolitan area, including the North Shore.

JDS Homes 3.5 3 4 3.5
6212 Elm Street, Burr Ridge, IL 60521
(630) 789 - 6202 www.jdshomes.com
Custom home builder

JDS considers itself a custom-home "boutique" that offers complete design/build services, including, if needed, a property search. It operates along a large area reaching to Chicago's southwest and northwest suburbs. JDS has housing lots and an array of spec-built homes that have won awards in national home-building competitions. On custom work, however, clients can use their own architect.

Regardless of the approach they take, clients report that owner James Slesser walks them through every aspect of planning and design and also functions as the team captain throughout construction. They credit JDS for its high degree of personal attention, quality craftsmanship on the job, and professional management. The company is said to give good value in the area's big-budget housing arena.

JMD Builders, Inc. | Quality 4 | Cost 3.5 | Value 4.5 | Recommend? 5

444 Lake Cood Road, Suite 10, Deerfield, IL 60015
(847) 945 - 9670

Custom remodeling and home building

Clients give this high-end residential remodeling specialist and custom home building contractor straight "A's" for service and quality and also say it delivers work at a fair price. JMD's services run the gamut from hanging a troublesome window, to restoring historic architecture or creating a custom, luxury home at the four-million-dollar level or higher. Its market encompasses downtown penthouses and townhouses and North Shore estates. Kitchen and bath remodels are among its specialties.

Principal Jerry Dardick worked as a carpenter with his father and has a B.A. in architecture. These credentials, clients say, combine with JMD's crews of construction-industry veterans to deliver work that is highly professional and also creative. The carpentry, we're told, dazzles. They also credit the company with good, technologically-advanced communication and cost-containment.

"High recommendation to anyone in a remodeling project." "Quality excellent! Subs excellent!" "Keeps budget in mind and produces along those lines." "On top of everything. Makes sure you know where you are in process." "Genuinely cared." "I've dealt with a number of contractors. Jerry Dardick is heads-and-shoulders above." "Wouldn't let anyone else touch my apartment." "Knew how to work around apartment building. Never used constraints as an excuse."

John G. Harty Ltd. | Quality 4 | Cost 3 | Value 5 | Recommend? 5

657 Laurel Avenue, Highland Park, IL 60035
(847) 266 - 1845 www.yourbuildingconsultant.com

High-end remodeling and new-home construction management

The Harty boys' approach to construction management is no mystery. Under Harty Ltd., the clients themselves contract with individual trades crews and Harty handles payments and project administration for a fee that is based on the total job cost. Clients call it an "open-book" approach and say it saves them money, time and grief. It is hailed by clients who favor this alternative to hiring a general contractor for their upper-end remodels or custom homes. They believe, they tell us, that it gave them greater input and more control over the design and building process. Some say it also eased their fears of hidden costs and high mark-ups.

The talents of brothers John and Rich Harty are complementary, according to clients. John walks clients through initial design work and communicates with them during construction. He works at the jobsite, overseeing progress and attending to details. From company headquarters, Rich manages every contract and scheduling, then walks clients through final punch work, without missing a detail.

Remodeling clients that do not have an architect pay Harty a deposit for the initial design and a cost-estimate that is accurate to within 10 percent of the final cost. Clients say the estimate and design drawings are highly detailed and accurate. Last year *Remodeling* magazine confirmed clients' claims by including John G. Harty on its list of the nation's Top 50 remodelers.

"So easy to work with. Use him again in a heartbeat. I've recommended them to lots of people, and everyone's been thrilled." "Love John. Love everyone he brought in. Couldn't imagine doing it another way." "Incredible, absolutely incredible."

John Marshall Construction, Inc. | Quality 3.5 | Cost 3 | Value 4 | Recommend? 3.5

1583 North Barclay Boulevard, Buffalo Grove, IL 60089
(847) 279 - 7840 jmcinc1976@aol.com

Residential general contracting

	Quality	Cost	Value	Recommend?

North Shore clients have been calling on the services of this 20-person contracting firm since 1976 with good results. John Marshall Construction typically farms out design/build service, but tackles total contracting for large additions and high-end kitchen and bath remodeling as well as new custom homes. Crews are willing to handle small repairs for past customers. Principal John Marshall is a student of high-end work and once replicated a Frank Lloyd Wright home.

John P. Teschky Inc. **5** **5** **4.5** **5**

824 Waukegan Road, Northbrook, IL 60062
(847) 753 - 8271 www.teschky.com

High-end remodeling and custom home building

Chicago's most prominent architects and discriminating residents rank John P. Teschky, Inc. among the best general contractors in the area. For 23 years the company has delivered high-end custom homes and produced top-quality additions and remodeling projects for houses and apartments that we are told excel in both esthetics and structural soundness. Principal John Teschky is said to be particularly skilled at orchestrating complex jobs that require a high degree of coordination. The company has a reputation for anticipating problems, providing options and, often, for developing low-cost solutions that don't sacrifice quality.

This is a family operation headed now by two generations of husband-and-wife, hands-on principals and their siblings, plus a loyal work crew, most of whom have been with the firm for decades. The carpenters are credited with museum-quality craftsmanship, and the professionalism of every member of the team wins clients' praise. The family-orientation, John Teschky says, carries special responsibility: "If we let down a client, we're letting down our whole family." He needn't worry according to the references we reached, all of whom call their experience with, and results from John P. Teschky "exemplary."

"Top drawer, first rate." "Did exactly what he said. Stood by all his work. What else can you ask for?" "Realized a number of things the architect made very difficult, but never compromised quality." "Right there if anything goes wrong, only there isn't anything that goes wrong!" "Just a gentleman."

Keystone Builders, Inc. **3** **2** **4** **4**

3435 Old Mill Road, Highland Park, IL 60035
(847) 432 - 4392 www.keystone-builders.com

Residential general contracting

Inspired by the philosophy expounded in Sarah Susanka's book, "The Not So Big House," this North Shore family-run firm prefers remodeling and building projects that call for charm and detail in every square inch to projects that are measured in sheer square-footage. While Keystone's owners, Stan and Joanna Szymel, will consider jobs of any size, their attention to detail has won them referrals that reflect their philosophy.

Keystone is praised for the Szymel's personal attention to projects and its crew of fine, European-trained craftsmen. Every project has an on-site point person, and a Szymel visits daily. The company provides complete design/build service and, by all accounts, remains mindful of its clients' budgets.

"Everything was better than our expectations." "Stan was very responsive to phone calls." "Fair price, good work, no problems." "Still maintain a relationship." "Good at solving problems." "Stuck to quoted price."

Larson Builders **3** **2** **4** **4**

2328 Cowper Avenue, Evanston, IL 60201
(847) 866 - 8404

Remodeling and restoration

Clients call Jeff Larson a "real straight shooter," and we're told that he and his field-staff of four are easy to work with. The company handles interior remodeling and restorations ranging from small projects to quarter-million-dollar additions, and is known as a problem-solver. Larson specializes in window replacement, particularly in duplicating old windows and trim. Clients say the company does good work and sees the job through to the finish. Much of its business is in Evanston, but Larson tackles challenging projects up and down the North Shore. Clients praise Larson's personal commitment to each project, and we hear his company employs quality subs for even the smallest of jobs. Larson also works closely with clients on the budget and its relation to clients' expectations for fit and finish, delivering at a price clients tell us is moderate and represents good value.

"Pleasure to work with. Honest. On time." "Wonderful, small crew became like family." "Said six weeks. Got it done in four-and-a-half." "Very conscientious. Did a fine job." "Absolutely recommend."

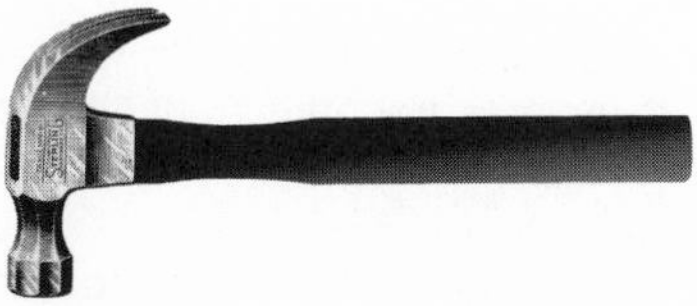

LDC Custom Homes **4** **3.5** **4** **4.5**
27W 031 North Avenue, West Chicago, IL 60185
(630) 293 - 9660 www.ldchomes.com

Residential restoration, remodeling and custom home building

By all accounts, LDC has a PhD in the restoration and enlargement of Victorians and townhouses and the building of high-end custom homes. The firm works primarily in Dupage and Cook Counties, but, we are told, will tackle any North Shore work that involves premier architects, challenging plans, and top clients and budgets.

Considered very attentive and trustworthy, principal Joseph Lichtenberger has a reputation for developing good relationships with architects and implementing their plans with skill and strict attention to the smallest of details. The LDC subcontractors are considered first-rate, and special praise is given to a company carpenter who is a master of interior millwork. Remodeling clients and those who have used LDC to add to their historic homes rave about LDC's ability to seamlessly blend new work into the existing architecture and period interiors.

Lichtenberger's hands-on attention is said to continue through completion and clean-up. Pricing is at the upper end of the scale, but, according to grateful and satisfied clients, well worth the extra dollars. Some vow they would never put anyone else in charge of their house.

"The only builder I'd ever use again." "Joe was wonderful." "A lot of detail work." "Great. I'm happy to bring prospective clients through our home. Chicago Magazine listed it among the top 30 most beautiful in Chicago." "Excellent job."

McKnight + Partners, Inc. **3.5** **3** **4** **4**
1132 Florence Avenue, Evanston IL 60202
(847) 864 - 2329

High-end remodeling, restoration and custom home building

When an older home's flaws and mysteries must be reconciled with new work, and the new work has to fit in with the old neighborhood, architects often recommend McKnight + Partners. This firm specializes in historic preservation and retrofits, does exterior work and additions and occasionally builds a new home. We're told principals Jonathan McKnight and Bruce Hidner are hands-on from up-front conceptual development to dropping by the job site daily. The concept stage is where this company brings special value, we're told, because the principals know immediately how an idea affects budget. McKnight + Partners is very detail-oriented and maintains its own in-house carpenters. Good subs help sustain the quality of work for the duration of every project, and its principals stay ahead of potential work and budget threats. Does this company hold its clients' hands? How about paws? It recently watched the dog for a vacationing client.

Metzler/Hull Development Corp. **4.5 4.5 4 4**

1103 West Webster Avenue, Chicago, IL 60614
(773) 871 - 2258

High-end design/build

People seeking ultra-custom homes in Lincoln Park that are characterized by one-of-a-kind interior details and start at the two-and-a-half-million-dollar mark, appreciate the one-stop service offered by Metzler Hull, the area's premier design/build firm. With this company, design/build is, indeed, comprehensive. It owns prime lots with a selection of spec-built, ready-to-occupy homes in place, but will also start projects from the ground up, occasionally working either with a client's architect or typically providing one from its in-house staff of certified architects.

Clients say they are guided through the entire process, from design concept through permit approval and each phase of construction and finishing until they're handed the keys. Investment banker, Jay Metzler, and carpenter, Andy Hull, formed the company in 1991. Devoted to a well-heeled niche, the company is dedicated to providing it with the quality it demands. That quality, clients tell us, encompasses business professionalism, hands-on attention and exemplary craftsmanship. No surprise, given that Lincoln Park is more than just Metzler's market—it's where he lives.

Clients praise the in-house work crews and say the partners hire only top-tier subcontractors. One of the partners spends a half day at each site every day, ensuring that quality-control measures are in place and that schedules proceed on time. All work is covered under a single contract, another hassle-free feature clients appreciate.

"Quality is outstanding. Everything is outstanding. It's everything I dreamed it would be." "Very good about coming back."

Mirco Builders

595 Elm Place, Highland Park, IL 60035
(847) 433 - 1270

High-end remodeling and interior build-out

This commercial and residential general contractor has been serving the greater Chicago metropolitan area for 40 years. Brothers Mike and Robert Brenner inherited the company from their father and specialize in top-dollar remodeling and addition projects that start at $250,000. The company is always on the lookout for well-conceived design and top architects. Mirco subs out all work, except carpentry, and its lead carpenter acts as site supervisor. We're told the brothers Brenner are always involved with the day-to-day progress of their company's projects, from the pre-construction phase to handing over the keys, and Mirco likes to retain customers long after that. It often does, because clients say Mirco knows the meaning of high-end quality and service.

Nayer Construction

2035 South State, Chicago, IL 60616
(312) 243 - 3335 www.nayercrue.com

Residential remodeling and historic renovation

This is the company to call for very special custom projects, we are told. The restored facade of Old St. Patrick's church is one example; another is restoration of a downtown 19,000-square-foot mansion. Despite the large projects on the company résumé, clients say principal Rich Nayer prefers smaller, "funkier" jobs that call for head-scratching and rely on his and his troupe of artisans' multi-media skills.

While all ten members of the Nayer team are carpenters by trade, expertise with chrome, copper, stained glass, tile, stone and marble is among their talents. Restoration architects are also on the staff. Nayer's in-house work extends from routine concrete pours to sublime custom cabinetry, we're told, and is executed with strict attention to detail. Special mention is made of its wood carving capabilities. High-end bathroom remodels that bring all the company's resident disciplines into play, are also among its specialties. Small wonder that Nayer's business has thrived only through referrals for 19 years.

Northridge Builders Inc. **3.5 3.5 4 4**
15 Spinningwheel Road, Hinsdale, IL 60521
(630) 654 - 3817

High-end home building and renovation

This prolific builder, known primarily for luxury custom homes, takes on a couple of major renovation projects each year. Its specialty is in duplicating traditional styles such as English Tudor and Country French. Principal Dave Kniecht has a background in architecture and engineering that adds both creative and practical insight to design concepts and the construction process. This is not a design/build firm, however. It works with clients' architects or refers them to one. The company's principal area of operation is in Hinsdale and Burr Ridge, where it is highly regarded. Occasionally, Northridge performs construction management, and will handle jobs downtown and on the North Shore. Working with Kniecht and team is such a delight, we're told, that clients invite team members to dinner when the project is complete.

"So authentic, the homes look like they came over on the boat."

Northstar Homes **3.5 3.5 4 3.5**
3100 Concord Court, Northbrook, IL 60062
(847) 714 - 0054

High-end remodeling and custom home building

Like its cosmic namesake, this North Shore builder guides the direction of high-end custom homes and large-scale remodels and additions. Clients often approach Northstar without an architect, calling on principal Allan Sherman to walk them through the design process and assemble a team of subcontractors specifically able to handle it. We are told he is good at brainstorming ideas with clients, has an eye for design and is equally adept in the field. This is a small company with an in-house staff of two. Sherman manages all projects from start to rough carpentry. Then his own master carpenter adds the final finish, which, clients report, ensures them of hands-on attention. Northstar enjoys a reputation for solid workmanship and honest, open-book business integrity.

Orren Pickell Designers & Builders **4.5 4 5 5**
2201 Waukegan Road, Suite W-285, Bannockburn, IL 60015
(847) 914 - 9629 www.pickellbuilders.com

Residential design/build and general contracting

Clients say Pickell earned its ranking as "2001 Custom Home Builder of the Year," an honor bestowed on the firm by *Custom Home* magazine. From Lincoln Park to Lake Geneva and west to Barrington, they rave about this company's across-the-board services, ranging from thoughtful attention to design to top-notch quality.

The Pickell resources run wide and deep. Within this large firm's umbrella are: a custom-home building group, responsible for what is considered the company's "signature" top-to-bottom design/build service; a design group that offers only architecture; a remodeling group that handles the gamut from gut renovations to kitchen and bath remodeling, historic restorations and maintenance; CabinetWerks, which makes custom cabinetry (see review under Millwork) and a real estate group. Despite its size and reach, however, clients say Orren Pickell has not lost touch with his roots, which dig back to a painting and remodeling business that supported his architecture schooling. He built the first Pickell home by himself, 25 years ago.

Now, supported by a stable of highly trained specialists in the full range of disciplines required for quality custom work, Pickell has garnered numerous awards for design and construction and a long line of very satisfied customers. Either Orren Pickell or his chief architect meets initially with a prospective client to determine what the client wants, then assigns the in-house architect that best matches the client's personality and project. Under Pickell's design philosophy, a house should be married to the land. Once plans are finalized, a construction supervisor is assigned. While some clients report that the super was always on top of the job, even making improvements to the design, another complained that the super did not check the site as much as expected and assumed he was busy with additional assignments. All the clients, however, said they were impressed with follow-up and told us Orren Pickell was personally available for any problems or questions.

"My father was a retired builder. He watched Pickell's men work and was ready to jump on them. But what he saw only impressed. For the first time in his life, he had nothing to say." "Very strong on design, very strong on quality. Even underneath, in the wall, it's done right." "Did everything we wanted, exactly the way we wanted it." "People are now raving about our house!" "I settled for a smaller house with Pickell to stay within budget. But I could rest assured. Now it's been six years and every day I'm very grateful."

Raswick Concepts Construction Design
3248 North Troy, Chicago, IL 60618
(773) 478 - 5889
Residential remodeling

This second-generation general contractor concentrates on high-rise remodels and loft build-outs on the Gold Coast and in Lincoln Park. It also does some new construction and commercial work. Peter Raswick, the current owner, is personally involved with clients' architects and designers and guides clients through conceptualization. He is said to welcome their consideration and reconsideration of options until final decisions are reached. They credit him with a keen sense for detail.

At a minimum the firm handles jobs with the scope of a high-end kitchen and bath remodel, and if Raswick can't help a prospective customer, he'll direct them to someone who can. All work is subcontracted, and clients say Raswick selects subs with care, matching them to both the project and the budget. They report that the quality is good in respect to price.

Reese Classic Residences/
Classic Design Studios
350 Old McHenry Road, Long Grove, IL 60047
(847) 913 - 1680 www.rclassicres.com

Custom home builder

The Reese piece of the contracting market is custom homes in the $750,000 to two-million-dollar range from Barrington to the North Shore. It's a small firm with expanded capabilities borrowed from its sister company, Classic Design Studios, which designs and installs kitchens, baths and audio/video systems and also offers custom millwork. For new homes, Reese's founder, Mark Farrahar, will work with a client's architect or devote himself to conceptualizing the house and have the plans drafted by an outside architect. Clients say this streamlines the process and cuts cost. All work is subcontracted.

We hear that Farrahar is always accessible—from start to finish. The firm is a leader in utilizing technology, such as a website to keep its customers informed and a database of warranties to help clients track their service agreements.

RGB Construction Management Ltd. — 4 | 3.5 | 5 | 5
736 North Western Avenue, Lake Forest, IL 60045
(847) 234 - 9900

High-end design/build, construction management and period restoration

A second-generation architect, Ray Basso says he's had a T-square in his hand since he was four. Maybe that's why clients are so enthusiastic about RGB's work, which includes construction management and general contracting for high-end remodeling and new homes in Chicago and along the North Shore. The firm is also responsible for a number of award-winning historic preservation projects.

We're told that because Basso is an architect, when clients relate ideas to him, he comes back the next day with detailed drawings. Clients also say RGB gives painstaking attention to the stickiest of details, including the faithful replication of old-master work in historic estates. Clients enjoy one-on-one service, and tell us that Basso's creativity is matched by his enthusiasm.

Basso also heads the architecture firm, Ray Basso and Associates (see review), and continues to work alongside his father, an architect since 1953. A jack of many trades, Basso is familiar with passive solar and other energy-efficient technology and designed and built the largest solar-heated pool in the Midwest.

"Everyone I've recommended him to says 'thank you, thank you, thank you!' This one's a prize." "As true to the period as possible." "When we went out of town, he checked on our house. After construction was done!" "Great job."

Rizzolo Brothers' Co., Inc. — 4 | 3 | 4.5 | 5
15670 West Birchwood Lane, Libertyville, IL 60048
(847) 247 - 8901

Custom home building and remodeling

Clients can't say enough good things about the craftsmanship, delivered personally every day, by owner Jeffery Rizzolo and his small and talented crew of carpenters. Rizzolo carries on his family's tradition of honesty and hands-on, hard work and quality in building luxury homes, one at a time, since 1953. We hear Rizzolo Brothers' also handles remodeling projects with the same great care, from installing a pitched roof to custom door hardware and everything in between. Wife Laurie complements Rizzolo's on-site supervision by managing the office. With one of these two "better halves" always accessible, clients say the Rizzolo's follow-through is outstanding, and they also tell us the couple is lovely to work with. Clients describe the soft-spoken Rizzolo as not only an excellent contractor, but also a fine person. The area's most established architects and tradespeople agree. The company's greatest asset may be that it offers a level of attentiveness at a cost other high-end North Shore builders don't always match, making many past clients say that Rizzolo is a superior find.

"I'll absolutely use again." "A joy to work with." "Definitely high end." "He is absolutely wonderful. Follow-through is terrific." "On site every day. No problem that Jeff couldn't handle. Knows how everything works in a house."

Ron Carani & Associates Inc. **5** **4.5** **4.5** **5**

P.O. Box 1544 , Highland Park, IL 60035
(847) 433 - 4090

High-end remodeling and custom home building

When the name's Carani, clients can bet it's a class-A company. Ron Carani has 40 years of experience in living up to the family's standards, which clients say he does with great care and meticulous workmanship. He and partner/wife, Sharon, have earned clients' full trust, we're told, by using only the best of subcontractors, hovering over jobs as if they were for their own home and avoiding shortcuts and inferior materials. Carani takes projects to the "nth degree," we're told, and does all the extras that lead to excellence.

The firm works primarily on the North Shore and occasionally in the city. Carani clients insist this company ranks with the best in the business for high-end custom homes and challenging upper-end remodeling projects. Its work is limited to approximately four major projects a year, ensuring that each gets the attention that's required. The firm's pricing, like its work, is at the upper end of the spectrum. Yet, clients rave about the work in general and the carpentry in particular—"superb in every shape and form"—and they can't seem to keep from telling us how much fun it is to work with the company. Some say they miss this couple once the job is done.

"No question his people are the best in the business." "If something doesn't look right, you don't have to tell him." "He's perfect." "A pro." "Honesty is synonymous with Ron." "Always called right back. Never had to chase him." "Can't say enough. A wonderful experience." "Now that it's over, you miss them. It was like they were friends for two years." "The quality of the work is outstanding."

S.N. Peck Builder Inc. **4.5** **4** **4.5** **5**

650 West Grace Street, Chicago, IL 60613
(773) 248 - 8883

High-end residential remodeling and additions

Peck's work unearths rave reviews by the bushel. Big enough to handle king-size renovations, yet small enough to provide personal service, S.N. Peck is known for satisfying downtown's most demanding clients on their most challenging remodeling projects, renovations and additions. We're told Peck's dedication to clients is remarkable, especially in emergency situations. A top architect called on the firm to repair fire damage in his own home.

Neil Peck and his wife, Barbara Rose, work as a team, ensuring clients that a principal is always within reach. S.N. Peck performs all its own carpentry and has an organized, responsive team of highly skilled tradesmen. Clients say Peck is inspired at solving tough problems, and keeps after subs, demanding that no detail is overlooked.

To meet past and present clients' demand for smaller work, such as minor alterations and maintenance, Peck purchased the local franchise unit of Case Handyman Services (312-431-0010). Clients call this their good luck and tell us that Case's service has been elevated, under Peck's management, to the standards of its new parent, and, when necessary, the company utilizes veteran Peck personnel.

"His perspective is always service-oriented." "Very pleased." "Would work with them again." "Wouldn't use anyone else." "Stood by everything they've done." "Never had any problem." "We had just moved into our Peck-built home when it was struck by lightening. We called Neal at 7:00 pm on a Sunday night and he had men there by 8:30 pm. And it was the Fourth of July!"

Schwall Builders | 3.5 | 3 | 4 | 4.5

1611 Techny Road, Northbrook, IL 60062
(847) 272 - 5743

Residential general contracting and interior renovation

For 40 years, Schwall has handled general contracting for custom home building, room additions and high-end remodeling projects along the North Shore from Gurnee to Skokie. Five sons now run the business in accordance with their Dad's admonition to "say what you do and do what you say." Clients have nothing but positive things to report about this company. Since 1963, Schwall has grown solely on word-of-mouth referrals, confirmation of its competence and quality. It facilitates complete design/build service and employs its own staff of carpenters. In addition, it has a separate division that specializes in window repair and replacement, and several clients have singled out its painters for praise. We're told Schwall's people are ever courteous, non-invasive of clients' homes, and that they clean up at the end of every workday, making this firm a preferred choice at live-in construction projects.

"Not only do they have skilled people, but personally, one-on-one, they are concerned about what we want and listen to what we think." "Remarkably professional. Quality of work is amazing." "Zero complaints. Recommend 100 percent." "They treated our home like it was theirs. So good to work with." "Anticipated things before they happened."

Scott Simpson Builders, Inc. | 3.5 | 3 | 4.5 | 5

1848 Techny Road, Northbrook, IL 60062
(847) 714 - 1107

Residential remodeling and additions

Scott Simpson says his company's mission is to provide architects and customers with the best craftsmen at a fair price. Clients say: mission accomplished. All members of the eight-man crew are carpenters. After an experience with this eight-year-old general contracting firm, many clients tell us they'd never consider using anyone else. Simpson Builders specializes in renovations and additions on the North Shore, and we are told it is conscientious, staying ahead (and out) of people's lives during the process. The key is in preparation, which includes erecting temporary walls to contain dust and limit intrusions into occupied space. We're told Simpson is astute at studying and following plans, but is also open to suggestions and often contributes valuable ideas. A lead carpenter provides daily, on-site supervision and conducts weekly meetings to keep reigns on quality and scheduling. References say Simpson and crew follow through on all aspects of a project and they rank the quality very high. The company is also said to be up front and honest in pricing.

"Absolutely fabulous." "Did what he said he'd do." "Great guys on the job. Respectful of home." "Very careful to prevent the unforeseen from happening." "A fine job. Good subs all the way." "Loved them." "Reliable and trustworthy, stayed with us until the finish." "Very conscientious of our lives. They'd come in while we were sleeping in the morning and we'd never know."

Spicak Construction | 3.5 | 3 | 4 | 4

27864 North Irma Lee Circle, Suite 103, Lake Forest, IL 60045
(847) 680 - 9292

High-end residential remodeling and additions

Only two years old, Spicak Construction is grounded in the two decades of North Shore building experience of owner Jim Spicak, who brings an impeccable reputation for high-end remodeling and room additions. Spicak, an architect by training, assists clients in a design/build capacity and will take on new construction. A team player, he keeps his architectural background under wraps when working with architects, allowing their work to shine and using his knowledge to implement their plans with precision and some creative enhancements. In construction, he doesn't look for the lowest-bid subcontractors, but ones that have above-par quality and match the specific demands of the job. He brings his own gifted carpenters and an in-house millwork shop to projects, along with a reliable foreman who oversees each site from start to finish. His loyal employees like him as much as his clients do, we're told. Often Spicak's remodels begin on a small scale and then, on the basis of the company's fine work, mushrooms to include other rooms and additional work.

"I think he's great. Honest, fair, not into playing tricks."

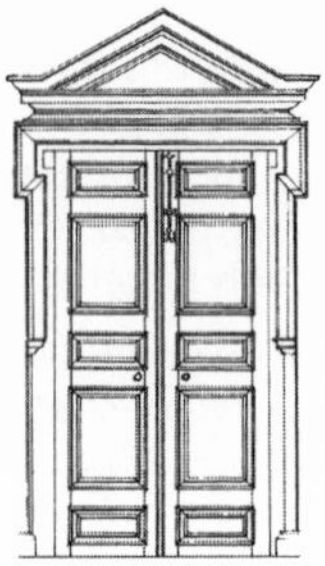

Sylvester Construction Services Inc. 5 4 5 5
2742 North Lincoln Avenue, Chicago, IL 60614
(773) 281 - 6094

High-end remodeling contracting and construction management

Historic restoration, stem-to-stern renovation and additions of 3,000 square feet or more are Sylvester's leading services, which are said to leave clients in awe at the workmanship. Experience in high-end masonry and interior finishes has led the company to many kitchen and bath remodels from downtown to Hinsdale and along the North Shore to Geneva. We're told that owner Barry Sylvester limits the firm to challenging projects that match the level of quality it supplies. References say he's a perfectionist who thinks through every construction ramification from the outset and attends to the tiniest details.

Demanding clients also credit him with good taste and an education to match, which they say contributes to the firm's ability to give jobs the appearance they want along with exemplary quality. Additional strengths, they report, are the firm's long-standing relationships with subcontractors and on-the-job coordination by seasoned, discriminating supers.

Sylvester, no stranger to landmark or architecturally significant buildings, restored a David Adler home to its previous perfection. Clients say the firm works well with the city's best architects and interior designers. On the philosophy that "you get what you pay for," clients say they not only do not balk at this company's prices, but, despite the high total tickets, end up feeling they got more than they paid for.

"I love Barry." "As seasoned home builders, we hold Barry in the highest respect!" "Compared to our other experience, it was night and day." "Phenomenal attention to detail." "If there was any glitch, he was very quick to say what was wrong and fix it." "Like them so much I'm going to use them again."

T&T Construction Co. 4.5 4 4.5 4.5
3351 South Parnell Avenue, Chicago, IL 60616
(312) 326 - 2782

High-end interior build-out and remodeling

For the serious remodeler, T&T is a dynamite choice for interiors on Chicago's Gold Coast and the North Shore. Its special forte, we're told, is breathing new life into vintage homes and houses by David Adler and other renowned Chicago architects. Empty-nesters and other well-heeled homeowners say T&T's combination of flexibility and persistence works well with top-tier architects and interior designers and is a perfect tonic to these professionals' potent personalities. Considering the company it keeps, T&T's costs are quite competitive.

The company handles small and large projects, many of which it gets through repeats or referrals. That it once worked on three apartments in the same high-rise based upon three unrelated recommendations, confirms clients' pleasure in passing on good words. The company uses 10 in-house carpenters and its own job foremen. Furthermore, one of the two owners, Anthony DiVittorio or Anthony Nudo, show up at jobsites almost daily, according to clients who appreciate such attention from the top. In fact, although the partners may want to keep this under wraps, we're told they are as highly skilled as their craftsmen and have been known to roll up their sleeves to bring a job in on time. The partners formed T&T more than 20 years ago and have maintained a reputation for fabulous quality work with a personal touch.

"The work is to perfection." "Really pleasant to work with." "Recommend to anyone!" "Subs were all good. If there was a problem, it got fixed immediately." "Even my neighbors were satisfied." "By far the best experience. Tony's word is his word. I won't trust anyone else."

The Meyne Company **4 4 4 4**

1755 West Armitage Avenue, Chicago, IL 60622
(312) 207 - 2100

High-end renovation, remodeling and additions

The Meyne Company is a favorite for interior build-outs and new construction along Chicago's Gold Coast. The firm opened its doors in 1906 and is now the high-end residential arm of Bully & Andrews, a large family owned and operated construction company that has served Chicago since 1891. The Meyne Company's projects typically fall at $300 per square foot, and begin at $500,000.

Pre-war co-op owners swear by The Meyne Company, and notable architects as well as discriminating private clients say its work is worth the money. A project manager and supervisor are assigned to each job, and The Meyne Company's ability to match these overseers to a client's personality is reportedly the company's secret strategy for not only completing work on time, but also gaining what some describe as a "cult following" of happy clients.

While The Meyne Company gives the hands-on personal attention these projects require, it also has the support of its parent's wealth of resources and expertise. Among those resources is a field staff of between 150 and 250 tradesmen, including qualified carpenters, masons, plumbers and even people trained in such specialties as excavation and demolition. The full family gives clients Main Street attention with industrial-strength support.

"Liked their approach." "Responsive. They got it done." "Apartments in my building are the most expensive per square foot in the city and Meyne's work lived up to it."

The Poulton Group, Ltd.

268 Market Square, Lake Forest, IL 60045
(847) 615 - 1178

Residential architecture

See The Poulton Group, Ltd.'s full report under the heading Architects

	Quality	Cost	Value	Recommend?
Tip Top Builders Inc.	4	4	4	4.5

8255 Kimball Avenue, Skokie, IL 60076
(847) 679 - 5010

High-end residential general contracting

Tip Top is the high-end residential remodeling arm of a 38-year-old firm that began as a small home improvement business, and now splits its prized services between commercial installations (under the identity of TRW Construction) and remodeling for blue-chip clients. Among the latter was the gut renovation and total remodeling of Chicago's famed McCormick Mansion. On projects of that scope, owner Howard Dardick draws on TRW's considerable resources to fill any gaps.

Tip Top's expertise is in period homes and older, difficult buildings, such as the stately, pre-war high-rises on Lake Shore Drive. Each client is assigned a project manager and working foreman, who marshall the forces of the company's in-house carpenters and labor crews. We're told that Dardick carries on his father's reputation for integrity and the highest level of quality. Architects and private clients tell us the company is not surprisingly "tip-top" among Chicago's fine general contractors.

	Quality	Cost	Value	Recommend?
TLC Construction	4	3	5	4.5

750 North Pine Avenue, Arlington Heights, IL 60004
(847) 259 - 8779

Residential remodeling

Clients tell us that owner Tom Chatel is responsible for the tender loving care TLC gives to home-remodeling clients. Described as a boutique operation, TLC has been in business for 17 years, concentrating, one job at a time, on upper-end kitchen, bath and home-addition work along the North Shore. Chatel, we're told, is on site for 90 percent of each project's duration, often doing his own carpentry work and also handling tile and stone installation alongside the good-quality subs he hires.

TLC jobs range from small ones that Chatel finds interesting to projects that bill for $500,000 or more. Regardless of a project's size, TLC is universally credited with excellence, and clients say prices are reasonable in comparison to the quality. The soft-spoken Chatel, they tell us, never disrupts their lives and treats their homes as if he were a houseguest. They describe him as a no-nonsense, honest, intelligent guy. Referrals from architects and contractors, as well as satisfied private clients, keep TLC in demand and selective.

"Didn't start job and leave. Stayed on it from the get-go!" "A lot of integrity; stays within cost." "Reasonably priced." "Hassle-free." "Did everything they were supposed to and more."

	Quality	Cost	Value	Recommend?
Triodyne-Wangler Construction Company Inc.	4.5	4	4.5	4

5959 West Touhy, Niles, IL 60714
(847) 647 - 8866

High-end residential and small contract remodeling

So impressed was a client—the Triodyne Company—with the masterful carpentry brothers Bill and Joe Wangler applied to Triodyne's penthouse suite in the Bloomingdale Building in 1993, that it formed a partnership with the two craftsmen. We're told Triodyne's owners demand as much from the modest and talented Wangler brothers on other people's projects as they did on their own.

Working with only the best of subcontractors, Triodyne-Wangler selects challenging projects throughout Chicagoland that call for a high level of quality and superb craftsmanship, and promise a creative collaboration between the contractors and a talented design professional. Primary projects include a mix of condos and single-family homes but also encompass landmark residences, law offices, condo lobbies and school-building additions.

The company's greatest strength, clients say, comes from the Wanglers' understanding of construction from the ground up and the perspective they gained from years of swinging a hammer. References characterize them as a couple of hard-working guys who love what they do, and applaud the level of skill they bring to a job. References not only love the results, but also tell us that working with the Wanglers is a delight.

"Remarkably attractive and efficient work."

Walter Slager 4 4 4 4

2841 West Belden, Chicago, IL 60647
(773) 489 - 1090

High-end interior build-out and remodeling

Originally a plaster specialist, Walter Slager has become designers' "secret" for upper-end interior build-out and remodeling in commercial spaces and select Gold Coast residences. Slager's crew of top-tier carpenters, plasterers and laborers generally begin projects at the demo phase. We are told the company tends to shy away from working for homeowners without a designer attached and from projects that are not high-end in every aspect. Once on board, however, references say Slager is ever ready, willing and extremely able to do anything a client asks and pick up any pieces of the construction package.

President Walter Slager brings a wealth of experience to his craft, having worked under his father, who founded the business a half century ago. We're told Slager never fails to finish a job until the client's expectations are fully satisfied. By leaving every client with a feeling of pride and satisfaction, Slager earns and maintains his place among the elite.

Weiss Enterprises, Inc.

501 Bank Lane, Highwood, IL 60040
(847) 266 - 8811

Remodeling and custom home building

References attest, this high-end custom remodeler can tackle anything from a $20,000 bathroom-remodel to a 6,000-square-foot gut renovation. Its market is the North Shore, and references tell us principal John Weiss knows the ins and outs of the old homes in that area and the high expectations of its clientele. He's been doing carpentry along the North Shore for 21 years, and clients report that this hands-on experience results in quality craftsmanship on their jobs. The company is now in its 13th year of general contracting, and clients tell us Weiss never misses a beat on either quality or service.

It's not surprising that this carpenter by trade runs his own company's in-house carpentry crew, which provides both ready-made cabinets and custom designed millwork. Complete design/build service is the next step for Weiss, a service which is presently in its infancy.

	Quality	Cost	Value	Recommend?
Windsor Builders Inc.	**4**	**3.5**	**4.5**	**4**

320 Melvin Drive, Suite 9, Northbrook, IL 60062
(847) 562 - 9545

High-end residential remodeling, additions and custom home building

Windsor's work is generated principally from a small cadre of top architectural firms and from friends of previous clients who laud principal Matthew Kurtyka's superior work and his crews' delivery of service that exceeds expectations. Windsor focuses mainly upon high-end additions and remodels, plus an occasional new home on the North Shore, where the nature of the work is challenging and the demand for quality is high. Kurtyka maintains, however, that Windsor's pricing is less than its respected competitors.

We hear Kurtyka is honest, conscientious, on time, well-spoken, business-like and highly responsible. Clients say he gives projects personal attention and always maintains control of their progress personally and through a hands-on project manager. Communication, they say, is clear and concise. The carpentry crew wins clients' special praise, as do the subcontractors, which one client calls "neatniks," in appreciation of their respect for his surroundings. Windsor attempts to always use the same team. The firm has cultivated longstanding relationships with subs that have the same level of skill and experience in working with these old stately homes as the Windsor carpenters do.

"Good builder. Honest man." "I didn't keep things as tidy." "Surprised to get quality as good as I did." "Kurtyka's a quality person." "Came right out and fixed troubles." "Superior work." "No complaints."

	Quality	Cost	Value	Recommend?
Windward Builders	**4**	**3.5**	**4**	**4**

1492 Minthaven Road, Lake Forest, IL 60045
(847) 295 - 5132 www.windwardbuilders.com

Custom home builder/developer, general contracting and remodeling

This big builder/developer firm has the capacity to offer complete home-building service, literally from the ground up. And, from property listings to final punch-list, clients tell us Windward is always on top of the job and say they are more than pleased with the result. Windward custom homes reach to 22,000-square-foot estates, and it also does major remodeling, such as alterations in the $100,000 range. For custom homes, Windward can package the entire project. It will assist clients in finding the right lot, either within one of its own boutique subdivisions or outside, where its close ties to the North Shore real estate community gives it an edge in locating choice lots.

Clients say builder/principal Ross Friedman sticks to his commitments and is especially good at offering options, working within budget, taking suggestions and explaining all aspects of a project and its progress. Clients also can't say enough about Windward's reliable and sharp project managers, who remain on site all the time and are, we are told, sensitive to the anxiety that accompanies a major investment and move.

Friedman uses a team-based approach in which professionals with different disciplines interact and communicate during construction to keep the project organized from day one and bring in a coordinated project with uniform quality. Clients applaud this formalized "Windward Way" operating system, which provides them and the crew with a manual that literally keeps everyone on the same page. Though Windward is not seen by clients as the cheapest in its class, neither is it seen as a "prima donna." Instead, clients say it delivers a really solid product, accompanied by a very agreeable experience.

"No complaints. Great job. Delivered on time." "Phenomenal." "A year later, can call him today, doesn't hesitate to jump." "As long as you stick to your word, he'll stick to his." "Artisans more than builders." "Sad they left." "A year later, drywall tape popped up. The sub blamed the house settling. Ross fired him, got another to repair and repaint my bedroom before I came home from vacation. I forgot it was even done."

	Quality	Cost	Value	Recommend?
Wujcik Construction	5	4.5	4.5	5

8322 North Lincoln Avenue, Skokie, IL 60077
(847) 673 - 5000 www.Wujcik.com

High-end residential remodeling and additions

The quality of a Wujcik job, according to clients, outshines that of competitors who also rank at the top of the market. Quite simply, clients marvel and recommend this company unequivocally for build-out and remodeling. The quality difference, in comparison with others, is stark, they say. The company specializes in high-rise co-ops and condos on the Gold Coast and the North Shore, where principal Mike Wujcik knows the territory, its challenging spaces as well as its demanding clientele. He wants the community as well as his clients to appreciate Wujcik work. The firm is also an expert at building additions and custom homes.

Wujcik works well with notable architects and designers. We're told Wujcik's demands of subcontractors are as high as his eye for detail. Sites are meticulously maintained, and neighbors are left relatively undisturbed, which clients at these particularly picky buildings are especially grateful for.

Regarding the workmanship and the whole Wujcik experience, clients say they could not do better. Often the relationships continue. They tell us Wujcik maintains ties with clients by caring for such maintenance as changing light bulbs and taking down screens. Small wonder clients say they'd hire Wujcik again in a heartbeat, and many of them do.

"I'd build a home with him on a handshake." "It was an experience meeting Mike, seeing the properties he'd done, meeting the people he'd done them for. I miss my interaction with him." "Workmen were very pleasant and on the job everyday." "I'm very critical. There are only two contractors I've ever been pleased with. He's one."

Hiring an Electrician

Dealing with electricity and wiring is intimidating, and with good reason—you are placing your family and home at risk if it is not handled properly. This is not the area for cutting costs by doing it yourself, or by choosing the lowest-priced service provider. Think of Chevy Chase putting his Christmas light cords into one giant, sagging cluster of adapters in *National Lampoon's Christmas Vacation*. Hilarious, but a little close to home. Quality, reliability and experience should be the determining factors in selecting an electrician for your needs.

Most electricians do both commercial and residential work, small repairs and large renovations. This versatility means that once you have found a professional that you like and trust, he can help you with all of your electrical needs over the years.

Renovation Work

For a large renovation, your general contractor (GC) is typically responsible for choosing and directing all of the subcontractors. Most GCs have several electricians with whom they prefer to work on a regular basis. For the most part, if you are pleased with your selection of a GC, you should entrust the process of choosing the subcontractors to him. Of course, you should also feel comfortable asking your GC to include another electrician in the bidding process if you feel strongly enough about that person. (Perhaps you have heard some wonderful things about an electrician whom several friends have used for years with great results). This also helps to make estimates competitive. You want the electrician who wires your entire residence to be the professional you use for general maintenance and repair work in the future because he will establish warrantees and gain familiarity with your residence.

When doing renovation or installation work, your electrician may suggest adding additional wiring for future use. This may sound like he's just trying to charge you more, but it's actually a very good idea. It is easier to add wiring and setups in the beginning for that dreamed-of central air conditioning system or six-line phone system or computer network you envision in your future. This avoids the headache of having to tear up walls and floors several years down the road, and saves a great deal of money, too.

It is very common for your electrician to work closely with your A/V specialist, telephone system analyst, computer consultant and security company when installing wiring. Your GC coordinates all of this, but you will need to think about exactly what you may require before everything starts.

If your renovation is relatively small and a GC is not involved, get several estimates for the proposed work. As with hourly rates, lowest is not necessarily best. Quality is very important, since this work will affect your entire family's comfort and health.

How to Choose an Excellent Electrician

Of course, recommendations from friends and contractors can be very useful in deciding which electrician to hire, but the final decision rests with you. Whether you are having an outlet rewired for a larger appliance or rewiring an entire renovated wing of your residence, quality and service should be your first priorities.

A good start is to contact each electrician you are considering. Do they return your calls promptly? Are they willing to provide references? Do they listen well? If they take days, even weeks to return your calls, this may be a good indication of the level of professionalism and attention you will receive once they are on your project.

Ask how long they have been in business and in what types of work they specialize. Many electrical professionals working in high-end are very active in commercial projects, and do both large renovations and smaller repairs. Others focus exclusively on "designer" electrical work such as the lighting of artwork and retrofitting museum quality finishes.

CHECK THE REFERENCES

Since an electrician's work is virtually invisible, the best way to get an idea of quality is to speak to others who have had electrical work done. When asking the electrician for references, inquire as to whether they have worked on any projects similar to yours, particularly if it is a large and complex project. Most will be happy to provide you with these.

When you are speaking with the actual references, a few areas that are useful to discuss are timeliness, cleanliness and reliability. Were they respectful of surroundings while they were there? Did they clean up when they left, or did they leave their tools everywhere until they came back the next day? Did they show up when they were expected or always arrive late? Did they finish the project on schedule? Did they come in on budget? Did they place safety first? These are good questions to ask of an electrician's references.

IMPORTANT PRE- AND POST-PROJECT CONSIDERATIONS

Many times electrical work requires cutting into a wall to gain access to the wires. There are two issues to think about here—cleanup and repair. Sheetrock debris and plasterdust are very difficult to clean up, so the electrician should either inform you of this at the time or put up protective plastic sheeting to keep dust from infiltrating your entire house. Some will repair the wall with plaster, but it is unlikely that they will sand and repaint it. Be sure to discuss this beforehand, clearly identifying the extent of the electrician's responsibility—and get it in writing.

Also, before your electrician leaves, make sure you know what switch controls what and that all circuit breakers are labeled properly. Do not let him disappear without doing this because he is the only one who knows.

LICENSING, INSURANCE AND PERMITS

You should only consider a full-time licensed professional for your electrical needs. A license from the Department of Labor is required for any electrical work, and all work must be filed with the city. This includes any installation related to light, heat and power.

Upfront, you should ask your electrical professional to provide you with an estimate describing the work to be done, the price and the payment, the contractor's guarantee as well as proof of worker's compensation and liability insurance.

Your electrical contractor should always be responsible for obtaining all permits necessary for your job.

ON COST

When hiring an electrician for a larger project, each electrical contractor submits its bid to the GC, who will then incorporate it into an overall bid which is submitted to the client. All of this should be available to you upon request.

For smaller jobs and service calls, which include repair and maintenance, most companies will charge an hourly fee. The standard in metropolitan Chicago these days is $55 to $75 per hour for a master electrician (not including transportation or materials), reflected in a baseline rating of 3 for cost in *The Franklin Report*. However, please remember, a company's standards in relation to product and safety, the depth of its resources and the demand it's in can all affect cost on top of hourly rates, and are factored into the rating. Some companies charge a set fee for a visit, then have flat-rate charges for each task peformed, such as per outlet relocated or fixture installed. Others insist on doing a consultation to provide you with an estimate before any work is started. This is a must for larger jobs. Fees for contract renovation work are typically higher than those for new construction per hour and per square foot. In the end, it should come down to the company with the best reputation for quality and service, not just the low bidder.

Before any work is begun, request a written estimate. Keep in mind that it is easier to estimate the cost of an installation than a repair. Even seemingly simple electrical repairs may require extensive labor and troubleshooting procedures.

GUARANTEES AND SERVICE AGREEMENTS

Your service provider should always stand behind all work that is done. Be sure to ask about service agreements. Many electrical professionals provide regular "checkups" and inspections. It may seem like wasted money at first, but over time these measures can prevent an emergency.

SAVE MONEY BY SAVING TIME

With a little preparation, you will be able to save money by saving the time of the service provider. Many times an electrician will need to cut into walls to gain access to wires or to replace fixtures. This is something you should think about before the workmen arrive. You may want to move or cover up that priceless antique sideboard near where the sconces are being installed rather than leaving it to the electrical crew.

Consolidating working hours will save time and money, too. Think about any jobs that may need to be done throughout the house and compile a list. Present the list to the service provider upon arrival so he can prioritize the various tasks, allowing his team to work simultaneously, if possible. This prevents having to call the professional back in several weeks for another minor repair.

If the electrician needs access to the electrical panel in a closet or a fixture above the sideboard, clear out the area beforehand to avoid wasted time and possible damage to any objects that may be there. By taking care of these little things in advance, you allow your electrical professional to get right to work, you will not have to worry about the safety of various objects and your billable time will be less.

By following these general guidelines, you can help any future electrical projects run smoothly. And remember, an electrician's work—if truly successful—is invisible.

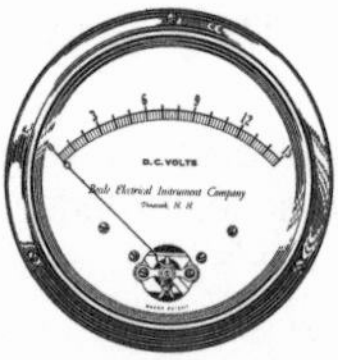

THE BUZZ ON CIRCUIT BREAKERS

It's tripped. What now? Check the breaker in the panel and reset. All breakers should be labeled, marking the locations of the outlets, light fixtures and other energy users on the circuit. If it trips again, you can troubleshoot for:

- **An overload:** Unplug or turn off the circuit's big energy users. Some users may have to be split onto a different, less crowded circuit.
- **A short** caused by connections that have pulled loose in electrical boxes.
- **A short** caused by frayed or nicked insulation that exposes wires (can be repaired with electrical tape).
- **A short** caused by using a lightbulb with higher wattage than required for the fixture (this melts the wire insulation).

+	$	◆	★

ELECTRICIANS

Abbey Electric
3.5 3.5 4 4

1140 West 47th Place, Chicago, IL 60609
(773) 247 - 8800 www.abbeyelectric.com
Electrical installation and remodeling

For half a century Abbey Electric has been helping commercial and industrial clients and high-end homeowners see the light. Abbey will tailor integrated lighting and heating controls to individual clients' lifestyles and special needs, and it guides customers through each phase of the process, including the selection of fixtures. Architects enlist Abbey solely for its engineering ability, and contractors turn to Abbey for actual installation. The company acts primarily in a design/build capacity and does not make service calls.

Abbey's clientele is principally in high-end condos and large homes on the Gold Coast and North Shore. Typically, per square foot, Abbey is more expensive than other electricians, making its work competitive only in higher-end projects. Owners Bernie Petchenik and Jerry Himmelfarb are adamant about maintaining a good rapport with clients, and we're told the company stretches to meet clients' needs. It has engineered heated floors and ceilings and, in one case, devised a way to light up a client's bathroom floor tiles. "Saturday Night Fever" anyone?

AM&L Electric
3.5 3 4.5 4

951 Garfield Street, Oak Park, IL 60304
(708) 524 - 1133
Electrical installation and service

AM&L is a family affair, owned and operated by three brothers and founded by their parents 50 years ago. Clients appreciate that an owner is always represented on jobs and say that it has a positive impact on performance and customer satisfaction. The company works on remodeling and new construction from the North Shore to Hinsdale and performs most of its service work downtown from its central-city headquarters. We're told it always accommodates the small needs of good clients. Premier builders employ AM&L for their own projects, and the company has also been trusted to rewire many of the area's Frank Lloyd Wright homes.

B-Electric Inc.
▭ ▭ ▭ ▭

8125 North Skokie Boulevard, Skokie, IL 60077
(847) 674 - 9200
Electrical installation and service

Many "A-list" general contractors count on B-Electric, as do some notable Gold Coast and North Shore homeowners.

Barry Gold
4.5 4 4.5 5

200 Fontana Drive, Glenview, IL 60025
(847) 724 - 2962
High-end designer electrical installation

This is of the gold standards of upper-end lighting and electrical work. An art collector himself, Barry Gold is often hired to design lighting and handle electrical contracting at area galleries and for designers whose clients prize their artwork.

Gold studied physics, has a degree in teaching and learned his craft under his father's tutelage. References tell us Barry Gold is a perfectionist, yet his manner tames concerns of the fussiest of artists and designers. They say he tackles projects other electricians turn down and is often called on to trouble-shoot and fix jobs that have been short-circuited by other, less exacting electrical contractors.

Gold rarely does new construction, but will handle routine electrical work. Devoted to projects that call for his specialist expertise, he works primarily on retrofits, and clients say he'll travel wherever a challenging project takes him. For big jobs, he brings a helper. While competitively priced in relation to his specialty, Gold's attention to detail comes at a premium. We're told his bids are realistic and he holds firmly to them, even if he has underestimated the demands of a particular project. At the same time, some clients contend that his initial designs result in cost savings over time. Furthermore, we're told he gets jobs done on time. A drawer full of thank-you notes from happy, demanding clients is testimony to his skills.

"Fabulous. Very sensitive to nuances of lighting, color and shape. Very creative solutions to problems." "Goes the extra mile." "Great people person." "Trust him totally." "Researches what he does very carefully. Educates me about what I'm buying." "Barry is my only choice, his expertise is so refreshing."

Bonus Electric Co., Inc. **3.5** **3** **4** **4**
112 Main Street, Lemont, IL 60439
(630) 257 - 1666

Electrical installation and remodeling

Bonus provides electrical contracting for remodeling projects and new construction, and, with 100 field personnel serving all of Cook County, it boasts that it is "large enough to serve you, small enough to serve you well." References generally agree with the claim. The company, they say, provides engineering plans and lighting design at reasonable pricing. A bonus, they add, is the company's ability to install integrated low-voltage cable for lighting, computer networking, telecommunications and fire- and life-safety systems. Condo-dwellers appreciate these electricians' experience in navigating the often-complex electrical systems in high-rise buildings. This company, however, strictly focuses on new installations and remodels, and does not make service calls. The firm has been in business for 20 years and is now run by second-generation owner, Jay Haberkom.

Current Electrical Contractors Inc. **4.5** **3.5** **4.5** **4.5**
1946 Lehigh Avenue, Glenview, IL 60025
(847) 832 - 0700 www.currentelect.com

High-end electrical installation and service

Current, we're told, is on the right current for high-end residential lighting design and complete electrical installation, regardless of a project's size and scope. This mid-size firm serves the city's top Gold Coast and Lincoln Park neighborhoods and communities that extend north to Lake Forest. Established in 1990 by veteran electricians Jim Eberle and Glenn Maxwell, Current works with up-market new-home builders, remodeling contractors and homeowners. Maxwell, we're told, is especially knowledgeable about recessed lighting options, and the firm is able to structure cabling for computer networks and integrate multiple electrical systems that can be controlled by a single switch. Equipped with cell phones, two-way radios and its own fleet, Current takes service calls, and we are told the field staff is polite, efficient and neat.

"A pleasure to work with. Great service, great value, great people." "They never let me down." "Current's workmen were very polite and clean." "I am extremely satisfied."

Quality	Cost	Value	Recommend?
	$	◆	★

Deerfield Electric

4 3 4 4

3680 Commercial Avenue, Northbrook, IL 60062
(847) 272 - 6700

Electrical installation and service

We're told this company satisfies the North Shore's most discerning and established architects and private clientele.

Kennedy Electric

4.5 3 5 4.5

1956 Raymond Drive, Northbrook, IL 60062
(847) 564 - 9863

Electrical installation and service, computer networking and telephone systems

Kennedy is said to be a top-notch electrical designer and installer, capable of providing the full complement of electrical systems in high-end residential and commercial projects, new or remodeled. Owner Mike Kennedy plugged into this career more than 20 years ago by meeting the electrical needs at North Shore residential remodeling sites, and clients tell us he's "very bright." In addition to installing traditional wiring, the company also specializes in the design and installation of telecommunications and computer networking hardware and systems for large estates and home offices.

The firm also provides ongoing service in each of its specialties. From a simple service call to a wholescale installation, Kennedy's care and communication with clients gets particular praise from clients. He understands clients needs, comes up with innovative suggestions and saves money where it can be saved. We're told workmen arrive with a vacuum cleaner and drop cloth and leave homes spic and span as well as fully wired.

"Can't do any better. Exhibits a lot more than what is expected." "Mike's IQ is higher than most people's I know. Can analyze a problem and follow through on a solution." "Always adds something to the pot; not just there to take orders."

Kordick Electric Company

4 3.5 4 4

225 Anthony Trail, Northbrook, IL 60062
(847) 446 - 7744

High-end electrical installation and service

An expert in residential service work and new construction, Kordick is highly recommended by the city's premier architects, designers, contractors and private clients, many of whom have had a long relationship with the firm. Established in 1915 by Joseph Kordick, it remains family-operated, now under the direction of Dennis J. Lauer, who took the helm in 1973. Customers say there hasn't been a short or a disconnect in Kordick's high-quality workmanship and service since its inception. The staff of approximately 20 electricians operates throughout Chicago, the North Shore and northeastern Illinois, often serving homes that were originally wired by Kordick. The company also offers a 24-hour emergency service. The Kordick staff, customers tell us, renews its historic-based commitment to customer satisfaction on every call.

North Shore Electric

3 2.5 4 4

2121 Ashland Avenue, Evanston, IL 60201
(847) 869 - 0606

Electrical installation and service

Working primarily with residential customers, North Shore provides complete electrical contracting for new homes, additions and remodeling projects, including the design and installation of lighting, structured cabling, computer networking and systems integration. There are eight electricians and a field service crew of two. As the name implies, North Shore's market encompasses the large swath of real estate that extends from Lake Forest to Lincoln Park and west to Des Plaines. Since North Shore was founded by Brian and Ann Lamberger in 1983, its business has grown almost soley through referrals, a testimony to the company's service. Customers especially appreciate that workers describe all options using layman's terms and stand behind their work.

Northern Electric Service 4 2 5 4
707 West Smith Avenue, Lake Bluff, IL 60044
(847) 234 - 6614

Electrical installation and service

Clients love to recommend this father-and-sons team for keeping homes in the upper North Shore suburbs wired. We hear the company principals are firemen, which means they know the importance of electrical work done safely. Clients say Northern Electric charges reasonable prices.

Omni Electric 4 3.5 4 4
1752 West North Avenue, Chicago, IL 60622
(773) 252 - 6000 www.omnielectric.com

High-end electrical installation and service in older homes

When not upgrading and servicing the electrical demands of the Chicago city schools, area hospitals and other commercial projects, Omni practices its considerable electrical expertise among its base of loyal, high-end residential clients on the Gold Coast and the North Shore. In addition to upgrading electrical systems for older homes—an Omni specialty—the company is also recommended for its skills in lighting design, home automation and voice- and data-communications for home offices. Whereas larger jobs take Omni as far as Lake Forest, the company only makes service calls within a tight two- to three-mile radius of its downtown location. We're told that principal John Ciurla and his crew of 10 seasoned electricians, many of whom having been with Omni for most of its 20 years, blend high-voltage knowledge with comfortable and reliable low-key delivery.

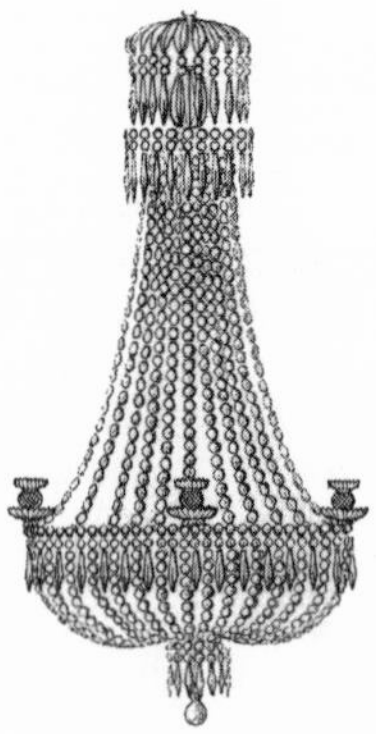

RJR Electric
4333 North Ashland Avenue, Chicago, IL 60613
(773) 230 - 8997

Electrical installation and service

RJR has been doing good, conscientious work in the city for 20 years. Contractors and clients look to this firm for service, remodeling and new construction. Whether at established north side communities or hot spots on the south side, we are told that RJR gets the job done right.

	Quality	Cost	Value	Recommend?
Romitti Electric Corp.	**5**	**3.5**	**5**	**5**

Highland Park, IL
(847) 831 - 4471 www.romitti.com

High-end electrical installation and service

Clients are vocal in their praise for Romitti Electric, and many state without equivocation that this is the best electrical contractor in Chicagoland. Others add that they would not use anyone else. The majority of Romitti's work is residential, in both new and remodeled homes, and it also handles some light commercial work. Its market area is the North Shore—Lake Bluff to Wilmette, Glenview to Deerfield.

Owner and founder, Ron Romitti, is said to treat clients and electricity with equal respect. He puts safety first, and he and his staff are known for integrity and professionalism. It's a "100-percent quality-driven shop," we're told. Although short-term solutions and inferior materials are not permitted, clients say that Romitti is creative in designing electrical solutions within his standards and applies "value-engineering" whenever possible. The company's capabilities encompass standard electrical work plus lighting, telecommunications and computer cabling, custom design and installation, and standby generator systems.

Romitti's customer service is as highly prized as its technical expertise. Employees arrive on time, are efficient, courteous and neat, according to clients, many of whom tell us that they're perfectly comfortable leaving these workers alone in their homes. Estimates are provided quickly and accurately. In short, Romitti is top-of-the-line in every respect, and references are eager to sing its praises.

"Exceptional." "Trustworthy and professional people." "Quality and concern for safety is above and beyond." "They demonsrate pride in their efforts." "Mr. Romitti is always there to answer a question" "Ron and his workers are simply the best! They are the neatest, most punctual and most professional workers we have had through our house." "Donated time to make our Adult Benefit dinner and auction a safely lighted event." "I told my contractor I wanted Romitti no matter what!" "Intelligent personnel: competent, responsible, honorable."

	Quality	Cost	Value	Recommend?
Simon Electrical Contractors, Inc.	**4.5**	**4**	**4**	**4.5**

2926 North Lincoln Avenue, Chicago, IL 60657
(773) 472 - 4666

High-end electrical installation

Whatever Simon says, Simon does and does well, references report. It does complex electrical wiring installations and unravels the ills of previous inferior work at high-end residences along the North Shore. Its specialty, clients say, is low-voltage lighting, especially where it's desirable to highlight architectural details and fine art. This specialty, along with owner Ron Simon's knack for keeping holes, drilling and other spatial intrusions to a minimum, has made Simon a favorite with interior designers who tell us they use the company for their own homes. When patching is needed, we're told, Simon knows who to call to render any marks invisible. Ron Simon evaluates each project himself and consults with each client.

Clients tell us he's as good at meeting the exacting demands of North Shore residents as he is at navigating the existing wiring labyrinths in high-rises. While Simon is more expensive than many competitors, clients at the upper end of the market consider the company's creativity, workmanship and concern for safety worth the price.

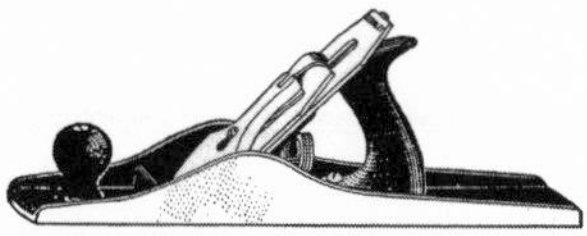

Hiring a Flooring Service Provider

More than any other element of your home, flooring creates the most basic ambiance of a room and gets the steadiest use. Does your personal style call for wood floors or carpeting in the living room and bedrooms? Do you prefer a marble bathroom floor or a softer vinyl tile? In the kitchen, do you make clean-up a priority and prefer function over form? Your floors should be attractive as well as durable, and it's important to do some research so that you do not invest in flooring that scores high marks on looks but low points for practicality.

Where Do I Start?

Take note of your flooring needs before you speak to any flooring professionals. What type of flooring exists in these rooms now, and what lies beneath them? How much traffic will be in the room you want to recover? Is the subfloor suitable, or will it cost you money to fix it before installing the new floor? If you have children and/or pets, do you want to select a floor covering that is more practical than exotic? Or do you want to invest in imported hard tile to complement your new state-of-the-art gourmet kitchen? To get ideas, look through home furnishing magazines and pay a visit to a flooring showroom or two. Internet sites that will help you learn more about flooring options include Floorfacts, a consumer site filled with links and information (www.floorfacts.com), the National Wood Flooring Association's site (www.woodfloors.com) and the Carpet & Rug Institute's site (www.carpet-rug.com).

Service and Warranties

The flooring company as well as the flooring material manufacturers should have warranties for your new floor coverings. Before you sign a work agreement, find out exactly who will be installing your floor: will your contact from the firm be doing the job himself, or bringing in a different crew? Check the work agreement to make sure that the firm will supply nails, glue and other installation accessories.

Know Your Floor

Insist upon receiving written information about the care and maintenance of your new flooring. What cleaning products should you use, and what should you definitely avoid? Is there a standard timetable for cleaning your hardwood floor or carpeting? Does your carpet warranty come with a consumer hotline for stain emergencies? Who can you call for advice about stains and/or damage?

What Are My Choices?

There are many options in flooring, each falling into five basic categories: wood, laminate, vinyl, carpet and hard tile (see section introduction to Tile, Marble and Stone). After considering the following descriptions of the basic floor types, you should be able to choose flooring that best meets your specific demands for beauty and maintenance.

Wood

A real wood floor never goes out of style. It complements every décor, from minimalist to Louis XIV, and generally ages gracefully. The most popular woods used in flooring are oak and maple, which can be stained or color washed to your exact specifications. Wood flooring can be designed in numerous patterns, limited only by your imagination (and budget). Some of the most popular are parquet, plank, strip and herringbone. When choosing a stain color, have your contractor apply a few color samples and look at them in different kinds of light. Think of the ambiance you are trying to create in the room—traditional or modern, casual or formal, spacious or cozy. Wood floors can also be bleached for a light and airy look or painted. Hardwood floors can be customized to satisfy every taste and personality and installed in any room regardless of what type of flooring—concrete floors, existing floorboards or particleboard subflooring—is already there.

Aesthetically, a wooden floor is stunning. But consider a few issues before you make this your final choice. How much traffic does the room get every day? Hardwood floors can be dented and scratched, especially from high-heeled shoes. Although a variety of urethane finishes provide excellent protection (and shine), they do not completely prevent dents and scratches. These same finishes, however, make wood floors much easier to clean and maintain than previous generations of wood flooring. Humidity is another factor to consider. If the humidity in your area varies from season to season, a wood floor may expand and contract with the rise and fall of moisture in the air. Storing the wood on site for a period of time before installing will allow the wood to acclimatize to the specific humidity level in the home. The service provider should consider whether the floor is being installed in a particularly humid or dry time of the year, and make his measurements accordingly.

Laminates

If you love the look of real wood but have an active household, laminate flooring may be the perfect choice for you. Laminates are plastic- or wood-based products that look like hardwood. They come in various textures, are durable and easy to maintain. Laminates can also imitate the look of stone, marble or tile, offering a wide variety of creative looks you may not have imagined. A wood-patterned laminate floor has some significant advantages over the real thing; for example, it will not be discolored by sunlight and is very scratch-resistant. Laminate floors wear well and usually come with a guarantee of ten years or more.

Cleanups are also a breeze with laminate flooring. Laminates repel liquid and do not allow stains to set in. This point alone saves your floor, your time and your psychological well-being. Design snobs will, however, look down their noses at laminate as as imitation.

Both hardwood floors and laminates, while possessing the great qualities of longevity and beauty, are quite expensive. If you are looking to invest less money, you may want to explore vinyl or carpet floor coverings.

Vinyl

Vinyl floor covering (linoleum) is the least expensive choice and offers more options than any other type of flooring. Patterns range from classic black-and-white squares to brick, stone, abstract shapes, animal prints—just about anything you can dream up has already been manufactured in a vinyl print. Vinyl is a very popular flooring, but it's important to consider that this material is vulnerable to cuts, rips and scratches from furniture that may be moved across it or sharp objects that fall to the floor. Although it resists moisture, vinyl can stain, so spills need to be handled quickly and carefully according to the manufacturer's directions.

Carpeting

A cozy, lush floor covering, carpeting adds warmth, soundproofing, texture, color and insulation to a room. When considering carpeting, inquire about the carpet's durability and consider whether it will receive light-, medium- or heavy-duty use. Industry experts suggest light duty for occasionally trafficked areas, medium duty for the bedroom or office, and heavy duty for hallways, stairs and other high-traffic areas. Carpeting requires extra maintenance as stains are more difficult to remove and general cleaning is more work. Wool is a whole lot easier to deep steam clean than nylon, but more expensive Also, a protective sealant may be applied for future spills and stains. Lastly, if you or someone in your home is allergy prone, carpeting is not a good option because it retains dirt, dust and other particles.

HARD TILE

Ceramic, quarry (stone, including marble) and terra cotta make up this premium category of floor covering. The look and feel of a hard-tiled floor is unlike any other, with grooves and textures that can be felt underfoot. Often used in kitchens and baths, tile flooring can give a distinct look and originality to any room in your home. In light colors, these materials do take on stains, so it is important to keep this in mind when choosing hard tile for particular rooms. Tile may be one of the most expensive kinds of flooring, but its remarkable beauty and longevity make it a good investment.

ON COST

Some floor installers charge by the square foot and others by the job. Most providers charge by the hour for cleaning and repairing. If your service provider charges by the hour, confirm whether this fee is per person per hour or for the whole team. Will they charge for moving furniture around? Make sure your order includes extra quantities of flooring in your dye lot to replace broken, worn or stained parts in the future. This is especially crucial with hard tile which can crack if something heavy is dropped on it, and any material which stains easily.

QUESTIONS TO ASK YOUR FLOORING SERVICE PROVIDER

Does the company have its own workshop? If so, it will have more control over the product than one that purchases its materials from another supplier. Ask the company if it does repairs as well as installation. If you need repairs done at a later date, you will probably have more clout if you also had the same contractor install your flooring.

FLOORING COMPARISON CHART

RATINGS:

Very Poor * Poor ** Average *** Good **** Excellent *****

BASIC FLOOR TYPES

	VINYL	WOOD	LAMINATE	HARD TILE	CARPET
Ease of Maintenance	****	***	****	****	***
Damage Resistance	**	***	****	*****	***
Moisture Resistance	****	*	***	*****	*
Stain Resistance	***	**	*****	*****	**
Fade Resistance	***	**	*****	*****	***
Scratch Resistance	**	***	****	****	N/A
Ease of Repairing	*	***	**	**	*
Softness Under Foot	**	*	*	*	*****
Design/Color Selection	*****	**	**	***	****
✧Price Range (sq. ft.)	$.50 - $4.50	$2.50 - $6.00	$2.50 - $5.00	$2.50 - $8.00	$.50 - $5.00

✧The price range is for material only and is to be used as a general guideline. Prices will vary from supplier to supplier.

FLOORING INSTALLATION & REPAIR

A American Custom Flooring Inc.	**3.5**	**2**	**4**	**4.5**

3221 West Irving Park Road, Chicago, IL 60618
(773) 588 - 6200 www.aamericancustom.com

Flooring installation and repair

A American Custom Flooring installs, repairs and sells hardwood, laminates, vinyl, tile, cork and rubber flooring as well as wall-to-wall carpets. Mike Biban and his dedicated staff have been serving clients in downtown and suburban Chicago since the company's establishment as a corporation in 1992. Clients are pleased with the firm's excellent work and affordable rates and confirm this with repeat business.

A Quality Floors	**4**	**2**	**4**	**4.5**

2409 Main Street, Evanston, IL 60202
(847) 864 - 2100

Flooring sales, installation and repair

A Quality Floors lives up to its name. The firm's market is primarily residential, and it provides installation, maintenance and repair for wood, vinyl, laminate, tile, marble and granite flooring as well as wall-to-wall carpet. All of these types of flooring are displayed in, and sold at retail from its showroom. The company has operated throughout Chicago's suburbs for 15 years. Described as very reliable and extremely hardworking, the staff at A Quality Floors can handle everything in flooring—from smaller projects in existing structures up to and including large new construction installations. Clients tell us the rates are affordable and give good grades to the firm's availability and its efficient service.

"Did a phenomenal job." "Worked hard even on weekends."

Birger Juell Ltd.	**5**	**4**	**5**	**5**

Merchandise Mart, Suite 1337, Chicago, IL 60654
(312) 464 - 9663 www.birgerjuell.com

Wood floor installation, fabrication, custom design, repair and maintenance

A jewel of a find for custom-designed wood flooring, hand-scraping and antique floor reproductions, Birger Juell has been in operation for more than 50 years. Its specialty is hand-scraped and hand-finished wood floors, created by European artisans using old-world methods. Special indeed. Its staff takes justifiable pride in its attention to such details as the use of four different grades of sandpaper to sand wood floors, and its meticulous reach into all edges and corners of floors for an exquisite finish from wall to wall. Clients confirm that pride, and, as a result, the company is not only popular among Chicago's high-end decorators and residential clientele, but has also been commissioned to work in other states and as far away as Bermuda and Japan. It also does commercial work.

Birger Juell is a member of the National Wood Flooring Association and The American Society of Interior Designers (ASID). While clients tell us the company's prices are high end, they also say such excellent craftsmanship and efficient service make it worth every penny.

"Excellent!" "True craftsmanship." "The only firm I would consider for wood flooring as I know my clients will be happy."

	Quality	Cost	Value	Recommend?

Chicago Hardwood Flooring 4 2 4.5 4
3853 North Newcastle, Chicago, IL 60634
(773) 685 - 9955

Hardwood flooring installation, custom design and repair

True to its name, Chicago Hardwood Flooring specializes in the installation, sanding, finishing, repair, and maintenance of hardwood floors only. It was founded in 1999 by Marek Staniszewski and serves downtown Chicago and nearby suburbs. Described as meticulous and skillful, Staniszewski serves mostly residential clients, though the company does some commercial work. The firm usually charges by the square foot and gives free estimates. It will also help move light furniture free of charge. Sources simply rave about the company's skill, and also appreciate what we are told is its very reasonable pricing.

Clark's Floor Service 4.5 3 4.5 4.5
3900 West Dakin Street, Chicago, IL 60618
(773) 725 - 8585

Hardwood flooring installation, custom design and repair

Known for its custom hardwood flooring designs, including inlays, Clark's Flooring Service works with interior designers, architects and private clients. It specializes in installing, sanding, finishing, cleaning and repairing hardwood floors. Clark's was established in 1975 by Jeff Clark and operates throughout Chicago's metropolitan and suburban areas. While the majority of the company's work is in existing buildings, it is equally adept at installations in new construction.

Clients say the company's work is superb and extremely detailed. They describe owner Clark as reliable, precise and thorough. The firm usually charges by the job and offers free estimates. There is an extra charge for moving furniture. Sources extol the service of this small firm and are just as pleased with its moderate pricing.

"There's nobody I know that can do better." "He's the best." "The floors are meticulous and beautiful."

Elite Hardwood Flooring 4 2.5 4 4
3344 North Avers Street, Chicago, IL 60618
(847) 233 - 9213

Wood floor installation and repair

Clients appreciate the personalized service given by Elite Hardwood Flooring, which installs, repairs, cleans and refinishes hardwood floors. Elite has been in business for two years and owner Daniel Matis has five years of experience in this specialty field. The company works throughout downtown Chicago and the surrounding suburbs. Customers describe Elite's prices as moderate and tell us its service is outstanding. While Elite's business currently caters to residential clients, it anticipates expanding to commercial clients in the near future.

"I'd absolutely recommend them."

Floors By Vinci 4 3 4 5
1230 North Roselle Road, Schaumburg, IL 60195
(847) 885 - 2400

All types of flooring, installation and repair

Vinci is a full-service flooring company that sells, installs and repairs all types of floors—from wood to tile to wall-to-wall carpet. Now operated by Michael Vinci and Gary Baldassari, this family business was founded by Vinci's father, Joseph, in 1953 as a company that sanded and refinished wood floors. Today, it has approximately 70 employees working from a

40,000-square-foot building that houses its offices, workshop and showroom. The company operates under the tagline, "walk on the finest," and we are told it lives up to this motto among its primarily high-end residential clientele and several commercial customers. Its services are offered throughout most of metropolitan Chicago and the northwest suburbs. Sources describe Vinci as honest and reliable, and many show their appreciation through return visits for additional flooring needs.

"Cannot say enough good things about him." "Very reliable." "They always come out responsibly."

Heritage Floors, Inc. **5** **4** **5** **5**

444 Lake Cook Road, Deerfield, IL 60015
(847) 940 - 7440

Wood floor custom design, installation and repair

Heritage has a strong legacy in wood flooring, and references tell us the company honors its legacy beautifully. Owner Scott Norris is the son of Anne Juell of Birger Juell, Ltd. (see review), and he and his staff are described in superlatives. Norris, described by clients as an excellent craftsman and "ideal contractor," has 25 years of experience in the business and established Heritage in 1993. The company specializes in hand-finished wood floors with custom inlay designs for high-end residential and commercial customers. Since its founding, customers in downtown Chicago and along the North Shore have been raving about the quality of its workmanship and service. The company works with architects, interior designers, contractors and private clients. Estimates are free, and Heritage generally charges by the job. Pricing is at the upper level of the market, but considered well worth the cost.

"The best in the city." "The best job for your money." "If this company was a car, it would be a Mercedes." "Creative." "Excellent craftsman." "Always my first choice."

Home Carpet One

3071 North Lincoln Avenue, Chicago, IL 60657
(773) 935 - 9314 www.carpetone.com

Rug and flooring sales and installation

See Home Carpet One's full report under the heading Rugs: Cleaning, Installation & Repair

Northwestern Hardwood Floors **4** **2.5** **4.5** **4.5**

5213 North Meade, Chicago, IL 60630
(773) 792 - 3147

Wood floor installation and repair

Blessed by a reputation for church flooring, Northwestern also provides residential customers with the installation, repair, maintenance, sanding and finishing of hardwood floors. Owner Cecilia Farfan and her team operate throughout greater Chicago, its suburbs and parts of Indiana and have been doing so since 1987. In 1998, the firm's skill was confirmed with a "Floor of the Year" award from the National Wood Flooring Association. Typically, Northwestern charges by the square foot and will gladly provide a free estimate. Clients say they appreciate the company's reasonable prices and fast, efficient service.

"They are really terrific!"

Quality Cost Value Recommend?

Pedian Rug Company
6535 North Lincoln Avenue, Lincolnwood, IL 60712
(847) 675 - 9111
Rug and flooring sales, installation, cleaning, restoration and repair

See Pedian Rug Company's full report under the heading Rugs: Cleaning, Installation & Repair

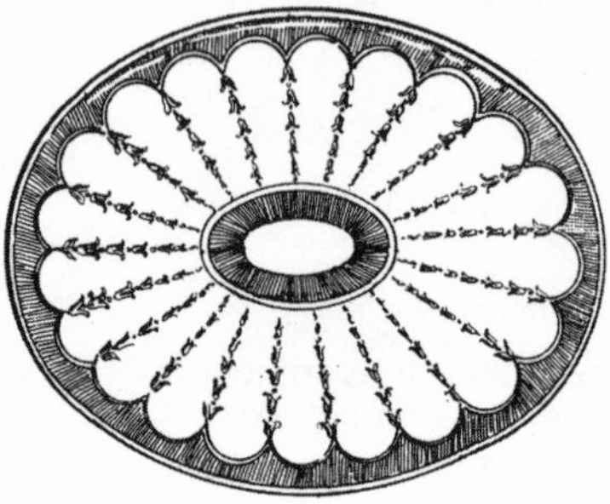

Peter Flooring Inc.
4 2 4.5 4

3352 North Neva Avenue, Chicago, IL 60634
(773) 481 - 2244
Wood floor installation, repair and custom design

Residential clients and professional experts cannot say enough good things about Peter Flooring. Described as very professional, clean, meticulous and extremely hardworking, this team, headed by Peter Gasinski, has been in the flooring business for 15 years. Its specialty is hardwood floor installation and maintenance, which encompasses additional services such as bleaching, staining, leveling, testing subfloors for vapors and moisture, removing old carpeting and disposal of debris. The company also creates custom designs at its in-house workshop.

Several grateful clients of Peter Flooring tell us that when other companies turned down their difficult repair jobs and badly damaged flooring projects, Gasinski and crew came to the rescue and produced a superb result. Pricing is moderate, which represents excellent value for such fine work, we're told. Satisfied customers return to this company and also recommend it to family and friends.

"Very good work ethic." "Managed to make new wood match my old wood. You couldn't tell a repair was done!" "They are very careful about clients' belongings. Very clean." "Phenomenal. They worked 'til late at night. I am very impressed."

Raymond Hardwood Flooring, Inc.
4 2 4 4

6115 North Pulaski Road, Chicago, IL 60646
(773) 866 - 2200
Wood floor installation and repair

Everybody loves Raymond. Since its establishment in 1992, the company has been installing, repairing and cleaning hardwood floors all across Illinois and leaving satisfied clients in its wake. Raymond handles both residential and commercial clients and works with architects, interior designers and directly with homeowners. Owner Raymond Souri and sister Brenda frequently attend classes to keep abreast of trends and techniques. Clients say the company's excellent service comes at reasonable pricing. The company is a member of the National Wood Flooring Association.

Quality	Cost	Value	Recommend?
	+	$	◆	★

S.G. Campbell Inc.

4.5 3 4 5

1721 West Winona Street, Chicago, IL 60640
(773) 878 - 0242

Wood floor sales, installation and repair

Serving high-end clients and satisfying discriminating tastes are not easy tasks, but Scott Campbell has been doing both since he established S.G. Campbell in 1976, following completion of a four-year apprenticeship with the Chicago District Council of Carpenters. The company installs, hand-scrapes, sands, refinishes, cleans and repairs wood flooring. Its market is high-end residential and commercial clients in Chicago's Gold Coast, Lincoln Park and North Shore neighborhoods who sometimes take the crew to second homes in Palm Springs, Florida and elsewhere.

Campbell is said to meet discriminating clients' demand for detail, and the company provides a lifetime guarantee on floors it installs. Customers tell us they are delighted with the firm's work. Pricing, like the quality and service, is at the top of the market, but definitely worth it, we are told.

"Definitely top-notch."

Svoboda Floor Service LLC

4 2 5 4

35082 Edgerwater Lane, Ingleside, IL 60041
(847) 587 - 1442

Flooring installation and repair

Svoboda Floor Service has been installing, repairing, refinishing and cleaning hardwood floors for residential and commercial interiors since 1981. Headed by Norm Svoboda, the company works with architects, designers, contractors and homeowners throughout the Northwest suburbs of Chicago, the Southwestern suburbs of Milwaukee and other areas in Michigan. Svoboda Floor also specializes in installing and creating custom designs and inlays, particularly with an antique finish. Clients tell us the firm excels at keeping to a schedule and budget, and produces exquisite floors for a very reasonable price

Turk Floor Company

4 3 5 5

1216 Bellevue Avenue, Elgin, IL 60120
(847) 741 - 8094

Wood floor installation, maintenance and repair

A hardwood flooring specialist of the first order, Turk Flooring installs, maintains, repairs, sands and finishes floors for residents throughout the greater Chicago area. It was begun by Paul Turk in 1976, and clients say he and his team live up to their most demanding standards for quality. Turk is described as a true craftsman, and the team is said to provide outstanding results. Although, technically, charges are based on square footage, we are told that the company's services are sometimes negotiable. Estimates are free and there is no required minimum. The company was started work has been featured in such prominent publications as *Architectural Digest* and *The Chicago Tribune*.

"I've been working with him for years." "Their craftsmanship is amazing!" "Their installation is just superlative. Very professional."

Victor Hardwood Flooring Inc.

4 3 4 4

4464 North Elston Avenue, Chicago, IL 60630
(773) 283 - 9333

Wood floor sales, installation, restoration and repair

In addition to selling, installing and repairing any type of hardwood flooring, Victor Hardwood also specializes in intricate inlay patterning and in the restoration of antique and aging hardwood floors. To this Victor belongs the spoils of a high-end residential clientele and architects and interior designers who call its inlay designs "masterpieces." Founded in 1975, Victor has amassed a sizeable following of loyal, satisfied clients who tell us the workmanship is outstanding.

Vincent's Flooring Company **4** **2.5** **4.5** **4.5**

3812 North Elston Avenue, Chicago, IL 60618
(312) 504 - 5457 www.vincentsflooring.com

Flooring sales and installation

This company's got you covered in wood, vinyl, rubber, cork, laminate or tile flooring and wall-to-wall carpet. It sells, installs and repairs them all. Vincent's is a family business, established in 1991 by Vincent Ardelean. It provides its services throughout Chicago and generally charges by the square foot. Estimates are free. Enthusiastic customers say the crews are punctual and reliable, and the prices are a great deal for such high-level service. The company also makes cabinets and designs bathrooms.

"Does lovely work."

Wood Floors by Lien **4.5** **3.5** **5** **5**

579 West North Avenue, Elmhurst, IL 60126
(630) 279 - 2191

Wood floor installation, custom design, repair and maintenance

Wood Floors by Lien have stood the test of time since 1985. Principal Don Lien provides services to discriminating commercial and residential clients along Lake Shore Drive to the North Shore and other metro Chicago areas. The company installs, repairs, waxes, sands and refinishes wood floors and is also known for its exquisite custom inlays and designs. It works in new and existing homes with designers, architects, contractors and homeowners. All business comes from referrals, another confirmation of its quality.

Sources rave not only about the beauty of the floors, but also about the company's reliability, thoroughness, punctuality and cooperative nature. We also hear that the crew will go out of its way to follow up and ensure that every aspect of a job is perfect. Although Wood Floors by Lien is expensive, customers say the quality and service are worth the price tag.

"One of my favorite vendors." "Excellent." "Can handle a difficult task." "I highly recommend."

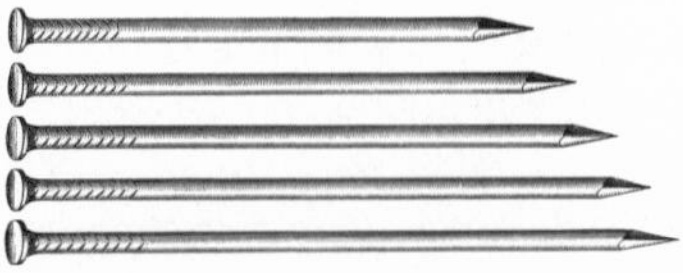

Hiring a Furniture Repair & Refinishing Service Provider

Does your prized baroque chair need restoration? Do you refuse to get rid of your comfortable thrift store couch but admit it needs sprucing up? Will your bedroom finally be complete with the addition of a twin reproduction of your favorite antique bedside table? Or perhaps you have a piece that has survived fire or flood damage, a teething puppy, climate changes or just general wear and tear. Before surrendering it to the hands of a professional, you should know a few things about it and the artisan who will repair, restore or conserve it.

Where Do I Start?

Before locating a professional, take the time to verify that your thrift shop bargain isn't a priceless antique in disguise and your heirloom isn't actually an ordinary reproduction. Inappropriate restoration of an antique can greatly compromise its value. Sometimes a seemingly simple repair can actually cause further, irreparable damage. So be sure to have your piece's history and condition closely examined before allowing any work to be done on it.

Research on your piece should go beyond a consultation with the encyclopedia. Consult a professional—preferably several. Most professionals will visit your home to provide a price estimate and a detailed explanation of how your piece should be treated. Some charge fees for on-site verbal and written estimates; others don't. Estimates should include the cost of labor, materials and transportation. You should also discuss how your piece will be insured and whether or not a warranty will be provided for the work and under what conditions.

Knowing the value of your piece is important not only in determining the type of work that it needs and how well it should be insured, but also how much to invest in the work. If your thrift store table simply needs its broken leg replaced, you may not want to pay top dollar for labor fees. However, if you're concerned about transporting your original Louis XIV dining room table, you may opt to keep it at home and pay for a specialized professional to work on site.

On Cost

Many professionals base their fees on an hourly or daily rate that is subject to increase, depending on the condition of your piece, the work it needs and where that work takes place. As a general guideline, hourly rates can range from $45 to $150. Be sure you receive a written contract for the amount of work agreed upon and the cost. If additional work is needed, the professional should notify you before taking action and a new fee should be agreed upon.

Choosing the Right Specialist for You

No licensing bureaus or governing boards regulate furniture restorers, so it is crucial that you take the time to find the right professional for your particular piece. Although furniture restorers tend to be well versed in all styles and periods, each has a specialty. You wouldn't take a broken toe to an allergist, nor would you want to take your japanned armoire to a caning specialist. Inquire about the professional's area of expertise. For example, if your dining room table needs to be refinished, be wary of a craftsman who wants to use French polish and says you'll be eating from your table within a day or two. French polish is typically saved for show pieces such as game tables and armoires and not used on surfaces that are prone to spills or burns. It is also a time-consuming process that requires numerous layers of shellac and alcohol to be applied, dried and rubbed before being reapplied. Keep in mind that moisture captured between the layers can cloud the surfaces irrevocably, so humid weather will prolong the process. Be patient because a good professional will not want to rush the job.

Also, be wary of someone who is eager to refinish your Federal bureau, or any of your antiques. Much of the value of any antique derives from its rarity, quality and condition, and an original finish is an important part of this. Be sure to find a professional who is as interested in preserving the unique qualities of your piece as you are.

Questions to Ask a Furniture Professional

Although your main contact will most likely be the firm's principal, most firms have numerous employees, each with a different area of expertise. Be sure you know who is working on your piece and what they will be doing. The person who re-creates the leg of your table may not be the person who finishes it.

Don't be afraid to ask about the firm's expertise, including whether individuals have been trained in a particular style or period. Ask where they've worked and with whom. Also, ask to see their portfolio and to speak with numerous references. Make a point of speaking with the references. They know the work, and will tell you if actual fees exceeded the estimate, if the work took twice as long as expected or—the best scenario—if the work was beautifully done.

Furniture Care Tips

- Protect furniture from direct sunlight, which fades colors, bleaches wood and clouds polished surfaces.
- Avoid exposure to excessive heat, such as placing furniture near a radiator or setting hot objects upon the piece, as this damages surface coatings, veneers and underlying adhesive.
- Place coasters on surfaces to protect them from liquids, which can stain.
- Wipe up water-based spills with a towel, but dab alcohol spills carefully to prevent spreading the spill; alcohol breaks down finishes.
- Invest in a humidifier/de-humidifier to minimize large fluctuations of humidity.
- Use a buffer when writing on a table top, as pens and pencils can cause unsightly indentations.
- When moving furniture, lift by the strongest units or rails—never drag!

Furniture Repair & Refinishing

	Quality	Cost	Value	Recommend?
Ancient Tree Furniture	3.5	2.5	4.5	4.5

104A Skokie Valley Road, Lake Bluff, IL 60044
(847) 295 - 2740

Furniture restoration and refinishing

Ancient Tree's restoration and refinishing services are in high demand among well-heeled private clients on the Gold Coast and the North Shore. Michael Schoenhoft and his brother Robert started Ancient Tree 22 years ago, with some equipment Robert received in lieu of payment from a prior employer. We hear they've since put that equipment to good use.

Michael is charged with most of the in-shop antique restoration and finishing work, aided by two craftsmen, while Robert handles in-home touch-up and restoration assignments. Polishing, carving, finishes and reproductions of small pieces round out the company's repertoire, with dining room table refinishing a noted specialty. Clients report that Ancient Tree's service and quality are both excellent, and, what's more, its prices are reasonable. The firm charges hourly rates and offers free estimates.

"Unbelievable refinishing work—also fast and efficient." "Their work is beyond excellence."

Andrew Upholstery

2234 West Roscoe Street, Chicago, IL 60618
(773) 528 - 5599

Retail—upholstery and minor furniture repair

See Andrew Upholstery's full report under the heading Upholstery & Window Treatments

	Quality	Cost	Value	Recommend?
Armand Lee & Company, Ltd.	4.5	3.5	5	5

840 North Milwaukee Avenue, Chicago, IL 60622
(312) 455 - 1200

Antique furniture conservation

In addition to Armand Lee's primary business of framing, the firm has offered a wide range of furniture and art restoration services to Chicagoans for more than 60 years. The services include antique conservation, art installation, mirror work, furniture restoration and refinishing and custom finishes. We hear that current president Norman P. Olson and his 28-person team do museum-quality framing and provide exceptional workmanship and fine service, too. Clients tell us they are amazed at the extent of the company's skill and creativity. The firm works mainly with the trade, but also takes on a few private clients, and most work is done in its studio. Prior to commencing with a piece, Armand Lee provides estimates for a fee. The firm charges an hourly rate for its services.

"Very much a boutique operation, providing services you can't find anymore." "They do incredible work—I depend on them for all sorts of things" "Can finely refinish anything." "It's amazing that they'll handle or source out everything from making a zebra skin mirror to gold leafing crown molding."

Quality | Cost | Value | Recommend?
+ | $ | ◆ | ★

Bernacki & Associates
4.5 4 4 5

424 North Oakley Boulevard, Chicago, IL 60612
(312) 243 - 5669

Restoration and conservation of art and furniture

There are few furniture or fine art restoration challenges that Bernacki & Associates cannot address. The firm's principal, Stan Bernacki, established the company in 1988, and we hear his staff of nine experienced craftsmen offers a wide range of expertise, including a few hard-to-find talents such as hand carving. Custom furniture work and a close affiliation with a premier upholstery business, Oakley Interiors (see review), make this a true full-service company.

The firm's furniture conservation department is headed by a master gilder and conservator, and its services include finish conservation (French and English polish and lacquer), structural repairs (including veneer, inlay, chinoiserie and boulle work), gilding (oil and water gilding on various surfaces and objects), tooling and leather work. The painting conservation department offers icon conservation; painting restoration services for canvas, panels and walls; repair of cracked, peeling and damaged surfaces; and structural repair, such as tear-patching and restretching, along with cleaning and touch-up services. Both departments offer complete assessment and documentation services, including insurance claims.

Clients concur that the firm's customer service skills are exemplary and mention its constant and up-front communication as exceptional. There are never any surprises, we're told. We also hear that turn-around time is "amazing" and that quality and craftsmanship are superb. The firm works with private clients and the trade and willingly takes on large and small projects.

"If we have a problem that we can't figure out, they have the solution and the ability to put something together extraordinarily well." "They're magicians." "They are an old-world operation and can do practically anything I ask of them." "There is constant communication—if there is ever an issue, they are on the phone with a report and a handful of solutions." "They are expensive, but right in the ballpark for the level of quality they offer."

Caledonian
4.5 4 4 4

820 Frontage Road, Northfield, IL 60093
(847) 446 - 6566 www.caledonianinc.com

Antique furniture conservation and restoration

Though primarily a high-end antique and reproduction house with a 10,000-square-foot showroom, Caledonian also offers premier in-house restoration and conservation services, focusing on 17th-, 18th- and 19th-century English antique furniture. We hear that the staff of five conservators combines modern scientific methods with traditional techniques to bring a balanced and conservative approach to the care of clients' pieces. The firm works with both the trade and private clients in Chicago and beyond, charging an hourly rate and offering free estimates.

✚	$	◆	★

Danlin Furniture Conservators
4 3.5 4.5 4

5919 North Ravenswood, Chicago, IL 60660
(773) 271 - 6311
Furniture restoration and refinishing

This 40-year-old family-run business specializes in fine finishes, but also restores antiques and works on fine contemporary furniture. The current principal, Dan Schubring, learned the trade from his father, who studied under European craftsmen. Schubring and his 10-person team work all over the Chicago area for a client list that includes designers, private clients and large companies. Most of the work is done in the studio, and pick-up and delivery service is available. Estimates are offered over the phone for free, or on-site for a small fee.

Deller Conservation Group, Ltd.
4.5 4.5 4 4

2600 Keslinger Road, Geneva, IL 60134
(630) 232 - 1708 www.deller.com
Conservation of historic furniture and objects

Clients interested in "museum-quality work" seek out Craig Deller's conservation skills and praise his helpful nature and cautious approach to the objects he conserves. Deller studied conservation at the Smithsonian Institution and is on the faculty of the Masters in Historic Preservation Program at the School of the Art Institute of Chicago. As a Professional Associate member of the American Institute for Conservation of Historic and Artistic Works, he is bound by its conservation guidelines and code of ethics.

Deller and his partner Wendy Leeds specialize in the preservation and conservation of historic furniture and objects and have a particular interest in the identification and treatment of early plant-resin coatings and historically important coatings, including original surface recoveries. Much of their work involves the de-restoration of inaccurate refinishings and repairs, resulting in a more visually appropriate surface. The firm's clientele includes museums and private clients, and most of the work is done in its 5,000-square-foot lab. Examinations and Condition Reports are not free, but if the object is brought to the lab, the first half-hour of consultation is free. The firm charges an hourly rate.

Deller has made a name for himself, as confirmed by appearances on such television programs as "The Antiques Roadshow" and "At the Auction with Leslie Hindman" and mention in numerous magazine and newspaper articles. His client roster includes the Lincoln Home National Historic Site, the Chicago Historical Society, Sotheby's and the Adler Planetarium and Astronomy Museum.

"Non-invasive, with a great deal of concern for the integrity of the object." "Excellent at marquetry and French polishes." "He's very detail-oriented and conservation-minded." "It depends on the job, but for most conservation work he's great."

Devontry Workshop
📁 📁 📁 📁

920 Pitner Avenue, Evanston, IL 60202
(847) 475 - 7962
Antique furniture restoration

Evanstonia Furniture Restoration
📁 📁 📁 📁

4555 North Ravenswood Avenue, Chicago, IL 60640
(773) 907 - 0101
Furniture restoration and refinishing

	Quality	Cost	Value	Recommend?
Everlasting	**4**	**2.5**	**5**	**4.5**

2999 Deerfield Road, Riverwoods, IL 60015
(847) 948 - 1724

English and French antique furniture restoration and conservation

Bogdan "Bogie" Gwarnicki has been restoring fine furniture on his own for 12 years, as an additional business to his work at Caledonian (see review), a high-end antique and reproduction house. The son of a multi-talented teacher, bee keeper and cabinet-maker from Poland, Gwarnicki apprenticed in London and worked for various antique dealers there before coming to the United States in 1987.

Clients speak warmly of Gwarnicki, praising his refinishing talents and his eagerness to take on challenging projects. He specializes in English and French antique furniture restoration, but will also refinish less-valuable items, such as turn-of-the-century reproductions, for example, and give them a "proper antique look." His repertoire of skills encompasses antique restoration and conservation, French polishing and lacquer refinishing along with handcrafted and custom-made furniture. He works mainly with private clients and charges an hourly rate. Estimates are free.

"A master craftsman and fabulous restorer and refinisher of furniture." "Absolutely extraordinary; I wouldn't use anyone else." "I hate to share my secret sources—I don't want the word to get out about him." "Great at the old English look, but I wouldn't ask him to do some things, like Italian." "As good as they come."

	Quality	Cost	Value	Recommend?
Feuille de Chéne	**4**	**3.5**	**4.5**	**4.5**

804 Dempster Street, Evanston, IL 60202
(847) 475 - 8410

Restoration and conservation of 17th-, and 18th-century European furniture

Benoît de Larauze has been doing conservation and restoration work for over fourteen years, the past five in the Chicago area. Originally from France, Larauze studied centuries-old techniques of fabrication for three years in Belgium, and is self-taught in restoration. Clients tell us that the combination of de Larauze's knowledge of old-world structural techniques and his deep respect for conserving the history and integrity of a piece produces high-quality results.

De Larauze's company, Feuille de Chéne (Oak Leaf in French), specializes in the conservation and restoration of 17th- and 18th-century European furniture—English, French and Italian—as well as some American furniture. We hear veneer work is one of his strengths (de Larauze makes his own veneer out of precious materials), as are French polish and marquetry. He also makes furniture on a limited basis and runs informal workshops on conservation and restoration. Private clients on the Gold Coast and North Shore comprise the majority of his business, and work is done either in clients' homes or in his studio.

"I was extremely pleased with the results, and I felt his prices were pretty comparable to others at his level of quality." "He took such interest in the history of the piece–he really tried to preserve its integrity, instead of just trying to make it look better." "When he uncovered the desk and I saw what a wonderful job he had done, I burst into tears and hugged him. I was so excited."

	Quality	Cost	Value	Recommend?
Finishes by Bruno	**5**	**4.5**	**4.5**	**4.5**

792 County Line Road, Bensenville, IL 60106
(630) 350 - 7822

Fine furniture finishing

Bruno is Joseph Bruno, and his business card reads: "Unique ideas in furniture finishing." From what clients tell us, it's a fitting description. Bruno learned his craft from his grandfather in Calabria, Italy, and carried his talent for fine finishing to the United States almost 20 years ago. In 1989 he started his current business, which he runs with his two daughters and a team of six talented craftsmen. While antique and distressed finishes comprise the bulk of the firm's work, we are told it also excels at the demanding art of French polishing.

Both professional and private clients seek out Bruno's skills, which have been applied at some of Chicago's most famous residences. All work, with rare exception, is done in the Bruno shop. Although the firm does not pick up or deliver, it can arrange for these services. In order to provide a fair estimate, the company insists on assessing the condition of a piece, on site or from a photograph. Costs are based on time and materials.

"No one can touch this guy." "His ideas are unbelievable. Nobody can match his technique." "Can tackle any kind of finish that's required." "Bruno has an artistic eye—a rarity these days. He's a real master at what he does."

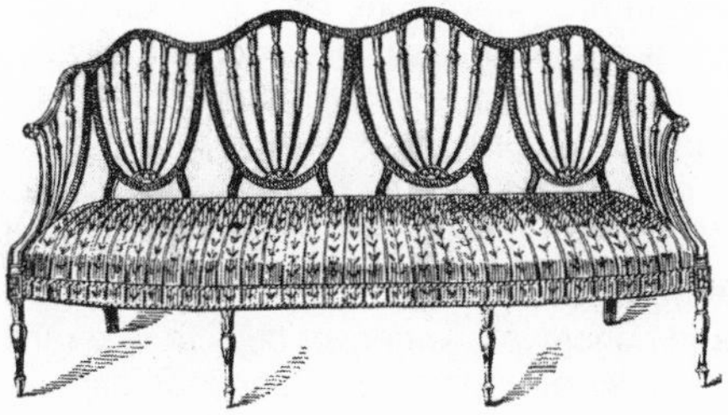

H. Lanny Green **4 4 4 5**
16W710 Red Oak Street, Bensenville, IL 60106
(630) 766 - 9063

American, English and Eastern antique furniture restoration

H. Lanny Green is a one-man show with an extensive repertoire of skills for the restoration of fine antique furniture. He's been in business for more than 25 years and specializes in American, English and Eastern pieces. We hear that Chicago's major art collectors entrust their Chinese lacquer, ivory, mother-of-pearl, tortoise and boulle work to Green. He also is a master of a wide variety of techniques that include French polishing, wood inlay, chinoiserie and wood carving. Clients report that Green's love of antiques and passion for his trade are apparent in the quality of his finishing.

While Green's to-the-trade work is offered exclusively by one interior designer, he does take on jobs from private clients. He has a studio, but also frequently travels to clients' homes for maintenance and touch-up work. He can transport small objects for a minimal charge or arrange for pick-up and delivery with one of the several freight companies that meet his requirements for care during transport. Estimates are free, and fees are based on a combination of time and materials.

Jeff Grund Restorations **3.5 2.5 4.5 4**
7127 North Ridge Boulevard, Chicago, IL 60645
(773) 338 - 1310

Conservation of wooden objects

Jeff Grund has been conserving and restoring wooden objects all over the Midwest for 28 years and around Chicago for the past 18. In addition to his work with private collectors, he handles assignments from museums and antique shops. Grund works primarily with European and American Colonial pieces, but also is equipped to restore Chinese antiques. Sources tell us that he has a real affection and affinity for gilding, and Grund himself says he'd happily work through his retirement doing just that. French polishing rounds out his talents.

Clients praise his top-notch skills, which Grund acquired during working under several teachers, including a master Czech gilder and a Jamaican cabinetmaker. He also spent many years at Caledonian, a high-end Chicago dealer in antiques and fine reproductions (see review). Grund provides free estimates and charges an hourly rate.

"Very satisfactory, very conscientious, very honest and very inventive." "His work is top-rate, and his rates are reasonable compared to others."

Kennedy Furniture Conservation Ltd **4.5** **3.5** **5** **5**
409 North Main Street, Mount Carroll, IL 61053
(815) 244 - 9789

Conservation of furniture, decorative arts and historical objects

Ralph Kennedy is lauded by clients for his complete professionalism, his flexibility and creativity in solving problems and his gentlemanly attitude. For the past 40 years, he and his wife Mary have conserved and restored furniture and historical objects for the finest museums and collectors in the Midwest. Self-trained in conservation, the Kennedys continue to build and share their expertise through speaking, teaching and consulting assignments and extensive coursework. As associate members of the American Institute for the Conservation of Historic and Artistic Works, they are committed to upholding its standards and ethics.

Together with a staff of five experienced craftsmen, the Kennedys restore, reupholster, repair and conserve a variety of objects in a range of media including wood, metal, veneer, silver and gold leaf and leather. It seems that nothing is beyond this firm's scope, which has included birch-bark canoes, Louis XV furniture, classic Harley Davidsons and Frank Lloyd Wright pieces. We hear it is expert at post-trauma conservation work on pieces that have suffered fire and flood damage. The firm recently added capabilities for custom furniture design and production, and sources tell us the quality of this division's work mirrors the firm's work in conservation.

Museums, private clients, corporations and trade professionals are among its clientele, which includes such notables as the Frank Lloyd Wright Home & Studio, The Chicago Public Library, the Art Institute of Chicago and the Lincoln Home National Historic Site. It charges an hourly rate, which we hear is competitive for the quality offered.

"An exquisite craftsman. For fine work, he's really my first and only choice." "He does a tremendous amount of work for museums, but he gives his private clients the same level of expertise as he does the museums." "He's treated pieces that have been in my husband's family for generations and brought them back to life." "His understanding of how furniture is put together is exemplary." "I highly recommend him—my only reservation is that he is very busy and has a full schedule."

Marshall Koral Pro Furniture Service **4** **3.5** **4** **4.5**
3148 A West Lake Avenue, Glen View, IL 60618
(847) 998 - 1355

Antique furniture restoration

Marshall Koral, a third-generation European craftsman, has been in the business for almost 50 years. He follows in the footsteps of his grandfather, who built custom furniture for the Tsar, and his father, who also crafted custom furniture. Although Koral no longer makes furniture, he applies the depth and breadth of his skill to antique restoration, French polishing, refinishing, caning, reupholstering, metalwork and on-site touch-ups and polishing. His main business is restoration of American and English antiques, but he also works on Chinese calamander screens. Sources tell us that both the trade and private clients seek out his refinishing skills on the basis of his expertise, knowledge and competence. Estimates are generally free, unless extensive travel time is required.

	Quality	Cost	Value	Recommend?
Mastercraft Furniture Refinishing Co.	3.5	3	4	4

3140 West Chicago Avenue, Chicago, IL 60622
(773) 722 - 5730

Retail and trade—furniture refinishing and custom upholstery

Principal Jim Antoni and the Mastercraft staff have a solid reputation for refinishing furniture of all styles, including antiques, as well as providing quality upholstery. As a result of the firm's competence with both, some decorators tell us they have switched their upholstery business to Mastercraft. Many comment on the company's reliability and friendly service, in addition to its excellent work. This 61-year-old company with 21 employees also makes custom furniture.

	Quality	Cost	Value	Recommend?
Recherché Inc.	4	3	5	5

3346 Main Street, Skokie, IL 60076
(847) 673 - 7172

Conservation and restoration of fine antiques and decorative objects

Clients say Paul Shanks of Recherché breathes new life into antique furniture, some of which initially seems beyond repair. They praise not only the quality and creativity of his work, but also his reverence for every piece he works on. Recherché means "to look again" or "see once more," and Shanks takes this translation to heart. One client describes a 19th-century sawbuck table as "splintered into bits and pieces" from a move. Believing it was destroyed forever, she turned to Shanks as a "last ditch effort." After he applied his master touch, no one could tell it had ever been damaged, she reports.

Shanks has worked in the conservation and restoration of fine antiques and primarily wood decorative objects for more than 25 years, and established his own firm 10 years ago. We're told that he'll take on most anything in addition to high-end antiques—weather vanes, totem poles and even a 280-pound hippo head. "If you can't imagine who can do it, I'd hope that we would come to mind," Shanks says. His talents include sculpture-base design, art and objects installation, plaster casting, gold leafing, brazing, concrete statuary repair and ivory carving.

Private clients, dealers, galleries, historical societies and museums seek out his skills. Cost is determined on a time-and-materials basis, and estimates are either given as a price, a range or a not-to-exceed figure. He will also transport items.

"One woman I know sends everything to him—she'd be lost without him." "I've used other people in other parts of the country to do similar types of work, but I feel truly blessed to have Paul so near to me." "I can't think of anything Paul can't do; I don't know anyone else who I would entrust my items to." "He's fastidious. People trust him and his work and go to him because they don't want to compromise on quality."

Restorvation

0 North 039 County Farm Road, Winfield, IL 60190
(630) 665 - 8000

English antique furniture conservation and repair

A cross between restoration and conservation, Restorvation aptly describes the combination of skills Robin De Groot embodies. He studied conservation with Ralph Kennedy at Kennedy Conservation (see review) and at West Dean College in England. In addition, he spent almost 18 years at Caledonian (see review) before starting his own business four years ago. His training is in English antique furniture repair and conservation, and his techniques include carving, gilding, French polishing, structural and veneer repair and hardware restoration. He also works with Federal American furniture and has recently started to make period-furniture reproductions.

Clients appreciate De Groot's strong sense of personal service and complete involvement in a project, from the initial consultation to the written proposal with photographs to the final delivery, which he does himself in order to explain what's been done and provide tips on maintenance. The bulk of his work is with private clients in the city and northern suburbs. Almost all of work is done in his studio. Estimates are free and pricing is based on the demands of each job.

Steiger Custom Furniture Upholstery

2201 South Union Avenue, Chicago, IL 60616
(312) 738 - 1882

Retail and trade—custom upholstery and furniture finishing and repair

See Steiger Custom Furniture & Upholstery's full report under the heading Upholstery & Window Treatments

Superior Custom Furniture Restoration Inc.

4557 West Diversey Avenue, Chicago, IL 60639
(773) 645 - 0300

Furniture repair, refinishing and custom upholstery

The Furniture Shop

1200 West 35th Street, Chicago, IL 60609
(773) 376 - 2525

Retail and trade—custom upholstery, furniture and restoration

See The Furniture Shop's full report under the heading Upholstery & Window Treatments

Weber Furniture Service

Quality	Cost	Value	Recommend?
3	2.5	4	4

5915 North Ravenswood, Chicago, IL 60660
(773) 275 - 9061

Furniture repair, refinishing and custom upholstery

The service from Weber Furniture Service is both extensive and far-reaching. For more than half a century the firm has offered furniture repair, refinishing and reupholstering, as well as antique and piano restoration, to customers as far north as Wisconsin, as far south as Indiana and throughout Chicago and the suburbs.

Weber employs a staff of 15 and works with both residential and commercial clients, including banks, hospitals, hotels, country clubs and major department stores. While much of the work is done in Weber's warehouse, the firm will also travel to clients' homes or offices to work on a piece. The company has changed owners several times, but our references tell us it consistently maintains the same level of quality, reliability and customer service that clients have come to expect.

"I use them for everything." "They generally come through with top-quality work, and if they don't, they will fix it." "Good Craftsman."

Zaroff Restoration & Painted Finishes

2173 North California Avenue, Chicago, IL 60647
(773) 384 - 8420

Decorative painting and finishing

See Zaroff Restoration & Painted Finishes's full report under the heading Painters & Wallpaperers

Hiring an Interior Designer or Decorator

The decoration of homes has captivated people throughout recorded history. In 67 B.C., Cicero commented, "What is more agreeable than one's home?" Interior designers put their style, creativity and experience to work to help a home reach its full potential—be it a studio or a multi-million-dollar spread.

The Franklin Report has uncovered over 70 design firms that clients constantly praise for their abilities and professionalism. Clients believe that these firms saved them considerable time and money by finding unique objects and avoiding costly errors. Each firm has its own style and personality, which is described on the following pages. For our first Chicago print edition we have tended to highlight the most prominent designers, which often translates into higher costs and minimums. Additional firms may be found on our website (www.franklinreport.com) which is updated regularly.

Finding a Match

After you fully assess your needs and your budget (see What You Should Know About Hiring a Service Provider, page 5), we recommend that you gather photographs from magazines and books to share with potential designers to communicate your preferences. Through our research, we have found that the best interior decorator-client bonds are founded on common ideas of style and taste. Even the best designers can falter and lose interest in a project if they are not excited by the end goal. So as you gather potential names from *The Franklin Report* and from friends, focus on the preferred style of the designers and ask to see their portfolios—even if they say they can do anything.

As you narrow down your list and begin the interview process, think about your working relationship with the interior designer, who, for better or for worse, will become a big part of your life. Will you be working with the "Name-on-the-Door" on a regular basis or less senior project managers? Are you interested in a collaborative process or looking for strong direction? Will you be offered a wide range of budgetary choices? Finally, the prospect of working with this person should feel positive and enjoyable. Given the amount of time and money you are about to spend, it ought to be fun.

On Cost

Only a client can determine the worth of an interior designer's services. The "great masters" of interior design are considered exceptional artists who may charge whatever the market will bear. No one ever valued a Picasso based on a markup over the cost of materials. That said, the vast majority of designers are not masters, but competent professionals looking for a reasonable profit.

Interestingly, very few designers earn huge sums, due to the inherent unscalability of the process. Since clients generally want to work with the principal designer and not an associate, a name designer can only handle so many major projects a year, usually about six to ten. Therefore, even with an average job size of $200,000 and an overall markup of 50 percent, annual profits to a designer working with six clients equals only about $80,000—a good living but not a fortune (especially compared to their clients).*

*Assumes net cost of products of $133,333 with a designer markup of 50 percent (includes hourly fees and product markups of about 33%), totaling $200,000 of cost to the client and $67,000 of gross revenue to the designer. With a 20% profit margin (after all operating costs), net profit to the designer is only $13,400 for a client, or $80,400 for six clients before tax.

Just a handful of designers have the clout to make serious money. This can be done by charging unusually high markups or hourly fees, employing multiple senior project managers, selling custom products (which carry very high, undisclosed markups) and/or accepting only clients with very expensive purchasing habits. While you should know standard industry pricing practices, many clients are willing to pay more for additional services or amazing talent.

Standard Industry Pricing

There are three fundamental services for which interior designers receive fees: 1) up-front design plans, 2) the shopping and purchasing of products (new and antique) and 3) the oversight of construction and installation. The pricing indications described below are what you can expect from a very competent, experienced professional—neither a part-time designer nor a grand master.

Up-Front Retainer: Most interior designers will usually charge an up-front design fee or retainer of about $1,000 (for a cosmetic rehab) up to $5,000 to $10,000 (for larger projects). These fees are generally applied to the first hourly bills, but are sometimes held until the last project payments are made. The extent of these plans can range considerably, from loose sketches to extensive architectural drawings with coordinating furniture memos, swatches and a detailed electrical plan. Qualify these expectations before you sign on.

Some, but not many designers (especially in a robust economic climate), will operate on an hourly consultation basis, with the client doing all the subsequent shopping, purchasing and implementation.

Hourly Fees: Most Chicago designers charge clients on an hourly basis for all time spent on the design concept, shopping for product and about half also charge an administrative fee for processing the purchasing (it takes longer than you think to order all the trims and fabrics for a sofa). These fees generally range from $75 per hour for an administrative assistant to $250 per hour for a grand master, with $150 as the typical, "standard" well-established Name-on-the-Door designer rate.

Thus, if *The Franklin Report* review describes a decorator as having "standard hourly rates," in the Chicago market, that means that they are in the $150 per hour range. Under $100 per hour is denoted as "very low," about $100 is said to be "low," $125 to $150 is in the "lower" range, over $160 is "higher" and over $200 per hour is classified as "very high" hourly rates.

Generally, hourly fees are charged by Chicago designers in addition to a product markup. This is not true in the more competitive New York market, where designers usually charge either a product markup or an hourly fee (but these New York hourly fees tend to be a bit higher). Some Chicago designers follow the New York methodology and just charge an hourly rate, passing the product through to the clients at cost (particularly the New York-trained designers or architecture-trained designers, as that is how architects usually charge). This methodology eliminates confusion and uncertainty on product pricing, but increases any issues with hourly accountability.

NEW PRODUCT FEES BY PERCENTAGE: Chicago designers generally earn a second fee when clients purchase new products including upholstery, case goods, window treatments, rugs or accessories. The vast majority of Chicago designers charge clients a 30 to 33% markup over the net (or wholesale) price. Designers who search high and low for the lowest-cost materials might charge a substantial markup, but still offer a very good value to clients. Similarly, there are some Chicago decorators that charge higher than a one-third markup, but no hourly rates, so they also would be considered a good value.

- ✧ **Product Markup Over Net:** Three-quarters of the designers in Chicago charge a flat 30 to 35 percent markup over net on all new products, including workroom costs. This pricing is considered "standard" in *The Franklin Report's* interior designer reviews (as it is about 11 percent below the suggested retail price on fabrics).
- ✧ **Retail:** Certain designers charge "retail" on products or 50 percent above net cost on fabrics, 66 percent on new furniture and 33 percent on new rugs. These percentages are based on the discount the decorators receive off the manufacturer's suggested retail price. For example, if the decorator were charged a net price of $100 per fabric yard, the client's retail price would be $150. Workroom costs are usually marked up 25 to 50 percent at Retail (this is a very squishy number that should be clarified). This overall retail pricing is considered "high" in *The Franklin Report*'s interior designer reviews unless an additional hourly rate is not also charged.
- ✧ **Pricing Structure:** Remarkably, virtually no one charges under any other price structure—it is either retail or about one-third up for new products. This is an interesting unifying principle in an industry that contains so many variables.

ANTIQUE PRODUCT FEES: Antiques are much trickier. First, the retail and net prices are usually negotiable with the dealers. Further, once retail price is established, most dealers offer designers a further discount of 10 to 20 percent. This presents a conundrum. For the designers to make their normal 33 to 50 percent markup, they may have to charge the client substantially above the new retail price (which could be above or below the original retail price). This is further complicated by the fact that most antique dealers are happy to sell directly to the public.

The most satisfactory solution used in many successful client-designer relationships seems to be full disclosure with a sliding scale. These designers charge a markup over the new net price, with their usual 33 to 50 percent markup for lower priced items and a much smaller markup for larger items (often a lower percentage for items over $50,000, etc.). Most designers further guarantee that clients will never pay over the original retail price. The most prominent designers appear to be able to hold to a set markup and/or not disclose the net prices. For expensive antiques, an independent appraisal may be warranted (see our listings of Appraisers).

There is an additional point that needs clarification between a client and the designer on antique purchasing. If a client happens to walk into an antique dealer on West Kinzie Street or an auction at Sotheby's and finds the perfect sideboard that has been eluding the decorator for months, should the decorator get a fee? Arguments may be made both ways, especially if that piece has been specified in the design plans, the decorator has spent time shopping for that piece (educating the client along the way) or the client seeks approval from the decorator before making the purchase.

Most decorators have a strong enough client bond to withstand these issues, and the client usually will not balk if, in fact, the designer deserves the fee. In New York, designers usually demand and receive a fee in these instances, and in Chicago, the designers usually forego this particular fee to fortify the longer-term relationship. But specific contracts help in these stressful times. An elegant solution that some of the more sophisticated designers use is to charge an hourly consultation fee under these circumstances, or to take a much larger up-front design fee to cover all subsequent antique and auction purchases.

OVERSIGHT FEES: Many Chicago designers charge their standard hourly rate for the management of the subcontractors from whom they are not already making a profit, and some charge for every minute they are on your job. Products and services not usually brought in by the designers (where the designer is not making a fee otherwise) would include the items and subcontractors focused on architectural and structural elements such as bathroom and kitchen, architectural woodworking, etc. Given this uncertainty on billable hours and large potential cost, these hourly issues should be clarified in advance.

In addition, a very few of the top-name Chicago designers will ask for 15 to 20 percent of the general contractor's net product costs to coordinate the overall artistic direction of the project. This service may be unnecessary if you are using an architect who takes on the project manager's role.

FLAT FEES AND OTHER NEGOTIATED TERMS: A limited but increasing number of designers will consider a flat fee for all of the services listed above. This fee would remain stable within a specified expenditure range, and go up or down if the product costs far exceeded or came in significantly lower than the estimates. But the key lesson here is that most interior designers are fairly negotiable on pricing and other terms, within reason.

CONTRACTUAL AGREEMENTS

Given the wide variance of markups and methodologies, it is highly recommended that you and your designer agree upon an explicit price scheme for each type of product and service before embarking upon a renovation. While not normally necessary, it is reasonable to ask to see all bills and receipts.

Also, before you sign, it is customary to speak with one or two past clients (and occasionally, see the projects first hand). Once the contract is signed, a retainer will be paid, the design plans will be drawn and purchases will be made. Timing expectations should also be addressed in the contract, but in many cases the timing of materials is out of the control of the designer. Therefore, if you have specific deadlines, the designers should be directed to order only in-stock items.

LICENSING OF INTERIOR DESIGNERS

The debate over the potential licensing of interior designers has been spirited. Currently it is not necessary to hold any type of degree or license to legally practice interior design in Illinois. While the American Society of Interior Designers (ASID) and the National Council for Interior Design Qualification (NCIDQ) administer qualifying examinations, only a minuscule percentage of the top residential interior designers have complied. Most designers describe these tests as having more to do with health and safety issues (generally handled by architects) than with design competency. In fact, the tests do include sections on space planning, historical styles, fabric selection and all the necessary algebra, but do not really test creativity or focus.

All this may change with a bill that is expected to be introduced shortly. The bill would limit the use of the interior designer title to those with certain educational, experience and testing credentials (including the passing of the two-day NCIDQ exam). Those who are not certified would be classified as interior decorators rather than designers.

From a residential consumer viewpoint, there seems to be little correlation in *The Franklin Report* data between the passing of the NCIDQ exam and the satisfaction of the customer. However, so few designers in our list of top 70 have taken the exam that the sample size is just too small to judge. As discussed in What You Should Know About Hiring a Service Provider, it is incumbent upon the homeowner to do a thorough investigation of the competency of any potential service professional through extensive interviews, referral information and a competitive analysis.

FINAL CONSIDERATIONS

As further described on the following pages, an overwhelming majority of the countless clients we talked with had very positive feelings toward their interior designers. While it may be possible to purchase "trade-only" fabrics and furnishings in other ways, truly successful decorating is about creating an intangible upgrade in mood and lifestyle that only an expert can accomplish. Professional designers also have the creative energy and resources to manage projects in a cohesive manner from start to finish, realizing clients' dreams more effectively and efficiently.

WHAT YOU SHOULD NOT EXPECT FROM YOUR INTERIOR DESIGNER OR THE DESIGN PROCESS

- That the designer will maintain interest in the project if you cannot make any decisions.
- That you attend each shopping trip or are shown every possible fabric in the Merchandise Mart.
- That the designer can read your mind.
- That there will be no misunderstandings or mistakes along the way.
- That the designer will bid out every subcontractor. There is a reason that the designer has been working with the same upholsterer and decorative painters for years. On the other hand, if you have a favorite supplier, the designer should be accommodating.
- That the designer will supervise other's work without an hourly fee. (The designer should be there, however, to oversee the installation of their products at the contractual rate.)
- That the designer becomes your new best friend.

WHAT YOU SHOULD EXPECT FROM YOUR INTERIOR DESIGNER

- The sense that your interests and opinions matter.
- An accessible and proactive effort, taking the initiative to complete the job.
- That some of your existing furnishings will be integrated into the new design, if you wish.
- Assurance that the designer will stick to a budget (and not tempt you with "the best" unless you request).
- A full understanding of your lifestyle and use of your living space.
- To be shown a full range of options and products—creative ideas well beyond the Merchandise Mart. However, you should not feel forced to take whatever they purchased on their last worldwide jaunt (and pricing is really fuzzy here).
- The ability to see the net cost of every item, if you desire.
- As hassle-free a process for you as possible.
- Open communication with you to avoid surprises.
- That you love your new home after the job is complete.

Interior Designers & Decorators

A.S.I. Interiors 4 4 4 4.5
980 North Michigan Avenue, Suite 1085, Chicago, IL 60611
(312) 932 - 9400 www.asi-interiors.com

Diversified, tailored, timeless interior design

Denise Antonucci and Jerry Sanfilippo are creating designs of quiet dignity, timeless appeal and diversified style according to satisfied supporters. This pair is said to take their design cues from the client and is equally capable executing traditional effects, contemporary-edged interiors or eclectic modern designs. Clients comment that the firm often takes an integrated approach, successfully orchestrating the composition of furnishings, artwork, accessories and lighting.

Both Antonucci and Sanfilippo worked with Bruce Gregga before creating their partnership in 1994. Antonucci previously worked on the floor of the Board of Trade and then studied at the Art Institute. Sanfilippo attended Harrington before joining Gregga. Each principal brings with them over 20 years of design experience. There are seven at the firm, with patrons remarking on their strong professional demeanor. About twelve to fifteen projects are active, with roughly five majors at any one time. References say that phone calls are returned promptly. Recent projects include a Park Hyatt penthouse, several Lake Shore and North State Parkway residences and a substantial Winnetka renovation. A.S.I.'s work has also taken them to Palm Beach, Vail, Santa Monica and St. Lucia.

Projects tend to evolve, at the client's direction. A low upfront retainer is taken against hourly design fees (none for shopping) and standard markups are charged on products. Living rooms are often in the $75,000 to $150,000 ballpark, with much room for upside. The very best resources are called upon by A.S.I. to create a look clients applaud and often return to more. Both partners are ASID.

"Jerry and Denise are responsible professionals and they work design magic." "They are always available when you need them." "They have been working together for 15 years, and are very smooth." "Their designs are comfortable, with clean lines, excellent flow and restrained continuity." "The lighting was particularly interesting and added warmth." "They are particularly helpful working closely with architects on new homes, stretching the design boundaries to include improvements in lighting, finishes and the windows." "These guys are pros, completing the project a few weeks before the deadline with excellent teamwork."

Agustin Fernandez 4 4 4 4
70 West Hubbard Street, Suite 400, Chicago, IL 60610
(312) 527 - 9876

Iconoclastic, uniquely eclectic interior design

With a defined client following, Agustin Fernandez works in an urban baroque style: "truly eclectic mix," highlighted by period-pure furnishings. There is said to be a creative balance and tension which is highly disciplined and simultaneously exuberant.

Fernandez works primarily on large downtown residential refurbishments, in an integrated fashion. It is not unusual for a commission to take from three to six years, with work developing in layers. Projects have taken Fernandez to second homes in Paris, Rio and Lyford Cay. There are six members of the firm which was established in 1985, after Fernandez graduated from Parsons, studied at the Harvard School of Design and then worked with Robert George. Living rooms tend to be in the $125,000 to $150,000 range. The firm charges a design fee and then either high+ hourly rates or standard hourly rates and standard markups on product. Clients appreciate the "hands-on" approach, saying Fernandez treats projects with the care one would expect if the project was in his own home.

"Quite a character." "Beautiful work—glamorous and subtle all at the same time." "His personality definitely factors into the design—you either love him, or not." "While we had a detailed budget, it did not restrain us." "We had great fun and created something uniquely special."

Arkules & Associates **4** **3.5** **4.5** **4**
5224 East Arroyo Road, Paradise Valley, AZ 85253
(480) 443 - 9901

Elegant, understated, personal interior design

An understated, personal and timeless feel to her work is what draws clients to the services of Linda Arkules Cohn. While she favors a classical style, we hear that Arkules Cohn is also conversant in modern and traditional vernacular, sometimes creating a harmonious mixture of periods within a project.

Arkules Cohn is a second-generation designer learning the craft from her mother and partner, Barbara, who has 40 years of experience in the industry, working mostly in Paradise Valley, Arizona. Arkules Cohn has collaborated with her mother on a growing number of projects in Arizona, but still keeps an office in Chicago. The majority of the firm's work comes from established clients, with a wide scope of projects, ranging from the renovation of a room or two to a 10,000-square-foot single-family home, designed by the renowned David Adler.

Arkules Cohn works on about a dozen projects each year, almost exclusively residential and mostly in Chicago and Arizona. Of her Chicago-area endeavors, Arkules Cohn works in the city as well as the North Shore and Gold Coast. She determines any retainer and design fee on a case-by-case basis and charges a lower hourly rate and standard product markups. Working with the top notch service providers, Arkules Cohn is said to deliver a high quality product.

Arlene Semel & Associates **5** **4.5** **4** **4.5**
445 North Franklin Street, Chicago, IL 60610
(312) 644 - 1480

Modern eclectic with spirit

Arlene Semel is consistently praised for her polished modern designs, knowledge and placement of fine objects and antiques, and for her professional operation. She is particularly known for "inspired" designs that incorporate a fulsome range of worldwide selections into a neutral ground. White upholstery, dark woods, African stools and English antiques are said to live together in "symbiotic harmony." Others commend her skills with more traditional settings, saying that she works towards the stylistic goals of the client.

The firm has been a part of the Chicago landscape for over three decades, and is an acknowledged industry leader. Clients range from superstars to young couples renovating their first home in the suburbs. The firm has an "excellent" group of project managers who handle the day-to-day. While not at every meeting, Semel is said to be involved with each project. About a third of the commissions are outside the Chicago area, usually second or third homes for delighted past customers. The firm works particularly well with leading business titans, due to its detailed project planning and excellent problem-solving capabilities.

Retail is charged on product with an oversight fee for structural and non-product consultations (the NY system). Living rooms can range from $75,000 to $125,000+ with a minimum total project cost of about $100,000. Alternatively, the level of cost and quality can be taken as high as the imagination. ASID.

"She is obsessive in her quest for perfection." "There is such spark and imagination in her work and a consistent degree of finish." "I find that I had to push to achieve a look beyond the predictable scope." "It is truly amazing the way she can have country folk art and Asian and African art live side by side in a cohesive manner. If others did this, it would just look like a jumble." "She is so wise and so skilled, but not a hand holder." "She loves to reupholster, and did a great job reusing my existing furnishings." "Arlene is a person with vision and, thank goodness, she does not waiver from the plan."

Art & Design **3.5** **3.5** **4** **4.5**
711 North Milwaukee Avenue, Chicago, IL 60622
(312) 491 - 1400

Contemporary traditional to funky modern interior design

Clients hail Michael Syrjanen and Roger Ramsay for their devotion to creative design, unusual color palettes and good organizational skills. They are known for their innovative skills in the design of everything from racing horse silks to the excellent placement and reupholstery of IKEA furniture. Often there is a "wow factor" built into the designs, with the rest of the furnishings complementing the site but keeping down the costs.

Ramsay and Syrjanen have partnered for 16 years, with clients speaking of the great teamwork. Previously, they both were in interior design for many years, and Ramsay also directs the Roger Ramsay Gallery, specializing in contemporary fine art. Syrjanen is said to be an expert in period furniture. Clients range from the city to many in Lake Forest, with a wide scope in age, and a strong interest in "real" art. Sisters, grandparents and parents all pass along Art & Design's name, with as many as six projects done for one such situation.

Living rooms are generally in the $50,000 to $75,000 area, but can go much higher with lots of period furniture. An initial retainer is taken, with standard product markups and standard hourly fees. Interesting sources are used by the firm, offering a diversified and economically broad range.

"They are both so well trained that it is like having two for the price of one." "The back office is terrific. They return phone calls immediately and follow up with furniture." "They brought the warmth of our Spanish architecture inside to the house." "They worked on just a few rooms and did not push." "Michael is a frustrated teacher. I learned so much about antiques." "Since Roger has so much knowledge in fine art, I felt comfortable working with him to begin my collection." "While they are on the high side of the budget, they are definitely smooth."

Berta Shapiro **5** **4.5** **4.5** **5**
225 West Huron Street, Suite 214, Chicago, IL 60610
(312) 951 - 7464

Refined, enhanced, eclectic interior design

Praised for her designs of balanced refinement, relaxed elegance and eclectic equanimity, Berta Shapiro is admired by clients and peers alike. Using a mixture of 19th- and 20th-century furniture, she is said to be a "lesson in balance." Shapiro will add contemporary whimsy to traditional settings or fine antiques to more modern interiors for depth and warmth. Best known for her particular strength with a sophisticated country effect, Shapiro has a loyal following. Projects are generally quite integrated and Shapiro is said to have a specific point of view.

With training in painting at Isabel O'Neil, Shapiro embarked upon an interior design career in the late 1980s. There are four people in the firm, including a licensed architect. Clients appreciate the boutique nature of the firm and the excellent attention they receive from Shapiro, who takes on a limited number of projects a year. Patrons say that Shapiro encourages them to be fully involved with the project, and that they learn a great deal from the experience.

Budgets tend to evolve based on the interests of the client, with living rooms generally in the $75,000 to $150,000 range. Product and hourly rates are in the standard range with the more junior members of the team at lower rates. Sources are of the highest quality and reflect long-standing relationships with Shapiro. Said to have an "eye for the finer things," Shapiro will slipcover but will not downgrade.

"She is a big believer in comfort and creates exceptionally beautiful rooms full of unusual handmade or reworked furnishings." "As an architect, I appreciate Berta's excellent design sensibilities—she is a connoisseur." "Berta is the only designer in Chicago who can make eclectic resonate." "Her knowledge of art and textiles helps to achieve a truly polished look." "During the project, it was like Christmas everyday." "She educates you, but does not push you." "Not only professional, Berta is also articulate and smart. A joy to work with." "We trust Berta implicitly and would never consider using anyone else." "She offers the epitome of gorgeous comfort."

Blutter Shiff Design Associates **3.5 3.5 4 4.5**
1648C Merchandise Mart, Chicago, IL 60654
(312) 467 - 9054

Tailored, timeless, client-oriented interior design

Joan Blutter and Janet Shiff are known for their thoughtful and timeless designs, their strong collaboration with clients and their professional work habits. This mother-and-daughter team can do English country and American contemporary with equal ability, often adding architectural personality to their interiors with useful built-ins. Clients remark that another strength of the firm is its understanding and creative adaptation to family lifestyle patterns.

Blutter began the firm in the 1950s and has been a mainstay of the national and regional ASID throughout her career. Shiff studied art history as an undergraduate, attended the University of Wisconsin and the Harrington Institute and joined Blutter in the 1970s. Their office has been located in the Merchandise Mart for over 35 years. There are five people at the firm, which handles over 50 active projects a year. About half of the Chicago-area work is in the city and the other half is in the northern and western suburbs, often with repeat customers. Other projects have included a range of second and vacation homes in Naples, Boca, Palm Springs, Aspen and Vail. The firm is always interested in new projects and will start with just a few rooms.

Blutter Shiff will work on a hourly consultation basis or on a project basis, which includes hourly fees for design work (not for shopping or administration) and a standard hourly fee. A typical living room is in the $50,000 to $75,000 range, and clients report that the firm stays within budget by offering a range of economic choices. The principals are consistently complimented for their strategic use of space and accommodating nature. ASID.

"These guys will do whatever it takes." "They did my high-rise apartment, ski house and suburban home in three completely different styles, all with great aplomb." "They are excellent designers with great attention to detail and also practical businesswomen." "Joan and Janet are easy to work with and really want the space to reflect the client's personality." "My first house was rather small, but they did a great job and I never felt like a second-class citizen." "They make everything lovely and comfortable."

	Quality	Cost	Value	Recommend?
Borg Design Studio	3	3	4	4.5

220 West Scott Street, Suite C, Chicago, IL 60610
(312) 280 - 4919

Imaginative, warm, versatile interior design

Overall creativity and a methodical workflow are characteristics that clients admire regarding the work of Wendy Borg. Borg takes her cues from her clients and relies heavily on their input and taste. This sort of collaboration has led Borg to create spaces that range from country kitchens to modern, zen-influenced and English Country spaces. In addition to Borg's design sense, she is also a skilled millworker and artist, practicing the art of glass blowing, weaving, sculpture and painting. Clients praise Borg for her use of organic influences to create a calming element.

With more than 20 years experience in the industry, Borg is the sole practitioner of the firm, established in 1994. The majority of her projects are in the city, but Borg occasionally takes on projects in the Winnetka area. Most of her projects are entire homes, but clients say she remains flexible enough to take on smaller projects, working with a client room by room. Living rooms are typically in the $50,000 range. Borg works on a retainer and extremely low hourly rate and charges standard markups on products.

"I adore Wendy." "She is really creative and a great listener." "She does things step-by-step and doesn't overwhelm you." "Really educates you." "Brought in the earthiness of the home with brick walls, granite fireplace and wood floors." "It's about what you like and who you are, not about her." "Very communicative—had a sofa made and it took a long time, but she never promised anything she couldn't deliver." "She is flexible and sensitive, something I never thought I would say about an interior decorator." "We were really partners." She always gets back to you and holds your hand."

	Quality	Cost	Value	Recommend?
Branca Inc.	5	5	4	4.5

1325 North State Parkway, Chicago, IL 60610
(312) 787 - 6123 www.branca.com

Luxurious, stylistic, exuberant Continental interior design

Peers and clients roundly laud Alessandra Branca for her lavish Continental design style, intense creativity and stylistic flourish. She is on most everyone's top ten design list, and consistently responds with unique twists on historically based, yet updated traditional elegance. Credited with extraordinary flair, she tends to work best in the classical genre, updated with exhilarating color and a multitude of details. Upholstered walls, multiple patterns, rich glazes and exquisite millwork often factor into the design plans. Italian-born, fine arts-trained and a mother of three, Branca uses all skills and experiences to develop her characteristic design creations.

Branca begins with a physical inventory and plan, and much is retrofitted to the new composition. Clients range from the most established to the young, who may begin with just a few rooms, but usually have high quality expectations, classical views and substantial budgets. Very often these clients continue to use Branca, expanding year-by-year to other rooms and, finally, to multiple locations and then the yacht. European shopping trips often factor into the picture.

Most of the products are custom, with many unusual European sources, creating a relatively expensive, but unique setting. There are eleven people at the firm, including three project directors. The firm's hourly rate ranges from low to high, depending on seniority, with a high markup on product (none on millwork). Typical living rooms are in the $25,000 to $125,000 range. The public may purchase selections of Branca's work, including tulipieres, porcelains and watercolors, at her new showroom, Atelier Branca, at the address above. Clients tend to be quite loyal, albeit exhausted, and clearly enthralled by the end result. HB Top Designers 2000.

"Alessandra has the temperament of an artist, and she produces design masterpieces." "I think that you are born with great style and Alessandra has more of it than anyone else in Chicago." "She gives new life and vibrancy to historical spaces, while retaining their original character." "While there were times when I wondered if we would ever make it to the end of the project, I would not consider using anyone else." "As an architect, I applaud her ability to add a multi-dimensional, detailed, layered warmth to the architectural renderings. While it is not always easy, her undeniable talent makes me want to do it again." "I have become a great friend of Alessandra's through this crazy, exciting and rewarding process."

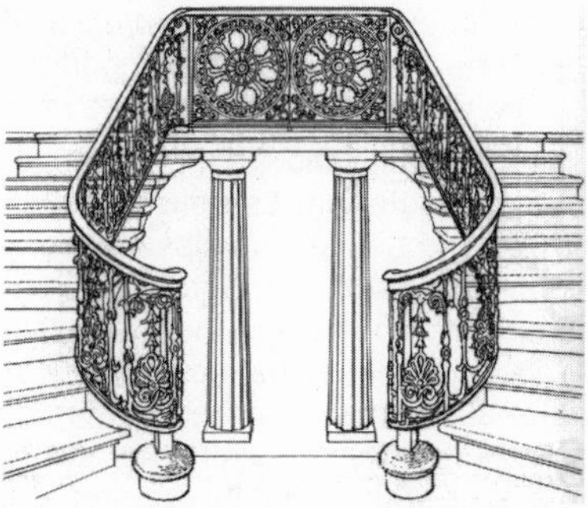

Bray-Schaible **5** **4.5** **4** **4.5**

80 West 40th Street, New York, NY 10018
(212) 354 - 7525

Tailored, contemporary, sleek interior design

Robert Bray and Michael Schaible are the acknowledged forerunners of avant garde interiors. Patrons say their designs are as crisp and innovative today as they were over three decades ago. The pair is commended for its mastery of architectural perspective, streamlined furnishings and effective execution. Their current clientele tends to have serious design aspirations and serious budgets, and Bray-Schaible responds with inspired levels of design and equally inspired levels of quality.

The two principals trained at Parsons. Mitchell Turnborough joined the team in 1988. Their design talents range from Modern-with-soul to edited traditional to 70s-style rejuvenated. Often, they fundamentally reconfigure spaces to achieve their trademark clean lines, incorporating comfort and clever detail, such as hidden areas for storage. Only a few new commissions are taken on each year, but are generally quite large, including the recent interior design of Jasper Johns' house in the Carribean. A good percentage of the current work is in Chicago, with clients reporting on the firm's good availability.

The firm works with an upfront design fee, standard markups on product, no hourly product fee and standard oversight fees. Much of the work is custom and built in, using the finest materials. Sculpture and art work often factor largely into the picture. Bray and Schaible are consistently recommended as dependable, accommodating, diligent and professional. AD 100, 2000. ID Hall of Fame.

"They realize that bones dictate, and follow that with decoration that is not fussy." "They did a great job flying out to Chicago whenever it was appropriate." "Incredible, quality people." "The masters of sleek." "While they are known for their more forward-thinking designs, they can also do a more traditionally classical take, indigenous to the surroundings, but to the max." "Great to work with, if you can afford them." "They are an old-school couture house of interior design." "Their designs are still the best in the country." "They just do not run out of new ideas." "I would highly recommend them for the project of a lifetime."

Firm	Quality	Cost	Value	Recommend?
Cannon Frank	4	4	4	4

340 West Diversey Parkway Suite 2516, Chicago, IL 60657
(773) 327 - 4099 www.cannonfrank.com

Versatile interior design with personality

A highly collaborative approach is what many say differentiates John Cannon, who is known to weave an eclectic mix of styles as dictated by the client's personal taste. Cannon is described as an extremely down to earth person who views each project as a learning experience—and believes he learns as much from clients as they do from him. With a client-described obsession for details, Cannon takes an active role in every phase of a project. While the firm doesn't focus on a particular style, new homes in a contemporary style is a strength, and, a French/Italian mix are also done to the client's strong satisfaction.

With Cannon as the lead designer and Cary Frank heading the back office, the firm has a very professional reputation. Established in 1981, the firm employs seven, typically taking on eight to twelve commissions per year. Projects are evenly split between the city and suburbs, and boast a diverse clientele, including established suburban families and their younger, city-dwelling second generation. The firm will do renovations one room at a time for repeat customers. With an in-house computer-aided-design system, Cannon Frank designs a large amount of its own custom millwork, with skill. The firm has worked on many substantial-sized commissions with specialty requirements, including train rooms and movie theaters.

Cannon Frank generally takes on larger first-time projects and works on a standard retainer with standard hourly rates or standard markups on products (not both).

"As an architect, working with them on an exceptionally high-end project, they were a pleasure to work with—clear in intent and excellent in follow through." "John will tell you if you are making a mistake, but it is your choice." "From plumbing to tile work, John gets involved in every detail." "He takes it ten steps beyond what I imagined."

Firm	Quality	Cost	Value	Recommend?
Cara Young & Associates Inc.	3.5	3.5	4.5	5

1750 Braeside Lane, Northbrook, IL 60062
(847) 753 - 9999

Streamlined, practical interior design with flair

Appreciated for her refined integration of natural woods, distinguishing accents of color and excellent business sense, Cara Young is strongly recommend by clients. While favoring a contemporary sweep, including a strong element of built-in furniture, she brings comfort and livability to her designs, and responds to clients' interests.

The firm was established ten years ago, after Young received her MBA and worked in advertising. Young takes on just a few clients a year, and then is fully involved in most every detail. Most clients are within a ten-minute drive of her Northbrook office for increased efficiencies. Patrons appreciate her hands-on approach and often hire her for their second projects.

Clients commend Young for her practical, good judgement and for making the most of their budgets. She will judiciously use Pier I or Target products and mix them with the finest quality woodwork. She charges an upfront retainer, a very low hourly fee (not for administration) and a very low product markup. Living rooms are generally in the $75,000 to $100,000 range, despite her low fees, because she favors the best upholsterers and painters. Clients say she is much more interested in the process and in making clients happy than in making a profit. ASID.

"She worked with me to find something beautiful within my budget and she encouraged me to keep a lot of what we already owned." "She had great taste and took great care to make the home comfortable for my children." "She is

beyond smooth and organized. We would discuss something, she would jump into her car and 30 minutes later it was done." "She is so capable, has fabulous resources and is always available." "She watches my money more closely than I do." "I am very grateful to work with someone who has such great taste, is so reasonable and also remarkably smart."

Carol Wolk Interiors, Ltd. 3 3.5 4 4.5
340 Tudor Court, Glencoe, IL 60022
(847) 835 - 5500

Clean-edged, updated traditional interior design

With an updated take on traditional, the designers of Carol Wolk Interiors incorporate lean forms, modern materials and classic textiles. Ethnic or regional touches often accent the contemporary lines, adding depth and color. The firm's spaces are developed with clients' interests and lifestyles as a basis, with detailed accessories often highlighting the clients' influences and offering warmth and comfort.

The firm was established 27 years ago by the late Carol Wolk. Anne Wolk Stolar, her daughter, carries on the tradition. She joined the firm seven years ago and is now the company's principal designer. With two experienced additional designers, Marilyn Wittenberg and Myla Frohman Goldstick, the firm handles about fifteen active projects a year. There is a strong mix in the client base: younger and older, suburban and city and new homes and renovations. The designers are found to be reliable and available, often shopping with customers for major pieces.

A non-reimbursable design fee is charged along with quite low hourly rates and a standard product markup. The firm is known for developing good working budgets, and typically clients spend from $75,000 to $125,000 for a living room. Clients are encouraged to intermix antiques with repro for richness, texture and patina. Clients remark that the firm has the skills to extend the context of a setting to the interior motifs, thereby expanding and "transforming their living space." ASID.

"They are really on top of all aspects of the design and the process." "I love it all—particularly the subtle blend of colors, and the interesting mix of contemporary furniture and eclectic details." "When you walk into the Mart with them, you know that they are respected." "I have a large family of growing boys and all the right fabrics were chosen for every room. They are beautiful and durable." "They have a great relationship with their vendors, and I was a happy beneficiary." "They are decent and reliable—a real find."

Carole Post, P.C. 4 3.5 4.5 5
330 West Diversey Parkway, Suite 905, Chicago, IL 60657
(773) 281 - 5290

Clean, serene, contemporary-tinged interior design

Noted for her contemporary, neutral backgrounds leaning toward modernism, Carole Post has a high-end following. The interiors are warmed with fine artwork and antiques of diverse provenance, including Viennese successionalist furnishings and Asian accents. Post will often use her architectural interests to enhance the background elements, adding character and depth to the interiors.

After an architectural apprenticeship, Post received a degree from the Harrington Institute and trained with Shelly Handman. Post then established her firm in 1987. As a sole practitioner, she takes on about six active projects a year, and is said to work very closely with clients. She is known to confidently integrate her design and fine arts background with the interests and lifestyle of the client. Most projects tend to be downtown and in the near north suburbs, generally with "forward-trending" clients. Regardless of the size of a project, Post is said to have wonderful initiative and follow-through, both with clients and with other members of the project team.

Clients commend Post for establishing a budget before embarking upon a project, setting a realistic basis from which to work. Living rooms are generally in the $45,000 to $65,000 range, and supporters credit Post for offering a wide choice of products at various price points. The firm works on an hourly consultation basis with an upfront retainer and a standard product markup. Friends pass on Post's name with confidence and pride.

"She is very forthcoming with all things financial, something my husband particularly appreciated." "Carole is remarkably good at creating elevations and design drawings for millwork that works. We thought that we would have to hire an architect as well, but Carole did it all." "I felt so enriched by the experience—she opened my eyes to a more modern and serene palette." "By shopping well beyond the Mart and by creating a lot of our furniture, Carole created a unique and remarkable look for our family."

Dale Carol Anderson Ltd., ASID **5** **5** **4** **5**

2030 North Magnolia Avenue, Chicago, IL 60614
(773) 348 - 5200

Sophisticated, classical, elegant interior design

Recognized for her designs of timeless grace, refined colors and graceful patina, Dale Carol Anderson is considered to be a master by her clients. Rooms will often include fine French furniture or English antiques, expertly mixed with modern, comfortably-sized upholstered pieces in muted hues. Accessories figure largely in the designs, and clients remark that no detail is too small for Anderson to do to perfection.

Recent work includes a mix of projects for downtown and suburban Chicago clients and others throughout the U.S. Most patrons are more established and many have multiple homes, all done by Anderson. The firm is small, with five employees, and Anderson takes pride in working closely with clients and subcontractors, supervising all aspects. Her team is consistently noted to be effective and highly service-oriented.

Supporters report that the quality of the firm's products can be as high as the clients want to take it, but not all has to be of the ultimate quality. However, typical living rooms are in the $200,000+ range. The firm works with an upfront retainer, standard markups on products and high hourly rates (lower for design associates). Anderson is considered to be a well-kept secret, passed among close friends. ASID.

"Dale is divine to work with—she goes above and beyond." "All other interiors pale in comparison to Dale's." "She knows her stuff, be it a French antique or the ultimate silk tassel." "She remains cool and collected, yet so effective even under stressful situations. The day before a big party, she made the electricians move the sconces so they were exactly centered, just as they should have been." "The upholstery is all big enough for relaxed afternoons and long naps." "I am particularly enamored of Dale's millwork—it has just the right amount of patina, looking as if it had been there for generations." "She is the consummate professional with the client's interests at heart."

✚	$	◆	★

Daniel Du Bay Interior Design, Inc.

📁 📁 📁 📁

1512 North Fremont Street Suite 104, Chicago, IL 60622
(312) 787 - 7766

Luxurious interior design with spice

Darcy Bonner & Associates

4.5 4.5 4 5

205 West Wacker Drive, Suite 307, Chicago, IL 60606
(312) 853 - 3470

Graceful, transitional interior design and architecture

With balanced composure and extraordinary architectural detailing, Darcy Bonner has distinguished himself among a sea of eclectic transitionalists. He favors the grace and background proportions of the 19th century with the furnishings, elegance and inventive spirit of the Moderne era. Clients laud Bonner for his ability to transform a new space into a home that appears to have existed for generations and also for his stylistic strength with furnishings of various provenance.

Bonner began his career in architecture and design with Scott Himmel in 1979, after receiving a master's in architecture from the University of Chicago. Bonner set up his own firm in 1994, retaining the Mattaliano Furniture business. Bonner takes on about seven large projects a year, generally for the more established of Chicago and beyond. Landmark Gold Coast and suburban residences in the 10,000-square-foot range are typical. Patrons report that Bonner's communication skills are strong, and that he is always available to them. The staff of ten is also reportedly very helpful and responsive, with project managers running the day-to-day.

While using the finest resources in Chicago, Bonner also reaches out to a creative array of alternative craftsmen to help keep costs in check. The firm charges a standard architectural rate for new construction, hourly for interior design (high to lower, depending upon seniority) and a slightly lower than standard markup on product. A typical living room is in the $150,000 range with significant latitude, between $100,000 and $500,000. Bonner is highly recommended among friends and relatives.

"I don't know how they do it. The simplest of lines look gracious under Darcy's direction." "While they love buying original Jean-Michel Frank, these are practical people who also scoop up similar pieces from the period." "Darcy is an all-around great guy as well as an exceptional professional." "His designs are simultaneously comfortable, classic and progressive—who could ask for anything more?"

Elise Schreiber

4 4 4 4

636 North Orlin Street, Chicago, IL 60610
(312) 664 - 3600

Edited, transitional interior design with flow

Acknowledged for her sweeps of individualistic modern, Elise Shreiber works in a collaborative yet innovative manner with clients. With simplicity, form and color, Shreiber is said to offer a personalized and updated take on English country, transitional eclectic or urban sleek, presenting various points of view. References state that she is extraordinarily professional and appreciate her diligent follow-through.

Raised in England and trained by Gregga, Shreiber then formed a partnership with Bill Olafsen for several years. This firm was established in 1998 and works on four to five major projects a year, mostly in the Gold Coast and northern suburbs. Clients range from the young to the more established, with all appreciating a high quality context.

The firm is said to be quite thoughtful in the design process—developing a detailed furniture plan to set the course. Budgets tend to evolve with the clients' preferences. Hourly rates and standard product fees are charged. Shreiber will shop with clients in the Mart and reportedly has excellent, unique European sources. ASID.

"I fired two decorators before I found Elise." "She is the most professional designer I have ever met. She turns paperwork around in 24 hours and leaves the most precise voicemails." "Elise creates great flow with color and light." "Communication is a strength." "Elise believes that there is a place for Georgian silver and chintz, but does not overdo it." "She forms a framework, but then encourages you to put our own personal stamp on the design." "With a marvelous eye for scale and proportion, and a distinct touch, Elise delivers a streamlined version of the very best traditional with modern whimsy."

Eva Quateman Interiors, Ltd. **3.5** **2** **4.5** **4.5**
399 West Fullerton Parkway Suite 3E, Chicago, IL 60614
(773) 472 - 0522

Clean, neoclassical comfort

Noted to be a cool traditionalist, integrating neoclassical lines into modern backgrounds, Eva Quateman has a loyal group of clients. Supporters say that Quateman works effectively and efficiently to achieve the client's vision, which is most often described as traditionally based, fun and comfortable, without the florals or flourishes. Quateman reportedly goes way beyond the usual interior design responsibilities, often managing the construction process as well.

Clients are generally younger, with homes ranging considerably from a very large Park Tower raw-space build out, to a new home on the North Shore, to just a few rooms for new graduates. The firm was established about ten years ago. Quateman learned the business from her father who was in contract renovation for 40 years. While most first-time clients will typically spend about $30,000 to $40,000 in the design of the living room, other clients will spend twice that. For the interior design services, the firm charges very low product markups and low hourly rates. Construction oversight fees are arranged separately. Although Quateman and her team offer a full range of services, only a handful of projects are fully active at one time, allowing the firm to be very responsive to clients' needs.

Quateman encourages clients to choose just a few good furniture pieces to distinguish the spaces. Patrons say she is quite practical about mixing in existing furnishings, suggesting low-cost alternatives and finding excellent, economic subcontractors. Quateman is known to search high and low for possibilities, including antiques in New York and Paris.

"She found some amazing, economical choices." "Eva is great at maximizing space and redesigning existing furnishings." "With a light hand, she has fun with the furnishings." "She is not constricted by traditional boundaries—if she cannot find the perfect piece, she has it made." "Eva's strength is in her ability to make each room comfortable with wonderful finishing touches." "What started as a living room rehab became a gut renovation due to my confidence in Eva."

Frank S. Perry, IIDA **4** **4** **4** **4.5**
1040 North Lake Shore Drive, Suite 6B, Chicago, IL 60611
(312) 280 - 0850

Bold, classical, luxurious interior design

The work of Frank Perry has become synonymous with the look of bold sophistication, ornate detail and resonant textures. With his signature animal-skin-print carpeting, Perry has created a style that incorporates dignified, clean-lined forms and various classical international motifs. Clients say Perry has a gift for creating drama throughout by incorporating surprises, such as a "little shimmering accessory" against a backdrop of simplicity. Unafraid to use bold colors to entice the eye and make an intrepid statement, Perry is said to have an aptitude for awakening the senses. Alternately, he can work in a more formal, traditional genre with a glint of the sublime. Perry is said to be an accommodating and delightful man with a strong sense of design possibilities and a commitment to historical and relevant design.

"Frank will focus on the client's sense of the ultimate and deliver that product." "A happy man with a focus on the classical traditions of the past." "His designs are the only ones in Chicago that offer an edge of intense drama, yet are simultaneously elegant in the traditional sense."

Freiwald Associates, Inc. 4 3.5 4.5 4.5

2748 West Sunnyside Avenue, Chicago, IL 60625
(773) 463 - 8501

Conservative, transitional interior design

Clients appreciate Freiwald's innovative designs, excellent resources and professional demeanor. With a strong ability to adapt to clients' styles and interests, the firm often mixes "investment-grade antiques" with cleaner backgrounds and build-ins. There is said to be a sophisticated consistency room-to-room in taste, style and attitude.

With a major in fine arts, Freiwald likes to incorporate the learning process into the design process. There are four at the firm, with Freiwald known for developing excellent relationships with clients. The firm was started about seventeen years ago and has a loyal following, mostly in the northern suburbs (Highland Park, Glencoe). Many second homes have also been done including commissions in Vail, Aspen, Snowmass, the Chesapeake Bay and Nantucket. He will happily do a few rooms, which generally leads to more.

Freiwald loves to move furniture around and reupholster, giving designs and furnishings new life. A retainer is taken upfront, with low markups on product and low hourly rates. Clients are amazed at his array of interesting resources.

"As a designer, I find Richard's concepts fresh, innovative and timeless. I can learn from him." "Richard is very forward thinking, and also is very happy to allow people to express their taste." "Any glitches are handled in a helpful and timely manner." "He is best at an updated design with a few quality, anchoring antiques." "Richard has amazingly wide resources—he is not using the same names as everyone else." "He is a designer, advisor and teacher." "He was so sensitive to my needs." "He did each of our three houses in completely different styles, each with great energy and aplomb."

Gelis & Associates, Inc. 3.5 3.5 4.5 5

222 East Pearson, Suite 204, Chicago, IL 60611
(312) 943 - 7464

Architectural, elegant, serene interior design

Be it a farmhouse or a penthouse, Madeline Gelis delivers calm and serene interiors with character. With particular skills in historic preservation and space planning, she often contrasts traditional architectural elements with warm colors, natural materials and modern textiles to soften and enhance the look. Very high-quality millwork and strong structural details, such as neo-classical fireplace surrounds and handsome moldings, are often incorporated into Gelis's work. References also compliment her innovative perspective, detailed orientation and highly professional manner.

Gelis is a graduate of Harrington and has taught several design courses at her alma mater. Starting in the corporate arena, she evolved into residential properties and now works mainly on the North Shore and in the city. The firm was established seventeen years ago and includes five people. Clients tend to be interested in excellent quality and generally work with Gelis on multiple projects. Based on her corporate training, she holds comprehensive discussions upfront with clients and provides detailed budgets and extensive floorplans.

Charges are based entirely on hourly fees, ranging from standard rates to lower ones for project managers and staff. All products are passed through to clients at net or wholesale with no markup. Given the firm's hourly-fee philosophy, all product price ranges are taken into consideration, including Crate & Barrel for children's rooms, as appropriate. Living rooms are generally in the $50,000 to $75,000 range. Patrons often return for more, confident that Gelis will enhance their space with care and creativity. ASID.

"Madeline saved us by being there early on in the project, incorporating innovative design into the architect's plans." "She helped us understand that we should splurge on a few good pieces and she was absolutely correct." "The value she added to our new house, particularly in enhancing the bones and the flow, easily covered her fee—and we get to live there!" "When she is with you, she is so efficient." "She worked within a budget and stayed within budget." "She is always a lady and very dependable." "We have the most beautiful home in the neighborhood thanks to Madeline."

Geoffrey Bradfield **4** **4.5** **4** **4.5**

105 East 63rd Street, Suite 1B, New York, NY 10021
(212) 758 - 1773

Opulent, modern interior design

Known for his unique perspective, Geoffrey Bradfield brings opulence, quality and verve to his projects. While he often bases his designs on a classic modern genre, Bradfield combines antiques and objects from different centuries and continents to energize his interiors. Art collectors often become clients and clients often become art collectors, owing to Bradfield's passion and knowledge of contemporary art. Clients say he is particularly adept at designing backgrounds that make a statement, yet feature the art.

After working with McMillen for a brief period, Bradfield joined the late Jay Spectre in 1978 to pursue his more contemporary style. Recent projects include substantial apartments on the Gold Coast, grand private homes in Palm Beach, spacious Park Avenue apartments, private jets, yachts and offices with character. Chicago clients say his responsiveness makes it very easy to have a long-distance relationship.

The firm charges a standard+ upfront design fee, standard product markups and hourly rates only for hours where no commission is otherwise received (the NY system). These fees are actually lower than the normal percentage for Chicago, but Bradfield tends to work with only the highest-quality materials. While many enjoy Bradfield's fulsome personality, others say he can be a bit much. Overall, clients roundly praise Bradfield for his attention to detail, resourcefulness, accessibility and style. ASID. AD100, 2000. KB, 1993.

"Geoffrey is extremely professional and meticulous, working every angle until reaching perfection." "He took a shell of a house, my dream concept and my color scheme, and transposed the property into something magical." "While always respectful and professional, he was not thrilled when I pushed the aesthetic line toward practicality." "I feel as if I am happily floating on a cloud in my high-rise living room." "We were a team and I loved the experience." "I cannot tell you how many people are dying for a dinner invitation just to see the house." "I have never enjoyed working with anyone as much as I did Geoffrey."

Gomez Assoc./Mariette Himes Gomez **5** **5** **4.5** **4.5**

504-506 East 74th Street, 3rd floor, New York, NY 10021
(212) 288 - 6856 www.mariettehimesgomez.com

Modern, elegant interior design

Mariette Himes Gomez is consistently praised for her relaxed elegance, calming palette and professional manner. She is much admired for her uncanny ability to make minimalism appear luxurious. While she has a healthy respect for tradition, she is known as a master editor who refines spaces with neutral forms, textures and details. Best known for her trademark colors of whites and creams, she will also incorporate soft hues at the client's request. References say that Gomez is not, however, the person to hire for flounces or frills, and that she has a specific view of what she believes will work.

The firm is quite large by industry standards and is often recognized for its strong organizational abilities. Patrons feel that they receive a good amount of attention from Gomez herself and are very impressed with the follow-up. Clients include a large number of entertainment moguls, including Harrison Ford and director Ivan Reitman, and high-profile bankers. She is also known to accept the challenge of interesting, smaller projects, and recently created her own line of furniture and accessories. The firm does occasional commissions in Chicago, and is said to be available and accommodating.

While her fees are said to be as high as the quality of her work, she has an ever-increasing list of happy, repeat clients. ASID. AD 100, 2000. HB Top Designers, 1999, 2000. ID Hall of Fame, 1994. KB 1991, 1994, 1996, 1999.

Gray & Walter, Ltd. **4.5** **4** **4** **4.5**

159 West Kinzie Street, Chicago, IL 60610
(312) 329 - 1007

Traditional interior design with grace

Ann Gray and Ken Walter are praised by clients for their classical, traditional style, suffused with rich details of elegance and character. They are known to collaboratively build upon the client's interests, expectations and vision. With extensive high-end experience, strong vendor relationships and creative thinking, Gray & Walter has established itself among the very top traditionalists.

Gray began the firm in 1971 after training with New York's esteemed interior design firm, McMillan. Walter joined in 1981 with years of commercial design training in Atlanta. Residential Chicago clients have included many a CEO living in the Gold Coast or Lincoln Park, and these clients tend to have second homes further afield, also dressed by the firm. Commercial projects have included The Little Nell in Aspen, The Tremont Hotel in Chicago, The Ritz-Carlton in Washington, D.C., and The Standard and Mid-America Clubs in Chicago. The partners are said to approach each job thoughtfully and specifically, which often translates into a substantial investment in time and resources for the client.

The firm generally charges a higher hourly rate and low product markups, or, alternatively, works on a retail basis with no hourly fees. With a strong focus in historic renovation, most projects are expansive and expensive. More recently, the firm has worked with a number of younger clients, starting with just a few rooms. Living rooms are typically in the $75,000 to $100,000++ range, with Crate & Barrel used only in vacation homes. Supporters applaud the firm for respecting and tracking a budget, and recommend the firm for its professionalism and "high-caliber sensibilities." ASID.

"Gray & Walter took our basic concept of English manor house and transformed the space to realize the dream." "Ann's taste is impeccable—she was the only one we considered when we moved to Chicago, on the recommendation of our classiest friends." "Ken is meticulous, on top of every loose end and very communicative." "I was a little nervous when Ken did not want me to review our rather large living room in its various design stages, but I give him an 'A' in everything he did with it." "They took my stylistic preferences to heart." "Ann is the most gracious person I know." "They did a great job of making the house beautiful, yet also comfortable and livable for my young children."

	Quality	Cost	Value	Recommend?
Greg Jordan Inc.	5	5	4.5	5

504 East 74th Street, Suite 4W, New York, NY 10021
(212) 570 - 4470

Lavish, traditional, colorful interior design

With his lavishly creative interiors, strong client service and engaging demeanor, Greg Jordan has won his clients' hearts and minds. Jordan intricately combines historic backgrounds with eclectic ingredients to create texture and movement. This melange creates a relaxed yet stylish environment steeped in historical reference. Clients report that the firm can also develop more traditional interiors and produces sumptuous chintz-laden environments that do not look overdone or fussy.

Jordan was raised in Louisiana, and clients describe him as a true Southern gentleman. The business was established in 1984 and has a very impressive roster of clients including Blaine Trump, Libbet Johnson and various banking moguls. The firm is extremely client-service oriented, reportedly completing the gut renovation of a very large house in less than four months. The designer's own line of furniture and accessories will soon be available to the public in his retail shop in New York. AD 100, 2000. HB Top Designers, 1999, 2000. KB 1992, 2000.

"I feel that Greg is in perfect sympathy with my design vision and lifestyle requirements." "He's the nicest guy you would ever want to work with. He is a wonderful listener who not only hears what I am saying, but also what I am not saying." "He is a master with detail, color and timeless design."

	Quality	Cost	Value	Recommend?
Gregga Jordan Smieszny Inc.	5	5	4	5

1203 North State Parkway, Chicago, IL 60610
(312) 787 - 0017

Luxurious, layered, eclectic interior design

Bruce Gregga is the accepted master and creator of what has become a distinct Chicago design nomenclature consisting of warm textured backgrounds, tailored silhouettes and eclectic showpieces. Modern is reinterpreted into a lush, textural, even romantic notion. While many have followed this path, Gregga and his partners, Alex Jordan and Dan Smieszny, set the standard of excellence with their devotion to the highest quality products, exact proportions, attention to detail and inexhaustible energy. Jordan, focusing on design, has been with Gregga for thirteen years, and Smieszny, focusing on architecture, for twenty. While Gregga continues to be active, clients now happily rely on these two partners.

Clients are friends and friends are clients, including many prominent families and celebrities of Chicago. The firm's reputation takes it to homes throughout the U.S. and abroad, with about half of its residential work in Chicago. Many clients have three or four residences, all decorated by the firm. For one extended family, GJS has worked on more than thirty residential and commercial projects. There are fourteen people in the firm, which handles more than twenty active projects at one time. Clients report that the firm does Art Deco, French, country English or Moderne with equal aplomb.

The firm charges an initial retainer, retail on products and substantial+ hourly fees for drawings and supervision, but no hourly for product shopping or administration. Costs for most projects are considerable, typically reaching to well over the quarter-million mark. Most clients become lifetime devotees. ASID. AD 100, 2000. HB Top Designers 1999, 2000. ID Hall of Fame.

"Bruce will be as extravagant as allowed." "While notably expensive, the firm is scrupulously detailed in its financial accountability on a monthly basis." "Bruce knows the best when he sees it." "They deliver the highest standards of service possible—from fixing every nick immediately to serving caviar at the installation." "These are true professionals." "They think nothing of hand-brushing a dining room wall with eight coats of paint." "We usually blow the budget or don't have one, but we all know that it will be beautiful." "Everything they do is to their specific specifications and a labor of love."

Handman Associates **4 4 4 4**
222 West Huron Street, Chicago, IL 60610
(312) 951 - 8456

Casual, contemporary elegance

Shelly Handman is recognized for his clean, transitional, comfortable designs and professional attitude. Clients also credit Handman for his excellent space planning and considerable flair without embellishment. Meeting a balance between sophisticated styling and relaxed family lifestyles, he has a strong preference for a "less is more" contemporary blueprint with allowances for oversized, well-stuffed upholstery. Handman is said to be adamant that the furnishings enhance and complement the existing architecture, urging clients to "fulfill their interiors' potential."

After studying art history undergrad and design at the Harrington Institute, Handman worked with Arlene Semel, for eight years, leaving as director of design. He then established his own firm in 1987. There are seven people on staff, which is said to be very strong. Clients state that Handman is part of every design decision and that he is very approachable, accessible and client-service oriented. Projects are generally on the North Shore and the Gold Coast, with commissions further afield (Florida, California, Israel).

The firm charges no hourly rate for interior design work and retail prices on furnishings. For construction oversight, there is an hourly fee. Supporters say Handman is very open and organized about presenting economic design options often offering "Volvo, Saab and Mercedes" alternatives. Living rooms generally fall in the $70,000 to $125,000 range. He is highly recommended for potential clients seeking his soft modern design. ASID.

"Shelly is especially talented and very caring." "Recently we had a plumbing leak that was a disaster. Shelly was right over to help." "Besides his excellent design capabilities, he is very likable." "He calls you back and is always available." "Shelly does not nickel and dime you." "He has worked with us for thirteen years—first in the public rooms, then in the bedrooms and most recently with a new addition. He did exactly what we had hoped." "Each piece is special; Shelly has a great eye." "When some furniture arrived with a huge scratch, they came over immediately. They make decorating stress-free. It is like calling your mom." "Shelly serves two masters so well: his furnishings are sleek and modern, and at the same time comfortable and welcoming."

Harriet Robinson Interior Design **3.5 4 3.5 4.5**
900 Pinetree Lane, Winnetka, IL 60093
(847) 446 - 2590

Evolving, updated traditional interior design

While historically more of a traditionalist, Harriet Robinson has gracefully shifted along with her client base to a more modern, 21st-century framework, integrating mid-20th-century furniture with distinctive and far-ranging accents. She reportedly excels at adding rich colors, warmth and comfort to new homes as well as refurbishing older homes.

With her artistic background and a corollary antique textiles business, Robinson offers a range of design options. She has worked in interior design for over twenty years and manages about eight projects a year. Customers enjoy working directly with Robinson, saying she is quite available, and understands the timing limitations of a sole proprietorship. Most clients are well-established North Shore or Gold Coast residents, but Robinson also does smaller projects for younger customers.

Fees include a reimbursable upfront design fee, a standard product markup and limited low hourly fees for non-product consultations, such as architect meetings, etc. Robinson works with the very best subcontractors and product providers which results in higher costs, despite the below standard fees. Clients find the work exceptional, meeting every expectation. Living rooms generally are in the $75,000 to $125,000 range, and budgets typically evolve. Clients trust and believe in Robinson's instincts, and appreciate her quality focus.

"She has so much experience and still does such exciting things." "She doesn't make mistakes and doesn't waste money, but sometimes takes longer than I had hoped." "She has impeccable taste and is so knowledgeable, especially in the textile area." "She always worked through design choices with me and took great care of us." "After the main project, Harriet was always helpful, even if there was no fee involved." "I fired two decorators before I found Harriet, but I will never interview again."

Heather G. Wells Ltd. **4** **3.5** **4.5** **4.5**

1 West Superior, Suite 605, Chicago, IL 60610
(312) 475 - 0477

Tailored, textural, architectural interior design

Heather Wells is respected for her intellectual focus, strong design range and project-management skills. Clients credit Wells for her creative abilities, whether it be for a traditional suburban "manor house" with a transitional edge or a downtown, contemporary loft. With warm tones, layered textures and architectural details, Wells offers clients a sophisticated, modern ambiance, thoughtfully composed for the setting.

A graduate of Smith College and Harvard Architecture School, Wells worked in architecture firms for several years and then with interior designer, Leslie Jones, for five years. Clients appreciate Wells's architectural training, saying that she contributes strongly to the bones of each project. The firm was established in 1997. With offices in both Chicago and Boston, about ten active projects are completed each year. Clients report that Wells is readily available and always prepared.

The firm is known to consciously and consistently offer economic choices and be responsive to budgetary issues. Living rooms tend to range from $50,000 for younger clients to $100,000 for the more established. A standard hourly rate and low product markups are incorporated into the fee structure. Clients highly recommend Wells for an educated viewpoint and excellent vision. ASID.

"Heather has such a refreshing and honest energy that we were immediately excited to work with her." "She has inspired us with her great knowledge and educated point of view." "While she may be a modernist at heart, Heather is doing a great job on our traditional project. She did a lot of research, which we really respect." "She has an architect's ability to visualize the end product." "While the budget evolved, it was our choice." "Aside from her professionalism on the job, we really like her as a person." "Heather and her team absolutely exceeded our expectations."

Ilene April Interiors, Ltd. 3 3 4 4

907 Rollingwood Road, Highland Park, IL 60035
(847) 266 - 0176

Versatile, client-oriented contemporary interior design

Ilene April has a more contemporary background and a love for color that we are told manifests itself in the numerous styles she uses for her various projects. April is the sole practitioner of the firm she started in 1994 at the age of 29. She takes on about eight projects annually—split between the city and its northern suburbs—and we are told she encourages the input and active participation of her clients. April, a graduate of Harrington, will not hesitate to take on smaller projects and insiders say she relates well to a younger clientele. A typical living room will cost about $25,000 and April charges a very low hourly rate and standard markup of products. ASID.

Insight Environmental Designs 5 4.5 4 4.5

1997 Lake Avenue, Highland Park, IL 60035
(847) 432 - 4606

High-end eclectic with warmth and character

Anne Kaplan and Bruce Goers are roundly acknowledged for offering the highest-quality eclectic designs with finesse and warmth. They rarely do "period pure," often blending timeframes, cultures and sources in a refined and sophisticated manner. Neutral palettes "take on life" with the rich patina of fine case goods and the character of unusual objets d'art. Alternatively, backgrounds can be full of color, tempered with elegant Old World antiques. Supporters credit the firm for using its expertise and knowledge to interpret and achieve the objectives of the client, taking them to the highest level.

As a small partnership, Kaplan and Goers accept a limited number of commissions a year, mostly very high-end and usually downtown. Clients say that the two designers typically work together on projects, "often trading places" for an excellent collaborative experience. The partnership began in 1980 after Goers had been in the design business for a number of years. Most clients say the firm is very communicative and responsive.

Insight can work on either a straight fee or on an hourly rate plus a standard product markup. Typical living rooms are in the $75,000 to $150,000+ range. Clients say the firm works with a general budget that evolves over time. Many design professionals say they, themselves, would choose Insight to decorate their own home—the highest compliment.

"They do the best work in town." "While breathtakingly beautiful, their designs are also livable." "Anne is not only a problem solver, but really a design psychologist." "They want their clients to have fun—during the process and after they leave the site." "Anne is a lovely lady with the finest reputation, but she can often be out of town." "There is a great feeling of creative trust between us and Anne and Bruce." "You have to be in the know to learn about Insight." "They are thoughtful, honest and extraordinarily expert at what they do."

	Quality	Cost	Value	Recommend?
Interiors II	4.5	4	4	4

1827 North Sedgwick Street, Chicago, IL 60614
(312) 280 - 8260

Luxurious, updated traditional with flair

Applauded for their high-quality, traditional designs with updated appeal, Barbara Lione and Jim Zidlicky are consistently mentioned among Chicago's very top traditional design firms. Patterns, florals and toiles are often combined for a layered, multi-generational effect. Clients say that the pair takes pleasure in incorporating their design interests and vision. While better known for their classical design sensibilities, they can also do more neutral palettes and more modern furnishings with ease. Regardless of the style, the firm is commended for their designs of notable grace, scale and proportion.

A small firm, Interiors II is known for being quiet and discrete. Clients include world-class art dealers, entrepreneurs and businessmen with an eye for the finest. While maintaining the highest standards and usually working with good-sized budgets, the firm has a variety of sources to offer economic choices.

"They are great listeners and most accommodating." "Colors, and particularly wall coloration and finishes, are a specialty." "Barbara adds joy, warmth and interest with delicate plays of fabrics, wall and floor coverings." "Their interiors are simultaneously comfortable and beautiful and look as if they could have been created over generations."

	Quality	Cost	Value	Recommend?
Jack Waddell Interiors	3.5	3.5	4	4

106 West Madison Street, Suite 25, Chicago, IL 60607
(312) 942 - 1225 www.jackwaddell.com

Updated traditional interior design

Clients say Jack Waddell goes to great lengths to study living patterns and create inviting spaces that not only present an aesthetic beauty, but also serve as a functional and intimate dwelling. Waddell takes pride in his strengths of space planning, layout, furniture design and a good understanding of art history. Clients say this combination of skills proves fruitful in creating sophisticated, yet practical interiors.

Waddell holds a B.F.A from Ball State University and an M.F.A. from the University of Wisconsin. The sole designer of this 20-year-old firm, Waddell follows a methodical seven-step project process that establishes the feasibility of the collaboration, design and budget. The firm charges an hourly rate with standard markups for products and has a strong client base that has sought his services repeatedly, and includes second-generation clients. IFDA.

"A clear sense of style and beauty." "A wonderful ability to marry differing styles together to accommodate our different tastes." "He really knows how to choose colors and fabrics that tie a room together—thank heavens, because we were practically color-blind when it came to that." "Jack offers subtle refinement that is comfortable and does not scream of a decorator's presence." "He really factored our everyday needs and current furnishings into the design plans."

	Quality	Cost	Value	Recommend?
James E. Ruud, Inc.	3	3	4	4.5

1410 North State Parkway, Suite 22B, Chicago, IL 60610
(312) 573 - 1951 www.jeruudinc.com

Traditional comfort with a twist

James Ruud is appreciated for his warm design sensibilities leaning toward traditional, his thoughtful incorporation of clients' interests and his accommodating nature. Ruud's designs are said to be tailored, comfortable and appropriate, often classical with a touch of contemporary whimsy. Clients report that he "rallies the troops" and gets the job done, whether working in a more defined palette of neutral tones or a more colorful integration of pattern and detail.

After majoring in psychology in college, running his own painting and contracting firm, studying interior design and working as a design associate for about eleven years, Ruud established his own firm in 1994. As sole practitioner, Ruud is consistently praised for his dedication to clients and for being a professional as well as a "friend." His client base is centered in Chicago's downtown and near-north suburbs. He also has successfully completed a range of large-scale renovations and is willing to take on just a few rooms.

The firm charges a very low hourly rate and a standard product markup, or can work at straight retail with no hourly rate, depending upon the preference of the client. Living rooms are generally in the $60,000 to $70,000 range, and Ruud is commended by clients for offering suggestions to help keep costs "reasonable" and creating lovely, livable designs. ASID.

"Whenever the general contractor would ask me a question, I would refer him to Jim, who would handle everything." "Months after the renovation, a curtain rod fell down, and Jim had someone there that very same day. He is almost telepathic." "Whatever your budget, Jim will work with you. He will often find excellent reproductions to substitute for antiques." "He is thoughtful about spending money in ways that make a difference." "He is only a phone call away and always gives a yeoman's effort." "I now consider Jim a friend, and it is a great pleasure to recommend him."

Janet McCann Associates, Inc. **3.5 3.5 4.5 4.5**

351 West Hubbard, Suite 103, Chicago, IL 60606
(312) 236 - 8766

Serene, understated, comfortable interior design

Janet McCann is appreciated by clients for her refined yet understated elegance, patient demeanor and excellent space planning. While working with a predominantly neutral palette, she tailors designs to customers' needs. References comment upon her strong communication skills, excellent understanding of clients' lifestyles and accommodating nature.

Most of the firm's projects are in the Chicago area, including Lincoln Park, the Gold Coast and the North Shore. Other projects have included second homes in Colorado, Arizona and Memphis. The firm includes about eight people, with McCann leading most major design decisions. McCann's background is in fine arts. She began her own design firm in 1976, partnered with architect Carl Klimek in 1984 and returned to an independent practice 12 years ago. She is known to work well with architects and builders and will often design custom furniture to meet the clients' needs.

While patrons say that she has "very high-end taste," she offers a variety of more price-conscious choices as well. Living rooms are typically in the $50,000 to $75,000 range, and McCann aims to work within clients' budgets. There is a very low retainer, standard hourly rates (lower for project managers and none for administration) and standard product markups. The firm is willing to do one or two rooms for new clients with long-term potential. Clients consistently speak of her strong professional manner and straightforward business practices. ASID.

"I still love what Janet did for me ten years ago." "While she is not an architect, she could be. She has an extraordinary sense of proportion and scale." "If everyone had the ethics of Janet, the world would be a better place." "She listens to what is being said and also what is not being said." "There is never just one answer with Janet, she always offers a range of choices." "I have been working with Janet for 18 years. If anything ever goes askew, she always fixes it at her own expense, if necessary." "She is always calm, and this balance and serenity translates to her work." "She is at least as interested in making my house perfect for me as I am—and that says it all."

Janet Schirn Design Group 4.5 4.5 4 4.5
401 North Franklin Street, Chicago, IL 60610
(312) 222 - 0017

Exuberant, contextual, high-end interior design

Consistently regarded as one of the finest designers and an industry-standard bearer in Chicago, Janet Schirn uses contextual references and client preferences to set the mood in her diverse portfolio. Known for her bold colors, dramatic use of light and strong professionalism, Schirn develops interiors that have a well-defined and educated point of view. Stylistically, the interiors range from Greco-Roman neoclassicism to Art Deco modernism to updated federalism, but all include integrated historical references, appointed with strong details.

With decades of experience, the firm often focuses on clients' multiple residences and fine art collections. While most projects include living rooms of $200,000 or more, the firm also maintains an enthusiastic group of younger patrons, including the parents of six newborns just last year. Half of the work is residential and half is commercial. Notable recent clients have included the Adler Planetarium, Holly Hunt LTD, Goodyear Tire & Rubber, Tootsie Roll Industries and McDonalds Corp. With six people in the firm, Schirn is the primary client contact and is focused on all major design decisions.

The firm charges a substantial reimbursable retainer, standard product markups and a range of hourly design fees depending upon seniority (from very low to high). There are no fees for administration. Schirn also manages JS Collections, a fine arts consultation and acquisitions firm serving corporations and individuals. Professional distinctions include past national presidency of the ASID and the former national treasurer of FIDER. Schirn's name is passed with conviction among friends and relatives. ASID.

"She sets really incredible standards." "I am always so impressed at how hard she works." "She is as much a student of human behavior as she is of design." "I would trust her to properly design and execute to the highest level, while adding a twist of the here and now." "She brings in her jobs to the penny." "Janet's prices are high, but she is able to do the same work in one hour that takes another designer ten hours to complete." "She wants the very best quality for her clients. This is wonderful when she is overseeing the painter, but can be tricky when budgeting for a sofa." "When my neighbor saw Janet's work, she hired her on the spot."

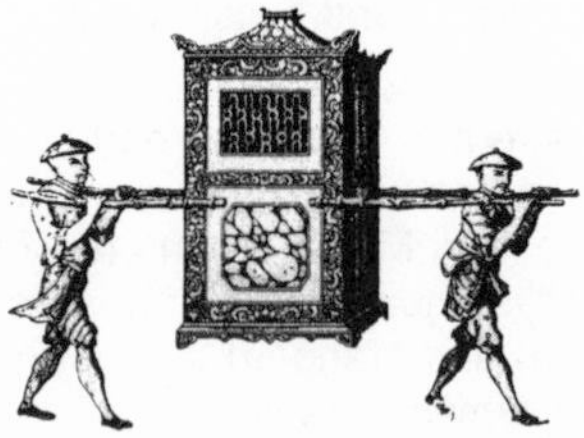

Jean Alan 3 3 4.5 4.5
2134 North Damen Avenue, Chicago, IL 60647
(773) 278 - 2345 www.jeanalanchicago.com

Sophisticated, yet off-beat interior design

Jean and Ruthie Alan are respected for their ability to balance comfortable livability and forward-edged, contemporary design. The mother-and-daughter team is adept at creating eclectic and unique settings that can combine the best of the mid-20th century, Art Deco, Asian and Italian styles. Connecting particularly well with creative-minded clients, this team will work on just a few custom pillows, a few pieces of vintage furniture or a whole house.

The duo's breadth of skills and flair for the dramatic is rooted in Jean's 20 years of experience in motion picture set decoration, including set work for The Blues Brothers, and Ruthie's degree in art and masters in business communications. The firm began in 1994 and has remained a boutique, taking on just a handful of new projects each year. While most of their projects are residential, commercial projects include work on the 404 Wine Bar and the women's clothing store, Ikram.

The firm charges a reasonable retainer based on the scope of work, standard hourly rates (administration included) and a standard product markup on all third-party products. Living rooms typically are in the $50,000 range for a full design. The team generally shuns mass-produced goods and reportedly searches "the ends of the earth" for interesting, lesser-priced, vintage alternatives. An excellent array of these possibilities are showcased in the firm's retail showroom. The Alans are said to be budget sensitive, flexible and expert at managing clients' design expectations. Clients remain very loyal, remarking that the designers always rise to the next challenge.

"I thought that I just wanted to buy one chair, but it was so much fun that I ended up re-doing the entire apartment." "My bedroom of chartreuse silk, accented with raspberry, makes me smile every time I see it." "I cannot imagine buying anything without Jean." "They use color in an artistic dimension to bring life to their works." "They quickly became the liaison/GC between the architects, engineers, building contractor and the city zoners—we were so appreciative." "Jean remains so hip and entertaining, she will always be on the leading edge with quite a following."

Jessica Lagrange Interiors LLC **4 4 4 5**

605 North Michigan Avenue, Suite 301, Chicago, IL 60611
(312) 751 - 8727

Updated traditional with flair and grace

Jessica Lagrange is hailed for her young and vibrant designs with traditional underpinnings, professional design experience and charming demeanor. References credit Lagrange for leading the design process in a collaborative, supportive and pleasurable manner. Noted for her skills with color, textures and modern lines, Lagrange is highly recommended for an integrated and balanced approach to comfortable and current design.

Lagrange worked at the renowned commercial architecture firm, Skidmore, Owings & Merrill, for several years, and then with Powell/Kleinschmidt. After working with summa architect-husband Lucien Lagrange for 15 years, heading up their interiors department, Ms. Lagrange established her own firm in 1999. A boutique firm with structural backbone, clients reportedly receive excellent attention and detailed budget updates. Many of the clients are younger with an appreciation of Lagrange's modern twist and developers who recognize the strong back office. Recent residential projects include a complete 8,000 square-foot Park Tower makeover and a substantial Winnetka renovation.

The firm charges low product markups and either an up front design fee or hourly rates. Living rooms are in the $75,000 to $125,000 range, with most projects of a substantial size.

"Jessica is an absolute joy to work with." "Not only is Jessica an excellent and thoughtful designer, but it is like working with a friend." "Her attention to detail is wonderful—we used four different shades of white to create depth." "Jessica would never box you into a particular decision, but does maintain very high quality standards." "As a mother herself, Jessica inherently understands the family-orientation of my household and all that implies for the design concept." "Everyone comments on the amazing color of ochre she picked for the front hall." "She has terrific taste and the good judgement to know that the apartment should look as if I did it myself." "Jessica works with style and grace."

	Quality	Cost	Value	Recommend?
John Robert Wiltgen Design, Inc.	3	4	4	4.5

70 West Hubbard, Suite 205, Chicago, IL 60610
(312) 744 - 1151 www.jrwdesign.com

Unique, dramatic, innovative interior design

Drama, color and flair set John Robert Wiltgen apart. Noted by many as avant garde, his designs are simultaneously reminiscent of the classical past. He is particularly expert at designing interior spaces and is known as "the loft king." His own loft is filled with ancient Greek pottery and Egyptian antiquities—limestone and hieroglyphs are everywhere. Bathrooms are yet another specialty. Clients report that each project has its own unique, quirky, unexpected design elements.

In over 20 years, John Robert Wiltgen has completed more than 350 projects throughout North America. He started his own firm at age 18, and, at 22, redesigned the model apartment of a condo complex that then sold out three months later, with 18 of the owners becoming clients. The firm takes pride in integrating the lines of architecture, art collection and design. There are ten people at the firm, including three project managers. The back office is said to be very professional. While all the work is residentially related, about half is directly for builders.

The firm takes a retainer, charges a high hourly rate for upfront design and retail on product, but no hourly fee on product. A typical living room is usually about $100,000, but can go much higher. There is a strong emphasis on customer service, with Wiltgen absorbing costs to get the subcontractors to rework a situation "to perfection." Many customers have done multiple projects with the firm, with Wiltgen becoming the source of all knowledge for some families who cannot seem to choose a pair of shoes or a new cereal without a consultation.

"John dares to be different, encouraging his clients to 'be brave' in their design decisions." "While always professional, John does not allow himself or his clients to take decorating too seriously." "No matter how ugly they may be, John accommodates family heirlooms." "He is passionate about his work and works seven days a week." "John is capable of working within budgets and is very generous, but he has demanding and expensive instincts." "He can be outrageous and daring and still be in good taste." "He insists on having lunch with you in your kitchen to better understand how you use the space." "John has fulfilled my design fantasy." "While we fell in love with John, he can be very opinionated." "Absolutely no regrets at all and we love his Halloween parties."

L Design	4.5	4	5	5

333 WN Avenue, PMB 385, Chicago, IL 60610
(312) 440 - 9363

Modern-edged, refined interior design

Doug Levine is thought by all to stand among the designers of greatest creativity, commitment and promise currently gracing the Chicago area. Pressing the design envelope, he reconfigures traditional silhouettes, incorporating them into clean, modern backgrounds in a manner which is described as nothing short of high-concept interior artistry. Levine is known to go to all lengths to offer a full breadth of products for his clients, often creating unique correlating fixtures, such as hand-made tiles, fireplace hearths and bronze, sculpted utensils.

Levine majored in art and design and was the design director for Holly Hunt for eight years, where he introduced the Christian Liege line to the United States. His firm, established in 1999, is a small boutique without an ounce of pretension. Levine, in fact, prefers to return phone calls from a seat in a café rather than from his office. Freelancers are used regularly to enhance and introduce continuing design waves. He currently is developing a high-end contract collection for Bright as well as doing about eight significant residential homes a year. Patrons say that Levine is particularly connected to the city pace, selectively working with those who share his passion for forward-thinking design.

The firm charges a non-refundable up-front design fee, standard product fees and standard hourly rates. Levine is just as happy developing a $100,000 studio apartment renovation as a multi-million-dollar Lincoln Park residence. His office is scrupulous about listing all net product prices in every bill. Supporters say he is ingenious in judiciously spending money to get the most design for the budget.

"He is the heart and soul of the next generation of design in Chicago." "Doug clearly has a gift and verve for design." "He is only capable of doing things one way—the right way." "He is a meticulous craftsman reconstructed for the modern age." "Over 300 pages of designs were drawn for my modern-edged home." "While I have seen some other clients' work that I thought was a bit funky, our project was perfectly polished." "My furnishings are luxurious, but not pretentious or overly dramatic." "You give him a budget and he dreams the dream and makes it work."

La Maison Custom Interiors, Inc. **3.5 3.5 4 4**
1230 North Western Avenue, Lake Forest, IL 60045
(847) 482 - 9705

Continentally-hued interior design

Clients say Renee Le Millier Young's French heritage brings a refined cultivated sense of style to her work. With this Continental viewpoint, Young has helped clients achieve a comfortable, yet luxurious and "uniquely un-midwestern" style. Clients tell us Young has an excellent eye and a strong commitment to developing the very best designs.

Young, a native Parisian, is said to have specific standards for design, and in turn, expects clients to provide budgets that will support custom furnishings and sources well beyond the Mart. Young devotes full attention to her projects and clients say she is easily accessible and always returns phone calls promptly. ASID.

"Renee really cares from her heart about the project and your home." "An amazing sense of style." "She works within budget, though it is high to begin with." "She creates homes that are well beyond what my neighbors would dream of." "Any glitches are dealt with swiftly and with great care." "Renee really elevated our design sensibilities and our lifestyle."

Larson Associates **4 4 4 4.5**
542 South Dearborn, Suite 610, Chicago, IL 60605
(312) 786 - 2255

Classic contemporary architecture and interior design

With a combination of architectural training and an eye for design, George Larson is said to integrate spacial sensitivity and stylistic flair into his designs. While Larson is adept at many architectural styles, he is best known for a classic contemporary look. Larson is also noted for his skills with glass and steel, furniture design and his productive European shopping excursions. The firm usually does both the architecture and interior design work on its projects.

Larson created his firm more than 25 years ago, after leaving Skidmore, Owings & Merrill, working initially with large commercial entities, including Sara Lee, GM and United Airlines. Eight years ago, he refocused the firm, switching its emphasis to residential projects. Since then, numerous houses have been built from the ground up in Chicago, and certain world-wide projects have been completed including a 175-foot yacht in Amsterdam. The staff now numbers eight, most with extensive training in architecture and interior design. Larson's furniture line, The George Larson Collection, is available at Holly Hunt.

We understand that Larson believes in providing one-stop service that includes furnishings and also takes great pride in delivering personalized service. Many clients insist, however, that his core strength is in architectural design. We also hear that working with Larson is a pleasure, and both his demeanor and professionalism are widely praised.

Leslie Jones, Inc. **5** **5** **4** **4.5**

754 North Milwaukee Avenue, Chicago, IL 60622
(312) 455 - 1147

Refined, tailored, yet inspired interior design

Leslie Jones is heralded as one of Chicago's top designers by clients and peers alike. Expertly blending clean architectural lines, classical furnishings and play of textural patterns and cultures, Jones creates a refined balance and a "delight for the senses." With a respect for both the modern and the traditional, Jones is said to work toward the highest quality, creating designs of integrated flow and clear reserve.

Jones's pedigree is made up of a Who's Who in Chicago interior design. With degrees in art history and interior design, work at a commercial firm was followed by experience with Himmel, Bonner and Bruce Gregga. The firm was established in 1993 and currently has nine employees, including several strong project managers. Jones works collaboratively with her team, completing about 10 to 12 projects each year. Most of the Chicago commissions are on the Gold Coast and in Lincoln Park, with several on the North Shore. Many patrons have serious art collections, while others are intent upon building one. All laud Jones for her refined design sensibility, professionalism and specific direction.

Jones shops way beyond the Mart, finding unique sources throughout the world. She is said to be particularly knowledgeable about contemporary art, but also loves contextual textiles: historic Indonesian skirts, Amish quilts, Indian saris, ancient Peruvian cloths and Oriental rugs. Living rooms are generally in the $125,000 to $300,000+ range. Detailed line-item budgets are prepared up front and updated regularly. The firm charges standard product markups and lower hourly rates (no fee for administration). Jones economically encourages her clients to share in her passion for the highest quality furnishings including exceptional collections. Customers are often lifetime subscribers, with Jones's skills passed from one family member to the next. ASID.

"Leslie is the captain of our design ship." "She took my fairly normal contemporary-style house and transformed it with discretion and clarity." "No one questions her design brilliance, but this focus tends to come in waves." "With defined touches, museum-quality fabrics and extraordinary woodwork, Leslie constructed a crystallized, yet comfortable setting." "She is always reachable, but she is not exactly sitting at my doorstep." "They did everything, including the sheets and candles." "Leslie offers the here and now." "Leslie inherently understands what is appropriate for our interests and our lifestyle, and offers the absolute best available."

Lovell Fridstein Ltd. **5** **5** **4** **4.5**

225 West Ohio Street, Chicago, IL 60610
(312) 595 - 1980 www.LFltd.net

Graceful, gallant, yet approachable interiors grounded in tradition

Clients and peers alike applaud Suzanne Lovell's design skills—she is known for creating rooms of unassuming beauty and spirited elegance. Most projects are classically based with a more modern, creative twist. Supporters embrace Lovell's passion for design and her articulation of a historic tradition warmed by the finest materials and textures. With a specific point of view, Lovell and her new partner, Darlene Fridstein, are said to follow a timeless, yet forward-thinking course.

Lovell has a Bachelor of Architecture degree and worked at the famed architecture house, Skidmore, Owings & Merrill, for six years before starting her own firm in 1986. Fridstein joined Lovell after eight years with Hardy Holzman Pfeiffer, leaving as director of the interiors group. The firm is quite large with 18 employees and an associated architect, and reportedly run as a "tight ship" with an excellent staff and regular, accurate budget updates. Projects range considerably from the office of a celebrated Chicagoan to a Lake Shore Drive transformation, to phased projects for younger clientele. Recently diversifying, Lovell launched an artistically transitional collection of furniture premiering in the NY Bergamo showroom.

The firm works with a standard up-front retainer, very high to standard hourly rates (depending on seniority) and a standard product markup (with hourly consulting fees for antiques purchased at auction). Living rooms are generally in the $100,000 to $150,000+ area. Clients report that the firm is quite expensive, but often come back for their second, third and fourth residence with great expectations. ASID.

"Suzanne has followed a calling into interior design. Her designs are extraordinarily and uniquely beautiful." "While I truly admire Suzanne's work, I do find it annoying when her assistant returns my calls." "You can tell that Suzanne grew up with a family of historians and is classically influenced by her years of exposure to Winterthur." "They have the highest expectations of themselves, the subs, their clients and the final product. While some probably cannot appreciate this exacting methodology, I could not be satisfied any other way." "They are to be admired for their good business sense as well as their exceptional design sense." "Suzanne takes common rooms and turns them into celebrations of design."

Lynn R. Hummer Interiors, ASID **4 4 4 4.5**
30 East Huron Street, Suite 1009, Chicago, IL 60611
(312) 943 - 2011

Traditional, high-end interior design

Mario Aranda **4 3 4.5 4.5**
1252 North Milwaukee Avenue, Chicago, IL 60622
(773) 782 - 9643

Eclectic, sensual, modern interior design

Mario Aranda is celebrated for his passion and knowledge of eclectic design, his strong spatial capabilities and his delightful demeanor. As the designer of Ikram, Chicago's acclaimed fashion boutique, Aranda has solidified his position among the city's most intriguing and resourceful interior artists. Aranda's "out of the box" thinking has won over clients who report that he can also do the more traditional, but never boring. Often classical European furnishings are set against flourishes of Asian inspiration.

As a small design firm, Aranda offers a personalized touch and is said to be very accessible and reachable at all times. Clients remark that he "sees the beauty and possibilities" in all design elements, and creatively restores their current furnishings into the new design plans. The firm was established in 1996, after Aranda worked at Skidmore, Owings & Merrill in Urban Planning and an architectural firm in Malaysia. There are a limited number of commissions taken a year, recently including extensive renovations in the Chicago suburbs, modernistic apartments in Lincoln Park and new wave in Miami. Many of Chicago's very top designers shop at Aranda's retail shop, Cielo Vivo, for Asian antiques and furnishings.

The firm charges a low retainer, very low product markups and a standard hourly rate. References laud the firm for offering a wide range of stylistic and economic choices.

"Mario is not content to use anything ordinary. In my bathroom, he used antique tiles and an old copper industrial funnel for the sink. We are thrilled with the result." "He takes budgets very seriously and understands that I am not a bottomless pit of financial resource." "He holds your hand through the process." "By slightly bumping out a wall, he created a completely new playroom for the children." "He is able to do whatever the client asks of him, making the design your own." "His skills in combination with his great sense of humor make the process fun."

Marshall Watson Interiors 4 3.5 5 5

105 West 72nd Street, New York, NY 10023
(212) 595 - 5995

Classical interior design with a twist

Marshall Watson has a strong group of clients who are fans of him and his work. His interiors are appreciated by clients for their classically elegant bones based on historical reference, with a hint of surprise. He often employs soft flowing fabrics, stately, yet comfortable seating areas and a welcoming palette of warm colors. Customers say he is a very engaging man who tries to please them by matching his designs to their lifestyles and interests. Younger clients on a budget, as well as more established patrons with very substantial projects, give the firm high marks.

Watson originally studied design at Stanford University and currently has his own line of furniture which is produced by Lewis Mittman. Resources applaud him for his dedicated philanthropy work, particularly in the area of the design arts.

The firm is based in New York, and many of Watson's clients are in Manhattan and Chicago, with others in the Hamptons, Nantucket, St. Louis, London and Spain. While certain clients suggest that Watson's follow-up could be a bit better, most find him highly effective. They consistently report that Watson is fair, honorable and helpful until the end. His up-front design fee and product and oversight fees are very reasonable, and he finds unusual and interesting pieces to fit a budget. The firm is highly recommended, noted for the beauty and comfort of each design.

"He has the warmth of a Midwesterner and the sophisticated design sensibility of a New Yorker." "He quickly understood what we wanted and became part of our family." "He designs for the real world, not for Architectural Digest photo shoots. There is good reading light near every sofa." "Many a Goldman partner has commented that we have the most stunning dining room they have ever seen." "Despite the fact that his home base is in New York, I found him remarkably accessible for my Chicago renovation." "He delivers great quality without killing you on the budget." "He listened well and delivered. A+."

Mary Rubino Interiors 3.5 3.5 4.5 4.5

620 Judson Avenue, Suite 3, Evanston, IL 60202
(847) 424 - 0432 www.maryrubino.com

High-end interior design

Clients are consistently impressed with Mary Rubino's calm yet glamourous take on soft modern design and her professional abilities. Rooms will often include streamlined Italian furniture or early 20th-century American in bold colors, with witty accents. She is said to translate the personalities of clients into the design plans, with an aim to create comfortable and practical living spaces.

Rubino received a bachelor's degree in psychology and economics from Brown, and a master's in social anthropology from the University of Chicago. She also studied design for two years in Italy, and continues to attend the Milan Fair annually. She began the firm in 1997, and tends to work with bachelor entrepreneurs or young married couples in their 30s and 40s looking for a design statement. Projects have included condos and homes in Chicago's Gold Coast, Streeterville, River North Printers' Row, Evanston and Highland Park. This sole practitioner wins accolades for her accommodating nature and availability.

Rubino generally works with a low up-front design fee and retail on products. Clients report that she will often present several various-priced schemes per room, allowing the homeowner to control the budget. Friends pass on Rubino's name with confidence.

"Mary is great about doing research and will look to the ends of the earth to find the perfect piece." "She is very good about listening to the client, but also has lots of helpful recommendations." "She is the type of person you become friends with because you trust her." "She is well connected to the design world and gets good deals." "When it looked like 'real' artwork was out of the budget, she found some really great old photographs." "While we started with a plan to do just two rooms, it was so much fun that we did the whole apartment." "I actually hired Mary to add spice to my fairly boring apartment, with the thought of attracting a potential wife, and it worked!"

Maxine Snider, Inc.	**4.5**	**4**	**4.5**	**5**

116 West Illinois, Suite 7E, Chicago, IL 60610
(312) 527 - 4170

Elegant, restrained, thoughtful transitional interior design

Maxine Snider is greatly admired and acknowledged for her award-winning Paris Series furniture collection, and is equally lauded by clients for her interior design capabilities. With great editing skills, Snider seeks and highlights the shared elements of various providences and periods, creating a stylistic interplay that "sings." She unifies minimalist furnishings, fine antiques and strong architectural details with complementary tonal colors, proportions and textures to create a balance of restrained harmony. References say that Snider works quite collaboratively and diligently throughout the process.

An interior designer for 25 years, first on the commercial side (the Saudi Arabian government, First of Chicago's executive offices) and for the last twelve years in residential, Snider impresses patrons with her breadth of knowledge and experience. The interior design side of the operation is small, with Snider as the primary client contact. About three large-scale projects are completed each year. She is said to be a great communicator, keeping clients apprised along the way.

The firm asks for a small up-front retainer, standard new product markups and higher hourly rate (lower for staff). Patrons say she is quite gracious when shopping for antiques, encouraging clients with economic breakpoints to attain the best. Living rooms are in the $150,000 range, which typically includes a fair percentage of fine furniture with a good patina. Clients adamantly recommend Snider without reservation, feeling fortunate to have found her. HB Top Designers, 1999, 2000, Chicago Athenaeum Distinguished Design Award for Paris Series.

"Working with Maxine is a dream. She is extremely creative and a great listener." "She creates rooms of timeless serenity." " It was a team effort—she did not overrule me, but also expressed her opinion with ease." "We used lots of antiques, but kept to the budget." "I so enjoyed the process—she is highly sophisticated, intellectual and worldly." "Maxine has a perseverance for perfection." "The interiors are so much about our lifestyle, that friends assume we did not use a designer, and think we are geniuses."

McNutt & Dennen
1400 North State Parkway, Chicago, IL 60622
(312) 397 - 9400

Refined, high-end, suburban interior design

Michael La Rocca **5** **4.5** **4.5** **4.5**
150 East 58th Street, Suite 3510, New York, NY 10155
(212) 755 - 5558

Opulent, fresh, elegant interior design

Michael La Rocca has one of the finest reputations in the business for his classic design sensibility, exquisite quality products and strong client service. Typically beginning with a classical framework, La Rocca mixes time periods and provenance, creating rooms with personality, character and wit. Designs usually include high-quality woodwork, Regency details and a symmetrical overlay. Clients say his vast experience allows him to make the "absolute most" of their rooms, often transforming the fundamental disposition of the spaces themselves. It is said that his interiors are very "balanced," creating highly livable environments with "serenity."

After 13 years as David Easton's partner, La Rocca has been on his own for about 12 years. He focuses on just a few very well-heeled clients each year, mostly in the New York and Chicago areas. Patrons say that he listens well, is quite accessible even for out-of-town projects and delivers a complete package. Patrons also comment on the strong back office.

The firm charges a standard up-front design fee, retail on products and workroom and standard oversight fees (but no ongoing hourly design fee). Subcontractors say he is among the most creative and most professional in the industry. Supporters comment on La Rocca's preference for the highest quality products, which are appreciated and considered well worth the cost. KB 1991.

"He is a gentleman and a scholar." "He can always find the perfect solution, even when there may have been a difference of opinion between my husband and myself." "He likes creating magic for his clients." "They develop constant checklists and punch lists, and really fight for their clients." "He is a finisher." "I have worked with Michael for over five years, and we have never had a disagreement." "While they are sensitive to budget, Michael really encourages you to use the best." "It was the most civilized experience you could imagine. Michael was always willing to hop on a plane and he never gets rattled." "A master at scale and proportion." "He makes you feel as if you are the most important person in the world."

Nancy H. Brennan, Inc. **4** **4** **4** **4**
2650 North Lakeview Avenue, Chicago, IL 60614
(773) 248 - 7566

Traditionally elegant interior design

Nancy Brennan is known for her classically traditional interiors warmed with refined details, offering excellent high-quality work of "the old school." Brennan takes her cue from the clients and from the inherent architectural forms, and is one of the few designers working on the Gold Coast and North Shore focusing on "period pure" rooms. Patrons say she considers it her obligation to surround clients with the most interesting and beautiful objects, without being overdone. Her designs are never a copy or a repeat, but are noted for "always being in good taste, the way it is supposed to be."

A graduate of Harrington, Brennan holds an M.F.A. and has both lectured and studied extensively at the Art Institute of Chicago. After working with the acclaimed Meredith Beals and Watson & Boaler, Brennan opened her boutique firm in 1976.

With this depth of experience, she works closely with clients, completing one or two major projects a year. More of the work has been with the renovations of historic suburban homes, usually with established clientele. Since all is done to particular specifications, supporters say this can take a significant amount of time.

Brennan will work on an hourly fee basis with markups or on a product markup in the high to retail range. Living rooms are typically $50,000 to $100,000+, with a good many projects done in stages. Brennan is credited for working with clients' existing furnishings, being sensitive to family "heirlooms" and consistently steering clients in the "right direction."

"A fabulous traditionalist, perfectionist and a great resource." "A delightful woman, she listens very well and has an erring eye for the correct." "While she is good at mixing historic period furniture, she is not one to call on for the latest trends or a quick turnaround." "I still absolutely love the living room and dining room she did for me ten years ago." "She knows where to spend the money to get the biggest impact." "Nancy was the only one we considered in the renovation of our private, historic club. She understands the meaning of understated elegance and classical drama, better than anyone."

Nancy Schencker/Visions **3** **2.5** **4.5** **4.5**
2715 Daiquiri Drive, Riverwoods, IL 60015
(847) 444 - 0904

Interior design with verve

Nancy Schencker is appreciated for her dramatic design flair, project coordination skills and ability to work with the client to create a unique result. She is particularity noted for her ability to add character, personality and depth to newly constructed spaces. Whether designing an interior with an abundance of chintz and traditional details or doing a stark, contemporary interior, Schencker is said to work with clients to make a notable design statement.

With an educational background in art and architecture and previous practice as an art dealer, Schencker has a great range of creative ideas to draw upon. A sole proprietor, she began work in the interior design field 20 years ago. As many as 20 active projects are completed a year, virtually all in the near-north suburbs including Riverwoods, Northbrook, Highland Park and Glencoe. Most clients seem to be in their 30s and starting a family or recent empty-nesters in their 60s, and all are looking for design inspiration. References say she is highly dependable and will go to great lengths to keep a project on track.

Schencker is said to be very accommodating about using clients' existing furnishings and has a good range of well-priced sources. Fees are charged on a very low flat-rate basis with all products passed to the client at net price. Living rooms are generally in the $50,000 to $75,000 range, with most product done on a custom run. References highly recommend Schencker for a smooth process and a special result.

"We have used other designers without much success. Nancy really gets the job done." "This is our fourth project with Nancy, and we will use her again." "She will do what it takes. On a rainy day, she will just put on her galoshes and make things happen at the site." "She doesn't make the layman feel ignorant and does not turn up her nose at your budget." "Our architect recommended Nancy after we had a rocky start with someone else, and now she is working with our daughter." "This is her life—she will happily pick up McDonalds for my kids to keep the process moving." "She added warmth and detail to our house, making it truly unique and very different than our neighbors. We love it."

Nate Berkus & Associates **4** **4** **4.5** **5**
311 West Superior Street, Suite 110, Chicago, IL 60610
(312) 632 - 0404

Modernist interior design with warmth and soul

Nate Berkus is recognized as one of the leading new design lights of Chicago. He has established a fresh minimalist style based on a carefully edited mix of antiques and innovative modern elements. While clients describe Berkus as clean, modern and "edgy," they also praise his ability to create environments with warmth and character. Natural surfaces, including limestone, marble, bronze and cashmere, are favored. Patrons say his spaces are always a window to the client's lifestyle and imagination.

Patrons wax effusive about Berkus's engaging personality, obvious love of the design process and knowledge of furnishings. He worked for Leslie Hindman Auctioneers for a few years before starting his own firm in 1994. Clients range from the young and trendy who are designing their first lofts, to the most well-established of the northern suburbs to empty-nesters looking for a whole new city look. Berkus is known to be as enthusiastic and creative in designing a basement as in creating a complete renovation. While spearheading most of the design decisions, he uses a number of experienced project managers to handle day-to-day operations.

The firm charges an up-front deductible retainer, a standard hourly rate and standard product markup. Project managers are billed at lower rates. Clients say that Berkus defines and keeps to the budget. Definite in his stylistic instincts, he works with either the "real thing" or a lower-price-point knock-off, but nothing in between. He searches for pieces in flea markets, old furniture shops and auctions, then covers these finds in rich, "intriguing" fabrics. When he cannot find the perfect furniture piece, he has it fabricated. Berkus's signature style can be seen at Maison, his River North showroom at the address above, which displays pieces found during his frequent forays to Europe and across the States.

"He is delightful and kept me happy throughout the entire process." "Nate was terrific about not offering any products outside our budgetary range." "He and his project manager almost drove the wood flooring guys crazy. They made them keep at it until the stain was just right." "While he has a well-defined opinion, he always works to find the right compromise." "He was so good about incorporating my existing furniture into the plans in a graceful and appropriate manner." "I have recommended him to all my friends."

Noah & Associates
1735 West Fletcher, Chicago, IL 60657
(773) 549 - 1414

High-end interior design

Olafsen Design Group, Ltd. — 4 · 4 · 4 · 4.5
233 East Erie Street, Suite 305, Chicago, IL 60611
(312) 664 - 4738

Refined classicism with a twist

Bill Olafsen is said to enrich his clients' lives with educated and comfortable design choices, an appreciation for the architectural surroundings and an engaging work style. His work is classically based, generously proportioned and dramatically furnished. With training in fine arts and a passion for travel, Olafsen wins accolades for his ability to incorporate clients' interests and collections and for amiably finding excellent design solutions under challenging circumstances.

After working with Bruce Gregga for five years and also collaborating with Elise Schreiber for thirteen years, Olafsen established his own firm in 1998. With just a handful of major projects each year and a relatively small, but able, support staff, this firm is said to give clients a lot of attention. Patrons are generally among the more established, with relatively large projects, and say they feel free to call Olafsen night or day. Living rooms typically range from $75,000 to $200,000 or more. The firm's younger clients tend to have a strong interest in design and a proclivity for developing an artistic collection. Olafsen has successfully worked on many houses from the ground up, where clients and architects commend Olafsen for his insights and contributions.

The firm generally charges a fixed design fee, based on the scope of the project, plus a high product markup over net. References credit Olafsen for his policy of not charging an hourly rate, saying they are more comfortable when the firm is "not on the clock." Clients are also impressed with the firm's willingness and ability to find sources outside the normal paths, resulting in a range of viable, economic choices. ASID.

"Bill was so tuned into my design aesthetic—and I am not easy to please." "His follow-through was notable and impressive." "He incorporated the soft earthtones of my view of Lake Michigan at sunset into the bedroom." "My husband and I would definitely be divorced by now if we did not have Bill to guide us, calmly, through the renovation of our house." "Bill was so good about reupholstering our existing furnishings and working them into the new design plans." "We were delighted with the process and the result." "We felt that it was a great partnership." "He is so dependable and such a sweetheart."

Pauline Laner Interiors 3 3 4 4

1240 North Lake Shore, Chicago, IL 60610
(312) 440 - 1550

Versatile, client-oriented interior design

Insiders tell us Pauline Laner takes an ultra-personal approach to dealing with clients—she encourages their ideas, welcomes them on all shopping excursions and incorporates the client as an integral part of the decorating process. We understand that Laner enjoys working with clients who have an opinion about interior design and who seek to be involved in the project. She is comfortable working in nearly any period of décor, doing anything from traditional to modern while striving to keep her spaces uncluttered.

Laner is the sole practitioner of this firm that has primarily served a well-established clientele on the North Shore for nearly 30 years. We understand that she limits the practice to several projects or less each year in order to preserve her highly personalized service.

Some clients have hired Laner continually for 30 years, and now she is working on the houses of their children. Because of Laner's highly accommodating and amiable philosophy, clients tend to become friends. A typical living room is in the $50,000 range and Laner works on a retainer, a standard markup on products with no hourly rate for product purchases. ASID.

Powell/Kleinschmidt Inc.

645 North Michigan Avenue, Suite 810, Chicago, IL 60611
(312) 642 - 450 www.powellkleinschmidt.com

Modern high-end interior architecture and design

See Powell/Kleinschmidt's full report under the heading Architects

Quality	Cost	Value	Recommend?
	+	$	◆	★

Richar Interiors, Inc. 4.5 4.5 4 4.5
1244 North Wells, Chicago, IL 60610
(312) 951 - 0924

Sumptuous, dramatic high-end interior design

Richar is well known for his sumptuous, dramatic take on gutsy, modern design. Clients appreciate his love of rich color and transitional dynamic with a twist. Often included in the plans are unique sculptures, leather furniture, glass accents and antiquities. He is noted to have a particular sensitivity to art, subduing the interiors to complement these works. While Richar has a favored look of his own, he develops his plans with clients to achieve their ideal.

A French-Canadian, Richar established his firm in 1983, following associations with interior design firms in Columbus, Palm Springs and with Bruce Gregga. Maintaining a boutique atmosphere, Richar is applauded for the attention he lavishes upon clients, often accompanying them on shopping adventures. The firm delivers fully furnished and integrated environments, including full audio-video systems, linens and even toothbrushes.

The firm usually works on full renovations, with a typical living room costing in the $100,000+ range for interior design. A non-reimbursable design fee is charged upfront, and there are standard markups on products, plus hourly fees only for drafting or non-product consultations. Furnishings tend to be of the highest quality with corresponding costs, but the firm can work within tighter constraints for weekend homes. Many clients become lifetime fans. IIDA.

"While some may say that my apartment is a bit rich, I feel engulfed and embraced by its warmth." "Richar was very efficient and timely." "If any pieces were too expensive, I just vetoed them." "He makes it fun and easy and has no decorator attitude." "He went through volumes of books with me to be sure he understood just what I wanted." "I like chintz and gilt and my husband is a meat-and-potatoes kind of guy. Richar made us both happy." "Like magic, the installation was conducted while we were away. The experience was delightful, exquisite and satisfying." "Visitors' jaws drop in admiration and amazement."

Robyn Shapiro Design, Inc. 4 3.5 4.5 5
220 West Kinzie Street, 5th Floor, Chicago, IL 60610
(312) 396 - 0400

Architecturally-inspired interior design with heart

Admired for her intellectual design integrity, organizational talents and warmth, Robyn Shapiro is thought to be a wonderful secret source by clients. With a strong preference for tailored, modern silhouettes and natural materials, she generally works in a restrained traditional genre incorporating furnishings "with character." It is said that Shapiro appreciates the traditional, with updated resolution. Customers also say that Shapiro focuses on all the details, has a wealth of expertise and enjoys "making people happy."

Trained and licensed as an architect, Shapiro worked in Bruce Gregga's firm for eight years and opened her own interior design firm in 1996. As the head of a boutique firm, she works closely with clients and takes on about three to four major projects a year. Reportedly, she has also had great success with smaller projects, working in stages as these clients' budgets allow. She acts as the architect on some of her commissions and with outside architects for more structural renovations or new homes.

The firm charges a lower hourly rate, a standard markup on products and very low markups on workroom items. After the furniture plan, budgets tend to evolve, but clients say that Shapiro is very flexible and resourceful. Typical living rooms are in the $50,000 to $75,000 range. Shapiro is often hired repeatedly, especially by supporters upgrading their homes a phase at a time.

"Four years later, and everything is still perfect." "She came, she fixed up someone else's mess and she left us with the most beautiful design." "Robyn's real strength is in her architectural training—she is amazingly organized." "She works within a budget without any hitches." "She will badger the subs to perform to her high standards." "She simplifies and enriches." "While you would expect her architectural details to be excellent, her eye for color and paint finishes are fabulous, too." "Robyn is an unrecognized treasure." "I trust her completely."

Sandra Saltzman Interiors 4 4 4 5

1430 North Astor Street, Chicago, IL 60610
(312) 642 - 8381

Bridging modern and classical interior design

Sandra Saltzman is applauded for integrating the classical nobility of historical reference into a modern expression of time and place. With a design sensibility rooted in the intellectual pursuit of evolving stylistic attitudes, Saltzman seamlessly embraces the inherent architectural elements, softened with the comforts of home. Interiors are often said to balance an old-world aesthetic, high-quality art collection and contemporary textures and materials.

With an education in anthropology, archaeology, fine arts and business, plus years of training with Robert Barrett, Solomon and Bruce Gregga, Saltzman is well suited for her wide array of clients. Recent projects range from substantial residential renovations on the Gold Coast to innovative new homes on the North Shore to commercial work. About one-third of the commissions are outside Chicago, including the Hamptons, LA, San Francisco, Florida and Europe. A one-woman show, Saltzman is fully involved with clients, who feel they learn from the process and are impressed by her efficiency and time management.

Saltzman charges standard product markups and standard hourly fees (no administrative fees). Patrons say Saltzman is very disciplined with budgets and offers economic choices. Also, she is noted for working well with architects and contractors and for managing subcontractors effectively.

"She is a wonderful listener with great intuition, really incorporating our lifestyle patterns into the design." "She is very sensitive and accommodating and did an amazing job of completing a gut renovation around my cats!" "Sandra was very supportive of using my existing family furniture." "By moving doors, Sandra was able to add great flow to the apartment." "She is so professional—everything is taken care of with no worries." "She integrated a rather random art collection into the apartment with a clever use of coordinating paint colors." "Sandra's personal mission is to enrich her clients' lives."

Scott Himmel Architects 4.5 4.5 4 4.5

360 North Michigan Avenue, Suite 1100, Chicago, IL 60601
(312) 332 - 3323

Updated, classical, luxurious interior design

With wide-ranging design and architectural abilities, Scott Himmel is lauded by references for designs with continuity, radiance and joie de vivre. While much of the work is modern 20th century, all of it is rooted in Himmel's classical, historical training. Because Himmel is a licensed architect, clients are highly confident that Himmel will get all the design details just right, and they often turn to him for structural advice. Others add that Himmel becomes their design advocate, encouraging them to fulfill their interior design vision and objectives.

Himmel and Darcy Bonner were partners for 15 years. In 1994, Himmel sold his share of Mattaliano furniture to Bonner and established his own firm. There are about twenty people in the company, including nine architects and nine designers. While the firm occasionally does just a few rooms for new clients, most of its projects are much more involved, with a typical living room at about $150,000 to $250,000. Staying on track and within budgets is very much the norm, especially since completion of the firm's substantial office expansion in 1999.

Himmel charges a standard markup for products and a high hourly rate for design work (none for shopping). On the architecture side, a standard percentage of the construction cost is billed. The firm designs a good deal of the furniture and unique built-ins with "gorgeous" details. While Himmel has well-defined and premium-cost design sensibilities, he is also said to offer two or three solutions to every situation.

"While Scott is happy to use Room & Board for the kids' rooms, he is very much about exceptional quality and established clientele, with a large, integrated machine to make it work." "I only have excellent things to say." "Scott literally figured out the entire apartment on the first day, in one meeting." "For a few years there, in the late 80's, Himmel got more work than the shop could handle. But now they are very much on course." "My family moved into the apartment last year, the very same day my husband had heart surgery, and no additional stress was caused by the move." "He worked within our budget and always made us feel good." "He stands by everything he does." "Scott is a first-class joy."

Settings, Inc.
725 West University, Arlington Heights, IL 60004
(847) 870 - 1800

High-end interior design

Sherry Koppel/Fine Threads **3.5 3 4.5 5**
1244 North Stone, 2nd Floor, Chicago, IL 60610
(312) 560 - 1978

Bold, exuberant, stylized contemporary interior design

With a strong aptitude and preference for exuberant color, saturated warmth and pizzazz, Sherry Koppel has jumped into the Chicago interior design scene with a splash. She is said to have a strong creative streak, knowing where she wants to take clients and gently leading them in that direction. The designer has a penchant for the mixture of various aesthetics, easily blending 40s French with modern Italian and lively Art Deco.

Koppel has always been drawn to design—first as a painter, then as a high-end costume jewelry designer and most recently as the creator of elegant and elaborate quilts, sold at her store, Fine Threads. Along the way, she completed interior design projects for 10(!) of her own homes and also for the homes of friends, who encouraged her to follow a calling into interiors. She formally began the interior design business three years ago, currently as a sole proprietor, taking on a few extensive projects a year. Most of her clients tend to live in the city and have a "young, downtown attitude," but are of all age groups.

The firm charges a low hourly rate and a very low product markup. All products are considered, from IKEA to the finest modern art. Koppel receives kudos for her extensive range of excellent and unusual sources, particularly craftsmen. She is highly recommended by customers who are delighted by Koppel's "imaginative transformations."

"Sherry invigorated my classic Victorian house with an intriguing combination of mid-century antiques, custom furniture and abundant color." "She thinks and works a thousand miles a minute." "Sherry absolutely stays on top of all the subcontractors, urging them on to perform their best." "While she does not

necessarily have all the technical experience of the trade, Sherry creates the most extraordinary results." "Sherry thinks decorating should be fun, and I wholeheartedly agree." "You would be lucky just to meet her."

Stephanie Wohlner Design
1442 Waverly Road, Highland Park, IL 60035
(847) 432 - 8735
High-end interior design

Studio One Design, ASID
9915 Capitol Drive, Wheeling, IL 60090
(847) 229 - 7000 www.s1d.com
High-end residential interior design

Suhail Design Studio — **3.5** | **3** | **4.5** | **4**
2041 West Carrol Avenue, Chicago, IL 60612
(312) 733 - 9411
Imaginative, thematic interior design

From lights made from plastic shopping bags to recycled plastic bar stools, Suhail is admired by clients for his innovative use of materials, striking visuals and unabounding imagination. Born in Pakistan, raised in London and settled in Chicago, Suhail is probably best known for his work at two of the city's most visually stimulating restaurants, the ultra modernist MOD and the Moroccan throwback Tizi Melloul. Insiders say Suhail firmly believes in creating spaces that are rooted in architecture, and have a distinct philosophy and an overall theme. His style strikes a balance between avante garde and lavish, international modernism.

Suhail is a sole practitioner who started the firm in 1992 after a brief period with Skidmore, Owings & Merrill. His clients tend to be a younger group, with the majority in Chicago, and he recently expanded to the New York City area. We hear Suhail travels extensively to revitalize his creative reservoir of multi-cultural inspiration. Clients report that Suhail thinks first about the concept and design, offering several budget frameworks to fit the vision. Suhail generally charges a flat fee, but is also known to charge an hourly or monthly fee, determined on a project-by-project basis.

Susan Fredman & Associates, Ltd. — **3.5** | **3.5** | **4** | **4**
425 Huehl Road, Unit 6B, Northbrook, IL 60062
(847) 509 - 4121 www.susanfredman.com
Transitional contemporary suffused with natural materials

Praised for her ability to incorporate warm, natural elements and colors in her work, Susan Fredman is also greatly respected for her holistic approach to interior design. Fredman is praised for her use of a unique Westernized approach to Feng Shui, using rich textures and melding traditional and contemporary styles accented by a love of natural materials. Clients say Fredman is evenhanded and works well with the client, sorting out any issues very professionally and quickly. Fredman gives back to the community through her nonprofit organization called Supporting the Spirit Foundation, which donates design services and materials to nonprofits which provide facilities for child care, assisted living and domestic violence survivors.

Fredman leads the team of 21 employees at the firm, which she founded 25 years ago. With fourteen ASID decorators, the firm has a seasoned staff, most of whom have between eight and fifteen years of experience. We are told the firm will never turn a client away because of budget and will take on projects as small as a single window treatment, as long as the quality is high. Approximately two-thirds of the firm's projects are renovations, with the remaining one-third being new homes. Fredman generally works on the North Shore with an established clientele, many of whom are repeat customers.

With more than 100,000 fabric samples, a new furniture line and a recently published book, *At Home With Nature*, insiders say Fredman ably manages a "mini-mart." Fredman and Associates generally works on a flat fee for new construction, standard hourly rates for design and retail product markups. Monthly statements are presented to clients who respect and appreciate the firms diligence and professionalism. ASID.

"Susie is always available despite being incredibly busy." "Often came up with immediate solutions, just walking through the house." "Wonderful, unique resources." "Susie worked with the architect and builder to make sure all the room sizes were appropriate and our existing furniture could be incorporated." "She has a no-nonsense style of getting things accomplished." "Her ability to visualize a room and concept is superior." "She absolutely takes the clients' point of view, taking that to a philosophical and empathetic level, understanding what would make them 'feel good' in their own space."

The Schwebel Company **4** **3.5** **4** **4.5**
311 West Superior Street, Suite 114, Chicago, IL 60610
(312) 280 - 1998

Period-pure house and garden restoration

Todd Haley Design Associates, Inc. **3.5** **3** **4.5** **4**
1512 North Fremont Street, Suite 104, Chicago , IL 60622
(312) 440 - 0855

Sleek, elegant interior design

A practitioner of sleek and elegant minimalism, Todd Haley has developed an innovative style that often includes incorporating unusual accessories in not-so-traditional contexts such as antiques in an industrial setting. The vast majority of the firm's work is residential with a cutting-edge style, mostly for city settings. Clients with older homes in the Lake Forest area also appreciate Haley's approach, offering a modern take in a more traditional venue. Often more neutral colors are given "spice and originality" with a strong mix of textures.

Haley studied at Washington University and is the principal of the firm, which he founded in 1992. Insiders tell us he handles roughly six to eight new projects each year and juggles up to nine projects at any one time. Haley enjoys a number of return customers who have called on his services from Florida and Nevada. We are told that the client relationship is paramount with Haley, who excels at small projects as well as large, especially with clients who share his vision.

Haley charges standard markups on products and works on a retainer and lower hourly rates. He is said to be excellent in working on $25,000 jobs or $350,000 jobs, and very sensitive to budgets, especially for young married couples.

"Todd offers minimalist with kick." "He gracefully took on the role of mediator between me and my husband, and we have very different tastes!" "He started with our bedroom, and is now doing the rest of our house, one room at a time." "Todd is a one-man show, but returns calls promptly." "He takes care of any glitches." "He is always calm and reasonable, finding lovely economic alternatives to match our budget." "Todd is perfect for those who do not feel they need a 'big name', but just quality work."

Tom Stringer, Inc. **4.5** **4.5** **4** **5**
62 West Huron Street, Chicago, IL 60610
(312) 664 - 0644

Modern interpretation of historically classical design

Clients laud Tom Stringer for his refined, classic design sensibilities tinged with a modern hue, his attention to detail and his thoughtfulness. While stylistically adaptive, much of the work is based on his love of historical design elements, including Palladin traditions, proportionate symmetry and fine Federal mahogany antiques placed in clean-swept, harmonizing backgrounds. These interiors are said to be equally compelling for relaxed family gatherings and for the most formal occasions.

Stringer brings a multi-disciplinary approach to each job. He studied architecture and interior design, designed furniture for several well-known manufacturers and was with Branca for several years. His firm was established in 1996, and has offices in Chicago and Los Angeles. Clients applaud the team spirit at the firm, from which no employee has ever departed. Stringer has similarly long-term relationships with clients, many of whom become good friends. The firm's clientele tends to be among the well established, many of whom start with Stringer on their Gold Coast renovation, then ask him to work on the northern Michigan summer retreat. Stringer goes to great lengths to assure client satisfaction, returning calls from planes and training staff members on the art of bed-making and ice-shaving for the bedside tables.

While clients say they are given excellent budget guidelines, the budget tends to evolve as the project progresses, at the client's direction. A typical living room costs from $100,000 to $200,000. There is a reimbursable retainer of about one month's billing, high hourly fees and standard product markup. No hourly fees are charged for administrative processing. References are emphatic in their desire to use Stringer again.

"He transcends style with his classical elements, fitted into more neutral settings." "He is always available and a joy to work with." "Nothing is by accident with Tom." "I like what Tom has done for us more that anything I have ever seen elsewhere." "Tom is amazing. In building our new house, he corrected the architects' drawings and thought of unique possibilities that transformed the space." "He can do French minimalist cowboy and avant-garde classic, both with the highest stylistic elegance." "While he is quite expensive, I would never dream of going ahead without him."

Winnie Levin Interiors Ltd. **3** **3.5** **4** **4**
595 Elm Place, Suite 202, Highland Park, IL 60035
(847) 433 - 7585

Versatile, high-end interior design

Clients appreciate Winnie Levin for her individualistic, transitional designs and accommodating nature. While many of Levin's interiors are based on a balanced mix including contemporary backgrounds, traditional wood furnishings and antiques, others are a more specific style such as Art Deco. Elaborate trim details and gold leaf often factor into the picture.

As the sole designer, Levin has developed a reputation for excellent client rapport, often shopping with customers. About five large projects are underway at any one time, generally on the North Shore, with a near-equal split of new homes and renovation projects. Formerly a professional artist creating oil paintings, Levin transitioned her passion for color to decorating, starting the firm 21 years ago. Levin generally attracts an established clientele, with typical living rooms in the $75,000 to $100,000 range. Budgets are established before the start of the project. Levin has developed standing relationships with her clientele and she will rework rooms for past customers. Many of these repeat clients do second homes with Levin, most in Wisconsin, Palm Beach and Arizona.

Levin charges a one-time design fee and high markups on products, but no hourly rates. Clients say Levin is conscientious of budget, often creating spaces that make the most of the investment. ASID.

"Working with Winnie is like shopping with a good friend." "She's phenomenal and can transform a room." "She is very accommodating and has great alternative sources, well beyond the standard offerings." "She can certainly work within budget and make it elegant while looking far more expensive than it actually is." "Winnie incorporates my design wishes while keeping the project on track." "She found a home for all the old upholstery we wanted to keep." "Winnie is a really good decorator and a really good person as well."

Hiring a Kitchen & Bath Designer

The perfect kitchen won't make you a great cook, and an all-marble bathroom will still need cleaning. But the fact remains that a kitchen or bath remodel can make your life at home enormously more pleasurable on a daily basis. They are often the two rooms that see the most use, and so their planning and construction deserve careful thought. A good kitchen and bath designer will listen attentively to a client's desires and incorporate them into rooms that are as functional as they are beautiful.

Finding a Designer

Some architects, interior designers, space planners and certified remodelers dabble in kitchen and bath design. There are even "designers" who work for manufacturers and home improvements stores. But if your sights are set on a specialist, you'll want to look for a Certified Kitchen Designer/Certified Bath Designer (CKD/CBD). To get certified, the designer needs at least seven years of hands-on experience in addition to coursework, and must pass a series of tests administered by the National Kitchen and Bath Association (NKBA), the field's main professional organization. Even after certification, continuing education will enable a designer to stay abreast of current styles and the latest advances in equipment.

Most designers have either a showroom or portfolio to give you a sense of their particular style. You may think that you are on the same page when you talk on the phone, but when you see the ideas embodied in a room you may find that you have very different ideas of what a word like "contemporary" or "traditional" means. You'll be a giant step closer to getting what you want if you can find a designer whose style is similar to your own. Take a look at your prospective designer's recent work history while you're at it. At the very least, a designer should be able to produce three current references, and a history of two or more projects per month shows a healthy demand for the professional's work.

Finding someone you feel compatible with will make the whole process more pleasant and productive—especially if you see eye-to-eye on budgetary considerations. It will also help alleviate some of the inevitable stress. With the right designer, you'll be able to openly discuss such issues as project cost, time frame for completion, product information and warranty issues. You should feel comfortable asking for advice on the logical and functional placement of appliances, how to make cabinets childproof, lighting alternatives, your storage needs, personal preference for gas or electric stoves, the upkeep involved in tile kitchens vs. stainless steel and other design considerations. Also, do you want to work with the appliances you have or completely replace them? If you want new appliances, the designer may or may not coordinate their purchase. Don't assume that a designer can read your mind and know that you will not—under any circumstances—part with your matching canary yellow refrigerator and stove.

On Cost

There are generally two ways in which designers can charge for their services. The first type of pricing structure is a percentage—about 10 percent—of the project's total cost. This type of fee schedule is common when the designer coordinates the entire project as well as supplies the artistic template. Coordinating the project includes ordering all materials and finding and managing the workers to install everything. This approach is often a good value. It also relieves you of having to find someone else to carry out the project, or of immersing yourself in the hassles of ordering and overseeing.

The second method of pricing is an hourly fee called a pure design fee. Your money buys only the designer's ideas and plans for creating the kitchen or bath of your dreams. The price will depend upon the designer's experience, education and general reputation. Hourly charges range from $65 to $200 or more per hour.

It is imperative to discuss total cost prior to starting the job, of course, so you know what to expect. If you have your heart set on a new kitchen layout that requires new plumbing and electrical work, for example, know that this will be a more expensive renovation than one that involves existing systems. If the cost of such a renovation is more than you'd like to spend, work with the designer to match your dreams with your budget.

Once you've chosen a designer, you'll need a contract to protect both parties. No professional will be offended if you request one. The contract should spell out the services you are expecting and include a timetable for payment. Expect to part with a down payment of 40 to 50 percent to secure a good designer.

Many designers are sole proprietors, which means that the designer may be the only employee of the company. Others are part of a large firm with designers representing a range of specialty areas. Deciding whether or not to use an individual or a firm is a choice that depends upon your own style and the scope of your project: a firm's diverse collection of talent may come in handy if your project is especially complex. Some clients prefer dealing with one person, while others may feel more confident having a number of designers available. If, after speaking to a few of the vendors in this book, designers from both large and small firms interest you, make some comparisons such as their availability to begin work and how long they anticipate it will take to complete it. Their answers may help you narrow your search.

As with any major home project, you'll go through a period of upheaval when everything—including the kitchen sink—gets overhauled. But the result will be worth the trouble, whether your fantasy is to cook dinner for 20 with ease or to sink into a tiled Roman bath.

TREND IDEAS

- **In the bathroom:** When space is at a premium, installing a bathtub may not always be possible. If you can't go without soaking yourself in relaxation, give your stand-up shower the capacity to be a "steam room." All it requires is the plumbing of the steam device, a tiled seat and sealed glass door.
- **In the kitchen:** Use an open cabinet for storing all your everyday dishes and glassware. This will break up the monotony of all-doored cabinets and come in handy when washing dishes—you'll duck beneath open doors less frequently. Placing your everyday dishes in open cabinets may also motivate you to clear out any missmatched pieces and to better organize your frequently used tableware.

KITCHEN & BATH DESIGN

	Quality	Cost	Value	Recommend?
Abruzzo Kitchens	4	4	4	4

1105 Remington Road, Schaumburg, IL 60173
(847) 885 - 0500 www.abruzzokitchens.com

Sales, design and installation—kitchen and bath

Abruzzo Kitchens has been a family run business for 20 years. This company offers one-stop shopping for designing and building kitchens and baths. Serving all of Chicago, Abruzzo carries the finest lines in kitchen and bath appliances, cabinetry and accessories, including Corian countertops, Sub-Zero refrigerators and Wood-Mode and Neff cabinetry. Abruzzo offers design, drafting services and installation.

	Quality	Cost	Value	Recommend?
Aquaworks	4	3	5	5

2308 Main Street, Evanston, IL 60202
(847) 869 - 2111 www.aquaworks.com

Sales, design and installation—kitchen and bath

Clients rave about the wide selection of high quality decorative plumbing fixtures, cabinetry and accessories offered by owners Barry and Annette Carnow of Aquaworks. Complete installation service is second only to the company's first-class customer service, we're told. Prospective customers should not be deceived by the strip mall surroundings. The Aquaworks showroom offers only the finest in cabinetry and hardware. Originally inspired by their own trials when remodeling their home, both Barry and Annette understand the importance of dependable service providers. Aquaworks has recently opened up a second showroom at suite 1326 at the Merchandise Mart.

"I was willing to pay more for the quality of assistance we received and would (and have) strongly recommend Aquaworks to others." "Good service and good relationships. They handle problems promptly." "Pleasant, professional and personal service. They stand behind their product and proactively provide solutions to questions or problems."

	Quality	Cost	Value	Recommend?
Artistic Kitchen Designs Inc.	4	3	4.5	5

1600 16th Street, Oak Brook, IL 60523
(630) 571 - 4567

Sales, design and installation—kitchen and bath

Artistic Kitchen Designs has been covering everything from concept to completion for kitchen and bath clients since 1985. The company has just four employees, all of whom have between 10 to 30 years of experience. There is a certified kitchen designer, accredited by the National Kitchen & Bath Association, on staff who reviews all plans.

Clients say that the price represents a great value for the quality of service provided. Artistic Kitchen Designs charges a standard design retainer of $1,000 at the start of a project, and customers say it's well worth it.

"If everyone who came into my life was as responsible, professional, knowledgeable and good on their word, I would indeed have a 'perfect' life." "We always felt that they really listened to us and that they cared about us."

Quality	Cost	Value	Recommend?
	✚	$	◆	★

Barrington Home Works

3.5 3 4.5 5

102 South Hager Avenue, Barrington, IL 60010
(847) 381 - 9526 www.barringtonhomeworks.com

Design and installation—kitchen, bath and cabinetry

From a snack to a multi-course meal, a quick shower to a luxurious bath, Barrington Home Works has been designing and installing kitchens and baths to meet diverse clients' needs since 1982. Headed by Jim Walker, a certified kitchen designer of the National Kitchen & Bath Association, Barrington Home Works will do as little or as much as clients want in a remodel. Although the company works primarily in the northwest suburbs, it services the entire Chicago area. Clients say Walker is very focused on customer service and always willing to go the extra mile.

We're told the company is capable of working within clients' budgets while still fulfilling their needs in both design and quality of appliances. The company carries a wide selection of cabinetry, appliances, countertops, plumbing fixtures and lighting fixtures.

Bath Resource and Design Center

4 2.5 5 4.5

22 Calendar Street, LaGrange, IL 60525
(708) 354 - 4770

Design and installation—bath

Known to customers and fellow professionals as the "bath man," principal Scott Laing has been in business since 1990. He started out as a plumber and now does complete bathroom remodeling. This company is also the area dealer for an imported line of Italian bath furniture. Most of its work is in the southwest suburbs of Chicago, but Laing is willing to talk with anyone anywhere about a planned bath project.

Half of the company's total business is with trade professionals, such as interior designers and architects, while the other half is with individual homeowners. The company provides free consultation and an estimate, but Laing encourages prospective clients to first visit the company showroom. Clients highly recommend Bath Resource and Design Center and say that Laing and his team communicate well and help clients in selecting the right components for their bathrooms. In short, the "bath man's" reputation is squeaky clean.

"Job done properly—looks great—no hassles." "Great guy, great worker, meticulous to a fault."

Better Kitchens Design Studio Inc.

3.5 3 4.5 4

7640 Milwaukee Avenue, Niles, IL 60714
(847) 967 - 7070 www.betterkitchens.com

Sales, design, installation and cabinetry—kitchen and bath

By most accounts, this company is accurately named. For 45 years, Better Kitchens has been a family run business that offers top-of-the-line cabinetry and appliances for kitchens and bathrooms. It carries both Wood-Mode and Brookhaven cabinetry, which can be seen on display in the company's 1,200-square-foot showroom in Niles. While some clients told us that phone call returns took longer than they would have liked, all agreed that Alan Zielinski and his company are a top-quality, one-stop shopping resource for kitchens and bathrooms.

"The work was really well done." "The kitchen went together as promised on time, on budget, without a hitch."

	Quality	Cost	Value	Recommend?
Bulthaup Chicago	4	3.5	4.5	5

165 West Chicago Avenue, Suite 200, Chicago , IL 60610
(312) 787 - 9982 www.bulthaup.com

Sales, design and installation—kitchen

Bulthaup is a German company that has been in business for 50 years and opened in Chicago in 2000. Each of the five employees in this Chicago showroom has a background in interior decorating and subscribes to the Bulthaup European design philosophy that considers the kitchen the center of the home. In accordance with classic, contemporary European design, Bulthaup's kitchens are clean, sleek and modern in appearance and also, clients attest, functional and practical.

"I have been pleased with the design of my kitchen. It is not only beautiful, but it is also functional." "It was a pleasure working with the kitchen designer at Bulthaup."

	Quality	Cost	Value	Recommend?
Cabinets at Danada Inc.	4	3.5	5	5

245 Rice Lake Square, Wheaton, IL 60187
(630) 260 - 1200 www.cabinetsatdanada.com

Design, installation and cabinetry—kitchen

Clients can count on custom work from this company that has four on-staff carpenters among its personnel. As a result, clients give rave reviews to the company's cabinetry and installation. Glenda Swanson has owned Cabinets at Danada since 1993. Seventy percent of the company's work is devoted to kitchens, but it also does bathrooms. While it operates mainly in Kane and Dupage counties, Cabinets at Danada has done work as far as Wisconsin, Michigan and Minnesota.

Cabinets at Danada has a showroom that customers say is a great place to review ideas when considering a kitchen remodeling. The company offers the Wood-Mode line of cabinetry among others.

"Glenda Swanson is a great and imaginative designer with a terrific flair for what will work and what won't, while listening to exactly what we told her our needs were." "We were pleased with customer service, product quality and commitment to the job, including carpentry expertise."

	Quality	Cost	Value	Recommend?
CabinetWerks, Ltd.	4	3.5	4.5	4.5

185 Milwaukee Avenue, Lincolnshire, IL 60069
(847) 821 - 9421 www.cabinetwerks.com

Sales, design, installation and custom cabinetry—kitchen and bath

CabinetWerks works from concept through final installation. It is a full-service custom cabinet company that operates along Chicago's North Shore and in the Barrington area. It has the staff and the know-how to manage every aspect of kitchen and bath remodels. The staff is headed by Dave Heigl, a certified kitchen designer, and a member of the National Kitchen & Bath Association. Clients tell us he is dedicated to providing reliable and friendly service and many decorators are devoted customers.

The showroom displays a selection of high-end cabinetry, ranging from Wood-Mode, Brookhaven, Neff and its own custom cabinetry. CabinetWerks has won numerous awards and its work has been published in the *Chicago Tribune*, *North Shore Magazine* and *Woman's Day*.

"This company only hires employees that are dedicated to their work." "They came up with ideas that no one else bidding on our kitchen remodel came up with." "They keep a close eye on manufacturing quality and act quickly on any concerns."

	Quality	Cost	Value	Recommend?
Cambium	4.5	4	5	5

113-119 West Hubbard, Chicago, IL 60610
(312) 832 - 9920 www.cambiumhome.com

Design, installation and cabinetry—kitchen

This is the place for those who don't want a cookie-cutter kitchen. Clients call Cambium a "must" among those who are looking for something out of the ordinary in kitchen design and furnishings. Although Cambium has only been in business since 1996, principal Brian Hudok, a certified kitchen designer, has more than 14 years of experience designing kitchens. This history led him to a niche of customers that he says, want "a splash of creativity" and designs that reflect their own individuality, along with solid, traditional furniture that is of the highest quality. And that is what Cambium supplies, clients affirm.

This approach has led Hudok and Cambium to projects throughout the United States. While its prices are not cheap, clients say that there is no comparison. Cambium charges a $300 fee to visit a client's home for an initial assessment and $150 per hour for design. Clients who must have a Cambium kitchen design in their vacation home also pay $75 per hour for travel time.

"My kitchen has a distinct look that few designers can achieve."

	Quality	Cost	Value	Recommend?
Canac Kitchens	4	4	4	4

1238 West Belmont Avenue, Chicago, IL 60657
(773) 404 - 5110 www.canackitchens.com

Sales, design and installation—kitchen and bath

Canac Kitchens of Chicago is a division of Kohler Company, and for 33 years it has provided home cabinetry for kitchens and bathrooms. At its large Chicago showroom, Canac displays its cabinetry in a variety of colors and finishes, and in styles that cover the spectrum from traditional to southwestern to contemporary. The company utilizes CANCAD, a proprietary computer software system that creates custom drawings and imagery, allowing customers to see and review a complete menu of options, based on their room measurements, and try them out visually on screen.

Quality	Cost	Value	Recommend?
	✚	$	◆	★

Chicago Kitchen & Bath

3.5 3.5 4 4.5

1521 North Sedgwick Street, Chicago, IL 60610
(312) 642 - 8844 www.chicagokb.com

Sales, design and installation—kitchen and bath

For those who consider the high-end German kitchen lines the top of the mark—and there are many who do—Chicago Kitchen & Bath is the showroom to visit. It carries the Leicht and Duravit lines and combines its offering of the full range of these companies' kitchen and bath cabinetry with equally high-end, high-style appliances. It has five designers on staff and provides complete kitchen and bath design and installation. While the designers will visit clients' homes, they ask clients to first come to the showroom and review the many possibilities on display.

Chicago Kitchen Design Group

4.5 4.5 4 5

1332 Merchandise Mart, Chicago, IL 60654
(312) 245 - 0100

Sales, design and installation—kitchen and bath

Known as much for doing its homework on clients' needs as for the kitchen and bath designs that follow, Chicago Kitchen Design Group has provided its services all around the world, including six installations in Japan. It is a six-year partnership between Lynn Larson, a trained architect, and Joe Lamantia, who practiced construction technology. With this combination of disciplines, the company treats kitchen and bath remodeling like high-end design firms treat whole-home remodels. It was Larson's notoriety for kitchens and baths in her previous work that led her to the company's kitchen/bath specialty.

At the start of a project, a client supplies answers to a 10-page question-naire, developed to give the partners clues to the client's personality, taste and style of living. No high-pressure salesmanship here. Following study of the questionnaire, Chicago Kitchen Design Group continues to learn just what its clients are looking for, according to a philosophy that Larson calls "design in metaphor." The "metaphor" is that aspects of the person are reflected in the kitchen or bathroom created for that client alone.

"I was impressed to see that Lynn emphasized the importance of knowing what I wanted." "Lynn and Joe were accommodating throughout the entire project."

Christians of Chicago

4.5 4.5 4 4

1300 Merchandise Mart, Chicago, IL 60654
(312) 755 - 1075 www.clivechristian.com

Design and installation—kitchen and bath

Christopher Peacock Cabinetry

5 4 4.5 5

1370 Merchandise Mart Plaza, Chicago, IL 60654
(312) 321 - 9500 www.peacockcabinetry.com

Sales, design, installation and custom cabinetry—kitchen and bath

Customers can't wait to show off their cabinets from Peacock. Christopher Peacock Cabinetry of Chicago migrated to this city in 1991 from Connecticut, where it opened nearly 20 years ago. In its almost two decades of existence, it has established a reputation for some of the finest cabinetry manufactured in the United States. Each piece is carefully constructed with strict attention to the smallest detail. Cabinets are primarily patterned on fine traditional English style and craftsmanship.

Once a customer's cabinets have been commissioned at the Chicago location and completed, the company's professional installers make sure that each piece fits perfectly and that moldings and cornices are scribed on site. Peacock offers a wide selection of stains and finishes, and its artists work to achieve the exact shade, including various painterly effects, that each client wants.

"Extraordinary." "Quality work." "I am so happy with my beautiful kitchen cabinets." "I don't believe people can be perfect all the time, but always accountable. That is Christopher Peacock."

Cucine del Veneto
1344 Merchandise Mart, Suite 1344, Chicago, IL 60654
(312) 644 - 9520

Sales, design and installation—kitchen and bath

Cucine Del Veneto uses cabinetry by Italian manufacturer, Val Cucine, noted for its sleek, clean, contemporary design. The company came to Chicago a year ago, and we are told it offers excellent design and cabinetry solutions for lofts and small spaces. Quotes are offered at no charge, and kitchens are installed by the company's chief installer who was trained in Italy. Once an order is placed, delivery takes 12 weeks. The time it takes a client to master Italian cuisine, however, is not guaranteed.

deGiulio Kitchen Design Inc. **5 5 5 5**
674 North Wells Street, Chicago, IL 60610
(312) 337 - 2700 www.degiuliokitchens.com

Design and installation—kitchen

Many architects, interior decorators and homeowners are unequivocal in their belief that deGiulio Kitchen Design stands in a class of its own. Clients not only marvel at the appearance of kitchens designed by Mick deGiulio and his team, but also tell us this company understands and accommodates their functional demands for this all-important room.

Designs from deGiulio, they say, have a layer of creativity on top of features that meet their own particular cooking requirements. Conceding that this company's prices are a little steep in comparison with its competitors, clients tell us its innovation, in addition to service that "takes headaches away," plus its dependability make it well worth the price.

"I was not only impressed with the customer service but also with the quality of the design and the final outcome." "DeGiulio understands that each kitchen design should be determined by the clients' needs as well as aesthetics"

Design Studio Ltd.
709 North Forest Avenue, Lake Forest, IL 60045
(847) 234 - 0800 www.thedesignstudioltd.com

Design and installation—kitchen

Since 1995, The Design Studio has been designing kitchens and supplying high-end appliances to the North Shore area. Eighty percent of its business is with individual customers and the other 20 percent is devoted to projects with design-industry trade professionals. Although the company is young, principal Mark Olmon has 20 years of experience in kitchen design, and customers say it has equipped him with the expertise to assist even the pickiest of clients in reaching choices that meet their aesthetic and functional needs.

Olmon is a member of the National Kitchen & Bath Association, where he served as vice president of education. The company recommends that prospective clients visit the Design Studio showroom for a complimentary consultation and a sampling of its abilities.

"The showroom gave me great ideas about what I wanted my kitchen to look like and the staff was more than helpful."

➕ $ ◆ ★

Distinctive Kitchen Design

📁 📁 📁 📁

201 South Main Street, Wauconda, IL 60084
(847) 526 - 7822 www.distinctivekitchens.com

Sales, design and installation—kitchen and bath

From the design and drafting of floorplans to the on-site installation of its high-end cabinetry and countertops, Distinctive Kitchen Design has the ability to meet demanding clients' needs in kitchen and bath remodeling. The company utilizes CAD (computer-aided design) drafting, which enables clients to visualize plans and also run through a variety of alternative "what-if" scenarios.

The company carries Wood-Mode and Plato custom cabinetry, Brookhaven and Kraftmaid semi-custom products and its own Distinctive Custom Cabinetry line. It also offers a variety of solid surface and granite countertops and has a show-room, fully staffed with trained design consultants, to assist customers in the often-daunting task of developing custom kitchen and bath designs and making appropriate decisions regarding the choice of equipment.

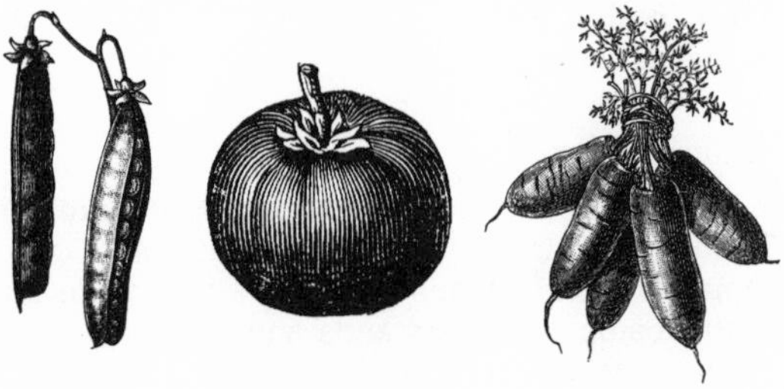

Dream Kitchens Inc.

4 3.5 5 5

3437 Dempster Street, Skokie, IL 60076
(847) 933 - 9100 www.dreamkitchens.com

Sales and design—kitchen and bath

This dream extends from the kitchen to the bath and to other rooms throughout the house that require cabinetry. The company offers a wide selection of cabinet style choices and carries such upper-end U.S. and European appliances as KitchenAid, Whirlpool, Bosch, Viking and Sub-Zero. Clients tell us the are very impressed with the company's response in interpreting their visions.

"Rick Glickman and his staff were extremely responsive." "Dream Kitchens went above and beyond what we had expected."

Drury Designs

📁 📁 📁 📁

534 Pennsylvania Avenue, Glen Ellyn, IL 60137
(630) 469 - 4980 www.drurydesigns.com

Sales, design and installation—kitchen and bath

An award for "best of show" in a National Kitchen & Bath Association competition among kitchen and bath designers nationwide attests to Drury Designs' stature in its field. The firm's projects have also been published in design magazines. The key to this success, according to principal Gail Drury, is understanding clients' needs. The firm's route to custom designs begins with an extensive client interview.

Glencoe Kitchen & Design 3.5 3 4.5 5
661 Vernon Avenue, Glencoe, IL 60022
(847) 242 - 9999 www.glencoekitchens.com
Sales, design and installation—kitchen and bath

This company is said to be a gourmet-class kitchen and bath remodeling firm. In addition to its own line of custom cabinetry, which includes units of stainless steel, it carries the Kountry Kraft, Prevo and Ultracraft custom lines. The showroom also contains a selection of antique French furniture to give clients' kitchens added spice. Clients begin with a visit to the showroom to preview ideas and potential plans. For an initial design fee, determined by the scope of the project, one of the company's qualified designers will discuss options, take measurements and develop a preliminary plan. Then the custom designing begins in earnest, and we're told the company provides a high level of attention throughout the specifying and installation process. Product delivery can take up to 12 weeks.

"The staff at Glencoe was knowledgeable and their showroom had a wide selection of brands and styles."

Idea Companies 4 4 4 4
1132 Waukegan Road, Glenview, IL 60025
(847) 998 - 1205 www.ideacompanies.com
Sales, design and installation—kitchen and bath

Idea Companies imports Scavolini brand Italian kitchens, Bagno Pui Italian baths and additional furniture pieces from Italy. Scavolini, the flagship brand of Idea Companies, expanded to the United States a decade ago. The staff at Idea Companies works with clients to tailor plans for their specific needs and specify cabinets in its brands that fit the plan. This company also handles installation. Depending on the complexity of the order, cabinet delivery typically takes from eight to twelve weeks.

"I decided to remodel my kitchen and I wanted a style that was not traditional. I was pleased with the sleek lines that Idea Companies offered."

Insignia Kitchen & Bath Design 3.5 3 4.5 5
1435 South Barrington Road, Barrington, IL 60010
(847) 381 - 7950 www.insigniakitchenandbath.com
Sales, design and installation—kitchen and bath

Insignia has won its badge of approval through publication of its designs in such magazines as the *Woman's Day Kitchen & Bath Remodeling* special edition and with an award from the National Kitchen & Bath Association's nationwide competition. It carries the full line of top-end Downsview cabinetry and Grabill Quality kitchens. It also offers custom countertops and upper-end faucets and fixtures. In-house designers are on hand in the showroom to answer clients' questions and guide them along the road to complete, custom-tailored kitchen and bath installations.

"Good quality, great staff and fabulous website."

Jean Stoffer Design 4.5 3.5 4.5 5
632 Lathrop Avenue, River Forest, IL 60305
(708) 366 - 6055 www.jeanstofferdesign.com
Design—kitchen

Jean Stoffer's career began as an interior designer. In 1993 she decided to stay in the decorating and design field, but limit business to expertise in kitchens. According to clients, this was a wise decision. Many of her kitchens have been seen on the annual Parenthesis Kitchen Walk. Having a kitchen designed by Jean Stoffer insures that it will be unique and especially suited to the client's needs, while still embodying flair and style. Stoffer's cabinetry is custom, made by a group of skilled Amish craftsman.

Stoffer offers a free consultation and interview with clients to determine their needs and wishes. Design fees range anywhere from $2,500 to $5,000 per design. By combining function with fashion, clients say Stoffer creates the hottest kitchens in Chicago.

"Jean is a creative person who integrates many different materials and design elements to create a unified space." "They use only the finest Amish craftsmen to fabricate their products. Workmanship, creativity and reliability are absolutely outstanding!" "Jean has exquisite taste and finds unique accessories (faucets and drawer pulls) that add so much."

Karlson Kitchens 4 4 4 5
1815 Central Street, Evanston, IL 60201
(847) 491 - 1300 www.karlsonkitchens.com

Design, installation and cabinetry—kitchen

By all accounts, Karlson Kitchens is 40-karat. David Karlson, who now heads the company, is carrying on the kitchen and bath design tradition established by his father, Ben Karslon, in 1965. The company works primarily downtown and to the north of Chicago. David Karlson is accredited with the National Kitchen & Bath Association and studied kitchen and bath design at a high-end kitchen cabinet manufacturing company in Germany. Karlson carries the Wood-Mode and Brookhaven cabinet lines and has a 3,000-square-foot showroom where prospects can preview the firm's products and design innovations. Customers tell us that the $3,000 up-front fee Karlson charges for design is a worthwhile investment.

"Karlson Kitchens was professional and well worth every penny." "Their showroom was huge and had everything you could possibly imagine."

Kitchen Classics 5 4 5 5
519 Fourth Street, Wilmette, IL 60091
(847) 251 - 9540

Design and installation—kitchen

Custom cabinets and installation by its own carpenter is what puts the "classic" in Kitchen Classics, according to this company's clientele. The firm is owned by a husband-and-wife team, Ed and Nancy Hillner, who have been designing and installing their cabinets for 25 years. The majority of the firm's work is in upscale residences on the North Shore, and 99 percent of all business comes from referrals. We're told that service stands alongside craftsmanship to keep clients happy during what customers describe as a good working relationship. When the inevitable problem arises, we're told Kitchen Classics' owners respond without hesitation. Homeowners and professional decorators who use this company say the showroom exemplifies both its quality of product and of service.

"These people are honest, reliable, punctual and creative." "The Hillners are a charming, creative team with wise problem-solving skills. Both are experienced and have a practical approach to the placement and selection of materials."

Kitchen Village 4 4 4 4
1081 East Golf Road, Arlington Heights, IL 60005
(847) 956 - 6800 www.kitchenvillage.com

Sales, design and installation—kitchen and bath

Kitchens Baths and More
817 West Devon Avenue, Park Ridge, IL 60068
(847) 825 - 6622 www.kitchensbathsandmoreinc.com
Sales, design and installation—kitchen and bath

North Shore Kitchen and Bath Center Inc. 4.5 4.5 4 5
3207 West Lake Avenue, Wilmette, IL 60091
(847) 256 - 5600
Sales, design, installation and cabinetry—kitchen and bath

A specialist in designing kitchens and baths in older homes along the North Shore, this company has earned its stripes with demanding clients since its inception in 1985. The business thrives on substantial numbers of referrals, which is confirmation of the quality of its designs and service. All work is fully custom, and while the company does not sell appliances, its designs include them and its in-house design staff will coordinate with suitable appliance distributors to help clients obtain products. The company will handle projects of any scope and size except for building room additions.

"I would recommend North Shore Kitchen and Bath to anyone." "Their kitchen design was original and the quality of work was truly outstanding."

nuHaus 4.5 3 5 5
1665 Old Skokie Road, Highland Park, IL 60035
(847) 831 - 1330 www.nuhauscabinetry.com
Custom cabinetry—kitchen

The nuHaus operation encompasses 35 kitchen designers, support staff and installers and was established in 1989. Its vast, 10,000-square-foot showroom provides an extensive display of kitchen vignettes that show off the skill of its designers and craftsmen. The firm is an authorized dealer of Downsview, Wm Ohs, Mark Wilkinson and Rutt Custom Cabinetry—all upper-end custom cabinet lines—in addition to cabinets by its own custom millwork company. Clients give high marks to the firm's customer service and knowledgeable staff and tell us the combination makes projects run smoothly and efficiently.

"The service, quality and timing were outstanding. This was the smoothest part of our entire project." "Every single person with whom we dealt was completely professional, courteous, efficient and knowledgeable of our project."

Poliform Chicago
1379 Merchandise Mart , Chicago, IL 60654
(312) 321 - 9600 www.poliformusa.com
Custom closet design and installation—kitchen and door sales

See Poliform Chicago's full report under the heading Closets

Schander Works
420 Uvedale Road, Riverside, IL 60546
(708) 485 - 2112
Custom kitchen and bath cabinetry

Smartrooms Inc. 4 4 4 4
222 Merchandise Mart, Plaza Suite 1356, Chicago, IL 60654
(312) 644 - 4446 www.smartrooms.com
Sales and design—kitchen and bath

Quality	Cost	Value	Recommend?
	+	$	◆	★

Soupcan Inc.

Quality	Cost	Value	Recommend?
4	4.5	5	5

1500 South Western Avenue, Chicago, IL 60608
(312) 243 - 6928 www.soupcan.com

Alternative sinks and countertops

Soupcan is a resource for high-end custom kitchen and bath sinks and countertops. Principal Gerry Santora has been designing and fabricating countertops since 1992, with various materials including zinc, copper, iron, steel and concrete, including 11 different colors of pigmented concrete. The products created by Santora and his crew of 12 provide designers' and clients' kitchens and baths with a distinguished alternative to commodity tops, routinely available in the marketplace. These are always original, and primarily sleek and modern in design. They are in demand in Chicago and throughout the United States. Pricing is by the square foot and varies according to material. Products are guaranteed against structural damage for three years.

"I ordered a fabulous, uniquely-colored kitchen countertop from Soupcan and everyone asks me who designed it."

Spaces and Views

Quality	Cost	Value	Recommend?
3.5	3.5	4	4

583 Elm Place, Highland Park, IL 60035
(847) 681 - 0300 www.spacesandviews.com

Sales and design—kitchen and bath

Clients give Spaces and Views good reviews. A division of Lee Lumber, this company opened its business with a showroom more than two years ago and has been accumulating loyalists ever since. Its design staff requires clients to complete a questionnaire and takes pains to develop designs that meet individual clients' wishes and functional criteria. Spaces and Views carries and installs the Wood-Mode and Brookhaven lines of custom cabinetry and also provides countertops and appliances.

"Spaces and Views had a great showroom and I was impressed by the lines of cabinetry that they carried." "Friendly and well-informed design staff."

The Kitchen Master

📁 📁 📁 📁

600 Industrial Drive, Naperville, IL 60563
(630) 369 - 0500

Sales, design and installation—kitchen and bath

Tomten Inc. Cabinet Designs

Quality	Cost	Value	Recommend?
3.5	4	4	4

211 West Burlington Avenue, Clarendon Hills, IL 60514
(630) 654 - 0051

Sales, design and cabinetry—kitchen and bath

Hiring a Landscape Architect/Designer

Every Chicagoan can benefit from a serene retreat, a peaceful oasis from the outside world. The ultimate refuge is your very own green space where sunlight, plants, flowers, walkways, trellises—or simply a colorful flower box in the window—create a delightful escape. The artisans who turn these dreams into reality are garden designers, horticulturists and landscape architects. Experts in both art and science, these professionals create natural havens in any type of space. Garden and landscape designers use plants and masonry to plan, design and construct exterior spaces—in the city, the suburbs or the countryside.

More Than Planting

Planning a garden paradise for your surroundings is a job for professionals, as many technical elements are involved. Garden designers create water and soil systems that are unique to city landscapes, and their craft requires a complex blend of botanical knowledge, construction expertise and creativity. Suburban or country projects can be more or less involved, incorporating large trees and bushes, masonry and rock formations, and constructed ponds and streams.

Service providers included in *The Franklin Report* reveal a common thread—artistry combined with a passion for creating the ultimate natural space to suit each client's unique habitat. Many Chicago-area landscapers adhere to native landscaping, eco-gardening and sometimes even ecological restoration, which involves prescription burns and bioengineered erosion control. One major influence, and a name that will pop up over and over, is the master landscape architect Jens Jensen, a Danish immigrant who founded the prairie conservation movement around 1900. As a designer he paid special attention to the beauty of a natural prairie setting and the history of the land, often incorporating signature Native American "players greens" and "council rings" into his designs. His masterpiece, Columbus Park in Western Chicago, showcases such native features as broad prairie meadows, natural perrenials and streams trickling over rockwork.

Where Do I Start?

The most general decision to make about your city garden or country landscape is what type of purpose it will serve. Are you a cook who loves using fresh ingredients and would like to build an herb, vegetable or cutting garden? Have you discovered the joy of exotic plants and wish to install a greenhouse for your orchids? Or are you dreaming of a superbly designed terrace with benches and several layers of growth? With your overall purpose in mind, take stock of the space available in and around your home. If you want to create a balcony or rooftop garden, are you primarily interested in shrubs, trees, vines or particular colors and species of flowers and plants? Is privacy—building a hedge to separate your yard from your neighbor's—an important issue? Do you prefer the informal charm of an English cottage garden or the elegance of a neoclassical French one? Keep in mind that the more complicated the design, the more maintenance of it is involved. Nurture your ideas by looking through home, garden and architecture magazines before you contact a garden designer.

Foremost in a landscape designer's mind is building a setting that can be enjoyed year round. The designer will have many ideas for you, but if you have done some research and fallen in love with specific plants and flowers, you will be a step ahead in designing your perfect oasis.

On Cost

The pricing system for landscape design varies from firm to firm. Some designers charge an hourly rate; others determine a flat fee after analyzing the job. Like other professional services, garden design companies will produce a written agreement for the client that lists what will be done and what it will cost. It is not unusual for these agreements to leave room for flexibility in scheduling and pricing, should unforeseen circumstances, such as bad weather delaying the work, affect the job.

Will a Designer Also Maintain My Garden?

Services provided by garden designers vary from firm to firm and depend on the scope of your project. Many companies provide a complete package of design, installation and maintenance, and thus establish a long-term relationship with the client. Other professionals are limited to design and consulting, and subcontract for installation and maintenance. Landscape projects can vary drastically in size and detail and therefore in degrees of maintenance. Discuss these aspects with your designer and make sure you're aware of the amount of attention your yard or garden will require. Like interior designers, garden designers, horticulturists and landscape designers work closely with clients on a one-to-one basis to bring their creative ideas to fruition.

Permits and Professional Considerations

A garden-design project may require a permit from your building management if you live in a downtown city apartment. Designers are well-schooled in this process and some will even intervene with a super-strict co-op board to get your plans set in motion. No license is required to be a garden or landscape designer, and these green specialists come from a variety of educational backgrounds, including degrees in horticulture, study programs affiliated with arboretums and botanical gardens, degrees in sculpture and other studio arts and lifetime experiences with plants and nurseries. Landscape architects, many of whom focus primarily on the hardscape aspects of garden design rather than on horticulture and maintenance, have degrees in the field and are licensed. All the men and women drawn to the garden design profession, especially those devoted to the challenges of city landscapes, undoubtedly share the view of Thoreau, who wrote, "In wildness is the preservation of the world."

Top Plants for All Seasons

Trees and Shrubs:

Japanese Maple: Great shape all year, especially in winter, with excellent fall color.

Kousa Dogwood: White flowers in June, exfoliating bark that looks good all year. Bears fruit and wonderful color in the fall.

Oakleaf Hydrangea: Great bark, huge white to purple (depends on ph balance) flowers in July and overall excellent foliage.

False Cypress: Very interesting evergreen variety that adds much to winter gardens.

Perennials:

European Ginger: Shiny, heart-shaped foliage for great evergreen groundcover.

Fountain Grass: Beautiful in every season—even in winter landscapes.

Lenten Rose: An evergreen with dark, leathery leaves. Flowers from March through May.

Silvery Sunproof or *Lily Turf*: Purple flowers in the fall, with brightly variegated foliage all year. Very hardy and pest resistant.

Yucca: Bright color and beautiful form all year, excellent in dry conditions.

LANDSCAPE ARCHITECTS/DESIGNERS

American Gardens Inc. — 3.5 | 3.5 | 4 | 4.5

P.O. Box 596, Warrenville, IL 60555
(630) 393 - 4000

Landscape design, installation and maintenance

The development of designs appropriate to different individual landscapes and settings is American Gardens's particular strength, according to clients. Its services are comprehensive and include landscape architecture; design and installation that encompasses patios, walks, decks, ornamental woodwork, ponds and fountains; plus planting and customized maintenance service. It has eight full-time and seventeen part-time employees and has been in business for ten years. Two of the partners are landscape architects and one is an engineer.

Artemisia — 5 | 3 | 5 | 5

875 North Dearborn Street, Chicago, IL 60610
(312) 988 - 7476

Landscape design

Clients are simply in awe of Maria Smithburg's mastery of garden art. Her knowledge and training are outmatched only by her devotion and sense of design, they say. Smithburg, the founder and head of Artemisia, has a master's in landscape architecture from Harvard and has been designing residential gardens throughout the Chicago area for 15 years. Her love of gardens and landscaping dates back to her childhood in Argentina and fond recollections of her parents picking oranges and pecans from the family's backyard groves.

Because she takes deep personal interest in every garden she creates and understands that a garden's evolution is as important as its roots, Smithburg oversees all aspects of the maintenance of her creations. Despite all this, clients say Artemisia's pricing is moderate, especially in relation to the quality of its work. Many view Smithburg more as an artist than a landscape architect. In Latin, artemisia means "muses of the arts," and delighted clients think this fits perfectly with the firm's creativity and philosophy of garden design.

"Maria is most knowledgeable about plants and trees, but her biggest sales point is her sense of design." "Artemisia is as talented and committed to client satisfaction as any design firm in the business." "However much they may already know about landscape design, clients will always learn more from Maria."

Avant Gardener — 4 | 4 | 4 | 4

411 Central Avenue, Suite 100, Highland Park, IL 60035
(847) 433 - 3003

Landscape design and installation

Seen as an up-and-coming landscape design firm, Avant Gardener embraces the philosophy that gardens are an extension of interior space. Partners Doug Kasmer and Kenneth Harder are known for creating original designs that require little maintenance. In doing so, they incorporate a great deal of "hardscape" in their gardens. Kasmer has a master's in landscape architecture, and Harder's background is in interior design.

The company has been in business for six years and has twelve employees. Avant Gardener works throughout Chicago and the surrounding area. The initial consultation is free, and all work is billed at $100 per hour. While this can add up to a pricey initial investment, clients point out that, over time, it can represent savings in seasonal maintenance costs.

Beary Landscaping
16201 108th Avenue, Orland Park, IL 60467
(708) 349 - 1500

Landscape design, installation and maintenance

Chalet Nursery and Gardens 4 3 4 4
3350 Martin Luther King Drive, North Chicago, IL 60064
(847) 688 - 0561 www.chaletnursery.com

Landscape design, installation and maintenance

This is a big firm with a reputation to match. Despite its size, Chalet follows a team concept that gives clients and their projects individual attention. Customers praise the firm's service and say the staff is quick to respond to their needs. Size also enables Chalet to handle every aspect of landscape design, installation and maintenance. The company operates its own nursery, which sells retail to do-it-yourself gardeners.

Chalet is a family-owned business that began in 1917 as a small landscaping company and blossomed into the current firm that employs more than 250 people at the height of the season. Larry Thalman III is now general manager of the company that was founded by his grandfather, L.J. Thalman, over 80 years ago. Chalet has received many local, state and national awards, including a "Best of the North Shore" honor from *North Shore* magazine.

"Chalet was responsive and listened to any questions that I had."

Cityscape 4 4 4 4
P.O. Box 482, Wood Dale, IL 60191
(630) 860 - 1116

Landscape design and installation

Summer in the city has been greatly improved by this specialist in townhouse and rooftop garden installations. Kevin Coogan, owner of Cityscape, has 30 years of experience in landscape design. He started Cityscape 20 years ago and limits its services overwhelmingly to downtown Chicago, although he can occasionally be persuaded to wander into the outskirts.

Craig Bergmann Landscape Design Inc. 4.5 4 5 5
1924 Lake Avenue, Wilmette, IL 60091
(847) 251 - 8355 www.craigbergmann.com

Landscape design, installation and maintenance

Called "the best in the midwest" for English gardens and the "dynamic duo" of perennials, partners Craig Bergmann and James Grigsby have won the hearts of many grateful clients, especially those who admire the relaxed and uplifting style of European gardens. The two, who have impeccable and complementary credentials, joined forces to found this company in 1982. Bergmann is a registered landscape architect with training in botany and biology. Grigsby is a former professor at The Art Institute of Chicago. The joyous informality of the company's garden designs comes from a combination of indigenous materials and plantings in naturalistic landscapes.

Clients and prospects can preview the quality of the company's work at its perennial flower nursery and European-styled garden center, located in Winthrop Harbor, Illinois. Once a Craig Bergmann design and installation is complete, the company provides a tailored garden care regimen. Although clients acknowledge that Craig Bergmann is expensive, they overwhelmingly conclude that the workmanship and design—and their enjoyment of both—are well worth the price.

The firm's award-winning work has been featured in *Better Homes and Gardens, House & Garden* and *Metropolitan Home.*

"My work with Craig Bergmann Landscape Design was one of the most extraordinary, exhilarating experiences of my life." "The design and care from Craig Bergmann has created one of the loveliest gardens on the North Shore of Chicago." "The communication between client and provider is open and easy."

Cummin Associates, Inc. **5 3.5 5 5**

114 Water Street, Stonington, CT 06378
(860) 535 - 4224

Landscape design

This Connecticut import has a following in Chicago and around the world. Peter Cummin is a Connecticut-based, English-born landscape architect, known for his exceptional talent as an English-style horticulturist. While his architect and interior design clients nominate Cummin Associates for inclusion in history's all-time "Who's Who" of landscape architecture, Cummin himself describes the company he founded in 1985 as a "boutique." It employs eight people.

Cummin's lifetime interest in horticulture began in childhood, and his dedication to the company's projects prompts him to visit them often, even after the plans are completed. Clients have high praise for the firm's professionalism and for Cummin's own talent and character. Various projects have been featured in *Architectural Digest* and *House and Garden.*

"Besides his talent as a designer and architect, he also has a degree in horticulture, which is an unusual and highly desirable attribute." "Very responsive and available when we need him." "Peter Cummin is a genius and one of the great landscape architects of our time." "I would not dream of using anyone else." "Creative, yet refined to offer a timeless, multi-generational look." "My garden could easily be located at the foothills of the Cotswalds."

Deborah Nevins **5 4.5 3 5**

270 Lafayette Street, Suite 903, New York, NY 10012
(212) 925 - 1125

Landscape design and installation

Another out-of-towner, Deborah Nevins, a small company of six, is located in New York but designs and installs gardens in Chicago and nearby Winnetka as well as Texas and California. Interior designers rank this firm at the top of the heap, which, in the world of horticulture, is a high honor. Nevin's interest in gardens and horticulture began in childhood, and she founded her company in 1983. She personally visits the company's gardens, regardless of location, to oversee maintenance plans and procedures.

Don Fiore Company Inc. 4 3 4 5
28846 Nagel Court, Lake Bluff, IL 60044
(847) 234 - 0020 www.donfiore.com

Landscape design, installation and maintenance

This company is characterized as a reliable "jack-of-all-trades" for outdoor work, including garden planning and maintenance. It employs a staff of more than 50, which encompasses qualified landscape architects as well as trained supervisors and others who perform a wide range of garden-related services in addition to landscaping. Among them are the design of flower pot arrangements and seasonal plantings, the installation of holiday lighting and even snow plowing.

In planning gardens, company representatives will host customers on field trips to local nurseries to review and select materials. Clients give the company high marks for its personal attention to their individual concerns. We're told the staff is also prompt and courteous.

"Great personal contact with primary people at the office and exceptionally responsive to phone calls." "While I can't depend on my wife on a weekly basis, I can always depend on Don."

Don Halamka Associates Inc.
11 South La Salle Street, Chicago, IL 60603
(312) 782 - 9575

Landscape design

Douglas Hoerr Landscape Architecture Inc. 4.5 4 4.5 5
1330 Sherman Avenue, Evanston, IL 60201
(847) 733 - 0140 www.dhoerr.com

Landscape architecture and design

Clients rank this company among Chicago's best in the field and even on the roof. While Douglas Hoerr, owner, is best known for his North Shore residential landscape designs, he and his mid-size company are said to be equally artful in designs for downtown terraces and corporate grounds. Over the past 11 years, the company's reputation has led it to landscape projects throughout the United States.

The firm employs 16 people who cultivate and care for more than 60 residential properties. Clients admire the team's attention to each site's natural setting, regardless of location, and they also like its willingness to listen to and incorporate ideas from homeowners and project architects and designers.

After practicing landscape architecture for 10 years, Douglas Hoerr took a two-year sabbatical to study horticulture and garden design in England, where, in 1988, he participated in the renowned Chelsea Garden Show. His work is highly respected and has been published in *Metropolitan Home, House and Garden, Elle Decor* and numerous other magazines.

"Doug Hoerr is an exceptionally talented and creative landscape architect who understands and complements building architecture." "Our only complaint is they are a little hard to get to do follow-up." "Very pleasant and responsive staff." "We have incredible landscapes in our three homes due to Doug's fabulous talent." Doug did a magnificent garden for us years ago which grew even more beautiful over the years. We recently sold that property, and I miss the garden very much. It was a wonderful solution to some difficult landscaping problems, and it was beautiful."

Dowden & Associates Inc.
P.O. Box 415, Libertyville, IL 60048
(847) 362 - 1254

Landscape design

	Quality	Cost	Value	Recommend?
Earth Developments Inc.	4	2.5	4.5	4.5

11016 Zarnstorff Road, Richmond, IL 60071
(815) 678 - 4177 www.earthdevelopments.com

Landscape design, installation and maintenance

Clients heartily approve of Earth Developments' professionalism and have particular praise for the company's sensitivity to how they use—or want to use—their outdoor areas. The firm's owner, Chris Marzahl, and his company of 25 work primarily north and west of Chicago and in the Barrington area. For 18 years, Earth Developments has been tailoring master landscape plans that integrate customers' expectations with their homes and property. The firm's in-house staff has the experience and capability to handle all aspects of landscape design and installation except for irrigation, which Marzahl subcontracts to qualified specialists. Earth Developments then oversees these subcontractors' work to ensure it meets the company's high standards. Earth Developments is a stickler for detail, we're told.

"Chris and his staff have proven time and again their professionalism and commitment to detail. A true breath of fresh air in a profession that has too many amateur and unskilled companies." "Able to design a landscape plan that beautifully integrated the home to our lot."

	Quality	Cost	Value	Recommend?
Everything Under The Sun	3.5	4	4	4

61 South Barrington Road, Barrington, IL 60010
(847) 842 - 1400

Landscape design, installation and maintenance

Greenview Companies

1501 Ogden Avenue West, Oswego, IL 60543
(630) 898 - 0200

Landscape design, installation and maintenance

	Quality	Cost	Value	Recommend?
ILT Vignocchi	4	3	4.5	5

25865 West Ivanhoe Road, Wauconda, IL 60084
(847) 487 - 5200 www.iltvignocchi.com

Landscape design, installation and maintenance

This big operation gets the kind of recommendations usually reserved for small, elite garden planners. That's because ILT Vignocchi's landscape design and services consistently exceed customers' expectations, Established in 1969, the company has a staff of 200 and offices in Island Lake and Vernon Hills as well as Wauconda. This capacity enables it to handle projects throughout the greater Chicago area and surrounding suburbs and also provide complete service, from landscape design through installation and maintenance. It will also do masonry work.

Despite its size and reach, the company is family-owned and managed by Harry Vignocchi and his daughter, Donna Vignocchi. Clients praise the calibre of Vignocchi work crews and say they are both efficient and pleasant. Initial consultation is free, after which a one-time design fee is developed by a company representative. Clients consider prices reasonable for the quality.

"It is extremely difficult for any firm to meet, much less exceed, my expectations and yet ILT has consistently exceeded our expectations." "Thoughtful consideration goes into their planning as well as execution. I would highly recommend them to others looking for landscape design services."

	Quality	Cost	Value	Recommend?
Kinnucan	3.5	4	4	4

28877 North Nagel Court, Lake Bluff, IL 60044
(847) 234 - 5327 www.kinnucan.com

Landscape design, installation and maintenance

From big landscaping projects to small gardens, Kinnucan can—and does. Tree care, the company's original specialty when owner Robert Kinnucan founded it, remains a specialty. However, in 1985, Kinnucan expanded to provide the full range of landscaping services, including even outdoor holiday lighting. It employs 60 landscape professionals and has the experience and earth-moving capabilities to tame a forest along with the knowledge and sensitivity required for smaller jobs. It takes what Kinnucan calls "a holistic approach" to landscaping with plantings that are designed to be self-sustaining as they grow.

	Quality	Cost	Value	Recommend?
Klaus Schmechtig Company	4	3	4	5

20860 West Indian Creek Road, Mundelein, IL 60060
(847) 566 - 1233 www.klauslandscapes.com

Landscape design, installation and maintenance

This company stands tall among Chicago-area garden lovers' best all-round resources, whether they are starting from the ground up or tucking in seasonal bedding plants. Klaus Schmechtig and his wife, Gabriele, both arrived from their native Germany with extensive backgrounds in landscaping to set up shop here in 1960. At its heart is a 40-acre nursery with a broad selection of trees, shrubs and flowering perennials. Because plants are grown locally, customers say the plants have an excellent survival rate and are also in tune with the area's growing season. One customer tells us that every Klaus Schmechtig plant that has been set in the family's landscape over the past 30 years is still healthy and thriving.

High quality landscape design, construction and maintenance are hallmarks of Klaus Schmechtig along with a commitment to service that clients prize. Son Michael is now in the business along with 21 full-timers, including landscape architects, horticulturists, certified landscape and pesticide technicians, construction supervisors, plus an irrigation designer and a lighting designer. These are all in addition to the company's skilled nursery manager.

"They can help on all aspects of the garden—plant selection, irrigation, lighting, maintenance, etc., for the most demanding client." "We have been very pleased with their high quality work, as have the friends to whom we have recommended their services!"

	Quality	Cost	Value	Recommend?
Mariani Landscape	4.5	4	4.5	5

300 Rockland Road, Lake Bluff, IL 60044
(847) 234 - 2172 www.marianilandscape.com

Landscape design, installation and maintenance

It's hard to find a better equipped, more comprehensive landscape resource than Mariani Landscape. What began as a small garden maintenance company in 1959 has grown to a multi-divisional firm that provides complete landscape design, installation, management and even environmental consulting to residents throughout the Chicago area. Specialist divisions now include landscape management as well as maintenance, and the firm also operates a 300-acre nursery.

Separated into divisions, the company's specialists address different customers' individual needs. Once the landscape architects perform site evaluations, budgets are established and the construction phase begins. The garden division, staffed by trained horticulturists, installs perennials and annuals selected for each particular design and location.

Clients recommend Mariani without hesitation and tell us they appreciate the company's specialist professionals and their ability to handle all aspects of even the most complicated landscape projects.

	Quality	Cost	Value	Recommend?
Michael Van Valkenburgh Associates Inc.	5	5	5	5

231 Concord Avenue, Cambridge, MA 02138
(617) 864 - 2076 www.mvvainc.com

Landscape design

There is a reason Michael Van Valkenburgh Associates is headquartered in Cambridge, Massachusetts. Michael Van Valkenburgh is the Charles Eliot Professor of Landscape Architecture at the Harvard Graduate School of Design. Yes, this company is at the top of its class. Chicago projects include select residences and a large project for Illinois Institute of Technology. The company also recently opened an office in New York City and has a roster of impressive projects throughout the United States and around the world.

Van Valkenburgh is known as a landscape innovator who sees landscape design, he says, as a vital link "between our culture and the land." While most of the company's projects are at commercial sites, clients tell us Van Valkenburgh and his team are receptive to residential work and promptly return phone calls. Not surprisingly, the company has won widespread recognition and numerous awards.

"I called to ask a question and five minutes later my call was returned. They are prompt, professional and have a fabulous eye for landscape design."

Milieu Design Inc.

48 East Hintz Road, Wheeling, IL 60090
(847) 465 - 1160

Landscape design, installation and maintenance

	Quality	Cost	Value	Recommend?
P. Clifford Miller & Company	4	4	4	4

11 North Skokie Highway, Suite 200, Lake Bluff, IL 60044
(847) 234 - 6664

Landscape design, installation and maintenance

	Quality	Cost	Value	Recommend?
Peter Lindsay Schaudt Landscape Architect	4	4	4	4

410 South Michigan Avenue, Chicago, IL 60605
(312) 922 - 9090

Landscape design

	Quality	Cost	Value	Recommend?
Pizzo & Associates Ltd.	4	4	5	5

10729 Pine Road, Leland, IL 60531
(815) 498 - 9988 www.pizzo1.com

Landscape design and installation using native plants

Pizzo & Associates is an unusual firm that bases its practice on sound ecological principles. Many of the 1,800 species that are native to the Midwest are grown in the Pizzo nursery. The company can create or restore a prairie, woodland, wetland, lake or natural landscape. Jack Pizzo and his team provide design services from a licensed landscape architect. Pizzo provides professional ecological restoration and natural landscape services to commercial and public sector clients throughout Illinois, Indiana, Michigan and Wisconsin.

Pizzo & Associates touts the many benefits of ecological restoration and educates clients on the importance of this concept and practice. Founded in 1988 by Jack and Kathy Pizzo, the company is headquartered on a 32-acre restored prairie and wetland. Although the initial fees can be more expensive than traditional landscaping, Pizzo says that, because the plants are native to the area, they require little maintenance.

Quality + Cost $ Value ◆ Recommend? ★

Rocco Fiore & Sons Inc.

4.5 4 4.5 5

28270 North Bradley Road, Libertyville, IL 60048
(847) 680 - 1207 www.roccofiore.com

Landscape design, installation and maintenance

This company has maintained its place in the top tier of area landscape firms for more than half a century. Located on the North Shore, Rocco Fiore has been a favorite among private clients and commercial businesses since 1947. Its numerous awards for landscape architecture, construction and site management confirm its ranking.

During peak season, the company employs as many as 200 people. Despite its size, however, loyal customers applaud the Fiore crews' expertise and personal attention. Clients recommend Rocco Fiore & Sons without hesitation and give it exceptional grades in design, service and value.

"If all other service providers were as good, there would be no need for guarantees." "Rocco Fiore has done a very wonderful job. Our home is a historic estate home and requires special attention. They have been very attentive and responsible in their work."

Rosek Landscape Contractors Inc.

3 2 5 5

1818 North Richmond Avenue, Chicago, IL 60647
(773) 772 - 4386 www.rosekland.com

Landscape design, installation and maintenance

Hardscape, the outdoor landscape's permanent counterpoint to nature's growth that gives gardens and outdoor architecture structure, is the specialty of this firm, which was founded in 1990 by owner Kenneth Rosek. The company employs nine people and customers appreciate not only its original work, but also its superb hardscape restorations. It also builds and restores retaining walls. Customers tell us the workers are dependable and finish projects on time and within budget.

"Ken is highly dependable and always follows up." "His work is always first class. I have recommended him to family and neighbors." "He did a terrific job of transforming my property from a 'pit' to a beautiful oasis."

Scott Byron & Co.

5 4 5 5

30088 North Skokie Highway, Lake Bluff, IL 60044
(847) 689 - 0266

Landscape design, installation and maintenance

Among the giants of suburban Chicago's landscaping firms—in both size and service—Scott Byron & Co. enjoys a very favorable ranking by a discriminating client base that includes many of the area's top architects, contractors and interior designers as well as homeowners. The firm has a staff of more than 325 people and operates primarily on the North Shore, designing, installing and maintaining to the highest quality standards.

The business has grown on the basis of referrals alone since the company's inception in 1983, another indicator of its high customer-satisfaction quotient. Work crews' technical proficiency is matched by their top-notch client service and an upscale design sensibility."

"I have never seen such high quality customer service from a large company." "They go out of their way every time, making my life easier. They would probably go grocery shopping if I asked."

	Quality	Cost	Value	Recommend?
Signature Landscaping Inc.	4	3	4	5

725 North Skokie Highway, Lake Bluff, IL 60044
(847) 234 - 3333

Landscape construction, installation and maintenance

Residents who want skilled personnel to handle a wide variety of landscaping disciplines call on Signature Landscaping. While this award-winning firm does not design, it installs plantings and hardscapes, provides tree care and offers a variety of comprehensive maintenance programs. Principal David Gorter, a Lake Forest native, provides one-stop convenience through parent company Sidney's Services (see review), established over two decades ago. Clients say that Signature sets itself apart with its professional management that treats each job with exceptional care and concern. The crews are described as well-trained and polite. Customers maintain long-term relationships with Signature and use them for a variety of services.

"They installed our original landscape eight years ago and have been maintaining it ever since." "Always take the initiative to suggest some way to enhance our setting." "They are not your typical lawn guys."

The Brickman Group Ltd.

3490 West Long Grove Road, Long Grove, IL 60047
(847) 438 - 8211 www.brickmangroup.com

Landscape installation and maintenance

Those who want local attention for outdoor maintenance, backed by standardized training and business procedures, will find that combination at this and two additional Chicago-area locations of The Brickman Group. This chain now operates in 17 states, providing a comprehensive array of specialty services that include irrigation, tree care management, snow removal and outdoor holiday decorating. It was founded 60 years ago as a local design firm and is headquartered in Langhorne, Pennsylvania.

The Dirsmith Group

318 Maple Avenue, Highland Park, IL 60035
(847) 433 - 3616 www.dirsmithgroup.com

Landscape design

Hiring a Millwork & Cabinetry Service Provider

Transform your den into an elegant library with a mahogany ceiling and walls, lined with matching bookshelves. Add a touch of warmth to your loft apartment with a gleaming spiral staircase, or renew your dining room with oak wainscoting and French doors with glorious beveled glass. From kitchen and bathroom cabinets to custom moldings and wall coverings, millwork enhances interiors with the beauty of finely crafted wood.

Choosing a Millwork Firm

After making a short list from *The Franklin Report,* you can learn about the process and make a choice by visiting select millwork shops. Surrounded by work-in-progress, you can get a first-hand look at the various qualities of workmanship, look at photographs of finished projects and speak to some of the craftsmen. You should feel comfortable with the woodworker's style and confident that your ideas will be listened to and valued throughout the process. During this visit, ask for references from customers who ordered work similar to yours.

Three Levels of Quality

Once you've determined the scope of your project, it is wise to determine the caliber of workmanship and quality of wood that is most appropriate for your needs. There are essentially three grades of woodwork to choose from, each with its own standards for materials and craftsmanship.

Economy is the lowest grade of woodwork and may be chosen for projects that will not put a lot of demand on the structure or materials. For example, a built-in desk and shelving in a guest room that gets very little use could be constructed at the economy level. Although the work must be attractive, it need not be made from exotic wood or constructed with intricate joinery.

The next grade is custom woodwork, the level of craftsmanship most frequently requested. Custom woodwork ensures good quality wood and workmanship and is suitable for such popular projects as household cabinetry and moldings. A beautiful kitchen makeover with glass-paneled cabinet doors and a new butcher block island could all be constructed using custom woodwork.

The highest grade is premium woodwork, top-of-the-line millwork that delivers the highest quality of craftsmanship, wood and finishing. Premium jobs include outfitting an entire room with elaborately carved wall and ceiling panels made of top-grade wood, or building a grand staircase using imported wood and marble.

Major Renovations

Millwork jobs that involve complex structural elements or that will affect your home's electrical or plumbing systems will require a contractor and, in many cases, an architect. The contractor will assure that the job is done properly and on time, taking into consideration any electrical, plumbing or heating issues that arise, and an architect will assist with the design and structural elements. A contractor or architect can also recommend millworkers with whom they've worked in the past, and you can explore those firms.

ON COST

Due to the specialized, diverse nature of the millwork business, there is no standard pricing structure. Most firms determine their fees based on the materials that are being used and the complexity and scope of the project, which is why it is important to collect several bids for your job. When requesting bids, it is also important to note whether or not the cost of installation is included. Some firms subcontract the installation process. Before you sign a contract, be sure that you know exactly who will install the work you ordered in its intended place in your home.

WHAT TO EXPECT FROM YOUR MILLWORK COMPANY

If the structure of your home will not be altered by your millwork project (as with replacement kitchen cabinets, for example), the job will not require a permit and can probably be done without a contractor or architect (if the millwork shop does detailed drawings). There are no license or permit requirements for millwork firms, nor are there any trade associations through which millworkers are generally certified. Before you sign a work agreement, request proof of the company's insurance and warranty policies, which vary from firm to firm. If craftsmen will be working in your home, you'll want to be sure that they are covered by the company's worker's compensation policy. You don't want to be held responsible for a misguided nail or toppled ladder.

Like all artisans, millworkers take pride in their work. You'll enjoy working with a wood craftsman who shares your enthusiasm for bringing a rustic, cozy or luxurious new look to your home.

MILLWORK MASTERY TIPS

- It's your millworker's duty to measure! If you do it yourself and give him the dimensions, you're only asking for trouble.
- Plan the electrical and plumbing layout meticulously or you may have to rip up fine work, send it to the scrap heap and pay to have it redone.
- Don't install millwork too early in a renovation project. Your millworker should be the last person in so that other workers won't scratch your beautiful new wood finish.
- Hire excellent professionals for the entire renovation. Millworkers must have a level surface, and shoddy workmanship from carpenters, drywall or plastic contractors will haunt the millwork.
- Remember to design backing structures where necessary. You don't want a cabinet that will store heavy cookware fastened to a mere one-half inch of drywall.
- Don't be afraid to reject a panel or piece of molding that doesn't match the quality of its brothers and sisters.
- Allow at least six and up to sixteen weeks for fabrication and delivery of the materials—and more for installation.

MILLWORK & CABINETRY

Abitare Inc. 4 4 4 4.5
1301 Merchandise Mart Plaza, Chicago, IL 60654
(312) 222 - 9922 www.abitare-inc.com

High-end custom cabinetry and millwork

For the past 20 years Abitare has designed, manufactured, finished and installed custom cabinetry and fine furniture in all styles, including traditional, Art Deco, transitional and contemporary. Abitare has a reputation for exceptional professionalism and reliability, and we're told that principal Barry Wachtel is friendly, open and attentive. The company works through designers, architects, and contractors and also directly with homeowners. Each piece is built by hand using the latest up-to-date equipment in the company's 40,000-square-foot facility. Clients praise Abitare's gift for intricate detailing and craftsmanship. The company offers a lifetime warranty on the furniture it creates, an uncommon practice among millwork companies.

"Meticulous craftsmanship." "Easy experience with superb service." "I love this company." "Price, professionalism and originality—A+."

Barrington Home Works
102 South Hager Avenue, Barrington, IL 60010
(847) 381 - 9526 www.barringtonhomeworks.com

Design and installation—kitchen, bath and cabinetry

See Barrington Home Works's full report under the heading Kitchen & Bath Design

Bruce Woodworking 3.5 3.5 4 4
1275 South Wolf Road, Wheeling, IL 60090
(847) 520 - 1995

High-end custom cabinetry and millwork

Bruce Woodworking has been supplying high-end custom cabinetry and millwork to clients throughout the Chicago area for nearly 25 years. Its capabilities include, but are not limited to: entertainment centers, mantels, computer desks, bookcases, home offices, libraries and wall units. While all work is custom, the company is capable of replicating cabinets of the same design in multiple quantities at customers' requests. Yet, this is no production-line millwork shop.

References praise the company's detail and say owner Bruce Egeland is from the old school. They describe him as a kind, friendly and professional craftsman. His workers are partners in the company, and we're told their vested interest may also help account for the firm's exemplary quality. References praise Bruce Woodworking's attention to detail and its options. It offers a choice of hundreds of veneers and utilizes only top-of-the-line materials in its practice of true, old-world craftsmanship.

"They're absolutely out to please."

CabinetWerks, Ltd.
185 Milwaukee Avenue, Lincolnshire, IL 60069
(847) 821 - 9421 www.cabinetwerks.com

Sales, design, installation and custom cabinetry—kitchen and bath

See CabinetWerks, Ltd.'s full report under the heading Kitchen & Bath Design

Cambium
113-119 West Hubbard, Chicago, IL 60610
(312) 832 - 9920 www.cambiumhome.com

Design, installation and cabinetry—kitchen

See Cambium's full report under the heading Kitchen & Bath Design

Cherry Valley Woodwork 3 3 3 3.5
809 Area Drive, McHenry, IL 60050
(847) 516 - 8869

High-end custom cabinetry

This small company has a big reputation for the custom cabinetry it creates for the upper end of the market. In addition to cabinet-making, it takes on a limited quantity of custom furniture work and can also create paneling and moldings. We're told that principal Matt Praxmarer, one of this company's two craftsmen, is comfortable with and capable of producing pieces in any style and is especially talented with intricate designs. Clients also say Cherry Valley takes great pride in its detailing and craftsmanship. It offers design, complete with shop drawings, and requires a non-refundable design deposit, after which it provides an estimate. Sources tell us the prices are reasonable. The company also handles installation. Although the firm works mainly with private clients, it has worked for some of Chicago's top builders.

"Always hits the deadline!" "Finally a company saving the client some money." "Can duplicate any cabinet." "Great small guy!"

Chicago Cabinet & Fixture Co. 3.5 3 4 4
3057 North Rockwell, Chicago, IL 60618
(773) 588 - 8699

Custom cabinetry and millwork

Artistic, helpful and friendly—that's how references describe this firm's principal, Kurt Stushek. With a staff of 10, Chicago Cabinet has been in business since 1979, providing custom cabinetry and other millwork for both residential and commercial installations. Its craftsmen work with all types of wood as well as plastic laminates. We're told the company is especially good with challenging designs and contemporary pieces that require strict attention to detail. The majority of its business is with interior designers and architects, but it also welcomes work from private clients.

"Contemporary straight lines—you can throw anything at them and they can design it in a contemporary voice." "They are willing to try new things." "They are very responsive and proactive to the needs of their clients."

Christopher Peacock Cabinetry
1370 Merchandise Mart Plaza, Chicago, IL 60654
(312) 321 - 9500 www.peacockcabinetry.com

Sales, design, installation and custom cabinetry—kitchen and bath

See Christopher Peacock Cabinetry 's full report under the heading Kitchen & Bath Design

Creative Wood Design
2965 North Campbell Avenue, Chicago, IL 60618
(773) 665 - 0090 www.creativewood.com

Custom cabinetry

Diebold's Cabinet Shop 4.5 4 4.5 4.5

1938 North Springfield Avenue, Chicago, IL 60647
(773) 772 - 3076

High-end custom millwork

Shunning growth in favor of meticulous work, this company was begun by a German immigrant in 1936 as a high-end custom millwork business that also offers refinishing, restoration and repair. Current principal, Rick Diebold, and a staff that never exceeds five craftsmen continue to produce some of the finest quality millwork in Chicago. Although it handles large projects, small residential pieces represent the core of its business. Top designers and architects recognize this firm as a leading source of fine woodworking, and references tell us they especially appreciate Diebold's development of full-size shop drawings that provide a clear picture of each piece and every detail.

"Their enthusiastic contributions to the design were thoughtful and appreciated. In every aspect of designing, scheduling and building they surpassed our expectations."

Dimension Woodwork 4 3 4 4

20448 West Rollins Road, Lake Villa, IL 60046
(847) 223 - 4989

Custom cabinetry and furniture

This full-service shop, run by husband and wife partners Jonathan and Tina Moe, specializes in custom cabinetry and furniture, large and small. Entertainment centers account for a large portion of Dimension's work, but clients also rave about its other custom-designed freestanding furniture pieces, which include bookcases, mantels, computer desks, buffets and benches. The company works primarily with homeowners, but also has a following among interior designers. It has been in business for 19 years and serves the complete Chicago area and southern Wisconsin, and we are told its stands by its workmanship.

"Workmanship was exemplary—finish and detail the best I've seen." "This company produces more than custom cabinetry. Friends who have seen the unit refer to it as the work of an artist!" "Easy to work with, very patient, the man is a perfectionist!" "In a heartbeat would hire again."

E. Dahlin & Associates

231 West Main Street, Suite 306, Carpentersville, IL 60110
(847) 428 - 2500

High-end custom millwork

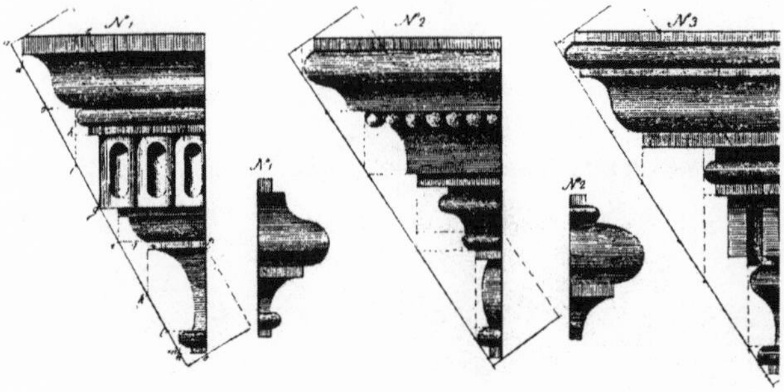

	Quality	Cost	Value	Recommend?
Eiesland Woodwork Co.	4	3.5	4	4.5

2041 Johns Drive, Glenview, IL 60025
(847) 998 - 6391

High-end custom millwork

After long hours building cabinets in his two-car garage, Arvid Eiesland, principal of Eiesland Builders (see review under Contractors), formed Eiesland Woodwork, a second company to complement his first. Together they represent a one-stop shop for builders' woodworking needs. The seven cabinetmakers at Eiesland Woodwork win clients' praise for what we are told is "perfectly beautiful" artisanship. Clients tell us the company can match any molding design. It maintains hundreds of molding profiles in inventory and grinds knives to accommodate each of them according to customers' exact specifications. Among its additional custom specialties are complete home paneling, kitchen cabinets, libraries and entertainment centers. Installation is handled by its parent company.

"Reliable and accessible." "I am so thrilled with this company and their work." "Very customer oriented." "A pleasant experience." "Old-school craftsmanship—Norwegian shipbuilders."

	Quality	Cost	Value	Recommend?
Exclusive Woodworking, Inc.	4	3.5	4	4

4050 Joseph Drive, Waukegan, IL 60087
(847) 249 - 5222 www.exclusiveww.com

Custom cabinetry and millwork

Exclusive has amassed an exclusive clientele among the area's top builders and architects, who have turned to this company for high-end custom cabinetry and millwork since its inception in 1983. Formed by brothers Douglas and John Durbin, it has grown to occupy 30,000 square feet in which a staff of more than 35 design, build and install libraries, kitchens, bathrooms, laundry rooms and other cabinetry in styles ranging from traditional to contemporary. In 1990, Douglas Durbin formed nu-Haus Kitchen and Bath (see review under Kitchen & Bath), an affiliated specialty company. Clients give Exclusive high marks for quality and workmanship, which has carried the company's work far beyond its headquarters north of Chicago to installations in nearby Michigan and Indiana and as distant as Florida, Utah and California.

"The millwork makes our home. It's wonderful!" "Great staff."

	Quality	Cost	Value	Recommend?
Fine Woodworks	3.5	3	4	3.5

5915 North Ravenswood Avenue, Chicago, IL 60660
(773) 334 - 6050

High-end millwork and custom furniture

An insider's secret source, this three-person woodshop has been producing made-to-order furniture and custom cabinetry for 15 years. The specialty clients tell us that what they value most is Fine Woodworks' ability to construct new pieces that match existing ones in style, color and finish. It does not, however, supply kitchens, and this is not the place for large volume jobs. References praise its custom designs and say its workmanship is meticulous.

"Reasonable prices for polished pieces." "Such fine, fine woodwork!"

	Quality	Cost	Value	Recommend?
Finer Woodworking, Inc.	3.5	3	4	4.5

25130 North Ellrie Terrace, Lake Zurich, IL 60047
(847) 540 - 6527 www.finerwoodworking.com

Architectural millwork and custom cabinetry

For wood turnings, moldings and all types of architectural millwork, including high-end cabinetry, Finer lives up to its name. This company, with it's staff of six, has been in business since 1988 and utilizes advanced technology to achieve sharp, precise cutting and fitting. The company works in all woods, including cherry, maple, walnut and mahogany, as well as the more exotic red ash, tiger maple, teak and lacewood. Whatever clients want, we're told Finer Woodworking can deliver. We hear their work on both large and small projects is exceptional. Finer Woodworking serves all of metropolitan Chicago and the North Shore.

"Very reliable." "Great people to work with." "Very ethical and responsive to needs." "Paul Weintz is honest and dependable. I would leave my back door open for him to work while I wasn't there."

Globe Custom Woodwork **3.5** **3.5** **3.5** **4**

1949 North Cornell Avenue, Melrose Park, IL 60160
(708) 345 - 3687

Custom millwork

When Globe Custom Woodwork rose from the ashes of a devastating fire two years ago, it re-emerged as an up-to-date company that married its original old-world craftsmanship with more advanced equipment and improved efficiency. This not only saved, but also enhanced, the company's reputation among Chicago's top builders. This rebirth is a credit, they say, to Globe's proprietor, Steve Wholgemuth, who began the business in his two-car garage in 1980. Clients laud the quality of Globe's custom millwork, which includes the creation of libraries, kitchen cabinetry and bathroom vanities. Much of the work is in mahogany, hickory, cherry and maple. Clients say the company offers a wide range of styles and takes justifiable pride in its craftsmanship.

"They made a major renovation in our home a positive, pleasant experience."

Hammer Design **4** **3** **4** **5**

228 West Illinois Street, Chicago, IL 60610
(312) 832 - 9115 www.hammerdesign.com

Custom furniture

People in the market for custom-made furniture with age-old looks turn to Hammer Design. The company is housed in a renovated 1887 three-story firehouse with a showroom on the property. Utilizing unusual woods, such as antique pine, white oak and other old-growth forest lumber, much of it rescued and recycled from Chicago-area barns and other antiquated buildings, Hammer Design specializes in custom pieces with a distressed look. It is said to be equally adept at creating new looks from old materials.

Clients compliment principal, Ari Smejkal, and his 13-person design team for creativity and for Hammer's ability to incorporate other materials, such as leaded glass and steel, into its pieces. Some of Chicago's most prestigious residences and corporations boast of Hammer Design's highly-detailed, hand-carved windows, doors, dining room tables, curio cabinets, bed frames and armoires. Hammer works with private clients and interior designers, and, although its work is concentrated in the greater Chicago area, it also has a following in upper-end areas of California, Florida and Colorado.

"Very creative." "Great follow-up." "Nice to work with." "What sold us on Hammer Design was a visit to their showroom and seeing the results of quality craftsmanship." "We keep coming back for more."

Highland Park Millwork, Inc. **5** **5** **4** **5**

1580 Old Skokie Road, Highland Park, IL 60035
(847) 831 - 2770

High-end custom millwork and cabinetry

Highland Park Millwork is a third-generation family business founded in 1929. Chicago's prominent families as well as several national television celebrities and sports stars are among its upper-end clientele, which also includes the area's top interior designers, architects and builders. Using the finest materials available, Highland Park Millwork creates custom cabinetry, paneled rooms, doors and architectural moldings. Its work can be found in homes across the nation. While many references comment on Highland Park Millwork's high prices and some on timing, most say the quality is worth the price, especially for the public rooms of a house. The firm's work has been featured in such top magazines as *Architectural Digest, House Beautiful* and *Interior Design*.

"Extraordinary work!" "Unparalleled quality and customer service." "Very knowledgeable and very, very professional project managers." "Expensive, but nearly flawless. . . I pay for the best." "Hit our schedule perfectly." "Their attention to detail and professionalism is clearly evident by their stunning woodwork." "Although they're a lot more expensive than everyone else, the results are exquisite, distinctive custom furniture and cabinetry."

Hylan Design, Ltd. **4.5** **4** **4.5** **4.5**
329 West 18th Street, Suite 700, Chicago, IL 60616
(312) 243 - 7341 www.hylandesign.com

High-end millwork and custom furniture

Hylan Design wins enthusiastic praise from references, which concur that this firm is one of the best in the Chicago area. Principal Ted Schultz, who studied woodworking and cabinet-making at Western Michigan University, founded Hylan Design in 1986. Hylan continues to impress clients with its multi-use built-in cabinetry, although the company can create the full range of custom millwork. Schultz and his staff of 10 are adept at designing all furniture styles from traditional to contemporary, and typically use an array of select domestic, exotic and figured veneers and solid woods. The company is particularly noted for its expertise with multi-medium design and both clients and industry peers tell us that Hylan Design produces some of the highest quality work in the industry. But clients should be prepared to pay, because the company's work does not come cheap. The prices have not discouraged the firm's high-end clientele and Hylan Design continues to be a first choice for many designers and architects who work in Chicago's upper echelon.

"They demonstrate tremendous expertise, care and focus on completing jobs." "Their work shows a great deal of precision." "Fulfilled all of my design intentions." "The caliber of work is superb."

Imperial Woodworking Company **5** **4.5** **4.5** **4.5**
310 North Woodwork Lane, Palatine, IL 60067
(847) 358 - 6920 www.imperialwoodworking.com

High-end custom millwork

Founded in 1963 by Frank Huschiti, a cabinetmaker from West Germany, Imperial Woodworking is a leader in the design and manufacture of quality cabinetry, our sources report. The firm's capabilities include built-in wall units, complete paneled rooms and freestanding custom furniture. A favorite among decorators, architects and builders for both residential and commercial projects, Imperial builds in styles ranging from traditional to contemporary and is facile with all domestic and exotic woods and veneers as well as plastic laminates. The company manages all phases of a project, from drafting to manufacture, installation and final touch-ups. Clients and peers repeatedly praise the firm for its high quality work and continuous efforts to stay updated in trends, styles and construction methods.

"Phenomenal!" "Exceptional craftsmanship."

✚	$	◆	★

Johnson's Custom Cabinets

| 4 | 2.5 | 4 | 4.5 |

28W147 Commercial Avenue, Suite 7, Lake Barrington, IL 60010
(847) 381 - 7774

High-end custom cabinetry and millwork

Top designers along with some of Chicago's well-known businessmen and even a few famous athletes extol the cabinets and made-to-order furniture produced by this small, four-person custom woodworking shop. Residential clients laud the talent principal Henry Johnson and his team have with end tables, dining room tables and built-in cabinetry throughout homes that sometimes extend to 10,000 square feet or more. Lake Forest Hospital is among Johnson's commercial cabinetry customers. While the company works throughout the greater Chicago area, we are told that Johnson prefers to—and usually does—avoid jobs downtown.

"They take great pride in their work." "Great prices." "He had the difficult task of laminating our kitchen and he held it all together with such smooth execution." "Very reliable."

Joseph's Woodworking

| 3.5 | 3 | 4 | 3.5 |

5680 Northwest Highway, Chicago, IL 60646
(773) 774 - 2996

Custom architectural millwork

The reproduction of period architectural millwork is a specialty of Joseph's Woodworking, and we're told that the firm can not only produce millwork in any style, but also that owner, Terry Lee, is an expert in determining which designs work well in particular interior spaces. Custom cabinetry, another specialty, accounts for approximately half of the company's business. Joseph's is a 20-person shop that has been in operation since 1990, providing complete service, from design development through manufacturing and installation. The shop blends old-world techniques with modern technology and typically works with cherry, maple and oak, but, on request, will use tiger wood and other exotic species. Our sources say Lee is friendly, easy to work with and very professional. These characteristics and the team's abilities have resulted in strong relationships with the area's high-end builders.

"Their patience in the planning, building and follow-through of our project is appreciated." "Every phase, from design to installation, was professionally managed, and we are so thrilled with the results."

Kempner Company

☐ ☐ ☐ ☐

629 West Cermak Road, Chicago, IL 60616
(312) 733 - 1606

Custom millwork

	Quality	Cost	Value	Recommend?
Kevin-William Inc.	4	3.5	4.5	5

1433-J Fullerton Avenue, Addison, IL 60101
(630) 620 - 0404

Custom cabinetry and furniture

Custom veneering and inlay work are among the fine woodworking specialties brothers Kerry and Sean Moran, the owners of Kevin-William, bring to the high-end residential market, where they work with top designers, architects and contractors as well as private clients. The company's workmanship has recently led it to commercial installations too, although it continues to serve primarily the residential market. The brothers opened the firm in 1994, and we are told they are particularly good at helping clients explore options and develop concepts. Kevin-William's made-to-order furniture and millwork is considered excellent and is offered in a wide range of styles. By all accounts, the firm is as reliable as it is skilled.

"They thought of things that we never would have." "Very accommodating and went out of their way to please us." "They were sensitive to the historic value of our Frank Lloyd Wright home and were careful to leave the original work intact."

	Quality	Cost	Value	Recommend?
Krumpen Woodworks Inc.	4	3	4.5	5

611 Walworth Street, P.O. Box 427, Genoa City, WI 53128
(262) 279 - 2001

Historic preservation

When it comes to historic reproductions and preservation, Krumpen is the ultimate insider's find. Located just over the Illinois border, the company works mainly in Chicago-area residences, where its expertise in Georgian, Colonial and French furniture styles is in high demand. We're told it can reproduce any period style and clients reserve their highest praise for the company's architectural moldings and period millwork.

Krumpen Woodworks is run by Van Krumpen and a team of five, and designs custom wood windows and doors along with contract furniture. The doors and windows are primarily made of mahogany, white oak or reclaimed cypress. Krumpen also does a limited amount of custom cabinetry, but avoids casework and prefers to stay out of the kitchen and the bath. Installation is generally done by the contractor, although Krumpen will handle it at a client's request. The company operates at the upper end of the market, primarily through architects, interior designers and contractors.

"Wonderful and creative craftsmanship." "Van Krumpen really knows his stuff, and he can speak authoritatively about any decorative molding." "Van is fabulous and really adds to the process." "A world-class architectural millwork and design furniture creator."

	Quality	Cost	Value	Recommend?
Lange Custom Woodworking, Inc.	3.5	4	4	4.5

6035 East Highway, Suite 50, Lake Geneva, WI 53147
(262) 249 - 0576

Custom millwork and church restoration

Lange offers fine custom detailing, including turnings, carving and exacting color- and finish-matching in high-end residential millwork. Among the firm's clientele are a number of churches and temples that have called on it for unusual carved forms. In addition to this higher calling, clients report the firm does excellent work with kitchen cabinets, libraries, entryways, door trim, architectural moldings, home entertainment centers and notable residential theaters. Lange is an eight-person shop that has been in business for 19 years and utilizes modern technology to implement its old-world craftsmanship. The firm provides complete service, from design, which includes highly detailed drawings, through installation. Detailed craftsmanship is Lange's main strength, supporters tell us, and the reason why its cabinetry can be found in some of Lake Geneva's most luxurious mansions and its millwork in Chicago's Park Tower.

"Stunning work!" "Excellent shop drawings."

Lee Lumber

Quality	Cost	Value	Recommend?
3.5	3	3.5	4

3250 North Kedzie Avenue, Chicago, IL 60618
(773) 509 - 6700 www.leelumber.com

Custom millwork

Family-owned and independent, Lee Lumber operates two full-service lumber yards—both in Chicago—along with a state-of-the-art window, cabinet and door showroom in Highland Park, called Spaces and Views. Lee's millwork specialties include the creation of unique residential entryways, with custom doors designed from scratch or from various sources. The company can also pre-hang doors, install glass in doors, assemble window sashes and run custom molding patterns. Established in 1952, Lee handles any job—large or small. The frim's range of skills is tremendous—Lee made the wood spacers inserted between the inner and outer skins of the Mercury and Apollo spacecrafts and also the elegant mahogany doors for Chicago's Orchestra Hall. This diversity equips the firm to produce moldings and window sashes that match original work in Chicago-area landmark buildings.

"A company you can count on!" "Consistent service." "They provided prompt responses to our questions."

Midwest Millwork Inc.

31W101 Schoger Drive, Naperville, IL 60564
(630) 236 - 7590

Custom cabinetry and millwork

Midwest Woodwork & Veneering

Quality	Cost	Value	Recommend?
3.5	3	4	3.5

130 South Lincoln Avenue, Carpentersville, IL 60110
(847) 428 - 3122

Architectural millwork, custom cabinets and countertops

Known as a high-speed producer that does not compromise on the quality of its custom cabinetry, countertops, paneling, moldings and millwork, Midwest Woodwork & Veneering has been in business for a decade. Among its high-profile projects are the Navy Pier food court and casework at the E.B. Smith Stained Glass Museum. It employs 75 union workers who work in two shifts at it's 25,000-square-foot plant. While general contractors and architects have been the firm's mainstay clientele, it has begun to also market directly to homeowners in response to increased residential demand for cabinetry in home offices, entertainment centers, mantels and expanded fireplace settings.

"Timely service—they finished the project three days ahead of schedule." "The value for the dollar is amazing."

Muench Woodwork

Quality	Cost	Value	Recommend?
3	3	3	3.5

2701 Jackson Avenue, South Chicago Heights, IL 60411
(708) 754 - 5561 www.muenchwoodwork.com

Architectural millwork

This is a big company with big capabilities. The quality of its architectural millwork is said to be high, although some customers caution that personal service is not always a strength. Muench operates from a 65,000-square-foot plant and designs, manufactures and installs mantels—a specialty—along with custom cabinetry, windows, doors, moldings, paneling and bookcases. The company works in new construction and with general contractors and homeowners on remodeling projects. Its résumé includes the provision of trim work for Chicago's Park Towers. Muench's size allows it to tackle large projects and give them consistency. Paneling, for example, will match doors, and radius edges on casegoods are sure to line up. The company has been in business since 1988.

Quality	Cost	Value	Recommend?
	✚	$	◆	★

Nu-Trend Custom Cabinet Co. 4.5 4 4.5 4.5
2680 American Lane, Elk Grove Village, IL 60007
(847) 238 - 9300 www.nutrendcabinets.com
High-end custom cabinetry and millwork

No longer new, Nu-Trend was established in 1963. It has, however, grown considerably since its inception, expanding from its original 1,500-square-foot storefront operation in Chicago to its current 17,000-square-foot facility in Elk Grove Village. This company was referred to us by top designers, architects and general contractors who rave about its residential, commercial and institutional custom cabinetry in wood, laminate and veneer, as well as its specialty hardware. With 22 employees, state-of-the-art drafting equipment and woodworking machinery, and a fully equipped finishing department, Nu-Trend offers superb products, we're told, and a full warranty on its craftsmanship.

"Results are spectacular!" "A company that backs up its work."

O'Baran Inc. 4 3 4.5 4
1147 South Wesley Avenue, Oak Park, IL 60304
(708) 524 - 8296

Trade only—custom millwork, cabinetry and furniture

One-of-a-kind furniture, including custom period reproductions, cabinetry and architectural elements are the forte of this company, formed in 1992 by husband and wife partners, Susan and Doug Barnes. O'Baran operates at the top end of the market and works only through interior designers and architects, who tell us they have the highest regard for the firm's innovative designs and the quality craftsmanship provided by its 10-person staff.

"True craftsmen." "They take a tremendous amount of pride in their product, right down to the smallest details." "One word—stunning!"

Paoli Woodwork Inc. 4.5 4.5 4.5 5
10150 Franklin Avenue, Franklin Park, IL 60131
(847) 928 - 2630

High-end custom millwork

This mid-size company is on the A-list of many of Chicago's most renowned builders, architects and interior designers. These sources tell us Paoli not only excels at woodworking details but also provides excellent shop drawings and, to top it off, is a pleasure to work with. Specializing in high-end custom casegoods and millwork, Paoli was established in 1992 and has 30 employees who work in a well-equipped 25,000-square-foot plant. Although it works primarily with trade professionals, the firm does take on substantial private residential projects, such as kitchen remodelings and libraries. While it builds primarily from designs supplied by architects, it is able to translate clients' concepts into sound designs and then implement these plans into unique finished pieces.

"Outstanding ability to solve technical as well as aesthetic issues; a fine quality not commonly found in millwork shops." "They produce beautifully crafted pieces every time, delivering quality, top-of-the-line work—it doesn't get much better than this."

Parenti & Raffaelli Ltd. 5 5 5 4
215 East Prospect Avenue, Mount Prospect, IL 60056
(847) 253 - 5550

Superior architectural millwork, custom cabinetry and furniture

Proof that big shops can do superb custom work comes from Parenti & Raffaelli, a landmark resource among top designers, architects and builders throughout the Midwest for one-of-a-kind furniture and first-class, superior high-end millwork. In operation since 1955, the company has a staff of 170 European-trained craftsmen who are in sync with the demands of Chicago's legacy of outstanding historic architecture, with a strong aesthetic sense and exquisite woodworking skills. The firm will tackle anything from refinishing a chair to refurbishing a home, and provides built-in and freestanding casework for both residential and commercial installations. Clients cite Parenti's impressive millwork and say its creations mark some of the finest buildings along the North Shore.

"Old-world craftsmanship." "The absolute best!" "Last group in the city that really knows the craft." "I would use them for the finest rooms in the home, but my clients will not pay these prices for the living quarters."

Profile Woodworking 4 3 4.5 4
101 Ambrogio Drive, Gurnee, IL 60031
(847) 249 - 8920

Custom cabinetry and millwork

Profile Woodworking is a prime source for custom cabinetry, large or small. It designs and creates high-end, one-of-a-kind pieces using domestic and exotic woods. Veneering is one of Profile's specialties. Free-standing furniture pieces, including bookcases, entertainment centers, bedroom furniture, tables, benches and desks, as well as designers' own visions of millwork, are all said to be very well done by clients. A full-service shop employing five experienced craftsmen. Profile remains small by choice in order to maintain quality. Its in-house design service provides detailed drawings. Clients tell us that Profile stands by its workmanship.

"The quality and craftsmanship are exceptional." "This company is the best-kept secret."

Reese Classic Residences/
Classic Design Studios
350 Old McHenry Road, Long Grove, IL 60047
(847) 913 - 1680 www.rclassicres.com

Custom home builder

See Reese Classic Residences/Classic Design Studios's full report under the heading Contractors & Builders

Roecker Cabinets Inc. 3.5 3 3.5 3.5
850 North Main Street, Morton, IL 61550
(309) 266 - 5051

High-end custom cabinetry

Established 50 years ago, Roecker Cabinets is devoted to custom millwork and specializes in high-end cabinetry. The company installs what it builds, and most of its work is for residences. Production includes solid surface countertops and products that are made of all types of wood or plastic laminate. The company employs 50 professional craftspeople and serves all of Chicagoland.

"Courteous and professional."

Ron Carani & Associates Inc.
P.O. Box 1544, Highland Park, IL 60035
(847) 433 - 4090

High-end remodeling and custom home building

See Ron Carani & Associates Inc.'s full report under the heading Contractors & Builders

Schander Works
420 Uvedale Road, Riverside, IL 60546
(708) 485 - 2112

Custom kitchen and bath cabinetry

See Schander Works's full report under the heading Kitchen & Bath Design

Sullivan Woodworking
2021 West Carroll Avenue, Chicago, IL 60612
(312) 733 - 1021

High-end custom cabinetry

Superior Millwork Co. 3.5 3.5 3.5 3.5
7310 North Milwaukee Avenue, Niles, IL 60714
(847) 647 - 8080

Custom cabinetry and furniture

Superior is a small, high-end millwork shop with roots dating back to 1926 and a continuing reputation for quality custom cabinetry and premium-grade windows and doors. The firm will also make custom furniture, including entertainment centers, computer desks, bookcases and occasional tables, but stops short of providing custom paneling. We are told Superior has the ability to design and build almost any furniture concept drawn on paper. Installation is handed over to subcontractors. References say the firm pays close attention to each client's project and requirements.

"I was so worried about our unusual size requirements, but Bill figured it out and it looks amazing."

The Cabinet Shop 3.5 3 3.5 3
431 Temple Avenue, Highland Park, IL 60035
(847) 432 - 2240

Custom cabinetry

True to its name, The Cabinet Shop specializes in, and limits its work to, custom cabinets. It will, for example, build entertainment centers but will not design and fit libraries. The company has been in operation for 25 years, working mainly in the Chicago suburbs for private residential clients. Occasionally, it does work downtown, but staffers will not travel there for estimates. References say the company's seven craftsmen can translate concepts into reality.

"Hit our schedule perfectly and exceeded our expectations."

Tri-Star Cabinet & Top Co. 3 3 3 3
1000 South Cedar Road, P.O. Box 338, New Lenox, IL 60451
(708) 479 - 2126

Custom kitchen cabinets

The three stars of Tri-Star are its showrooms in New Lenox and Schaumburg, Ilinois, and Dyer, Indiana, where it displays over 40 different door styles including traditional, European and contemporary, in both woods and laminates. Its custom cabinets are primarily for kitchens but also include entertainment centers and other residential and commercial cabinetry. Established in 1966, the company has a staff of 150. Staffers work in maple, pine, birch, oak, hickory, cherry and walnut, and provide countertops in solid-surface material and plastic laminate. Work is produced on state-of-the-art equipment. While Tri-Star's main business is conducted through contractors and architects, it also will also work directly with homeowners.

"Timely. Can get things done in a hurry."

United Woodworking Inc. **3.5** **2.5** **4** **4**

638 Lunt Avenue, Schaumburg, IL 60193
(847) 352 - 3066

Architectural millwork and custom cabinetry

High-end custom home builders represent the largest customer base of United Woodworking, which has been designing, manufacturing and installing custom cabinetry and millwork throughout greater Chicago for 20 years. The firm also works directly with homeowners, however, and does some commercial projects.

We're told that United's staff of 42 is professional and pleasant to work with. Sources especially praise its finishing and veneering departments and credit the company with old-world craftsmanship. It is capable of making, and will occasionally handle, furniture reproductions.

"At a price no one else in our area could do." "They are able to provide and work within budgets."

Wilmot Woodworks, Inc. **4** **3.5** **4** **4**

11475 Commercial Avenue, P.O. Box 250, Richmond, IL 60071
(815) 678 - 2170

Architectural millwork

Wilmot Woodworks specializes in custom premium-grade windows, doors and running trim in addition to casework and other millwork for private clients, architects, designers and builders. In business since 1990, the company has supplied custom millwork for some of the finest homes on the North Shore and surrounding Lake Geneva area. Recently it went further afield, supplying all the casework for an island resort in the Bahamas.

"As a builder, I support Wilmot as their work always brings words of praise from our customers." "Visitors to our new home never fail to comment on the beautiful woodwork."

Quality	Cost	Value	Recommend?
	✚	$	◆	★

Wood Logic

4 3 4.5 4.5

76 West Seegers Road, Arlington Heights, IL 60005
(847) 640 - 4500

Custom cabinetry and millwork

In business for less than a year, Wood Logic has already amassed a dedicated client base. The firm is a high-end custom woodworking shop that specializes in residential custom cabinetry and millwork. If it's to be made of wood, these professionals can produce it, we're told, whether the project is small or large, simple or complex. Its growing portfolio includes entertainment centers, home offices, wall units, libraries, fireplaces, kitchens, bathrooms and doors, but it doesn't do windows. Clients give Wood Logic outstanding marks.

"Great, fresh and fun!" "Very good, very nice and very easy to work with." "I absolutely love this company—brilliant work and craftsmanship." "A must have."

World of Wood, Ltd.

4 3.5 4 5

148 East Wisconsin Avenue, Oconomowoc, WI 53066
(262) 567 - 0188 www.worldofwood.com

Custom cabinetry and millwork

Words of praise pour in for World of Wood. This family business provides high-end interior millwork and cabinetry for private clients, building owners, general contractors, interior designers, architects and churches throughout southwestern Wisconsin and northeastern Illinois. Now, after 20 years, its fame also gains it projects nationwide. With 16 skilled craftsmen and two award-winning in-house designers, the company creates such custom woodworking as doors, staircases, kitchen cabinets, bath vanities, office furniture, church alters and podiums. Sources cite World of Wood for attention to detail, such as straight and curved moldings, wainscoting, wall panels, columns, turnings and mantels.

The company is said to be creative and especially good at solving sticky design problems. All drawings are done by hand. Clients tell us that working with World of Wood is pleasurable, professional and problem free. One client reported that the company tore out and replaced, at no cost to the client, solid beams that it had installed but later considered not quite right. World of Wood has won numerous awards and received special recognition for its restoration work on a historic, private three-story Italian Renaissance-style mansion on Lake Michigan.

"These guys walk on water." "High standards and integrity." "Work very hard to meet client needs." "Very professional tradespeople who want to do things right." "Their work is a passion." "Stands behind work." "Responsive and timely completion of projects. As good as it gets!"

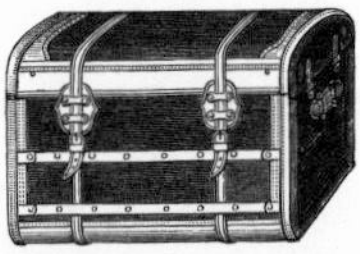

Hiring a Mover

Whether relocating downtown to a new hip apartment or moving the family and pets to the outer suburbs, just the thought of moving can bring the most stoic Chicagoan to tears. Even more worrisome than organizing the process is the thought of placing all of one's worldly goods into the hands of a truckload of burly strangers. The less-than-sterling reputation of the moving industry doesn't help either. According to the Better Business Bureau, moving companies consistently make the list of the top 10 industries consumers complain about. Even moving companies themselves admit that three in 10 moves result in a complaint against the mover. While those odds don't sound promising, there are several precautions you can take to ensure that you are one of the satisfied customers who end up providing glowing references about your moving company to your friends—and to *The Franklin Report.*

Where Do I Start?

Hundreds of moving companies are listed in the Chicago yellow pages. Consider four main factors in making your choice: cost, availability, reliability and reputation. Begin with an assessment of your needs. According to most movers, if you are a single city apartment dweller you will probably need 15 to 20 boxes for all your possessions. A family of two adults and two children will require approximately 120 to 200 boxes. Most companies will provide an informal verbal estimate based on your description of items, number of rooms, the availability of elevators on both ends of move, etc. If you're looking for a binding estimate, some movers will provide one after surveying your property and assessing your needs for themselves. Be forewarned that in this industry, a binding estimate is an elusive thing. Be prepared to consider any estimate a rough calculation rather than a binding agreement. In any event, be prepared with the requisite information before you call movers for estimates. Keep in mind that some movers only perform in-town moves while others are licensed to do countrywide and international moves as well.

Most movers provide packing services in addition to transportation. Packing, of course, incurs additional cost. If you choose to have your items packed by movers, you'll need to schedule packing days. Be sure to take inventory of what gets packed into each box, making sure to make a note of any existing damage. Keep a copy of the inventory list handy as you unpack to ensure that all your items have arrived safely. While movers assume liability for damage incurred by any items they packed themselves; they will not accept responsibility for items packed by you. Be sure to get estimates both with and without packing services in order to ensure that you opt for the services best suited to your needs and budget.

On Cost

Local moves are generally billed at an hourly rate, ranging anywhere from $80 per hour (a 1 on our cost scale) to $200 per hour (a 5 on our cost scale). This rate generally includes a truck and the labor of three men. Usually, moving companies will stipulate a minimum number of hours of moving time, and sometimes also a minimum amount of travel time. You should plan to factor in a gratuity of at least $5 per man per hour. Most movers will supply blankets and other padding material at no extra cost, but anything additional—rope, boxes, packing material, tape, bubble wrap, Styrofoam—will be supplied at a significant markup over retail. So you're better off buying your own packing materials ahead of time.

Weight-rated fees are usually used for long-distance moves. The charges are based on the weight of the goods and the distance they are moved. The truck is weighed before it is loaded with your household items and furniture, and then again after. The difference between the two weights will determine how you are charged. Again, get the best estimate you can before the move, but realize that the actual cost will be calculated after all the goods are loaded on the truck and weighed.

To keep the cost down, budget-minded consumers should consider packing their own books and clothes, but leave the packing of breakable items to the movers. That way the cost of moving can be contained and yet the cost of breakage and any other kind of damage can be absorbed by the moving company.

Summer is the most popular moving season. Not surprisingly, movers are generally over-extended during the summer months. The busiest time of year is generally also the most expensive. Many movers will offer up to a 30-percent discount on moves after Labor Day. Some will also charge less for weekday moves. However, these are options that movers don't readily mention, so make sure to ask about them when you're getting an estimate.

Contracts, Insurance and Licenses

As with most business relationships, make sure that you negotiate a written contract before you move. Most moving companies have a standard contract form. If it doesn't include every foreseeable detail of the move, insist on adding these details. As with any contract, scrutinize it carefully before signing it. Ensure that any agreed-upon terms such as mileage, packing, standard charges, additional costs and insurance are all included in the contract. The contract should state that the men will stay after 5:00 pm to finish the move if it takes longer than expected. If possible, attach a copy of the inventory to the contract as well. Retain a copy of the signed contract well after delivery has been completed, to ensure that all of your possessions are delivered in the manner that the contract dictates. Be aware that most standard contracts require that the movers be paid before they unload their truck at your new home.

For interstate moves, basic insurance usually provides 60¢ of coverage for each pound of goods transported (30¢ for local moves). While there is usually no additional cost associated with this kind of coverage, you do need to sign an additional contract to activate it. Unfortunately, the coverage itself is less than adequate: for instance, if your $500 television weighs 10 pounds, you can collect only $3. Several other insurance plans are provided at additional cost, and protecting the value of the $500 television might require purchasing one of these supplemental plans. Optional plans come at varying costs and provide different degrees of coverage. The American Moving and Storage Association (www.moving.org) can provide you with greater insights about moving insurance; they also supply guidelines to follow when planning a move.

Most Chicago moving companies belong to the Illinois Movers and Warehousemen's Association (www.imawa.com). This is a statewide not-for-profit trade association for moving and storage companies licensed to do business in Illinois.

COST-SAVING MOVING TIPS

- Packing items yourself will save you a bundle. However, movers are only liable for damage resulting from *their* packing, so limit the do-it-yourself items to unbreakables such as books and clothes.
- Packing materials cost significantly more when purchased from the moving company. If you're doing your own packing, buy the materials at an office products or packing products store.
- Insurance may seem like an expensive frill, but it can save you a lot of money and headaches in the event of damage. There are many types of coverage, so check out all your options before choosing one.
- The time of year and/or week during which you move will affect the cost. Since movers are typically busiest on weekends and in the summer, many companies offer discounts on moves that take place during the week and between Labor Day and Memorial Day.

MOVERS

A.C. Warehouse 4 2.5 5 5
7300 North Ridgeway Road, Skokie, IL 60076
(847) 673 - 2722

Specialized crate shipping services

A.C. stands for Angelo Colella, who has been receiving and crating furniture for high-end interior decorators for over 50 years. He began his business at the age of 18 and now his small company of five is trusted to ship even the most expensive of sofas and end tables throughout the Chicago area. Once Colella and his company receive the furniture, it is inspected for any damage before being crated and delivered.

Resources say that for the quality of work, the cost is moderate. For a large piece, for example a sofa, clients can expect to pay approximately $25 for crating. The cost for smaller pieces begins at $20. The delivery charge is based on the size of the piece.

A Thru Z Messenger & Driver Leasing 3.5 3 4 4
P.O. Box 55150, Chicago, IL 60680
(312) 563 - 0999

Residential and commercial moving

As its name indicates, A Thru Z will move anything, from the smallest item to the office furnishings for Xerox and The Chicago Tribune, just two of the corporate clients on its résumé. The company has been in business since the 1930s and serves both the residential and commercial markets. Headed by Colonel Bradford, this team knows the drill and avoids snafus, we're told. The company's troops are licensed, insured and bonded. There is on-site storage for the convenience of customers who need a safe place to store furniture or boxed items. Rates are calculated by the hour or by weight, and Bradford will provide an estimate for free. References say you can rest at ease, he'll choose the cheapest billing method for each assignment, and pricing, they say, is competitive.

A-American Moving Company 3 3 4 3.5
4455 North Elston Avenue, Chicago, IL 60630
(773) 777 - 9003 www.aamericanmoving.com

Residential and commercial moving

This company has extensive experience moving clients all over the country. Employees of A-American are licensed, bonded and insured through the Depart-ment of Transportation, an assurance that the job will get done honorably and well. A-American has been in business for over five years and is affiliated with American Van Lines. This affiliation gives A-American access to plenty of moving vans and moving professionals located in all major market areas for long-distance moves.

Pricing is determined by the weight and the mileage, and packing is extra. Having a kitchen, den or whole house full of items packed and moved can add up to a pricey sum. Medium boxes, for instance, run around $18 and large ones can be as high as $25, with labor and material factored into the price. The company provides an online estimate form that allows customers to submit detailed lists of what needs to be moved. And for customers in a crunch who need to move, say on Christmas Eve, A-American offers service 365 days a year, 24 hours a day.

A-Blankenship & Flowers Movers

Quality	Cost	Value	Recommend?
4.5	3.5	4.5	4.5

1624 North Cleveland Avenue, Chicago, IL 60614
(773) 282 - 3321

Residential moving, antiques and pianos

A-Blankenship & Flowers is a local-only mover with a specialized ability to move antiques, art and other prized possessions, such as pianos. For more than 40 years, the company has remained small and focused on giving customers' treasures immaculate care and attention to detail. As a result, 95 percent of its business comes from referrals from satisfied clients. Employees at this family-owned and -operated company are qualified and have plenty of experience. Blankenship charges an hourly rate of $102 with a two-hour minimum. The team is more than happy to pack boxes for $30 per hour, per man, plus packing materials—a charge that many Chicagoans tell us is well worth it.

Advantage Moving & Storage Inc.

Quality	Cost	Value	Recommend?
4	3	4.5	4

1300 Chase Street, Algonquin, IL 60102
(847) 658 - 3600 www.advantage-move.com

Residential and commercial moving

The advantage of Advantage Moving & Storage is personalized attention and service from a small, family-run business, augmented by its affiliation with Wheaton, a large, reputable international mover. Advantage has been in business for more than 13 years, handling moves from large country homes to small townhouses and vice versa. Belongings can be kept safe in the company's temperature-controlled storage.

Advantage charges hourly for labor and trucks. Two men and one truck, for example, cost $93 an hour, but customers say each truck can have as many as four men, increasing the price. This fee structure applies only to local moves. Long-distance charges are based on weight and mileage. Clients tell us they appreciated Advantage's combination of small-company customer care with large-company insurance and capabilities.

Affordable Moving Company

Quality	Cost	Value	Recommend?
4.5	4	5	5

5000 West Bloomingdale Avenue, Chicago, IL 60639
(773) 637 - 3131

Residential moving and storage

A high number of decorators and many high-end residents depend on Affordable for moving furniture and households. Although clients tell us Affordable is actually more expensive than other local movers, they believe they are clearly worth the extra cost. Our sources give the company high marks and also say its workers are efficient and friendly. Affordable has been in business for 20 years. We understand that even the most prized and delicate items are safe when stored in the company's 150,000-square-foot, climate-controlled warehouse. The company charges $125 per hour for three men and one truck. In addition to peace of mind, Affordable Moving offers clients additional insurance on valuables.

"They are so friendly and informative." "Affordable movers should be called the best movers."

Alexander Movers

Quality	Cost	Value	Recommend?
3.5	3	4	4

6535 South Cottage Grove, Chicago, IL 60637
(773) 955 - 7800

Residential and commercial moving

Although Alexander Movers is located in south Chicago, it operates throughout the city and handles moves to and from Michigan and Indiana. Owner Jerry Lightfoot has been in business for 30 years. He and his 20 employees are licensed, bonded and regulated by the state of Illinois. The company has six trucks and each holds, on average, six to eight rooms of furniture. Our resources tell us that pricing is $24 per hour, per man, and Lightfoot will come to small homes to calculate an estimate for free.

All My Sons Moving & Storage **4** **2.5** **4.5** **4.5**
2005 West 21st Street, Broadview, IL 60155
(773) 665 - 0700 www.allmysonsmoving.com

Residential and commercial moving and storage

This Chicago-area unit of All My Sons is family owned and operated and has been in business here for five years. The company has ten trucks providing local and long-distance moving and offers complete packing and unpacking services. It also has professional piano movers on staff. These sons are siblings of a larger 30-year-old company with numerous locations throughout the United States. For all moves beyond a 500-mile radius of Chicago, the company uses American Red Ball transit company, which is considered to be among the oldest and most reliable firms in the moving industry. Rates are by the hour, based on the number of men required and the amount goods to be moved. Customers say All My Sons is trustworthy, efficient and willing to do what it takes to get the job done.

"A lovely man who answered all my questions patiently and cheerfully!"

Antique Movers **4.5** **4** **4** **4.5**
4515 North Kedzie, Chicago, IL 60625
(773) 478 - 1911

Residential and commercial moving, art and antiques

Some of the best interior designers in Chicago rely on Antique Movers to get their one-of-a-kind furniture from one side of Chicago to the other. The company specializes in transporting antiques but also offers complete packing and storage services. It is privately owned and operated and is the trusted mover of such clients as Sotheby's auction house in Chicago. Most of the company's business comes from referrals by pleased past customers.

Although Antique Movers' hourly rates are higher than those of the average local moving company, discriminating clients tell us the care and time this team devotes to each move make the service well worth the extra cost. For three men, Antique Movers charges $100 per hour. We hear that there is an on-site warehouse, but it is not climate-controlled.

"Very efficient and friendly team."

	Quality	Cost	Value	Recommend?
Burrows Moving Company	4	3.5	4.5	4

Burrows Moving Company
6542 North Clark Street, Chicago, IL 60626
(773) 274 - 5500 www.burrowsmoving.com

Residential and commercial moving

Burrows Moving Company is an independent professional mover committed to providing customers with top-quality moving and storage services with workers who are exceptionally polite. Walter Burrows founded the company more than 25 years ago as a reliable moving company, and today many clients say that's exactly what he did. Burrows has a total of eight trucks and twenty movers. Up to 70 percent of Burrows' business comes from referrals and repeat customers, further confirmation of the satisfaction it provides. Clients praise the firm's ability to accurately estimate budgets and say that there are no hidden costs. The company takes great care in protecting clients' belongings, using rug protectors and special mats. Resources say that Burrows is expert in moving pianos and each staff member is trained in this delicate and demanding specialty.

	Quality	Cost	Value	Recommend?
Century Moving & Storage	4	3	4	4

Century Moving & Storage
951 North Main Street, Lombard, IL 60148
(630) 628 - 2400 www.centurymoving.com

Residential and commercial moving and storage

Well suited for this century's society of transient, demanding customers, Century Moving & Storage has been in business for 25 years. Century is a local family-owned company and an affiliate of Mayflower Transit, a reputable national carrier. With a 25,000-square-foot storage facility and professional crews, Century provides all move-related services including packing, unpacking and storage. Each client is provided with a customer service representative to help with the move from start to finish. The company is thorough in training their movers, requiring each to attend a program prior to handling people's possessions. Century's community commitment extends beyond moving services to membership in Discover America, a program in which its drivers correspond with fourth and fifth grade students, describing geographical and historic highlights from their travels.

	Quality	Cost	Value	Recommend?
Chicago Movers	3.5	3	4	4

Chicago Movers
1661 West Winona, Chicago, IL 60640
(773) 384 - 1000 www.chicagomovers.com

Residential and commercial moving

Chicago Movers aren't shakers. The firm's crew includes experts in the careful moving of antiques, art and other valuables, including pianos. Forty percent of their business comes from computer software and piano transportation. We are told the company rolls Oriental rugs onto a protective core, and then wraps them in an acid-free packing material that will not damage the fibers. The company has been providing full-service moving to Chicago families for 15 years and has ten trucks on the road at any given time. Clients say the company provides detailed estimates quickly. Above all, we are told that prized possessions are safe in the hands of Chicago Movers.

Chicago Movers relies on strong referrals from its customers as well as other moving companies who refer speciality projects that they cannot handle. Pricing begins at $70 per hour for two men and one truck. Piano moving is more expensive and ranges between $225 and $425 per hour or per project. But according to references, the staff's knowledge and experience in moving heavy yet delicate instruments makes the price a song.

Golan's Moving & Storage

4.5 2.5 4.5 5

7300 Lawndale Avenue, Skokie, IL 60076
(847) 673 - 8189 www.golansmoving.com

Residential and commercial moving

This full-service, independent moving company has been serving Chicagoland for the past 11 years. Known for being up-front with its customers, Golan's has built a reputation for trustworthiness by standing by its commitments and eliminating surprises. We're told this company sets the industry standard for professional, well-executed moves. Golan's handle's every aspect of both intrastate and out-of-state moves, from the provision of online estimates to safe storage of the most valuable possessions in its state-of-the-art, 20,000-square-foot climate-controlled warehouse.

"I was really pleased with the move." "I have recommended Golan's several times." "Everything went so smoothly."

Lake Line Delivery Inc.

5 4.5 4 5

2100 Greenleaf Street, Evanston, IL 60202
(847) 864 - 4022

Residential moving, antiques

Lake Line is highly recommended by a large number of Chicago's top interior designers. While the company does not handle large household moves, it is said to take extra care with those masterpieces that are the highlight of many a high-end residential collection. Fees are based on the size and quantity of the items to be moved. Lake Line is a small firm that limits its services to approximately 150 clients a year, it maintains strong customer relationships that are based on trust and the excellent reputation it holds in this field.

Midwest Moving and Storage, Inc.

📁 📁 📁 📁

1907 South Busse Road, Mount Prospect, IL 60056
(847) 539 - 7159

Residential and commercial moving

Whether you have a two-man office or a larger business, Midwest provides the labor and materials to make relocations run smoothly. Founded in 1983, Midwest is said to do an outstanding job of packing, moving and reassembling office and personal possessions. Because all aspects of the move are handled from one location, clients say they have greater control over the transition and the same crew that packed the goods can also deliver it. Midwest will do free on-site estimates and also provides tips for making moves stress-free.

Mini Moves

4.5 3 5 4.5

2154 Madison Street, Bellwood, IL 60104
(888) 256 - 9806 www.minimoves.com

Residential moving

Mini Moves specializes in—you guessed it—jobs of 2,500 pounds or less, and many top Chicago designers are among those who consider Mini quite mighty in its specialty. Some large national movers, in fact, pass small residential jobs along to this company. In business for a decade, Mini Moves now serves three markets nationwide—Chicago, Los Angeles and the New York City/New Jersey area. As a member of the board of the Better Business Bureau, Mini Moves' CEO, Jack Arslanian, makes sure his crews stay in line. The company's service has been recognized by *The Wall Street Journal, Crain's* and *ERC Mobility* online. While the moves may be mini, we're told the service is maxi.

"Best mover I ever used."

Samson Chicagoland Moving & Storage **4.5** **3** **5** **4.5**
3737 West Morse Avenue, Lincolnwood, IL 60712
(847) 475 - 4600 www.samsonmovingandstorage.com

Residential moving and storage, pianos and antiques

Samson Movers believes it is their obligation to see exactly what each prospective client is moving and to provide a witten estimate. The estimate covers all information clients need to know and describes all services. On moving day, Samson professionals will arrive in their purple trucks on time and ready to work, our sources say. Prices are based on an hourly rate with a three-hour minimum, plus truck and travel charges. Rates start at $80 per hour for three men and one truck and increase for additional trucks and men. Samson specializes in piano moving, packing, and crating fragile artwork and antiques. Many interior designers and art lovers put their trust in Samson for their relocation needs.

Terry Dowd **5** **3** **5** **5**
2501 West Armitage Avenue, Chicago, IL 60647
(773) 342 - 8686

Residential moving, valuables and antiques

Terry Dowd has the respect of many outstanding interior designers and artists in Chicago who consider it to be one of the finest moving companies. With more than 75 years of experience in delivering fine art by trained professionals, this company has a proven track record. It operates locally, regionally and nationally and will provide security service for valuables in addition to packing, crating and transporting. The team is licensed and well equipped and we hear that the workmen have a "can-do" attitude. Terry Dowd offers special insurance plans when required.

"The best without a doubt!" "So friendly and so professional."

Thompson Moving & Storage Inc. **3.5** **3** **3.5** **4**
153 31 South 70th Court, Orland Park, IL 60459
(708) 403 - 0008

Residential and commercial moving

Thompson's clientele encompasses businesses and residents throughout the Chicago area making both short and long-distance moves. The firm has been in business since 1952 and has a trained staff equipped to handle jobs ranging from as little as just seven or so pieces up to a full household of furniture and belongings. The same team packs and unpacks a particular job and takes pride in keeping tabs on the precious cargo. Estimated billing for local work is based on an hourly rate, and out-of-state jobs are charged by a combination of total weight and mileage. Should any scratches or nicks occur during a move, the Thompson team is trained to repair them without a trace. We're also told the movers are friendly and courteous.

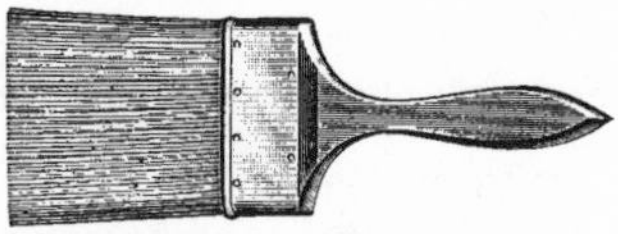

Hiring Painters & Wallpaperers

You walk into a room painted a beautiful celadon green and immediately your mood changes—you become calmer, more relaxed. By merely changing the color of a room, you can produce a feeling of drama or tranquility. Designers know that painting is one of the quickest, most versatile and cost-effective things you can do to transform a room. But painting can be a messy and hazardous proposition for the novice, so many homeowners opt to hire a professional contractor.

Paint contractors with a wide range of abilities and services abound in the Chicago area. Choices range from small start-ups to large established firms, and from straight painters to custom muralists. Depending upon the size of the job and the quality and complexity of the work, there is a paint contractor out there for you.

Where to Look for a Professional

Finding the right paint contractor for your job involves some research. It is very important to check references and ask to see a certificate of insurance. Each contractor should have worker's compensation and general liability insurance which protect you from jobsite-related liabilities. Several trade organizations, such as the Painting and Decorating Contractors of America, (PDCA), list paint contractors in your area. And of course, *The Franklin Report* offers a range of client-tested choices.

Contracts

Reputable contractors will encourage using a written contract. Your contract should clearly explain the scope of the work to be performed and include a list of the surfaces to be painted, a time schedule for the project, payment procedures and any warranty or guarantee the contractor might offer.

Pricing Systems

The cost for painting residential homes varies widely based on such factors as the cost of the materials used and the company's overhead costs. You should invite at least three paint contractors to bid on your paint job, and ask each to submit a detailed written proposal. Painting contractors charge on a per person per day basis, which generally runs in the $400 to $450 range for non-union jobs. Union jobs start at about $500 per person per day. The contractor should provide you with an overall cost estimate for the job that is broken down by room. Also ask for a step-by-step plan outlining how the job will be spackled, skimmed and painted. If colors are being matched, ask the painter to apply 24-inch square samples on the walls.

Ask for client references. They can provide valuable insight into the quality of work, timing and cost.

How Many Painters Will Be in My House?

The size of the crew needed largely depends upon the scope of the job involved. Some painters listed in this guide are sole proprietors who work on small jobs themselves and subcontract larger jobs; others are larger companies with complete crews. Ask how many men will be working on your job and whether there will there be a supervisor or principal on site.

The Elements of a Professional Paint Job

Typically, paint contractors offer the services of straight or flat painting (meaning no decorative textures, just one color in any finish, including glossy) and wallpapering. Flat painting a room involves preparing the walls, trim and ceiling surfaces for the paint as well as the paint job itself. To prepare walls, paint crews will do all the taping, plastering, plaster restoration, if needed, and skim coating. This prep work is considered one of the most important elements of a paint job as it provides the foundation for the paint. A primer coat, which prepares the walls for the paint, should be applied to dry walls. Two coats of high-quality paint should be applied to the wall surfaces.

Which Paint?

The quality of the paint is crucial in determining its longevity. Fine quality paint, properly applied, should last for six to seven years. If you or your contractor skimp on the quality of the paint, you may be facing a new paint job a lot sooner than you would like. The two most common types of paints are latex and oil-based paints. Latex paint is water based and dries quickly, which allows for more than one coat to be applied in a day. Latex paint is better at resisting mildew, easier to clean and lasts longer than alkyd paints, which are oil based. Alkyd paints are preferred by many painters because they are durable and long lived, but they take longer to dry, have a significant odor and can yellow over time. Most experts agree that oil-based paints are best suited for the doors and trim, and latex paint for the walls and ceilings.

Lead Paint Hazzards

The presence of lead paint presents health hazards in many homes. The federal government banned the use of lead paints in 1978, therefore, if you live in an older city building, your apartment is likely to contain a layer of lead paint if it was painted prior to that year. When sanding is done in advance of painting, the sanding may cause lead dust to enter the air in your home. Your contractor should provide you with a pamphlet that discusses lead issues in your home. Ask your contractor what measures he takes to ensure that lead particles are eliminated. If you need to have your home inspected or have lead removed, the Environmental Protection Agency (www.epa.gov) issues licenses for companies and professionals who work with lead control, including removal, inspection and risk assessment. Other good resources for more information about lead and asbestos include the American Lung Association (www.lungusa.org), the U.S. Consumer Product Safety Commission (www.cpsc.gov), the American Industrial Hygiene Association (www.aiha.org), the Department of Housing and Urban Development (www.hud.gov) and the Occupational Safety and Health Administration (www.osha.gov).

Wallpaper

Wallpaper can add depth, texture and visual interest to a room. Floral or striped wallpaper can make even small windowless rooms cheerful. It can be a costly investment, so it is important to find a qualified, competent professional to install your paper. Finding a wallpaper hanger can be as easy as talking to your paint contractor, as most of them also provide this service. Depending upon the complexity of the job, it may be appropriate to contact a professional who specializes in wallpaper hanging. One source is the National Guild of Professional Paperhangers (NGPP). For local referral, call (540) 370-4503 or visit www.ngpp.org.

Cost for wallpapering is based on a per roll basis with rates averaging about $50 per roll. Most wallpaper is sold in double-roll units which measure approximately 60 square feet. The price quoted should include trimming the sides of the paper if necessary. Professionals will strip your walls of existing paper and prep it for the new paper for an additional fee. Your wallpaper hanger should calculate the quantity of paper you will need for the room based on the room size as well as the "repeat" pattern on your paper. The larger the repeat, the more paper you will need. The newer vinyl wallpaper comes pre-pasted, while traditional and costlier papers need to be trimmed and pasted with wheat paste.

Decorative Finishes: The Art of Imitation

Decorative finishes, often called "faux finishes," are used by painters to add depth or to imitate materials such as marble, wood, paper, stone, metal and fabric. These finishes can be elegant, whimsical or dramatic, depending upon the artist and the paint technique utilized. Current trends today include fake wood- ("faux bois") paneled libraries and limestone facades. When done by a gifted artist, a faux finish can cost more than the material being imitated. Decorative finishes can customize a space through color and texture and dramatically reflect the owner's style.

Decorative Painting: A Master Tradition

A wall-sized mural that recreates a Pompeian gallery . . . majestic Greek columns beside the swimming pool . . . famous storybook characters dancing along the walls of a child's room . . . these enchanting effects are the work of decorative painters.

Decorative painting is an art form using techniques that have been passed down by artisans throughout the centuries. Today, decorative painters can come from a variety of backgrounds—some have fine art degrees, many have studied the techniques of the Old Masters in Europe and others have been schooled specifically in decorative painting. These professionals carry the legacy of a tradition that was once passed from master to apprentice. Both artists and craftsmen, many decorative painters have a thorough knowledge of specific historical and decorative styles and have the ability to translate this knowledge in a historically accurate artistic rendering. Others, however, are clearly unqualified to be attempting this work.

There are many forms of decorative painting. Some of the most popular today include fresco, murals and trompe l'oeil. Over time, techniques and materials have been enhanced and improved, allowing artists and artisans to produce works that have lasted—and will last—for centuries.

When you are considering any decorative painting style, ask to see a portfolio of the artist's work and, if possible, visit a home that has work of a similar nature. Decorative showhouses are also an excellent venue in which to witness the artistry of decorative painting. Many decorative painters use these showcases to demonstrate their talents. If working with an interior designer, consult with him or her on the project and how it will enhance your overall room design. If the designer finds the artist for you, ask how that affects fees. Artists should also provide you with renderings of the work being produced.

Fees vary widely for decorative painting and are based on many factors, including the scope and scale of the project and the expertise of the painter. Ask your contractor to provide you with a sample board of the paint technique you desire. Some charge for this service while others include it in the total cost of the project. Decorative finishes can be charged on a per person, per day basis or priced per job.

Decorative painting can be a major investment, but certainly one with exquisite results.

Paint-Choosing Tips

- Use oil-based paint for metals and trim; latex for wood and drywall.
- High-traffic areas need a durable, easy-to-clean paint job. Use delicate paint applications in light-traffic areas only.
- Use flat paint for base coats; gloss to set off trim and doors.
- Be alert to the number of coats required. Eggshell paints, for example, take at least one extra coat.
- Take into account the light in the room when choosing colors. They will look different in artificial and natural light.
- Note that darker colors make a room feel smaller and cozier, while lighter colors open it up.

PAINTERS & WALLPAPERERS

	Quality	Cost	Value	Recommend?
Alchemy Paint	4	3.5	4	5

P. O. Box 1179, Wayne, IL 60184
(312) 316 - 9234

Decorative residential painting

"Alchemy" is the perfect label for Joe Vajarsky's magical way with paint, according to those who call on him for faux finishes, special glazing techniques and proprietary textured surfaces that he created and developed especially for his interior designer and high-end residential clientele. A graduate of the Chicago Institute of Art, Vajarsky, clients say, "can do anything" in decorative finishing. While he will do straight painting, it is his decorative work that is in demand, not only on walls and ceilings, but also on furniture.

"He can do anything—his finishes are hard to beat."

Art Works Studio

7710 West 167th Street, Tinley Park, IL 60477
(708) 278 - 3365

Decorative painting

Roseann Jennings of Art Works Studio specializes in decorative painting, particularly murals, which have been gracing the walls of Chicago residents for over 12 years. This trained artist is also known for her Venetian plaster, tromp l'oeil, faux bois, stenciling and glazing finishes. A member of the Stencil Artisans League of Chicago, Jennings' work has been a part of many Chicago designer show houses and has been published in several Chicago area magazines.

	Quality	Cost	Value	Recommend?
Ascher Brothers	5	3.5	5	5

3033 West Fletcher Avenue, Chicago, IL 60618
(773) 588 - 0001

Decorative and straight painting and wallpapering

People who want absolute top quality in straight, as well as decorative painting, can look to Ascher Brothers for "museum-quality" work, we're told. The company has a staff of 300 masters in the preparation of walls—the crucial beginning of a quality finish—and in the painting of straight, or more demanding faux-finish and glazed, painting. The company is said to give the same meticulous attention to hanging wallpaper. Projects are measured and evaluated by an Ascher Brothers' representative before the work crew arrives, so crews are well organized and efficient on the job, according to clients. Interior designers and others also say workers are friendly and pleasant and the company is reliable. Most rank its customer service "exceptional" and also consider its prices quite reasonable for the resulting quality. Architects and desigers are avid supporters of Ascher.

"Why would you hire anyone else?" "They do it all with the best quality service available."

	Quality	Cost	Value	Recommend?
Bart's Fine Painting	3.5	3	4.5	4

2045 North Larrabee Street, Chicago, IL 60614
(312) 951 - 5227

Straight painting, emphasizing prep work

The forte of this painting firm is its attention to wall repair and prep work. Offering primarily straight painting services, it works on both new construction and older houses. Decorative work is available from the company's network of freelance artists. The firm does not offer wallpaper hanging. Established 11 years ago, Bart's keeps, conservatively, five painters on staff. The painters are at once polite to homeowners and capable of pleasing even the most picky of architects. Returning to fix a damaged area the client overlooked is no problem for Bart's, we are told.

"I use this great little painting company all the time." "Paint crew is really conscientious and respects your home."

Beatty Decorating Co. 4 3.5 4.5 4.5
28841 Nagel Court, Lake Bluff, IL 60044
(847) 234 - 9181 www.beattydec.com
Straight and decorative painting

A reliable source for high-quality straight painting and faux finishing at affordable prices, Beatty Decorating has a sizeable, loyal following among upper-end designers and residents in downtown Chicago and along the North Shore to Lake Geneva. This large firm is known for maintaining good customer relations, according to clients. They tell us that Miles Beatty's painters are meticulous in preparing surfaces. Complicated decorative work, such as trompe l'oeil and murals, are subcontracted by the firm to specialists.

"Conscientious, careful and a superb attention to detail." "Good, solid people to have in your home." "Punctual, friendly and courteous workmen with good daily clean up." "Everyone is highly trained and very professional—they always go the extra mile."

Bernacki & Associates
424 North Oakley Boulevard, Chicago, IL 60612
(312) 243 - 5669
Restoration and conservation of art and furniture

See Bernacki & Associates's full report under the heading Furniture Repair & Refinishing

BJ Decorating Inc. 5 3.5 5 5
905 Westgate Road, Prospect, IL 60056
(847) 255 - 7150
Decorative and straight painting and wallpapering

Joe Baltasi's knack for lacquering, a process that calls for extreme precision, has earned BJ Decorating the respect, if not awe, of top interior designers throughout Chicago. This is in addition to the firm's skill with other decorative painting techniques, including faux finishes, and in hanging wallpaper and fabric. We understand it gives equal care to straight painting. Customer service extends to having the principals act as project managers and personally oversee and work on each project. Established as BJE Painting in 1972 with brother Emerich, BJ is strictly residential, and while the overwhelming majority of its clients are professional interior designers, it accepts jobs from private clients as well. Professionals and private clients alike praise BJ's service and professionalism in addition to the quality of its work.

"A bit less pricey than others, but the same quality." "Their laquer finish is beyond amazing." "I love the personal attention."

	Quality	Cost	Value	Recommend?
Capriccio	4	4	4	4.5

1264 West Elmdale Avenue, Chicago, IL 60660
(773) 973 - 1870

Murals and decorative painting

Owner Mike Popilek's background as an fine artist gives him a well-rounded history on which to base his decorative painting service. Figurative, at times historical and realistic, murals are cited as excellent. Faux finishes, glazing and other decorative finishes are also well done. Though he also handles commercial jobs, Popilek appreciates the delicateness and attention to detail required in residential work. Popilek formed his own company 10 years ago and typically works alone, although he has a stable of freelance artists to call in for large jobs.

"Mike is very sensitive to design and researches his jobs to get it right." "He is an intellectual." "His trompe l'oeil is fabulous—he's certainly not just a fancy decorative finish painter."

	Quality	Cost	Value	Recommend?
Eric Ceputis	4.5	4	5	4.5

701 Ingleside Place, Evanston, IL 60201
(847) 864 - 1124

Trade only—decorative painting and historic patterning

Ceputis's work is truly at the top of the line. He advises on both color and pattern. References tell us they admire his ideas and creativity as much as his skill, and they also enjoy his friendly manner and good service. After studying graphic design and design history at Yale, Ceputis worked as an assistant muralist in Paris before returning to his hometown of Chicago 13 years ago. Despite this training and experience, he does not do scenics or murals.

One of his specialties is replicating historic graphic patterns on walls and floors. These are either stenciled or hand painted and glazed in several colors. Another is the labor-intensive art of applying tinted plaster. Ceputis mixes the plaster to achieve the perfect hue a client calls for and then applies it in a process that takes multiple layers, plus continual polishing and waxing. Residents say their walls invigorate and add such beauty and exclaim they have never seen anything like it. Ceputis is recommneded without reservation by many of the highest quality decorators in town.

"Eric's the best. He's terrific—he's full of bright ideas and makes intelligent decisions and choices. Then the execution of those ideas is fabulous." "He's very neat and clean on site." "He helped my decorator and me with colors and made custom walls that just glow." "A really nice guy, and he made my home go from lovely to gorgeous." "A unique young man."

	Quality	Cost	Value	Recommend?
Eurocraft Painting Services	4	3.5	4	5

409 Winnemac Street, Park Forest, IL 60466
(708) 503 - 8873

Decorative and straight painting and wallpapering

Eurocraft holds rank among the more competent and skilled practitioners of straight painting and decorative finishes such as glazing, textures, faux finishes and marble patterning. Clients also highly recommend this firm for wallpaper hanging. The company works for design professionals and private clients. Its crews do all wall-preparation work and will develop sample boards for clients prior to a project.

Our sources tell us that principal Thomas Strain, a Scotsman with a bit of a brogue, is detail oriented and that he and his staff are ever courteous and very tidy on the job. Strain has 25 years of experience and, not surprisingly, has a ready market among referrals from Eurocraft's satisfied, Chicago-based clientele.

"Every job that we've given them has been executed superbly." "Very detail-oriented professionals and attentive to special needs." "Tom is excellent and reliable." "Highly professional and well organized."

Quality	Cost	Value	Recommend?
	✚	$	◆	★

Gamera Studios Inc.

| | 4 | 3 | 4.5 | 5 |

1523 North Claremont Avenue, Chicago, IL 60622
(773) 636 - 4672

Murals and decorative painting

Paul Minnihan brings over 10 years of experience to his decorative painting business. His one-year-old studio services both design professionals and residential clients in the Chicago area. The company specializes in murals as well as trompe l'oeil, texture application, glazing, gilding and standard antiquing. We hear that Minnihan's pleasant and professional approach made him a favorite with many clients.

"He's really great. I use him whenever I get the chance." "Young and eager." "His work is beautiful."

Greg Hanson

| | 3.5 | 3 | 4 | 5 |

834 Crestfield Avenue, Libertyville, IL 60048
(847) 816 - 6437

Decorative and straight painting and wallpapering

Greg Hanson has the distinction of being one of a handful of painters in the city with a facility for applying decorative painting with a spray. Hanson is said to be particularly adept at striae patterning, lacquering and glazings. He and his crews also do straight painting, wallpapering and other decorative painting. References universally report that the firm's wall-prep and work is meticulous and service is excellent. Hanson founded this firm in 1981 after years of experience.

"A hungry young painter—Hanson can pull a crew together." "They get right back to you and get the job done." "He is great to work with, and the quality is very high-end." "Very honest with schedule and prices."

H&I Decorating

1161 Larkspur, Batavia, IL 60510
(630) 879 - 6822

Decorative and straight painting

Jim Hagermann of H&I decorating has been serving the northwest suburbs of Chicago for the past 18 years. This boutique firm specializes in straight painting as well as decorative finishes including trompe l'oeil, Venetian plaster, glazing and murals. H&I is known for stylized children's room murals but they are equally adept at painting in the old master style. Wallpapers and furniture refinishing are other offerings. Much of the firm's business comes from repeat customers, as well as the trade.

Hester Decorating

| | 5 | 4.5 | 5 | 5 |

7340 North Monticello Avenue, Skokie, IL 60076
(847) 677 - 5130 www.hesterdecorating.com

Decorative and straight painting and wallpapering

Perfection comes at a price, and those who seek perfection in color-matching and decorative finishes tell us Hester Decorating fills the "bill." A large firm, it has the specialist expertise for a full range of decorative painting techniques including faux finishes, marbleizing, wood graining and gold leafing, and it also applies Venetian plaster and wallpaper. Its wood graining and color matching earn special praise. Custom color formulas are created on site in order to perfectly match the clients' requests, even though the project manager's perfectionism may occasionally try their patience. The firm's painters' talent for wood graining is, one customer insists, "flawless." Four "Picture It Painted Professionally" awards from the Painting and Decorating Contractors of America attest to Hester Decorating's artistry. Clients say the quality is matched by superb service, professional conduct and efficiency. While acknowledging that this level of work comes at a high price, they conclude that Hester's projects are worth the extra dollars.

"The wood staining Hester did in our house was exceptional—they bond with the wood." "Never had an unsolvable problem in the past 25 years." "Whether it's working with drywall, wallpaper, tile, paint or any decorative medium, they excel in handling it all." "Creative, neat, thorough, versatile—the best!" "Competent and honest; trustworthy and fair." "When they leave, you don't even know they were there." "They charge a lot, but they get everything just right."

John Kny Painting **5 4 5 4.5**
1720 Holly Court, Long Grove, IL 60047
(847) 279 - 8753

Decorative and straight painting and wallpapering

On walls, beauty is more than skin deep. That's why, among interior designers, John Kny's diligent approach to prep work is as much appreciated as the stunning results. In addition to preparing walls with diligence and the highest quality products, Kny also masters his mixtures of pigments and oils to obtain just-right color and consistency, often on a series of sample boards. Following a job, Kny gives instruction on maintenance. Many clients rank him and his crew among Chicago's top ten for quality straight painting, wallpapering and decorative finishes. Some say he's the best, and all also say they appreciate the firm's reliability.

"One of the best."

John Roegge
951 North Wolcott Avenue, Chicago, IL 60622
(773) 384 - 2356

Speciality decorative painting

In business for 15 years, John Roegge is a university-trained decorative painter who's specialties include murals, faux finishing, glazing, stenciling and Venetian plastering. This boutique firm includes three decorative painters and a muralist who work with both residential and trade clientele. The firm's work has been featured in area show houses. Roegge has been known to accept decorative painting projects for clients in other cities.

John T. Olson Decorators **4.5 3.5 5 5**
P.O. Box 3068, Saint Charles, IL 60174
(630) 443 - 0303

Decorative and straight painting and wallpapering

This 20-year-old company's mastery of all decorative painting, including murals and trompe l'oeil, has put it among the top for Chicago-area's most demanding interior designers. It also does wallpaper hanging. Olson and his stable of painters and paperhangers have impressive credentials from the country's leading art institutes and their hand at graining, marbleizing, Venetian finishes, faux finishing and glazing has taken first place in area competitions as well as first-class ranking with clients. The firm's glazing, designers say, "is like glass," and the word, "wonderful," rolls from their lips when they describe their experiences with Olson.

	Quality	Cost	Value	Recommend?

Jordi Arnan
137 Rue Saint Pierre, Suite 303, Montreal, Canada
(514) 893 - 7072
Trompe l'oeil, murals and decorative painting

Although this specialist in murals and tromp l'oeil is based in Montreal, Chicago decorators call on him for his particular brand of artistry. Jordi Arnan hails from Spain and established his studio 14 years ago on his arrival in North America. His expertise and services span the full spectrum of decorative painting and finishing, but his true specialty lies in rendering such traditional styles as Louis XVI patterns and Neoclassical designs for ceilings and walls.

LJ&M Old World Creations — 4 | 3 | 4.5 | 5
P. O. Box 88935, Carol Stream, IL 60188
(630) 240 - 2030
Speciality stucco installation

Stuck on stucco? Leonid Kravchuck is the man to call. One of the area's few providers of old-style stucco, LJ&M uses only natural masonry to which Kravchuck applies custom colored finishes on exteriors and interiors of homes. This Russian immigrant's first job in America was in the restoration of damaged, often historic, stucco buildings where color-match was critical. Stucco application is a laborious process that can take up to two months. LJ&M's work, clients say is quite simply, "extraordinary."

"This company's European artisans do a fantastic job."

Landmark Arts Inc.
841 West Randolph Street, Chicago, IL 60607
(312) 491 - 1900 www.landmarkarts.com
Murals, trompe l'oeil and straight and decorative painting

Murals and trompe l'oeil are Landmark Arts' specialty, although it also does decorative and straight painting and some custom furniture finishing.

Lohre Painting Co.
1741 Harding Road, Northfield, IL 60093
(847) 446 - 4400
Straight and decorative painting and wallpapering

Mata Decorating
919 Brookwood Street, Bensonville, IL 60106
(630) 766 - 9373
Straight painting, textured finishes

For straight painting, Rudy Mata is recognized among both interior designers and residential clients for quality work and reliable service at a reasonable price. The company also applies textured finishes, but does not do decorative painting. Mata's friendly demeanor make him a favorite of clients, who he has been serving for over 25 years on Chicago's North Shore.

"Extremely dependable."

Mattingly Home Decorating — 4 | 3.5 | 4 | 4.5
P.O. Box 2230, La Grange, IL 60525
(708) 352 - 1711 www.mattinglydecorating.com
High-end straight and decorative painting and wallpapering

For top quality and a repertoire of decorative techniques that covers the field, from murals and trompe l'oeil to stucco, glazing, faux finishing, Venetian plaster and metallic textures, many of the area's best interior designers have been turning to Mattingly since 1981. The company, they say, is especially versatile in faux finishes with an extensive catalog of the various patterns it creates. The company also hangs wallpaper and fabric, ranging in textures from silk to suede, and restores architectural moldings. Add to this, fast turn-around and attention to service and clean-up, and it's no wonder designers and a circle of high-end private clients put this firm at the top of their list.

"I didn't want to give away this great source but everyone deserves this kind of quality service." "The best in the world." "Really reliable, I never had to wonder."

PaintCraft **3.5** **3** **4** **4.5**
1843 West Grand Avenue, Chicago, IL 60622
(312) 226 - 8082

Straight and decorative painting, wood refinishing and wallpapering

A versatile portfolio of skills makes PaintCraft a popular choice, especially in remodels and renovations at older homes in Chicago and its northern suburbs. Principal Rich Bauer represents the third generation of painters at this 12 year old company, which built its initial reputation on fine straight painting. It now offers a variety of surface techniques, including murals, glazing, plastering and wallpaper hanging. PaintCraft will paint or refinish fine woodworking moldings and will design millwork to match a client's antique moldings. Clients say pricing is reasonable and crews are respectful of homes while they work.

Peacock Decorators **3.5** **3** **4.5** **4.5**
7439 West Roosevelt Road, Forest Park, IL 60130
(708) 771 - 0160

Decorative and straight painting and wallpapering

Peacock has been offering high-quality straight painting, wallpapering and a range of decorative painting techniques since 1906. One of Chicago's oldest painting companies, it's said to stay on top of the most modern prep practices and products. The firm is also respected for its efficiency and fair pricing. Decorators say the firm is particularly adept at smaller jobs, and is respected for its workmanship and its all-round professionalism.

Professional Decorating **4** **3** **4** **4**
7149 North Austin Avenue, Chicago, IL 60714
(847) 647 - 2246

Straight and decorative painting and wallpapering

Professional Decorating, with principal Glen Giacinto, has been serving a large trade and residential clientele for over 18 years. This mid-sized firm specializes in quality straight and decorative painting, including faux finishes, glazing, murals and trompe l'oeil as well as gold leafing and restoration. Pigments are mixed on-site (a practice most consider a dying art) to ensure the perfect paint color. Clients give the company high marks for their quick, efficient and accommodating crews.

Ragsdale **3** **3** **4** **4**
709 Sheridan Road, Lake Bluff, IL 60044
(847) 234 - 4567 www.ragsdaleinc.com

Straight and decorative painting and wallpapering

Ragsdale is a family business that's catered to the upper-level market in Chicago's northern suburbs since 1977. The firm employs two master-trained painters for murals and trompe l'oeil and also is said to excel at faux boiserie and other fabulous fakes, glazing, striae and marble patterning and Venetian plaster. Cients also rely on owner Steve Ragsdale and his crew to "age" cabinets with crackled and distressed finishes and hang wallpaper. Ragsdale's prep work gets special mention from the company's mostly designer clientele along with its high level of customer service.

Sidney's Services
725 North Skokie Highway, Lake Bluff, IL 60044
(847) 615 - 0800

Residential and commercial window cleaning

See Sidney's Services's full report under the heading Window Washers

Simes Studios **4.5** **4** **4** **5**
1809 West Webster, Suite 200, Chicago, IL 60614
(773) 327 - 7101 www.simesstudios.com

Murals, trompe l'oeil and decorative painting

Decorative artistry from Simes Studios begins with walls and extends to floors and furniture. Cindy and Jorge Simes arrived from Buenos Aires in 1988 and established this small studio that applies murals, trompe l'oeil and a wide range of decorative finishes, such as faux bois and marble, glazing, textures and Venetian plaster. Noted for combining Old World techniques with contemporary styles and materials, Simes has won the admiration of interior designers for restaurants and residences in the upper strata. It does not prepare walls, but will recommend contractors that meet its high standards.

Steve Sciuto Ltd. **4** **3.5** **4.5** **5**
427 Kedzie Street, Evanston, IL 60202
(847) 424 - 9246

Straight painting, millwork restoration and refinishing

Steve Sciuto's boutique firm specializes in the restoration and authentic period reproduction, finishing and painting of architectural millwork. His attention to detail is well known among his top decorator clientele. Sciuto receives very high marks to the firm's decorative painting and paperhanging and its meticulous attention to wall-prep. His millwork restoration experience comes from his work in refinishing pianos and furniture for a New York company. His techniques, such as brush-dot application and French polishing, put the firm in a class apart, designers report. Service from Sciuto, they say, is "outstanding," making it a favorite resource for some of Chicago's best-ranked interior designers.

Tamara Studios **4** **3.5** **4** **4.5**
1130 West Monroe Street, 2nd Floor, Chicago, IL 60607
(312) 226 - 9066 www.backdrops.com

Murals, trompe l'oeil and high-end faux finishing

Seventeen-year-old Tamara Studios stands in the forefront of custom decorative wall art and fine art painting, not just in Chicago but also around the country. Interior designers say Tamara Morrison is able to replicate any design they want. At one client's request, Morrison and her artists copied a pattern from a swatch of intricate 17th-century wallpaper directly onto the wall. This team altered the original colors and used layers of fine glazes. The artists' specialty is custom murals in any style, usually on muslin. The murals can then be shipped directly to the client to be wallpapered to the wall. Designer clients say that the studio's skill with other decorative painting, including trompe l'oeil, faux finishing, Florentine ink staining and glazing, are also of the highest quality. The studio artists also paint furniture. It's no surprise that Tamara Studios serves the tip-top of the market.

"A real professionalism in their painting." "The work is polished and refined." "It's amazing—truly outstanding." "They're not only amazing craftspeople, they couldn't be nicer if they tried!"

Wallflower Painting & Design

1359 North Maplewood Avenue, Chicago, IL 60622
(312) 421 - 7282

Decorative and straight painting and wallpapering

Zaroff Restoration & Painted Finishes **4.5** **4** **4** **5**

2173 North California Avenue, Chicago, IL 60647
(773) 384 - 8420

Decorative painting and finishing

Tom and Julie Zaroff specialize in decorative painting on everything from walls to furniture, including traditional faux finishes, mural painting, trompe l'oeil and more basic treatments such as spongings, stenciling and striae. When they started their company in 1990, they focused primarily on furniture restoration and refinishing. The bulk of their business is now painting, but they still do the occasional on-site refurbishing, refinishing and restoration work on antique pieces (including French polishing). The Zaroffs, who are both art school graduates, do most of the work, with the occasionally help from freelance artists. The company works with both the trade and private clients in the Chicago area up to the North Shore. Clients tell us they appreciate the aesthetic touch they bring to their work, and praise their creativity and artistic eye.

"Tom and Julie are very helpful, easy to work with and have great ideas. They also work well with the painting contractor, which is a big help." "Very dependable, but pricey." "They take into account all the elements of a room when coming up with an idea." "We wanted a specific design, so they went to the library, researched ideas, came up with a plan for us, and then redid it a couple times until we agreed on it. Very thorough."

Hiring a Pest Control Service Provider

Roaches, mice, rats, termites, carpenter ants, ants, fleas, ticks, spiders and silver fish. These are the ten most common household pests, and according to the National Pest Management Association (NPMA), every house in America has been visited by at least one of them in the past year.

Even though do-it-yourself pest-control kits are readily available, they are not as effective as the services offered by professionals. The application of pesticides is just one part of a total pesticide management program which typically includes safety considerations, prevention methods and structural modifications. Whereas untrained homeowners may be able to apply pesticides with varying degrees of success, professionals rely on training, expertise and sophisticated techniques to control pesticide infestations in an efficient, economical and safe manner—protecting the long-term interests of the homeowner's family and the environment.

Not all pest control service providers are alike. While most work to eliminate a wide range of infestations, termite abatement requires a different kind of training and licensing and, therefore, a different kind of exterminator than most other pests. In addition to eliminating bugs from your living space, a lot of these professionals also specialize in removing birds and rodents, persuading squirrels to nest elsewhere, etc.

Generally, exterminators advocate that homeowners practice prevention to the greatest extent possible to minimize disease and damage to property. In fact, most reputable firms will happily provide training on standards of cleanliness in order to prevent infestations and mating, as well as counsel on clean-up of eggs and droppings.

Where Do I Start?

The first step involved in seeking the services of an pest control expert requires that you perform a preliminary inspection of your home yourself. Beware of exterminators who arrive at your doorstep unsolicited and offer free inspections. They tend to prey on homeowners' general ignorance about pests by intimidating them into authorizing immediate and expensive treatments. It has been rumored that some such service providers are known to bring bug specimens with them and release them into the premises of unsuspecting homeowners (a clever variation on the "fly-in-my-soup" routine).

When seeking an exterminator, be sure to have ready a list of the kind of infestation you have or suspect you have, the number of pets, children and adults that inhabit your home, any allergies these inhabitants have and the number of rooms in your home. These factors will determine the kind of exterminator you need to hire and the processes that will ultimately be used to eliminate infestations.

A Variety of Pest Control Methods

Pest control is a highly specialized industry and its jargon can be confusing. Be sure to ask the service provider for a description of each project and a success-rate estimate for each procedure. If, for instance, an exterminator advises fumigating your home with toxic gas to get rid of termites, ask for a detailed description of the method and its possible hazards. Not every extermination, however, requires you to leave the premises for a few hours and subsequently air out your home. New technology, such as microwave and electro-gun systems, may be safer for families with pets and children. Work with the professional to choose which option best suits your needs.

On Cost

Once you've conducted a preliminary inspection and suspect the presence of a residential free-loader, contact a licensed pest control service provider. Since large projects are often costly and require skill, expertise and knowledge, it is generally suggested that you get several bids from multiple vendors for large projects.

Different firms charge varied rates, depending on: 1) the scale and nature of the project, 2) the complexity of the infestation and 3) the potential need to remove walls and other structures. While there are no standard hourly or per-room charges, most exterminators are usually happy to give free estimates when they perform preliminary inspections.

Contracts and Guarantees

Once you decide on a firm, negotiate a contract and get it in writing. In the contract, specify the nature of the infestation, the extent of the infestation and the resulting damage, the exact services to be provided, description of guarantees, the desired end-result (abatement only or continuing control) and how long the treatment is expected to last.

Some exterminators do offer guarantees with their contracts. Be realistic about guarantee provisions that promise a one-time total solution! Cockroach abatement, for instance, needs to be renewed every six months in order to be completely effective. While this may seem a little excessive, remember that roaches are the only living creatures that can survive nuclear holocaust—one electronic or chemical application will only humor them.

Important Issues About This Highly Regulated Industry

Because exterminators handle highly toxic products, they should undergo rigorous training to practice their profession. A pest control specialist's membership in national or regional professional association is usually a good indicator that the service provider has access to the most cutting-edge technical information and is committed to ongoing education. Inquire about a service provider's affiliations and follow up by verifying membership with the professional organization. The NPCA is one of the largest and best known national organizations in the field and can be reached on the World Wide Web (www.pestworld.org) or by calling (703) 573-8330.

Insurance

Permits and licensing are not the only business issues to verify before hiring an exterminator. It is crucial to find out whether or not the exterminator carries liability insurance to cover potential damage to property and/or to people in the course of the exterminator's work. If the exterminator doesn't carry such insurance, check your home-owners' policy for coverage. In the absence of both, consider buying insurance to protect your belongings and yourself from liability.

Most good pest control companies in Chicago belong to the Illinois Pest Control Association, www.pestweb.com/ipca. This site tells you all you need to know about Pest control Insurance and government policies. Pest control companies in Chicago register with the State of Illinois, Department of Public Health (312-814-2608). It is advised that you also have a permit to work in the pest control Industry but it is not required. Permits and licensing regulations are the same for both the city and suburbs of Chicago.

What's Bugging You?
A few precautions to help prevent pest-nesting in your home

- **Termites:** Wet wood is every termite's favorite meal. Get rid of old tree stumps, form boards and wood debris around your house and rid your home of excess moisture, making sure gutters are unclogged and all pipe leaks promptly fixed.
- **Rodents:** Take out the trash. Daily! Garbage is a rat's favorite nesting ground, and they begin to mate at the tender age of five weeks to produce up to 48 spawn a year. Also, be vigilant about keeping all the entry points into your home clean and clear, including ducts, vents and chimneys.
- **Cockroaches:** While it is very hard to combat a cockroach infestation without professional help, a few tactics will go a long way toward keeping them at bay: proper ventilation, fitting all holes with screens, sealing around pipes where they come through the floor and ceiling and storing and/or covering all food (yours and your pets!).

PEST CONTROL

	Quality	Cost	Value	Recommend?
A&A Super Exterminators	4	2	5	4

4355 North Elston Avenue, Chicago, IL 60641
(773) 545 - 3650

Residential and commercial pest control

A&A stands for Arnold Limas times two, a father-and-son team that keeps common city pests away from the dwellings of more than 200 Chicago residents and commercial clients every month. The Limas duo uses only non-toxic products to control all rodent and insect infestations with the exception of termites, a specialty that A&A does not provide.

Clients say A&A is not only reliable and thorough, but also inexpensive. While prices vary according to the level of pest infestation and a location's size, initial fumigation of a three-story apartment, for example, is less than $100, and routine maintenance falls below $50 a month.

	Quality	Cost	Value	Recommend?
A Abate Termite & Pest Control Company	4	2.5	4	4

7907 South Champlain Avenue, Chicago, IL 60619
(773) 783 - 5888

Residential and commercial pest control

Owner Larry Jones has been in business for 20 years, and he operates his company with just two additional technicians in order to keep the company small and the service personal. It handles both residential and commercial customers in downtown Chicago and the surrounding suburbs, where it often gives furry pests a second chance by catching them live and releasing them in a nearby park. A Abate will rid buildings of all pests and offers a maintenance plan to keep pests away. Clients report that the staff is friendly, knowledgeable and provides good service at a fair price.

	Quality	Cost	Value	Recommend?
Aerex Pest Control Services	5	2.5	4.5	4

4674 North Elston, Chicago, IL 60630
(773) 545 - 7777 www.aerex.com

Residential pest control

This locally-owned exterminating company's reputation for pest control is as broad as its reach. Considered one of the best in the business, Aerex has a client list of more than 20,000 and has been ridding Chicago residences of rodents and insects for more than half a century. Under the direction of principal Richard Kirshner, fully-insured Aerex representatives practice up-to-date prevention techniques that clients say keep them and their homes free from unwanted pest guests.

	Quality	Cost	Value	Recommend?
Alpha Omega Pest Control Corp.	3	3	4	4

8444 Ashland Street, Chicago, IL 60630
(773) 233 - 3336

Residential pest control

Alpha Omega, the first and last name in top-to-bottom residential pest control, including all rodents and insects, services Chicago and the suburbs. The firm offers free inspection and free estimates, then guarantees results. Customers say Alpha Omega's certified technicians are dependable, trustworthy and hard working.

American Eagle Pest Elimination 5 3 5 5
3057 North Rockwell Street, Chicago, IL 60618
(773) 549 - 7320

Residential and commercial pest control

George Manning, the owner of American Eagle Pest Elimination for over 39 years, is said to be a true master in his field. A trained entomologist, he not only provides service, but also imparts fascinating facts about his prey. Many members of the American Eagle team have been with Manning since he founded the company and they, too, provide clients with an education as they offer relief from all types of pests.

While many companies offer general controls and press clients for long-term maintenance plans, American Eagle takes pains to understand each client's particular problems and conditions, and then prescribe immediate and enduring solutions, which may even include structural alterations. This methodology explains the company's nickname: The Problem Solvers. In addition to traditional pest control techniques, it also offers innovative and environmentally safe solutions.

Even more unusual, the company provides guarantees, some of which are unheard of in the business, such as the promise that squirrel trouble will be eliminated in a single visit. Prices, we're told, are a little above the norm, but is considered well worth the cost by satisfied customers.

"George Manning's expertise in the pest-control industry is wonderful." "This company is extremely honest."

American Exterminators 4.5 2.5 4 4.5
5860 North Lincoln Avenue, Chicago, IL 60657
(773) 763 - 8100

Residential and commercial pest control

American Exterminators has been eliminating pests in residences and businesses in Chicago since 1937. American deploys its troops on the basis of an individual client's particular problem, ensuring that whatever's bugging you, you'll be getting the right person for the job. Estimates for residences are typically given over the phone, and we hear that American's service is prompt, efficient and courteous.

Anderson Pest Control 3 3 4 3
1100 West Jackson Boulevard, Chicago, IL 60630
(312) 733 - 0100

Residential pest control

With eight Chicago-area locations, Anderson technicians know their neighborhoods. The company provides free estimates, and clients say the workers are extremely thorough, highly reliable and we're also told they are polite and courteous.

Chicago Exterminator Co., Inc. 4 3 4 5
100 South Lively Boulevard, Elk Grove Village, IL 60007
(773) 631 - 8383

Residential and commercial pest control

Now under fourth-generation management, this 100-year-old, family-run business operates throughout metropolitan Chicago and, we are told, enjoys top ranking with long-time grateful customers who consider the company's workers "experts" on pest eradication. Estimates and answers to pesty questions are given freely over the phone.

"Talk to the experts."

DL McDavis General Pest Control
6238 South Kedzie, Chicago, IL 60637
(773) 955 - 7322

Residential and commercial pest control

No job is too big or too small for DL Mc Davis, which cures both residential and commercial pest infestations with dispatch, then prevents any unhappy returns through monthly maintenance contracts. This company will take on any kind of pest, from the common to the unusual—bats, for instance. All employees are licensed, and clients say they give prompt, attentive service. This firm also offers a complete line of pest control products for do-it-yourselfers.

Logan Square Pest Control
3935 West Fullerton Avenue, Chicago, IL 60647
(773) 278 - 0966

Residential and commercial pest control

Lowe's Pest Control
1543 East 86th Street, Chicago, IL 60619
(773) 356 - 9748

Residential pest control

Furry pests as well as all unwanted insects, including troublesome termites, get the boot from Lowe's professional and competent teams of fumigators, we are told. The company specializes in residential pest control and is said to deliver excellent service at a reasonable price. Estimates are always free.

"Very happy with their service."

Mohorn's Exterminating Service 3 2.5 3 3
61 West 72nd Street, Chicago, IL 60621
(773) 224 - 2600

Residential and commercial pest control

NeverNest Extermination 4.5 2 4 5
3644 West Diversey, Chicago, IL 60647
(773) 772 - 9172 www.nevernest.com

Residential and commercial pest control

Thaddeus Mazuchowski and his small team of pest control experts have been discreetly "taking care of business" in Chicago and the suburbs for the past 15 years. Clients tell us that the company is quick to respond even on an emergency basis. Because NeverNest workers are experienced and reportedly "fantastic listeners," they are able to diagnose problems and provide estimates over the phone.

We also hear that the NeverNest team is particularly sensitive to households with children. It eliminates problems with any type of pest in the most environmentally friendly way possible, using formulations that are both odor-free and safe. They get a lot of referral business, which is a good recommendation, but not much repeat business, which clients say is an even better recommendation.

"I could not believe how quickly they showed up." "Really nice guys." "I am glad I never have to call them again . . . a good thing."

Nixalite of America, Inc. 3.5 3 4 4

1025 16th Avenue, East Moline, IL 61244
(309) 755 - 8771

Do-it-yourself pest control information and products

Nixalite manufactures its own brand of pest control products, including a formula for ridding homes of pigeon problems. Owner Marie Gellerstedt and her son, John, are scholars on the subject of pest control and provide practical information to harried homeowners on do-it-yourself cures using Nixalite products.

Original Pest and Termite Company

1941 West Armitage Avenue, Chicago, IL 60622
(773) 772 - 8052

Residential and commercial pest control

ORKIN 4 3 5 5

5840 North Lincoln Avenue, Chicago, IL 60659
(773) 334 - 1243 www.orkin.com

Residential and commercial pest control

This Chicago office of the ORKIN national chain is staffed with representatives who are very knowledgeable about all areas of pest control—rodents, termites, fleas and insects of every annoying ilk. Equipped with the parent company's proven products and trained in its techniques, Orkin technicians are nationally recognized as reliable pest eradicators. All are licensed, bonded and insured. ORKIN offers free inspections and ongoing maintenance contracts.

Pest Masters 3 2 3 4

1943 West 63rd Street, Chicago, IL 60636
(773) 737 - 6939 www.pestmaster.net

Residential pest control

Pest Masters' expertise in kicking unwanted pests out of Chicago homes is comprehensive and includes "wildlife relocation," a nice way of saying "pack your bags" to unwanted furry inhabitants. The company also terminates termite infestations and de-bugs buildings of any other crawling, creeping and flying creatures. The company has been in business since 1964, and clients tell us its workers are reliable and easy to work with. Estimates are free and the company has a 24-hour answering service.

Petty's Exterminating Co. 3 3 3 3

1515 South Polaski Road, Chicago, IL 60623
(773) 277 - 0437

Residential pest control

No pest that crawls, creeps or flies is immune from Petty's extermination tactics. These technicians have expertise in the elimination of problems with rodents, birds and all bugs, including determined termites. Service is available on a same- or next-day basis, and the references we talked with say they are delighted with the results.

	Quality	Cost	Value	Recommend?
Smithereen Exterminating Company	4	4	4	4

1635 South State Street, Chicago, IL 60616
(312) 922 - 5011 www.smithereen.com

Residential and commercial pest control

The very name, Smithereen, suggests that this company takes pest control seriously and we hear it does. It has been among Chicagoan's most trusted eradicators of rodents and insects for more than a century. Today it relies overwhelmingly on chemical-free, non-toxic solutions, but will declare all out war when necessary. Smithereen serves both residential and commercial clients who give it top-quality ranking for initial cures and ongoing prevention.

Smithereen realizes that there are seasonal pest problems, which are often neighborhood-related. It makes every effort to promote community cures, offering substantial discounts for next-door or whole-block services.

Hiring a Plumber

Whether it's trimming out a kitchen and bath remodel, installing an entire system for a new home, a routine repair or maintenance call or an absolute emergency, you need a plumber you can count on.

Obviously, you want to hold on to a plumbing contractor that has proved himself over the course of a major project. Hand-picked by your trusty GC, he knows the guts of your home better than anyone. Even if you aren't planning a renovation and just need someone to handle more mundane problems like leaky faucets, its worth putting in the effort to build a relationship with a plumber who can offer quality and service, so he'll be there before you're sunk.

Although most plumbers are available for a simple service call, some high-end service providers prefer to limit service calls, especially 24-hour emergency service, to existing customers. This practice ensures that you will receive the highest level of service and quality with a prompt response.

Where Do I Start?

You will want to ask prospective plumbers how long they have been in business and what types of work they specialize in. Many plumbing professionals do both commercial and residential work, dealing with both large renovations and smaller repairs. Specialties and focuses vary in this industry, so it is best to look to someone that has experience with your type of project.

When you call a plumber's references, you'll want to ask the usual questions about quality of work and whether the project was finished on schedule and on budget. Because plumbing can be a messy business, respect for surroundings and cleanliness are especially important.

A Job for Professionals

You should only consider a full-time licensed professional for your plumbing needs. Though a license is not required in Chicagoland to perform basic plumbing maintenance work, your service provider must be licensed for any jobs that require the filing of a permit. As always, ask about insurance, including worker's comp and liability insurance. Your plumbing professional should always be responsible for obtaining all permits necessary for your job.

On Cost

For larger projects, each plumbing contractor will submit its bid to the GC, who will then incorporate it into the overall bid submitted to the client. Often the GC for your project will bring in a trusted plumber for the job, but you are free to ask your GC to include another plumber in the bidding process, which also helps to ensure that bids are competitive. If your renovation is relatively small and a GC is not involved, get several estimates for the proposed work.

For smaller jobs and service calls, which include repair and maintenance, most companies will charge an hourly fee plus a flat transportation fee just to show up. Others will charge for the first half hour and per each additional quarter hour, eliminating the transportation/show-up fee. The standard in metropolitan Chicago these days is an $80 to $90 hourly rate for a master plumber and a $55 transportation/show-up fee, reflected in a baseline rating of 3 for cost in *The Franklin Report*. However, please remember, a company's standards in relation to product and safety, the depth of its resources and the demand it's in can all affect cost on top of hourly rates, and are factored into the rating.

Some companies charge a set fee for a visit, then have flat-rate charges for each task performed, such as unclogging a storm drain or replacing a sink. Others insist on doing a consultation to provide you with an estimate before any work is started. This is a must for larger jobs. Fees for contract renovation work are typically higher than fees for new construction per hour and per square foot. In the end, it should come down to the company with the best reputation for quality and service, not just the low bidder.

GUARANTEES AND SERVICE AGREEMENTS

When your equipment is installed, it should come with both a warranty from the manufacturer and a guarantee from the service provider. Be sure to ask about service agreements. Many plumbing professionals provide regular "check-ups" and inspections. It may seem like wasted money at first, but over time these measures can prevent an emergency.

SAVE MONEY BY SAVING TIME

If you inventory the state of your plumbing and think ahead about work that will need to be done, your plumber will be able to work more effectively. Check faucets, drains, radiators and fixtures throughout the house and compile a list. Present this list to the plumber upon arrival so he can prioritize the various tasks and work simultaneously if possible. This way, you won't have to call him in again for another minor repair in a few weeks.

If the plumber will need access to the pipes under your kitchen sink, clear out the area to save billable time. Also put away or protect anything vulnerable to damage. Your plumber will appreciate being able to get to work without having to wade through piles of children's toys or rummage around in a cabinet full of cleaning supplies.

Don't wait until your bathroom is flooded with four inches of water. Develop a good relationship with a plumber now, and you'll never have to page frantically through a phone book and throw yourself at the mercy of whatever plumber happens to be free.

MORE THAN PIPES

YOUR PLUMBER IS TRAINED TO DO MUCH MORE THAN FIX CLOGGED DRAINS. A FULL-SERVICE PLUMBER CAN:

- Provide condensation drains for air conditioning units.
- Install the boiler, lines and radiators necessary for household heat.
- Install hot water re-circulation and water pressure booster pumps.
- Hook up major appliances (gas stoves, washing machines).
- Make a gas-meter connection, install gas lines and provide gas shut-off valves.
- Install storm/slop drains for the kitchen, patio, garage, laundry room, greenhouse and roof.
- Label all shut-off, hot and cold, delivery and return lines, and provide you with a set of as-built drawings.

Plumbers

Angel Plumbing & Sewage
6248 North Pulaski Road, Chicago, IL 60646
(773) 685 - 9011

Plumbing service and installation

Arrow Plumbing, Inc. 3 2.5 4 3.5
Libertyville, IL
(847) 549 - 9600
Plumbing service and installation

Clients say this company hits the bulls-eye when it comes to plumbing remodeling and repair. Owner John Shull and his tight-knit team of six plumbers stick to smaller projects, such as bathroom change-outs and service work. We're told Arrow is discriminating about taking on new work, always conscious of keeping its current customers satisfied. Its fully equipped trucks will travel anywhere within a 10-mile radius of the company's Libertyville shop location.

BMW Plumbing 4.5 3.5 4.5 5
444 Lake Cook Road, Suite 21, Deerfield, IL 60015
(847) 948 - 8484

High-end plumbing remodeling and service

Characterized as an "excellent organization," BMW gets kudos from high-end clients, builders and the best kitchen and bath designers from Lake Forest to Chicago's Gold Coast. It is considered top notch for plumbing renovation, and we're told that it lets nothing slip—or leak—through the cracks. Co-owners Michael Dixon and Wayne Zonca are known for their can-do attitude and clients say one or the other is always available to field customers' questions and supervise the BMW team of ten "great guys." The owners are accessible 24 hours a day to resolve small annoyances as well as emergencies. Raves like "the best service company that's ever entered my home," roll from delighted clients' lips. Homeowners who live on the premises during remodeling are especially glowing in their praise of BMW's adherence to work schedules and the preservation of their personal space.

The BMW team is experienced and familiar with old and new products and plumbing-related systems. It's trained in the installation of top-of-the-line fixtures and fittings, such as Dornbrach and Hans Grohe, and is equally skilled in replacing pumps and piping in the aged recesses of turn-of-the-century homes. No wonder, when it comes to plumbing installation and service, specialists at the city's top kitchen and bath showrooms and many others ride with BMW.

"Absolutely the best. My husband is very particular and fastidious and wouldn't hire anyone else. You'll be hard pressed to find a better contractor. The only one I recommend!" "I work with three different plumbers, but for service work BMW is the only one I call." "They're great guys. Honest and on top of everything."

Bruno Francis Plumbing 4 4 4 4
3310 West Columbus, Chicago, IL 60652
(773) 436 - 6667

High-end plumbing service, installation and remodeling

Bruno Francis Plumbing is thought to be one of Chicago's premier plumbing contractor for the upper end of the residential, commercial and industrial markets. Since 1945, it has worked with the city's most celebrated architects and renowned residents. Long before the advent of off-the-shelf complex waterworks, Bruno Francis was designing and installing custom multi-jet whirlpools, steam rooms, waterfall showers and other luxury bath amenities, including towel warmers and heated floors. While it will tackle jobs ranging from $200 to $200,000 or more, it's made its mark in "showcase" penthouses along Lake Michigan from the North Shore to Wisconsin, and high-profile installations ranging from the ridiculous (the Playboy Mansion) to the sublime (The Art Institute of Chicago).

While the company's design of luxury amenities leaves the last best impression, clients are equally enthusiastic about Bruno Francis workers' consideration on the job. Clients say members of the 50-strong Bruno Francis workforce stick to schedules and create minimal disruption while they work. Crews will even construct temporary bath and kitchen facilities for clients during a remodeling project. The company's professional-level clientele appreciates its knowledge and understanding of such essentials as a structure's underlying architectural integrity and the building codes and restrictions that impact an installation. In creating and interpreting designs, it is said to be as facile with CAD software (unheard of for a plumber) as it is with rudimentary sketches.

Deerfield Plumbing **3.5** **3** **4** **4**

Highland Park, IL
(847) 948 - 7227

Plumbing installation and repair

Many high-end North Shore architects and contractors rely on the seven-member staff of Deerfield, headed by Jim Feid, for installations that are out of the ordinary and call for fine imported fixtures. The company works in both remodeling and new construction and also services existing plumbing systems. Clients give Deerfield high ranking for workmanship and reliability, and city inspectors also rate it A+. However, it's high marks and demand among industry pros means this small shop cannot always handle new service calls.

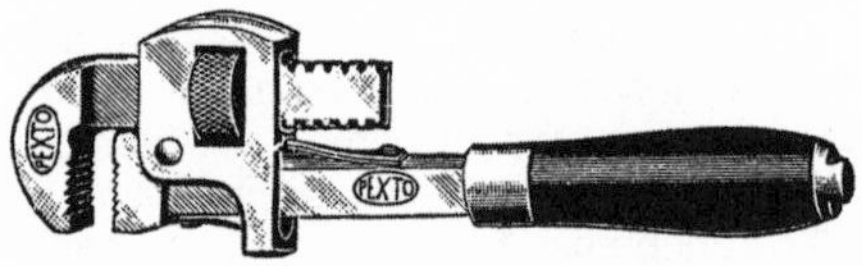

F.J. Kerrigan Plumbing Co. **4** **3.5** **4** **4**

811 Ridge Road, Wilmette, IL 60091
(847) 251 - 2695

Residential and commercial plumbing installation and repair

Jerry Kerrigan heads this versatile family operation that will put an O'Hare restroom in running order a lot faster than most flights leave the gate and also install plumbing exotica for top-of-the-line luxury homes along the North Shore and for select downtown clients. Kerrigan is a large shop with 50 years of experience and a talented staff of 65. Among its residential specialties are the provision of handicap accessibility in new and existing kitchens and baths, and custom-home jobs in which the plumbing alone costs out at $400,000 or more. However, the Kerrigan crew will also take on small jobs, and we are told, regardless of size or scope, this company stands behind its work.

HT Strenger 3.5 3.5 4 4.5

28915 North Herky Drive, Unit 101, Lake Bluff, IL 60044
(847) 234 - 9440

Plumbing renovation, repair and service

The second-oldest family operated plumbing and heating firm in the state, HT Strenger was founded by Henry T. Strenger in 1911. Grandson, John Strenger, now steers this excellent organization, which provides plumbing service repairs, retrofiting in remodeling projects, re-piping and also handles the repair of storm and sanitary sewers and tackles other drainage problems. Clients, both residential and commercial, tell us the Strenger crew is especially adept at taming quirks and navigating older homes. Strenger uses only premium materials and name-brand American products. Its area of operation encompass Lake Bluff, Lake Forest, Libertyville and Vernon Hills.

"They saved me—the gentleman who came was great!" "Excellent service on a Saturday." "I can always count on Strenger."

John J. Cahill III, Inc. 4 3.5 4 4

1515 Church Street, Evanston, IL 60201
(847) 491 - 1890 www.cahillinc.com

Residential plumbing, HVAC, kitchen and bath remodeling

Small wonder that Cahill specializes in the repair, restoration and replacement of plumbing systems in the historic houses along Chicago's North Shore. It is the oldest family-run plumbing company in Illinois, and chances are, the ancestors of today's third- and fourth-generation principals were the original installers. Since 1890, Cahill has updated its menu with a wide range of capabilities, including kitchens and baths and heating, ventilation and air conditioning as well as plumbing. It is a one-stop resource for design, product procurement, installation and service. A showroom displays its expertise in kitchen and bath remodeling and design and contains a store that will sell supplies to do-it-yourselfers. With 50 employees and a fleet of 30 trucks, Cahill handles both high-end residential and commercial projects from Highland Park to Lincoln Park. Its emergency service crews are available 24 hours, and customers so appreciate Cahill's employees' friendly, personal service, that when they need help again, they often call workers back by name.

Johns Plumbing

3116 North Cicero Avenue, Chicago, IL 60641
(773) 286 - 9030

Residential and commercial plumbing installation, repair and service

With a staff of 70, Johns serves residential and commercial clients from downtown Chicago to the North Shore and has been doing so since 1981. In the residential arena, it engineers and builds add-on baths and also remodels existing ones. It also handles plumbing repairs and provides 24-hour emergency service. For commercial clients, Johns provides engineering expertise, ushers plans through municipal certification, and handles complete installation.

Logan Square Plumbing Contractors 3.5 3 4 4

Northbrook, IL
(847) 291 - 8787

Plumbing and hot water heating repair

At many a North Shore residence, when the drain clogs or a pipe bursts, Les Epstein of Logan Square is the man to call. This strictly residential small shop has been committed to keeping loyal customers dry and warm since 1932. Its quick response to emergencies, 24 hours a day, along with a talent for troubleshooting that prevents new emergencies from occurring, has won Logan an excellent reputation. We are also told that Epstein and his crew of five don't make a mess or disturb the surroundings. Their skills and expertise encompass boiler repair, fixture replacement and tile installation.

"A reliable company with great service. We have been a customer for years."

Mahoney Plumbing Inc. **4.5** **3** **4.5** **4**

501 Bank Lane, Highwood, IL 60040
(847) 432 - 8696

Residential plumbing renovation and service

Comfort, not plumbing, is what Dan and Tom Mahoney, the second-generation owners of this family run business, like to think their company provides. Its customers agree. With a crew of just 11, Mahoney offers residential clients a wide range of plumbing-related capabilities that include the installation of gas lines and hydronic and radiant heat systems along with plumbing design and installation for kitchen and master bath remodeling. The company is equipped to "televise" pipes in detecting problems and keeps current with new technologies through regular training sessions and membership in professional associations. Customer service, a legacy from the brothers' standard-setting father, is being passed on, they say, to an upcoming third generation.

Northfield Plumbing **4** **3** **4.5** **5**

1749-B Harding Road, Northfield, IL 60093
(847) 441 - 0881

Plumbing renovation, repair and service

Clients give Northfield high marks, and say the integrity and competency of principal Mike Murrin sets the standard for the entire company. Murrin heads a staff of 11, and the company takes on plumbing subcontracting for everything from small kitchen and laundry room redos to six-figure kitchen and bath installations for custom builders.

At the same time, it continues to handle repairs and trouble-shoot for customers with old boilers, vintage gas pipes, and errant radiant heating systems. These long-time customers appreciate Northfield's familiarity with their plumbing landscape, and Northfield's 24-hour emergency service is limited to this loyal clientele. However, we're told that all calls are returned promptly.

"Top quality, prompt service. I recommend Northfield Plumbing every time." "Very accommodating. Pleasant people to work with." "I can only provide the highest possible recommendation."

Old Di Pietro Plumbing Corp. **4** **3** **4** **4**

440 Lake Cook Road, Deerfield, IL 60015
(847) 945 - 0044

Plumbing service and installation

Pasquesi Plumbing **5** **3.5** **5** **4.5**

3218 Skokie Valley Road, Highland Park, IL 60035
(847) 433 - 3426

High-end plumbing, heating, ventilation and air conditioning installation and service

There's a star next to Joseph Pasquesi's name on the Rolodexes of many of Chicago's best known families and top-tier contractors and architects. They turn to him and his team for everything from a leaky faucet to a sophisticated and complex bath installation that tallies out at a half-million dollars or more. Clients swear Pasquesi was born with the gift of good service, but he attributes it to his boyhood job at Sunset Hill Foods in Lake Forest, a name that also enjoys star ranking with much of this company's clientele.

Pasquesi employs 15 servicemen and 48 installers. All apprentice in-house, which accounts for their firms high and consistent standards of technical expertise. We hear they treat clients as if they were representing their own family. Pasquesi's family is proudly represented by his son, John, and a number of supers who have been with the company since day one. Calls are returned immediately; accurate price quotes for service are given over the phone, and no tool or serviceman's foot touches the jobsite floor unprotected by a dropcloth, towel or protective "booty." The company also handles HVAC replacement and maintenance, but does not do sheet metal work. It offers 24-hour emergency service and will travel into the city for jobs of significant size.

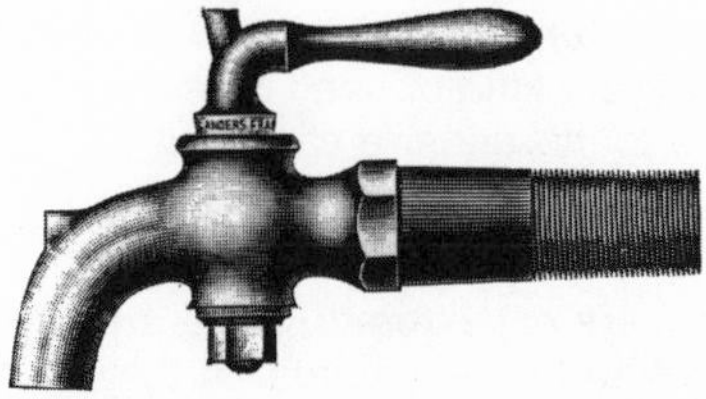

Ravinia Plumbing & Heating **4.5 3.5 4.5 5**
595 Roger Williams Avenue, Highland Park, IL 60035
(847) 432 - 5561

High-end remodeling, plumbing and HVAC repair, installation and service

Once voted best plumber on the North Shore by readers of North Shore Magazine, this company that set up shop in the 1920s has gone well beyond plumbing for its upscale clientele. It is a soup-to-nuts bathroom remodeling contractor that also sells and repairs home appliances and provides HVAC service, including furnace and boiler change-outs. It also sells parts over the counter. Customers praise its service as well as its comprehensive capabilities. Principal Don Ariano is an active member of professional associations and is highly respected within the plumbing community, we're told. Clients tell us he strives to get things right the first time. Assisted by son, David, and 29 employees, this firm gives clients first-class service. Ravinia operates from Gurnee to Evanston and also caters to its established customers in the city.

"Very thorough work. Always there for me." "The workmen really care about what they do."

The V.J. Killian Company **3.5 3.5 4 4**
939 Greenbay Road, Winnetka, IL 60093
(847) 446 - 0908

Residential plumbing and HVAC remodeling and repair

No job is too small or too sophisticated for Killian and crew, which specializes in repair, primarily within a five-mile radius of any of its four locations: Glenview, Winnetka, Lake Forest and Libertyville. It will also handle select downtown remodeling projects and tackles larger ones, such as retrofitting kitchens and baths with high-end fixtures or replacing old boilers and steam and hot water heating systems. It has a sheet metal shop for small-scale HVAC work, such as the replacement of built-in air conditioners and forced air heating systems.

Wayne Plumbing, Inc.
730 Van Dustrial Drive, Westmont, IL 60559
(630) 968 - 4151

Plumbing service and installation

Hiring a Rug Cleaning, Installation & Repair Service Provider

Does your heirloom Oriental display a record of your adorable yet hard-to-housetrain puppy? Did Uncle Mike spill a Bloody Mary on your Persian? Did your cat sharpen his claws on that hidden corner of your needlepoint? Or is your rug just overdue for its regular cleaning (every two to four years, according to The Oriental Rug Importers of America)? Not to worry: rug cleaners and restorers can address every kind of need on every type of rug, from museum-quality handmade rugs to inexpensive carpeting.

Gathering Information

When choosing cleaners or restorers, there are many factors to consider. Ask if they perform free, written estimates. If they make house calls, do they charge a travel fee, and do they have free pick-up, delivery and reinstallation? Before they quote you a price, you may wish to inquire how they set their rate: by the job, the hour or the size of the rug? Do they require a deposit? Will they arrange a payment plan if you need one? Do they offer discounts for multiple rugs or rooms? It's a good sign if they honor their estimate, even if the job overwhelms their expectations. It's an even better sign if they guarantee perfection, and don't consider the job finished until you are satisfied. Such an assurance (especially in writing) may be more valuable than letters of reference or membership in one of the professional associations, though both of these would add further reassurance of competence.

If your rug is handmade and you think it may be valuable, you may want to get your rug appraised by a rug-care service before having it cleaned or repaired. If it is valuable, you'll need to consider more expert (and expensive) services. On the other hand, you may also discover that the rug isn't worth nearly as much as you believed, and hence may not warrant lavish attention. Either way, a professional appraisal certifies the value of your belonging in case of mishaps; you may want to inquire beforehand whether liability falls in your court or whether the cleaner/restorer's insurance covers any mishaps. Many rug cleaning and reweaving establishments appraise rugs for insurance, estate sale, tax and charitable donation. Watching appraisers evaluate your rug also allows you to preview their professionalism. If their work instills confidence, hire them for the whole job; if not, you can still use their appraisal (and estimate, if they perform one simultaneously) as a first opinion in approaching another establishment. For complicated (expensive) repair or restoration jobs, ask how long it will take. Often the expert restorers have other jobs they must finish before they can get to yours. If your rug is valuable, it is worth waiting for the best.

If the rug needs repair before cleaning, confirm that the restorer knows the techniques of the tradition in which the rug was made: Navajo yarn-dying and rug-weaving methods differ from vastly those of Iran. Ask to see a portfolio of their previous repair work, which often displays side-by-side "before" and "after" pictures. Inspect how well they match colors, recreate designs, and blend repairs into existing weaves. If your rug is valuable, inquire whether an expert or an apprentice will perform the repair work. Also, see to it that all repair work is included in the estimate, from reweaving holes to renapping worn areas; restoring moth damage to rewrapping seams; and refringing to re-blocking your rug to its original shape. Particularly thorough rug conservationists will even unravel strands and overcast weaving in order to blend repairs into the rug's existing texture and design.

Cleaning and Drying Techniques

There are many different cleaning methods, each of which addresses different situations with varying degrees of efficacy and expense. Carpet cleaners typically have mobile operations, and will clean rugs in your home with hot "carbonating" systems, steam-cleaning or dry-cleaning. Will they move the furniture to clean under it or do they expect it ready when they arrive? Rug cleaners, on the other hand, usually perform the cleaning at their site. They may expect the rug to be rolled up and waiting for their pick up. Silk rugs, fragile tapestries and textiles with "fugitive" (short-lived) dyes, or bright colors that might "bleed" (run), should be hand-washed—the most delicate and expensive method. Luster cleaning immerses the entire rug in cleaning solutions, and thus achieves a deep clean while minimizing wear on the fabric. Soap washing involves running a vacuum-like machine over the rug; this vigorous method is only for particularly rugged or less-valuable rugs. Discuss in advance what problems the cleaner can and can't fix. For example, excessive wear on a hallway rug will still be there after a cleaning, though it will be much less noticeable. If you are health- or environmentally conscious, ask whether the company offers non-toxic cleaners.

Any rug that's washed must also be dried properly to avoid mildew and dry rot. Be sure to ask about the time and drying technique for in-home jobs; you should know beforehand if you need to reroute traffic through the patio for three days. For in-plant jobs, bigger outfits have dry-rooms where they control temperature and humidity levels. In the home, drying basically involves not walking on the rug until it is dry, which depends on humidity and other factors. Some businesses also offer stain protectants, which they apply directly to the rug to shield it from future accidents (should the tipsy uncle return). Other companies may take a purist approach, preferring periodic cleaning to chemical protectants.

Carpet and Rug Installation

Before the carpet or rug is put down, padding should always be laid first. Padding gives more cushioning for your feet and keeps the rug from sliding, which helps prevent slips, falls and spills. Ask what kind of padding the installer will use, as there are generally different quality and price options.

For wall-to-wall carpeting installation, the most common method is to lay wooden tack strips around the perimeter of the room. The tack strips have pins sticking up that grab the carpet and hold it in place. The tack strips are attached to the floor using small nails, which leave holes in the floor when the carpet is removed. The padding also is usually either nailed or stapled to the floor. If you must cover your nice wood floors (for the kids, maybe), you should discuss with the installer how to minimize the floor damage. Unfortunately there is not that much that can be done if you want wall-to-wall. Some installers may suggest attaching the carpet with double-faced tape, but most say that this doesn't hold well and the carpet shifts and buckles. If your floor contributes to the value of the apartment, it is simply better to stick with area rugs. Remember to ask whether or not there are any potential extra charges, such as for ripping up existing wall-to-wall carpeting before installing the new one or for disposing of the old carpeting and pads if you don't want to keep them.

Some rug cleaners focus on just stain and odor removal services to meet the needs of pet owners, smokers and families with small children (or just klutzes). Many providers offer stain protection for future spills, which, depending on your lifestyle, may be a sound investment. Other companies specialize in emergency services in case of fire, smoke or water damage, and may even be available round-the-clock. If you're moving, remodeling or otherwise in need of storage, look to the larger outfits for mothproofing and storage services. After storage or in-plant services, many companies will reinstall your rug over appropriate padding.

Rug cleaners and restorers also offer many other services for rugs and other furnishings. Many rug cleaners also clean curtains and upholstered furniture. Some businesses prefer to remove the draperies from the home and wash them at their facilities. In-home carpet cleaners are more likely to clean curtains in the house.

Since curtains, upholstered furniture and rugs dominate most of the space (not to mention the attention) in a room, rug cleaners and restorers emphasize the importance of maintaining these items. Their colors will be clearer, they'll last longer, you'll be inhaling less dust—and your home will look more beautiful.

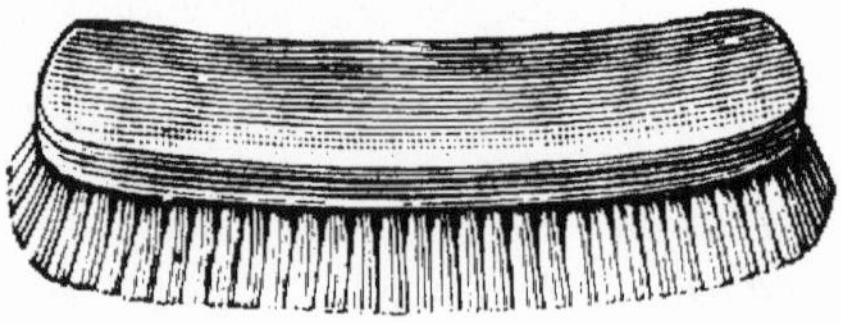

Don't Let the Rug Be Pulled Out From Under You!

- Get several bids. Prices among competent cleaners can vary quite a bit.
- When you have an estimate, ask if it's binding. Ask what factors might cause it to become higher (or lower) when the job is actually done.
- Is there a minimum charge for a house call? If the cost of cleaning your rug is below the minimum you might want to have them perform another service (such as clean or stain-proof another rug, piece of furniture or curtains) at the same time.
- Once they are in your house, the rug cleaners will often do another rug for much less money, especially if paid in cash.
- Some of the larger more commercial cleaners have regular "sales." Get on their mailing list to receive updates. If you're not in a hurry, wait for a sale.

RUGS: CLEANING INSTALLATION & REPAIR

A and L Carpet Cleaners **3.5** **2** **4.5** **4.5**
5306 North Virginia, Chicago, IL 62625
(773) 275 - 9648

Rug and upholstery cleaning

References rave about the service they get from A and L Carpet, and they're not just talking about A and L's way with rugs. While cleaning wall-to-wall carpet and rugs for residential and commercial clients is the company's primary business, it will also clean upholstery and furniture and it has won the greatest gratitude from customers who have suffered flood damage. A and L's all-round cleaning service includes flood water removal—a genuine rescue mission for fine interiors. This is a family-run business, begun a decade ago by Aurelio Aguila. Customers say the workers are good at their job, honest and reliable. Plus, they move furniture and put it back in place at no extra charge. For all of this, clients tell us that A and L's prices are very reasonable.

"Honest and reliable. I have entrusted them with the keys of my house."

A&R Professional Carpet and Upholstery Cleaning **3** **2** **5** **5**
2627 South Harding Avenue, Chicago, IL 60623
(773) 297 - 5460

Carpet, area rug and upholstery cleaning and repair

A&R has the staff, the equipment and the expertise to give nearly everything in a room a seasonal spruce-up. This full-service capability has gained founder, Abel Rosado, and his team a loyal following since it set up business in 1993. A&R is a steam-cleaning specialist that does draperies, blinds and upholstered furniture in addition to rugs and carpeting. It also handles odor-removal and applies stain-proofing. What's more, it offers 24-hour emergency service for untimely emergencies.

"He's excellent." "No complaints about him."

Allen Carpet Service LLC **3.5** **2** **4.5** **4.5**
6774-A Northwest Highway, Chicago, IL 60631
(773) 685 - 9697

Carpet and rug cleaning

For more than half a century, Allen Carpet Service has been giving carpets and rugs in metropolitan Chicago a like-new look. Many current residential and commercial clients have been using the company for years. They tell us Allen's service is as excellent as its cleaning, and recommend it highly. The firm is now headed by Philip and Wayne Allen, who grew up in the business that was founded in 1949 by their father. The company usually charges by the square foot, and customers say its prices are reasonable. Allen Carpet is a member of the Carpet and Rug Cleaners Institute of Illinois.

Herrington Carpet Service | 4.5 | 3 | 4 | 4.5

3429 North Tripp Avenue, Chicago, IL 60641
(773) 283 - 2562

Rug cleaning and repair

Herrington ranks at the top of getting stains out underfoot. Since 1927, three generations of Herringtons have been cleaning, repairing and restoring broadloom and all types and sizes of area rugs for Chicago's upper-end residential and commercial clientele. The company cleans furniture, too. Today, second- and third-generation customers tell us that Herrington's quality has remained excellent and unchanged over all these years. Sources also say Herrington is better than anyone at removing stains.

"Fabulous!" "Can get a stain out better than anybody." "Have been using them for thirty years. Now, my children use them too."

Home Carpet One | 4 | 2 | 5 | 5

3071 North Lincoln Avenue, Chicago, IL 60657
(773) 935 - 9314 www.carpetone.com

Rug and flooring sales and installation

Home Carpet One lives up to its name as a number-one source for flooring and rug sales and installation. Established in 1970 by Leon Engel, this firm serves Chicago's downtown, Northside and Lake Shore areas. It works with architects, designers, and homeowners. As a rug and carpet provider, Home Carpet One installs and sells all types of rugs. From Oriental to Sisal, this firm most likely has it in stock. It also specializes in custom-design carpets and area rugs.

Iloulian Antique Carpets | 3.5 | 3 | 4 | 3

1783 Saint Johns Avenue, Highland Park, IL 60035
(847) 266 - 1000

Oriental rug sales, repair and maintenance

Iloulian Antique Carpets specializes in the cleaning and repair of carpets of merit, and it also buys and sells antique Oriental rugs. The company was established in 1982 and works with designers, architects and residents. Pricing is per job and there is no minimum. Estimates on repairs and cleaning are free and so is pick-up and delivery.

Pedian Rug, Inc. | 4 | 3 | 5 | 4.5

6535 North Lincoln Avenue, Lincolnwood, IL 60712
(847) 675 - 9111

Rug and flooring sales, installation, cleaning, restoration and repair

Pedian Rug is one of Chicago's oldest flooring specialists. It opened in 1906 as a carpet and rug store that also handled repairs. Today it is a resource for the purchase, installation, repair and finishing of all hard and soft flooring, including vinyl, marble, hardwood, laminate and tile, in addition to area rugs and wall-to-wall carpets. It has a staff of 95, which includes specialists in the installation, cleaning and repair of area rugs and carpeting. Rug pick-up and delivery is free and so are estimates. There is, however, a small fee for the removal and replacement of furniture during flooring installation. The company's clientele is mostly residential. Today a second-generation Haig Pedian has taken his father's reigns. Clients appreciate this company's moderate prices and outstanding service.

"Quality is outstanding." "Always on time."

Press This Window Treatments 4 2.5 4.5 4
3041 North Cicero Avenue, Chicago, IL 60641
(773) 282 - 0660

Rug cleaning and repair

While this company name stands out in a crowd, it barely hints of the services available. While it does clean window shades, its primary claim to fame is cleaning wall-to-wall carpet, area rugs and upholstered furniture. It works in residences and commercial buildings, serving architects, interior designers and property management firms as well as homeowners. Clients say workers are efficient and reliable. Press This generally charges by the job and provides a free estimate. Rug pick-up and delivery is included in the charge, and so is moving the furniture on wall-to-wall installations.

Rugport 4 3 3.5 4
23 South Northwest Highway, Palatine, IL 60067
(847) 202 - 0600

Rug sales, cleaning, repair and restoration

This rug retailer also provides cleaning, repair and restoration of all types of area rugs. Fees are based on the price and condition of the rug, and Rugport provides a free estimate. Sources say pricing is in the upper bracket, but consider it a reasonable value in light of the company's service and workmanship. Rugport was founded in 1979 by Alex Torabi and partners.

Sealmaster, Inc. 5 3 5 5
425 Huehl Road, Unit 11B, Northbrook, IL 60062
(847) 480 - 7325 www.sealmasterinc.com

Application of stain-resistant coating for carpet and fabric

Sealmaster specializes in the application of a customized stain-resistant coating to new and freshly cleaned carpets, upholstered furniture and fabric wallcoverings. The formula gives the textile items resistance against permanent stains from water and oil-based spots. This company also cleans wall-to-wall carpets, area rugs, upholstery and fabric wallcoverings. Founded in 1987 by Hannah Malin, it operates throughout the entire Chicago area as well as neighboring states. Charges are based on the square foot, with the rate varying according to the type of carpet or material. Estimates are free, and workers move furniture, when necessary, at no extra cost.

Clients cannot say enough good things about this firm and tell us its workers are very prompt, professional, considerate of high-end surroundings and also very knowledgeable about caring for fine fabrics. Customers also appreciate the personal attention provided by Sealmaster's trained staff.

"Very professional." "They are the best!" "Respectful of my home and long-time employees." "Workmen very attentive." "The sealant used for fabric and carpet protection is superior."

Textile Restoration, Inc. 5 3 4.5 4
1801 West Byron Street, Suite 2V, Chicago, IL 60613
(773) 665 - 2259

Restoration and repair of rare rugs and textiles

We are told that Oriental and other antique rugs from all of the fine rug-making cultures of the world along with valuable textiles of every sort are in safe hands with Frank Connet of Textile Restoration. This is Chicago's premier resource for their restoration, conservation, cleaning and repair. Museums and collectors are among the company's clientele along with dealers, interior designers and residents with textile treasures. Work is by appointment, handled in the company's own workroom. This is, we are told, the unquestioned Chicago source for all things valuable that are made of fabric.

"He is truly an artist." "Has worked for us for almost 15 years." "His restorations are beautiful."

Village Carpets **4.5 3 5 5**
1455 West Fullerton Avenue, Chicago, IL 60614
(773) 935 - 8500 www.villagecarpet.com

Rug sales, installation, repair and restoration

Village Carpets sells, cleans, repairs and restores all kinds of rugs, including custom Tibetans, and also offers its complete range of services for wall-to-wall carpet, including sisal. In addition, it is a specialist in creating custom broadloom carpet and rugs and also cleans upholstery and furniture.

Area rug cleaning and repair is done at the company's workshop. It also operates truck-mounted equipment for on-premise cleaning. While Village serves primarily residential clients throughout the entire Chicago area, it also works with designers and architects. Sources describe its pricing as high end, but worth it for the company's excellent service which comes highly recommended.

"Fabulous!" "Their staff does a phenomenal job."

Wilson and Company
3726 North Lincoln Avenue, Chicago, IL 60613
(773) 929 - 0269

Rug cleaning and repair

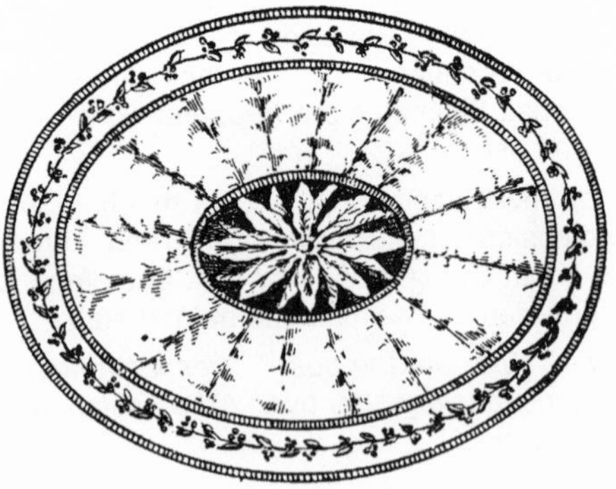

Hiring a Security System Service Provider

There are those of us for whom turning on the TV when leaving the house is considered a security measure. Of course, with an American home burglarized once every 11 seconds, it could also be considered hospitality. In fact, security systems, the first centrally controlled integrated system to make it into most homes, are branching out into fire/life-safety and the convenience/lifestyle sectors that are now becoming the backbone of home automation. So, if you really think "Three's Company" re-runs will scare away potential burglars, you can program your TV's routine, along with the rest of your security system, over your cell phone or the Internet while vacationing halfway around the world. Now if only you could get the vacuum cleaner to pick up your mail.

Like their A/V brethren, security system service providers are marketing themselves as the one-stop shop for your home's central nervous system. No one company may be best at everything yet, but security is a natural place to start to smarten up your home.

A Host of High-Tech Options

Options once reserved for technophiles, supervillains, museums or celebrities have become available to anyone. Closed circuit television (CCTV) can now be fed through your television or computer to eyeball for trouble and can be monitored online from virtually anywhere. Sensors can be installed that detect motion, change in temperature, smoke and carbon monoxide, fluctuation of sound waves, broken glass or breeched barriers. When tripped, they transmit the offended sensor's serial number to a central control panel, which in turn relays the home location and the point of alarm to the monitoring company. The monitoring company will immediately attempt to contact the homeowner to verify that a break-in has occurred. If there is no response, or the respondent fails to give the proper secret password, the police or fire department is notified. In addition, some monitoring companies will dispatch their own personnel to check out the situation, either from the street or, if keys are provided, from inside the home itself.

The explosion of cellular and wireless technology promises further protection and convenience to homeowners. Teamed with battery packs in the event of power failure, communication is fully safeguarded. Wireless modular components (touch pads) can be placed in convenient locations by homeowners themselves, as no cords or wires are needed. This is great for renters, too, who can take the wireless system with them when they move. Alarm devices range from the sounding of a voice wistfully repeating "fire" as if someone had left a car door open, to the crazed bark of a pack of 100-pound Rotweillers, to snapping on the lights in your home as if it were Wrigley Field.

All of these functions are managed through a central control panel, traditionally a keypad and display. But as this industry charges toward the home automation front, touch screens, or a platform on your PC, are increasingly becoming the way to go. This makes it much easier to program and manage your systems. You can keep tabs on the alarm history and security status, play back the sequences of which lights you turn on and off or kick on the air conditioning while driving home from work—and do it all remotely via computer or cell phone.

Choosing the right system for you is as much about the logistical characteristics of your location (i.e., apartment vs. house, rural vs. urban) and budget as it is about the degree of system integration you want in your home. The options range from an "I'm Protected" warning sticker on a window to a virtual HAL 5000. How sophisticated do you want to get? How intrusive? A homeowner's personal circumstances and susceptibility must also be considered.

ON COST

The cost of any security system depends upon the number of devices, the sophistication of the control unit, the degree of integration, the term and service of the monitoring and whether it's wireless technology or hardwired. Basically, the cost reflects the time and material for installation plus the monitoring agreement. The monitoring agreement covers three to five years. Shorter terms are available, aimed at renters, but these agreements may include higher-than-average installation costs. At the end of the term the monitoring agreement should be automatically renewable, with a ceiling for rate hikes spelled out in the contract. Payment can be made on a monthly, quarterly or annual basis. If you break your contract, don't be surprised to be held responsible for as much as 90 percent of the unexpired term as liquidated damages. If you sell your home, however, you should be able to transfer your monitoring agreement over to the new homeowners.

It is important to know the parameters of your monitoring agreement. Many people are involved in your security, and awkward mistakes will cost you. Security providers allow a familiarization period in which no signal will be acted upon. Use this time wisely. Once you're up and running, you will be charged for false alarms by both the monitoring company and the city for wasting their time. They will also charge you to reprogram controls. Be absolutely sure you're comfortable with the system setup and its use before signing the agreement. Warranties should cover parts and labor for one year and you can opt for a maintenance agreement that covers such extras as emergency service.

After you invest in a security system, check with your homeowner's insurance company. You may be able to get a reduction in your insurance rate.

GETTING PLUGGED IN

Finally, your security system provider may need a permit and certain components and installation methods may need to comply with local regulations. It's the municipality's call. As the homeowner, you must provide permanent electrical access and a permanent telephone connection.

WHAT TO CONSIDER WHEN CHOOSING A SECURITY SYSTEM

- Do you own or rent?
- Is it a house or apartment?
- How many entrances and windows?
- Are there children or pets in the home?
- How often are you around?
- Who has access while you're away (housekeeper, etc.)?
- Is the neighborhood crowded or isolated?

SECURITY SYSTEMS

	Quality	Cost	Value	Recommend?
ADT Security Services, Inc.	3.5	3	3.5	3

361 South Frontage Road, Suite 124, Burr Ridge, IL 60521
(630) 832 - 9610 www.adt.com

Security systems with central monitoring

This well-known national security firm has been in existence for 125 years. ADT installs residential and commercial security systems that encompass burglary, fire, flood and carbon monoxide detection. The company also monitors its systems 24/7. Chicago-area clients express satisfaction with the company's service and say they are always able to reach someone at the monitoring center. Sources report that costs are reasonable.

"A real solid company." "Great customer service."

	Quality	Cost	Value	Recommend?
Alarms Unlimited	4	4	4	3.5

6501 North Lincoln Avenue, Lincolnwood, IL 60712
(847) 410 - 0000

Security, telephone, audio/video and home automation systems

When it comes to preventing and detecting threats, Alarms Unlimited contains closed-circuit television, lighting control and intercoms as well as conventional security systems in its arsenal on a 24-hour monitoring basis. This broad range of capabilities is in addition to the company's other business, which include audio/video, home theater, telephone communications, data cabling, satellite dish and CATV systems.

"I was impressed and pleased by the service I received."

	Quality	Cost	Value	Recommend?
Alert Security Consultants	3.5	3.5	4	3.5

2453 West Morse Avenue, Chicago, IL 60645
(773) 465 - 5174

Security systems

This is a small firm that specializes in the design and installation of custom home security systems. Clients have been putting their trust and their property in the hands of Alert Security's principal, Dick Clark, since 1966. He offers safety tips along with safeguards that are tailored to each client's particular needs and concerns. His long-time loyal clients say they not only have confidence in Alert Security's work, but also find Clark's pleasant, calm demeanor reassuring.

"They were always available to answer my questions." "Mr. Clark is so wonderful. I love the safety tips he offers me."

	Quality	Cost	Value	Recommend?
ATS Residential	3	2.5	3	3

1080 Corporate Boulevard, Aurora, IL 60504
(630) 978 - 0878 www.atsresidential.com

Security, telephone, audio/video, home automation and central vacuum systems

ATS takes its initials and a wealth of expertise, too, from Aurora Tri-State, its parent company, which is a commercial security firm that has been serving the business market since 1953. Under the Aurora umbrella, ATS Residential and a sister company, J&T Security Plus, joined forces a decade ago to provide homes with an equivalent level of comfort and safety. In addition to systems that protect against burglaries and fire, ATS can install room-to-room intercoms, door speakers that are accessed by phone, and whole-home speaker paging. Beyond security, the company offers home automation, single or multi-room sound systems and central vacuum systems.

Bulldog Security & Comm
1981 Johns Drive, Glenview, IL 60025
(847) 432 - 9900
Security, telephone, audio/video design and installation

Certified Security Systems, Inc. **3 2.5 3 3**
2720 Thatcher Avenue, River Grove, IL 60171
(708) 456 - 9700
Security systems

Established in 1998, Certified Security and its 35 professionals develop and install security and fire alarms throughout the greater Chicago area. Principal Aaron Fisher is described as reliable and responsive.

"Their installation services were professional, efficient and neat."

Chicago Security Systems
508 East Camp McDonald Road, Prospect Heights, IL 60070
(847) 253 - 7360
Security systems

CSC Alarm System
411 North Illinois Avenue, Glenwood, IL 60425
(708) 799 - 6060
Security systems

Enterprise Service Corp. **3.5 3.5 3.5 3.5**
P.O. Box 855, Des Plaines, IL 60018
(773) 589 - 2727 www.enterpriseservicecorp.com
Security systems

Look, crook, no wires! Stealth state-of-the-art wireless security systems are a specialty of Enterprise. The company also develops hard-wired systems, and both types guard against burglary, fire and other unwelcome intrusions. If you need a DSS satellite dish installed, Enterprise can do that too. The company's technicians are bonded and insured. Enterprise's origins are in electrical contracting and date back to 1974.

"The staff at Enterprise is very knowledgeable and professional. Quotes are returned within a reasonable time frame."

Father & Sons Home Services, Inc.
22 West 421 Oldwoods Drive, Naperville, IL 60565
(630) 985 - 3600
Audio/video, security, telephone and home theater design and installation

See Father & Sons Home Services, Inc.'s full report under the heading Audio/Video Design & Installation

Fox Valley Security **3 3 3 3**
30 North Airlite Street, Elgin, IL 60123
(847) 931 - 7711
Security systems

Established in 1982 as an independent alarm dealer, Fox Valley Security develops and installs access-control systems, burglar and fire alarms and closed circuit TV for residents in the western suburban area only. It does not work in downtown Chicago. We hear Fox is dependable and we're told its employees are easy to work with.

Illinois Security Alarms 3.5 2.5 3.5 3
9525 South 79th Avenue, Suite 1, Hickory Hills, IL 60457
(708) 233 - 9393

Security systems

This company is a dealer in the ADT national network of security system providers (see separate review). Clients of Illinois Security tell us that the burglar systems and around-the-clock camera protection the company provides both residences and businesses are customized and comprehensive. Furthermore, we're told the personal attention they receive from the company's technicians gives them added peace of mind. They also like the price.

Keyth Security Systems 4.5 3.5 4 5
1575 Oakwood Lane, Highland Park, IL 60035
(847) 433 - 0000 www.keyth.com

Security systems and telephone systems

By many accounts, this firm is the professionals' choice for custom security systems. Designers, builders and architects consider Keyth Security a leader in home security, and the firm has also earned the trust of many Chicago-area residents in its 25 years in business. Its team of 35 technicians, headed by Keith Fisher, designs and installs custom alarm systems and telephone systems. The technicians are skilled and all staff members are finger printed and registered with the state. Although some clients say they'd like the service to be a little more personal, all universally praise the technicians' expertise and say the staff is responsible and reliable. Customers who have ever misplaced their keys—and who hasn't?—also appreciate that a full-service locksmith is on duty at Keyth 24 hours a day.

"They have mastered the art of blending high quality systems with the aesthetics of the home." "Future-ready, cost-effective systems."

Metronet Safe & Sound
67 East Madison, Suite 265, Chicago, IL 60603
(312) 781 - 0051 www.safesound.com

Audio/video, security, telephone and home theater design and installation

See Metronet Safe & Sound's full report under the heading Audio/Video Design & Installation

Omni-1 Electronics Inc. 3 3.5 3 3

128 Touhy Court, Des Plaines, IL 60018
(847) 699 - 0662

Security, telephone, audio/video, home automation and central vacuum systems

Systems that detect the intrusion of smoke, carbon monoxide and water are among the electronic precautions that can be wired into new and existing residences by Omni-1 Electronics, which has been serving Chicago-area homes since 1985. The company also handles the installation of systems for electricity, telephones, audio and video equipment and central vacuum cleaning. Following an on-site assessment of the client's needs, Omni-1 calculates a single fee for installation that includes the cost of labor and equipment. For that extra peace of mind, the company will install a panic button that alerts it's central station, which then radio-transmits information to field technicians.

"The experience was professional, very organized, and positive."

Tech Systems, Inc. 4 4 4 4

3150 Skokie Valley Road, Highland Park, IL 60035
(847) 433 - 8582 www.systemsbytech.com

Security systems, telephone systems and home networking

Known for top-of-the-line protection, Tech Systems is a favorite among architects, builders and interior designers and also receives accolades from its residential customers along the North Shore. Company experts design, install and monitor custom security systems that are often enhanced with intercoms and door speakers. The company has a team of ten technicians who are out on job sites everyday and who also design and install custom phone systems. Licensed by the state, Tech Systems retains membership in a slew of associations that require members to meet quality standards in their respective fields of security, automation and contracting. The credentials confirm what customers say: You're safe in the hands of Tech Systems' pros.

"I am so happy with their work!" "Very professional."

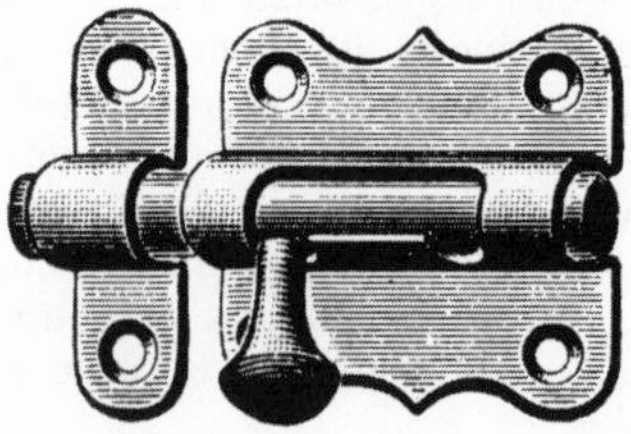

Hiring a Swimming Pool Service Provider

There's nothing like a cool dip on a hot summer day. Swimming pools offer an escape from the hustle and bustle of everyday life. So why should building one be stressful? Here's a primer on how to find a pool professional who won't leave you high and dry.

Most swimming pools are now constructed out of concrete and finished with a material called gunite. Those constructed of fiberglass present a lesser alternative. The classic rectangular, aqua-blue swimming pool still exists, but the options today are as varied as your imagination. For example, the texture and color of the gunite finish can affect the hue of the water, and consequently the character of the pool. Grays create a deep blue quarry feel, while whites speckled with flakes of color create a sparkling effect, not unlike that of crushed sea shells in beach sand. Your pool should reflect how you intend to spend your time there. Take size and shape. If you're a swimmer, a pool lengthy enough for legitimate laps is a must. However, if there are going to be a lot of young children around, the depth of the pool becomes an issue. Do you like to float aimlessly into little nooks and/or pull half-gainers off the diving board? A popular contemporary design is the "natural look." Natural pools, free-formed and employing rock or faux rock, blend into the natural surroundings. Another popular swimming pool is a "vanishing edge" pool where it appears that the edge of the pool drops off into the surrounding area. Also known as "negative edge" pools, they can be quite stunning overlooking a bluff across a body of water. For those Chicagoans resolute on not letting the bitter winter interrupt a good dip, indoor pools provide the ticket.

Swimming pools are certainly not cheap, but by being savvy about materials and design, your pool professional can help you get the most for your money. In-ground concrete and gunite pools range anywhere from $35,000 to $100,000. Cost is determined by the complexity of the design and quality of the materials. Although fiberglass swimming pools represent a less-expensive alternative ($25,000 to $50,000), we hear in-ground concrete pools wear better and live longer, and are, quite simply, more attractive. Other costs to consider are the pool deck (which may consist of concrete pavers, poured concrete, tile, stone or even sod), housing or camouflage of the mechanical equipment (not so easy on the eye), and fencing with a self-closing gate (often a code requirement.)

Pool contractors typically perform all the work themselves. This work includes site excavation, concrete work, irrigation and plumbing, mechanical and electrical, tile and stone work and the gunite overlay. Because much of the most complicated work becomes encased in concrete and buried under a deck (we are talking water here), an incompetent installation can be a disaster—expensive and dirty to fix. In fact, a great source for the best in pool design, construction and maintenance are many of the area's leading landscaping firms, who often coordinate with pool professionals. Your pool should complement its environment, so it's always important to have your landscape architect, architect, general contractor and pool professional talking to each other.

It is essential that the company you choose to build your pool be a member of the National Spa and Pool Institute (NSPI). Members of this organization are kept well informed of not only the technical side of pool construction, but are kept up to date on current state and national requirements for pool construction and developments in safety. The NSPI has a comprehensive website www.nspi.org that is targeted to both consumers and retailers. There is also the Masters Pool

Guild, which is comprised of 90 reputable swimming pool building companies from all over the world. Their website is www.masterpoolsguild.com. Another question to consider when searching for your pool builder is how long is the pool under warranty? If a sudden problem or emergency arises with your swimming pool, you want to make sure that someone will come and quickly fix the problem.

While swimming pools can be an incredible form of entertainment, they are also an enormous responsibility and potential safety hazard if used improperly. A dependable, respected swimming pool company can not only inform you of your aesthetic options, but can also inform you about safety options such as fences surrounding your pool area and different kinds of pool alarms.

WHAT ABOUT SAFETY?

- There are many types of pool fences on the market that will detract as little as possible from the overall appearance of your pool and backyard.
- Ask your pool builder about pool alarms. Alarms can alert you if someone or something unexpectedly enters the water.
- The most important safety reminder that is not on the market is supervision. Be aware at all times who is around your pool and if children are swimming, become their lifeguard.

SWIMMING POOL CONSTRUCTION & MAINTENANCE

Aqua Clear 3 3 3 4
444 Lake Cook Road, Suite 29, Deerfield, IL 60015
(847) 948 - 8310
Pool maintenance, openings and closings

Barrington Pools Inc. 4 3 4 4
P.O. Box 3906, Barrington, IL 60011
(847) 381 - 1245 www.barringtonpool.com
Pool design, installation and maintenance

This large company with a staff of 100 has been designing and building custom gunite pools for 27 years. Its reach extends throughout greater Chicagoland and into Michigan, Iowa, Wisconsin and Indiana. Our resources say that principal Dave Overson and his crews specialize in creating pool shapes and decking that complement the architecture of the home and its surrounding landscape. The company has the expertise to create pools in any shape, plus add such amenities as waterfalls and raised, integral spas. Barrington's in-house masons handle the deckwork. The company typically builds between 150 and 175 gunite pools a year. Costs are based on the square foot and the average, we're told, is approximately $60,000. Barrington offers original owners of its pools a 20-year guarantee on gunite pool shells. The company also offers pool maintenance services.

Boilini Pool Inc. 5 5 5 5
300 Rockland Road, Lake Bluff, IL 60044
(847) 615 - 7100 www.boilini.com
Pool design, installation and maintenance

No standard turquoise rectangles here. Boilini is known for the creation of original—even outrageous—pool shapes with sculptural spas, imaginative water features, outcroppings of natural stone and a full complement of amenities, including fiber-optic lighting. Customers rave at the results and spread the word, which has led Boilini to projects as far off as the Caribbean. The firm designs for both residential and commercial clients.

Owner Patrick Boilini dove into the pool business from working on bridges, where he gained expertise in shaping concrete. This firm charges by the overall design, rather than by the square foot, and prices typically range from $65,000 to $100,000—well worth it for the originality, we're told. Boilini pools carry a three-year guarantee.

"I wanted a pool design that was unique and creative. Boilini did it and I love it!"

Crescent Pool & Spa 3 3 4 4
14433 South California Avenue, Posen, IL 60469
(708) 687 - 6880 www.crescentpool.com
Pool design and installation

A supplier of high quality, if somewhat conventional, vinyl or gunite pools, Crescent works mainly in Chicago's southern suburbs. Before starting Crescent in 1980, principal Joe Dienes worked in the construction industry, which clients say equips the company with the skill and knowledge to come up with sound solutions to any problems that occur with a site. Vinyl pools from Crescent start at approximately $26,000, and gunite ones typically range from $45,000 to $50,000. Work is guaranteed for two years. Cresent also offers complete pool maintenance programs that include opening and closing pools in spring and fall, respectively.

"Joe provided good service at reasonable prices." "A reliable family- owned business."

Downes Swimming Pool Company Inc. 3 3 3 4

433 Denniston Court, Wheeling, IL 60090
(800) 939 - 9309 www.downespool.com

Pool design, installation and maintenance

Downes waded into pool building via its origins as a pool cleaning service company 30 years ago. It has since evolved to include a staff of competent pool builders that clients hold in high regard. They tell us the staff takes pains to understand exactly what the client wants in a pool and then builds accordingly. Downes also provides pool maintenance, and customers say they are satisfied with the service.

Esser Pool and Equipment Company 5 4 5 5

South 69 West 18011 Muskego Drive, Muskego, WI 53150
(414) 520 - 3651

Pool installation, service and repair

Don't be dissuaded by this out-of-state pool resource. We're told Joe Esser of Esser Pool will go anywhere, including to the North Shore, to detect a pool problem and fix it. Repair is the service that has won Esser Pool its highest recommendations. Clients say Esser is a master of leak-detection and underground pipe repair. Esser, himself, cautions, "I am not cheap, but I will fix it." The firm's facility for fixing also qualifies it as a fine pool builder, we're told. Three-quarters of the firm's business is in commercial pool construction, but it also handles high-end residential installations using a compound of poured concrete and fiberglass walls. Pricing is by the square foot and Esser pools generally run from $40,000 to $50,000. The workmanship along with Esser's willingness to handle all things pool-related makes this firm a favorite with both commercial and residential clients.

"Joe has been in the pool business a long time and he is willing to do any project or handle any problem—big or small."

Lakeside Pool and Spa Inc. 4 5 4 5

20370 Rand Road, Suite 212, Palatine, IL 60074
(847) 726 - 2391 www.lakesidepool.com

Pool design, installation and maintenance

Lakeside is a young, small firm with exceptional strokes, we're told. It opened in 1997 and has a staff of four, which limits its productivity to between five and ten pools a year. The company's speciality is custom in-ground concrete pools and spas with water features and decking that range, on average, between $60,000 and $100,000. Pool shells are guaranteed for five years. Lakeside works as far north as Lake Geneva and as far south as Burridge. The company also offers pool servicing, and when it provides the service, it offers a five-year warranty on every aspect of its pools. It is a member of the National Spa and Pool Institute.

"Lakeside offered us swimming pool designs that we had never thought of and their customer service was perfect."

Maverick Pools 3 2.5 3 4
20370 North Rand Road, Suite 208, Palatine, IL 60074
(847) 726 - 8564

Pool design and installation

Maverick in name only, this firm and its staff of 50 install gunite pools that start in the $35,000 range. The majority of its work is for commercial clients, although it designs and builds about six residential pools a year and also does the surrounding masonry and deck work. Price is based on the complexity of the design. The company has no showroom, but owner John Traff maintains a portfolio of completed jobs and also provides prospects with client references. All pool work is guaranteed for one year.

North Shore Pool & Spa Inc.
1849 Shermer Road, Northbrook, IL 60062
(847) 564 - 4910

Pool sales, service and maintenance

Pool Craft Inc. 5 5 5 5
1509 West Dundee Road, Palatine, IL 60074
(847) 776 - 5278

Pool design, installation and maintenance

Pool Craft earns a tide of glowing references from landscape architects and homeowners for its design/build capabilities and its service. The company has worked on the North Shore for nine years, and owner John Mitmoen's experience dates back 28 years to when he began servicing pools at the age of 17. Now, with a staff of 17, Pool Craft designs and builds luxurious gunite pools that average $90,000 and are said to be worth every penny. Clients assign the word "superior" to the staff's responsive service as well as its workmanship and talent for design. Initial consultation is free, and pools are generally completed within eight weeks.

"Over the years we have done several pools together and we have found them to be the highest quality and the most responsive of all pool companies." "Called to open up a pool in the morning and the work was completed that afternoon!" "Very reliable company for service and getting things done."

Pool & Spa Works
333 West Maple, Route 30, New Lenox, IL 60451
(815) 485 - 6162 www.poolspaworks.com

Custom spa design and vinyl pool installation

Quality | Cost | Value | Recommend?
➕ | $ | ◆ | ★

Rosebrook Carefree Pools Inc.

4 4 5 5

2310 Skokie Valley Road, Highland Park, IL 60035
(847) 432 - 0710 www.carefreepools.com

Pool design, installation and maintenance

Named one of the 100 finest pool and spa builders in the United States by *Aqua* magazine, Rosebrook stands at the front of the rankings when it comes to designing, building and repairing indoor and outdoor pools and spas. Owned by Gloria and John Bentley since 1973, Rosebrook works primarily throughout Chicago and the surrounding area. Its numerous design awards, however, have led the company to be hired for some high-end projects throughout the country. Clients say the work is gold medal. In addition to outstanding design, we're told the company often installs commercial-grade equipment to ensure its residential pools of superior, long-lasting quality. Rosebrook is a member of the National Spa and Pool Institute.

Strictly Spas

🗀 🗀 🗀 🗀

503 South Milwaukee Avenue, Wheeling, IL 60090
(847) 215 - 7727 www.strictlyspas.com

Spa sales and installation

Despite the name, Strictly Spas sells saunas in addition to spas. The company has been in business for twelve years and their large showroom displays many of the spas that the company installs. Strictly Spas carries popular brands such as Catalina, Clearwater and Jacuzzi. The firm has their own installers and the quality of work is backed by factory warranties. Clients are pleased with Strictly Spas and say that they were surprised at how quickly both the spas and saunas were ordered and installed.

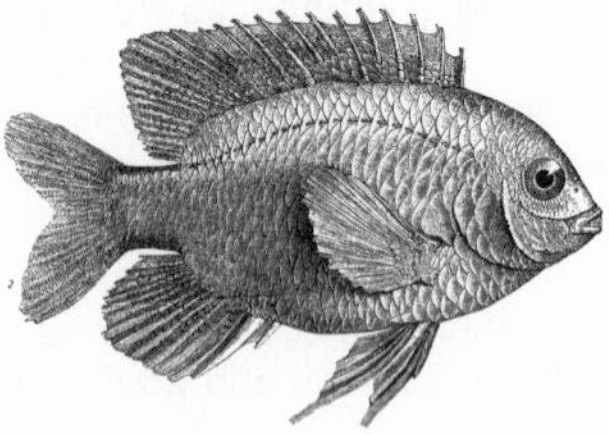

Hiring a Telephone Systems Service Provider

It all used to be so simple. One phone. Black. If you weren't around it just rang. If you were on a call, it droned busy. Now, telephone systems appear as high-tech as the Space Shuttle program. It's not really rocket science, though, if you know the basics and hire a great service provider.

Local telephone companies now offer a wide array of services: voice mail, call forwarding, three-way calling and caller ID (with or without ID block). The wealth of options combined with the rise of the Internet and the home office has changed the playing field for telephone system service providers. But for systems that integrate multiple phone lines, intercoms and door buzzers to a networked and net-savvy home office, these are still the people to call.

Plan Ahead and Allow for Expansion

The key to having the perfect phone system for your needs is to think, plan, discuss and think again. Figure out what you want and where. If you're putting in a home office, know how many lines you will need, where the fax and printers are going to be located, which computers will be networked and online and where you're going to sit. If you like to rearrange the furniture from time to time, consider putting phone jacks on both sides of the room. And always run more cable and reserve more lines than you need. Today's bedroom is tomorrow's office. Remember that running empty conduit gives you enormous flexibility to change with the times down the road. When you run phone, cable and other lines, the wires are usually buried in the walls or hidden behind moldings. This involves messy, disruptive and expensive construction, not to mention the need to redo your decorating touches. Avoid these problems by planning ahead and allowing for expansion. Also, don't overlook unusual spaces in your planning. You can hide that ugly fax machine in a closet, just don't forget to install a phone jack and electrical outlet.

Check the Brand

Most telephone system service providers have licensing agreements with certain system manufacturers and will only deal with those systems. If you're keen on a particular system, it's a good idea to contact the manufacturer for preferred service providers in your area. On the whole, they all perform the same functions (automated directories, voice mail boxes, multiple lines/extensions, on-hold music, interoffice paging, caller ID) and offer the same accessories (headsets, holsters). It's the brand of the system, sophistication, complexity of integration with other systems and convenience of use that affect the cost. Systems can be purchased outright, leased or financed.

It's All About Service

What really sets telephone system service providers apart is the quality of their follow-up service and support. If you're running a business from home, you can't afford to be stranded on the dark side of the moon, cut off from the rest of the planet for days or even hours. If you're just trying to live your life, non-responsive service is still a supreme annoyance. Find service providers with guaranteed response times and emergency service. Know that you'll be able to reach them in a phone-meltdown emergency. A good service provider will suggest and make additions and modifications to your system as times and technologies change. Warranties typically last six months to one year after installation.

SURF THE INTERNET AT TOP SPEED

Telephone system service providers should also be familiar with what type of Internet connection is best for you. A second line for data is becoming a necessity for anyone who spends time online at home. The speed of this connection is determined by both the type of cable in your home and the type of modem in your computer. Typically, homes are strung in Category 3 (CAT 3) cable. While that is fine for voice, Category 5 (CAT 5) is the way to go for your data lines, and can be had for only a modest increase in price per foot. Modems are a bit more complicated. Plugging a standard telephone or data line into the modem that comes built into your computer gives you about 56K of speed. If you don't have the time or inclination to watch your computer struggle to pull up a web page, you can add modem hardware to increase speed. ISDN provides about double the standard, with 128K. DSL, which is threatening to render ISDN obsolete, starts at 128K and can, if you're willing to pay for it, bring you up to the high-speed commercial level of a T-1 line. A mid-level DSL connection rides in at roughly $50 a month, and can handle streaming audio and video.

TELEPHONE SYSTEM TIPS

- An installer is only as good as his service.
- Plan and pre-wire for the future.
- Keep in mind a typical phone system lasts five to ten years. Build in excess capacity.
- Explore the new variety of telephone ring options—your life may change with a serene, low-key incoming call signal.
- Consider sending a request for proposal (RFP) to a number of vendors; having written proposals helps you compare features, service and price.

TELEPHONE SYSTEMS

Alarms Unlimited
6501 North Lincoln Avenue, Lincolnwood, IL 60712
(847) 410 - 0000

Security, telephone, audio/video and home automation systems

See Alarms Unlimited's full report under the heading Security Systems

Alfredo's Telephone Services Inc. — 3.5 4 4 3.5
7115 West North Avenue, Suite 286, Oak Park, IL 60302
(773) 481 - 0931

Residential and small business phone systems—Comdial, Inter-Tel, Panasonic, Vodovi

This one-man operation has been designing and installing residential phone systems of every size, scope and complexity in Chicago and the surrounding suburbs since 1993. The man is Alfredo Santiago Jr., and we're told that he responds to inquiries quickly and gives clients his undivided attention. He installs all brands of equipment and charges by the hour. We also hear clients appreciate his good sense of humor.

"Organized and efficient." "Mr. Santiago understood my needs and designed a phone system appropriately."

Allcom Inc. — 4 3.5 4 3.5
5621 West Howard Street, Niles, IL 60714
(773) 763 - 6100

Residential and small business phone systems—Fujitsu, Iwatsu, Nortel, Telrad

Although Allcom specializes in the design, installation and maintenance of telephone systems for small businesses, it won't hang up on jobs for large residences. The firm also wires homes and businesses for Internet service. Allcom is a large firm and has been in operation since 1960. References tell us the staff does excellent work and is also friendly and helpful with suggestions.

"Great service!" "Crew was well-trained, polite and on time."

ATS Residential
1080 Corporate Boulevard, Aurora, IL 60504
(630) 978 - 0878 www.atsresidential.com

Security, telephone, audio/video, home automation and central vacuum systems

See ATS Residential's full report under the heading Security Systems

Black Box Network Services — 4.5 4 4 4.5
1919 South Michigan Avenue, Chicago, IL 60616
(312) 808 - 5993

Residential and small business phone systems—Siemens

We hear that this downtown Chicago unit provides end-to-end telecommunications expertise. It sells, installs and maintains residential phone systems and offers ongoing support and repair. If you want your home wired for cable, Black Box will do that too and offers a lifetime warranty. Resources tell us the Siemens phone systems that Black Box installs are easy to use and that the staff is congenial, knowledgeable and reliable. All the technicians are union members.

"Five-star on follow-up!" "Prompt and friendly service." "Simple, user-friendly systems."

	Quality	Cost	Value	Recommend?

Gentel, Inc. 3 3 4 3
4750 North Milwaukee Avenue, Chicago, IL 60630
(773) 725 - 8100

Residential phone systems—Agere/Lucent, Comdial, Nortel, Panasonic

Gentel has been designing and installing telephone systems in homes for more than 20 years, performing the entire range of services: adding jacks, relocating existing phone systems and installing brand new ones. While it provides initial training and instruction on its systems to its Chicago-area residential customers, Gentel is not a service company. It will, however, provide customers with a referral to a qualified repair service. Manufacturers handled include Southwestern Bell, Agere/Lucent, Nortel, Panasonic and Comdial, among others.

"A solid, dependable company."

Good Vibes Sound Inc.
1807 South Neil Street, Champaign, IL 61820
(217) 351 - 0909 www.gvibes.com

Audio/video and home theater design, installation and service

See Good Vibes Sound Inc.'s full report under the heading Audio/Video Design & Installation

Integrated Telecom Systems 4.5 3 4 4.5
62 North Lively Boulevard, Elk Grove Village, IL 60007
(847) 437 - 4111 www.integratedtelecom.com

Residential and small business phone systems and service—Panasonic

References say there is no static on this company's line. Integrated Telecom Systems (ITS) is said to provide excellent system design using state-of-the-art products for both homes and small businesses. Its service also gets high marks from customers. This 15-person full-service provider of telecommunications systems has been in business for more than a decade. It sells and specializes in Panasonic products and handles some other brands. Service is available 24 hours a day, seven days a week.

"ITS installed the phone system in our home. First-rate service people, knowledgeable, helpful and reliable."

Jones Telecom Group 4.5 4 4 5
2425 North Greenview, Suite 2R, Chicago, IL 60614
(312) 296 - 8801

Residential and small business phone systems—Avaya, Nortel

We're told that Jones Telecom gives homes a clear signal and never puts customers on hold. Principal Travis Jones, Jr. and a staff of 15 certified technicians are said to be able to design and install the most complex of residential telephone systems and also make them easy to use. Technicians are called professional, reliable and responsible. Clients praise the staff's attention to detail and ability to communicate with them as much as they praise the communications systems the company installs.

"A company that delivers and honors a contract." "Travis Jones, Jr. is a fabulous individual, a class act." "Great follow up!" "They made a very stressful and frustrating process manageable."

Keyth Security Systems
1575 Oakwood Lane, Highland Park, IL 60035
(847) 433 - 0000 www.keyth.com

Security systems and telephone systems

See Keyth Security Systems's full report under the heading Security Systems

MicroAge Computer Center
9240 West 159th Street, Orland Park, IL 60462
(708) 349 - 8080 www.maop.com

Computer maintenance networking and training

See MicroAge Computer Center's full report under the heading Computer Installation & Maintenance

Mills Custom Audio/Video
358 Lexington Drive, Buffalo Grove, IL 60089
(847) 419 - 9990

Audio/video and telephone system design, installation and integration

See Mills Custom Audio/Video's full report under the heading Audio/Video Design & Installation

Omni-1 Electronics Inc.
128 Touhy Court, Des Plaines, IL 60018
(847) 699 - 0662

Security, telephone, audio/video, home automation and central vacuum systems

See Omni-1 Electronics Inc.'s full report under the heading Security Systems

R-2 Electronics
139 Heather Lane, Wilmette, IL 60091
(312) 807 - 5400

Audio/video, telephone and computer installation and integration

See R-2 Electronics's full report under the heading Audio/Video Design & Installation

Tech Systems, Inc.
3150 Skokie Valley Road, Highland Park, IL 60035
(847) 433 - 8582 www.systemsbytech.com

Security systems, telephone systems and home networking

See Tech Systems, Inc.'s full report under the heading Security Systems

Tele-Movers, Inc. **4** **2.5** **4** **4**
409 Lexington Drive, Schaumburg, IL 60173
(847) 969 - 1600 www.telemovers.com

Residential and small business phone systems—Agere/Lucent, Norstar, Toshiba

In today's wired world the phone system has to be at the ready, and Tele-Movers helps residential and small business customers make sure it is. The firm has been designing and installing systems for more than 10 years and provides training as well. It deals in systems from AT&T, Norstar, Toshiba, Agere/Lucent and the Partner Advanced Communications System (ACS). Tele-Movers has four technicians to handle service, maintenance and repairs on a "next-available" basis.

"We were making an unexpected change of location and needed our phone system to be installed quickly. We were quoted immediately and phones were installed within a few days. Have called for service and they responded immediately." "They make sure their customers are well taken care of and satisfied." "Prices are very reasonable."

The Audio Video Consultant
Neil Morganstein
2930 North Sheridan Road, Suite 1912, Chicago, IL 60657
(773) 528 - 5017

Audio/video, satellite, telephone, computer network and automation design, installation and maintenance

See The Audio Video Consultant Neil Morganstein's full report under the heading Audio/Video Design & Installation

Uantum Crossings, Inc. **4** **3.5** **4** **3.5**
141 West Jackson Boulevard, Chicago, IL 60604
(312) 377 - 4045

Residential phone systems and network installation—Agere/Lucent, Northern Telecom

Known for not getting its wires crossed, Uantum offers end-to-end design, installation and service for residential telecommunications systems using Agere/Lucent and Northern Telecom technology. Company experts will specify equipment, hook it up and provide ongoing maintenance. They also install computer wiring and set-ups. We're told the Uantum certified technicians are knowledgeable and friendly.

"Both telephone and voice-mail are easy to use."

Village Audio/Video
809 Ridge Road, First Floor, Wilmette, IL 60091
(847) 251 - 0250

Audio/video, telephone, computer and home theater installation and service

See Village Audio/Video's full report under the heading Audio/Video Design & Installation

HIRING A TILE, MARBLE & STONE SERVICE PROVIDER

Tile, marble and stone can transform a room. Marble kitchen counters make beautiful surfaces on which to work. Granite brings a dramatic flair to the bathroom, and carefully placed stones gives a fireplace earthy, Old World charm. Colorful, artistic tiles can brightly define the style of a kitchen—Spanish, French, Scandinavian. These materials come in a staggering range of types, qualities, shapes and colors. Tiles, for example, range in size from five-eighths of an inch square to one square foot and up. Marble can come in tile form or in slabs that can be as small or as large as you need. Slabs—pieces of stone larger than 24 inches square—can be cut in various sizes and shapes to fit the area.

WHERE DO I START?

The kind of tile that you choose will depend on your specific needs. For example, if you are selecting tiles for a high-traffic area like an entryway or kitchen, you'll want durable tiles that will not show wear and tear. If you are tiling your kitchen, you might consider a durable stone such as granite or a ceramic tile that is easy to clean and maintain. Smaller tiles tend to be used for decorative purposes because they are more laborious to install and harder to clean, while the larger tiles are used for more practical purposes such as covering a floor. Remember, each kind of tile has its advantages and drawbacks. The installer that you choose should be able to help you explore what kind of tile will work best for you.

Tiles, either man-made or natural, can be as plain as classic bathroom-white ceramic or as intricate as hand-painted/embossed pieces from Portugal. Man-made tiles are generally porcelain or ceramic and are durable and resistant to stains. Some manufacturers rate ceramic tile on a scale from 1 to 4+, from least to most durable. Porcelain is considered more durable than ceramic because porcelain is not glazed. Note that porcelain is actually a form of ceramic, but is fired at such high temperatures that it is more dense than the material labeled ceramic. Porcelain is vitreous, or glass-like—water cannot penetrate it—and this is one reason why porcelain is stronger than ceramic. Because of the firing process that ceramic tile undergoes, the color as well as the shape of the tile is permanent.

NATURAL TILE AND STONE

Most natural tiles—such as marble, granite, limestone and slate—will last forever. That doesn't mean it will look like new forever. Marble is one of the most classic, desired and expensive stones, and because it scratches and stains easily it must be sealed after installation. Even after the marble is sealed, it will still be more vulnerable to scratching than other stone, such as granite, so be prepared to care for and maintain a marble installation. There are many types of seals to choose from: a matte seal preserves the stone's natural color or texture, a glossy seal makes the stone appear shiny and smooth and gives it a more formal appearance, and a color enhancement sealer brings out the stone's colors and beauty.

Like marble, granite is a natural stone that comes in both tiles and slabs. Granite is one of the strongest stones, but it also needs to be sealed after professional installation. Granite is more impervious to stains than marble, and also less expensive.

In general, marble and granite slabs are more expensive than tile because the slabs are customized and take more of the installer's time. Slabs are commonly used for areas such as countertops and around fireplaces. Installing slabs requires different skills than installing tile; therefore, you should ask a potential installer if he normally installs tile or slab.

On Cost

With the exception of hand-painted tiles, tile is generally priced per square foot. This simplifies price comparisons of tiles that differ greatly in size or shape: once you know how many square feet you need for your area, it's easy to calculate the difference in total cost between tile choices. Basic ceramic and porcelain tiles range from $2 to $20 per square foot. Hand-painted tiles can cost anywhere from $8 to $150 each.

On the whole, stone tiles like marble and granite are more expensive than their ceramic counterparts. The price of marble and granite depends on color and type. Natural stone is quarried all over the world, and a particularly desirable origin can make it more expensive. Some stone is easier to find and is not considered as rare as other types of stone. Like ceramic tiles, natural stone tiles are priced per square foot. Marble and granite slab, however, is priced per project because there are so many variables in slab work. The price depends on the edges, customization and amount of work that goes into the actual installation. Slabs also have to be cut to fit the area precisely. The pricing of slab work depends on how difficult the stone was to get and how large the slab is. The larger the slab, the more expensive it is going to be to transport.

Tile and stone installers generally charge per project. The more custom work they have to do, such as edges and corners, the more expensive the project. Also, note that more artistic tile installation, such as creating mosaics, is much more expensive. Hiring a larger company can be cheaper because much work can be done in house, and the company can buy in bulk to save on materials. Also, installers will not have to be subcontracted and the materials will often be in stock. If you order from a smaller company and they do not keep a particular, expensive tile in stock, the price could be higher than from a larger company. With any installer, tile or marble that has to be ordered can significantly delay your project.

Who Installs the Tile, Marble and Stone?

Some of the service providers in this guide use their own installers and some subcontract the work out. If you choose a company that uses installers that are not in house, make sure that the company has used them before and ask for references. Some companies also keep a list of installers that they use on a regular basis.

Qualifications

No professional certification is required to install tile, marble and stone, but there are other ways of screening potential installers. For example, they should have a business license and, ideally, a general contractor's license. An excellent way to evaluate a potential installer is to ask for references, speak to them, and look at photographs of previous installations. Membership in professional organizations may also confer credibility to this service provider. These associations can offer general information as well as answer some of your simple questions about tile and marble installation. The main professional associations to contact for information are The Marble Institute of America (614-228-6194), Ceramic Tiles Distributors Association (CTDA) (800-938-2832), The Tile Council of America (864-646-8453) and the Ceramic Tile Institute of America (805-371-TILE).

Whether you decide to install simple ceramic tile in your shower or rare marble in your living room, the entire process will go more smoothly with a basic understanding of these special materials as provided above.

Decorative Ideas

- For the children's bathroom, use hand-painted tiles in favorite colors to make washing more fun.
- Scatter random tiles containing a thematic print (herbs for a kitchen or shells for the shower).
- Install mosaics around kitchen windows and in the window wells.
- Mix marble countertops with ceramic tile backsplashes.

TILE, MARBLE & STONE

Ann Sacks Tile & Stone — Quality 5 | Cost 5 | Value 5 | Recommend? 5

501 North Wells Street, Chicago, IL 60610
(312) 923 - 0919 www.annsacks.com

Handcrafted tile, marble and stone sales

Here, the hard-to-find and unusual in tile, stone and marble mingle with more predictable styles in creative displays that offer ideas for free along with the company's generally pricey product. This Chicago 1,900-square-foot showroom is one of a dozen Ann Sacks locations throughout the country. A favorite of upper-end interior designers, the company boasts an inventory that includes custom mosaics, leather tile, unique limestones, antique terra-cotta and Biblical stone from Israel in addition to handpainted tiles in designs associated with different countries around the world. Prices cover a wide range from $3 to $250 per square foot. Our references insist that if your heart's set on tile—from contemporary to antique—Ann Sacks is the place to begin your search. While the firm does not install, it will refer you to a cadre of recommended providers.

Aranda Masonry and Ceramics — Quality 4 | Cost 2 | Value 4.5 | Recommend? 4.5

1305 North Maplewood Street, Chicago, IL 60622
(773) 392 - 3610

Brick masonry, tile setting and handmade ceramic tiles

In just five years, Julian Aranda has amassed an impressive list of loyal clients who praise both his craftsmanship and creativity. A licensed brick mason and tile setter, he also works with marble, slate and other natural stone, and has recently added the glazing of ceramic tiles to his repertoire. He works on installations throughout Chicago and at local clients' summer homes in Michigan.

In addition to their high regard for his artistry, clients admire his knowledge of the materials and his ability to explain how he works. They also say he's dependable, "meticulous" and hard working. Aranda's fee structure is the only thing that's not set in stone. Depending on the project, he'll charge by the square foot or the hour. However he arrives at a price, clients seem to conclude that the outcome is near perfection.

"Julian is not only a skilled craftsman but he is also quite creative." "Great work ethic, very dependable and meticulous." "The work looks beautiful. Our basement is dry and I have recommended him to my friends. Julian seems to love what he does!"

Carrara Marble & Mosaics — Quality 5 | Cost 4 | Value 5 | Recommend? 5

2148 North Natchez Avenue, Chicago, IL 60707
(773) 237 - 0415

Tile, marble and stone sales and installation

Interior decorators and architects agree hands down that Carrara Marble is one of the best marble and stone fabricators and installers in the Chicago area. The family-owned company has been developing its outstanding reputation since 1975. Customers say that Carrara is responsive and works closely with clients. The company carries hundreds of varieties of marble, granite and natural stone. While Carrara's product pricing is competitive with other marble fabricators in the area, clients say its work tends to be more expensive because of the high quality craftsmanship.

"The best." "I would not feel comfortable recommending anyone else."

Chadwicks Surfaces International

Quality	Cost	Value	Recommend?
4	4	4	4

14045 West Rockland Road, Libertyville, IL 60048
(847) 680 - 3222

Tile, marble and stone sales, fabrication and installation

Chicago Granite and Marble Inc.

Quality	Cost	Value	Recommend?
4	3	4.5	4.5

415 Busse Road, Elk Grove Village, IL 60007
(847) 806 - 7000 www.chicagogranite.com

Marble, stone and granite sales, fabrication and installation

With four large showrooms, this company provides all of the Chicago area with a wide range of product options, sourced selectively from all over the world. Owner Anik Narula routinely splits his time between Chicago, London and New Delhi, and references say the firm's mangers stays in touch with their customers. Chicago Granite and Marble fabricates marble and granite countertops and vanities and charges by the square foot. Clients tell us the cost is a bargain in relation to the high quality of work. The company has been in business here for six years.

"Great customer service, good prices, nice showroom and very cooperative." "Chicago Granite and Marble did an excellent job for us in a short time frame." "Their prices were quite competitive."

Exotic Marble and Tile Inc.

8055 Monticello Avenue, Skokie, IL 60076
(847) 763 - 1863 www.exoticmarble.com

Tile, marble and stone fabrication and installation

One of Chicago's largest and most comprehensive resources for tile and marble, this company also fabricates and installs its "exotic" product on custom kitchen countertops, bathroom vanities and fireplaces. Clients appreciate the showroom's large selection of natural stone and marble patterns, which makes it a good starting place to assess the many options.

Frank Zanotti Tile & Stone Company Inc.

Quality	Cost	Value	Recommend?
4.5	3	5	5

6 Walker Avenue, Highwood, IL 60040
(847) 433 - 3636

Tile, marble and stone sales and installation

When private and professional clients rank Frank Zanotti "unparalleled," they are referring to the company's product selection as well as its installations. It imports granite, marble and ceramic tiles from Italy, Spain, Portugal and Brazil, ensuring patterns and styles to suit every taste. The company has 40 skilled employees and a 3,000-square-foot showroom to showcase the firm's abilities.

Owner Frank Zanotti learned the trade from his grandfather in Italy and has been practicing it since boyhood. The company's clientele includes many top architects, custom builders and interior designers. While they tell us that Zanotti is among the best in the field, they also say the company's work is reasonably priced for the quality. Aware of his professional clients' demanding standards, Zanotti says his goal is to "exceed their expectations." We're told he does.

"Our bathroom turned out more beautiful than we could have imagined. The quality of the workmanship was top rate. The workmen were prompt and polite." "Have dealt with Frank for more than 30 years on four different projects and he is the best!" "Work commenced promptly and was finished in good time."

+	**$**	**◆**	**★**

Granite Pro Company Inc. 3 3 4 5
1826 South Clinton Street, Chicago, IL 60616
(312) 432 - 1122
Tile, marble and stone sales and installation

It is a testimony to the growing demand for stone and marble surfaces as well as this company's skills, that, in just five years, Granite Pro has become one of the largest marble and granite fabricators in the United States, according to our sources. The company imports natural stone from Italy, Brazil and India. Services include design as well as fabrication and installation. Owner Greg Siwek can also advise on selection, and, we are told, the company works closely with clients, primarily builders and architects, on projects from start to finish. Jobs are priced by the square foot, and Granite Pro requires payment of half the fee up front and the remainder on completion of installation.

"The selection at Granite Pro was fabulous and the people were more than helpful."

Granitewerks Inc. 4 4 4 4
2218 North Elston, Chicago, IL 60614
(773) 292 - 1202 www.granitewerks.com
Marble, stone and granite sales, fabrication and installation

Customers report that this shop reliably works in a range of products, including imported granite, marble, slate and limestone from around the world. In business since 1992, it offers custom fabrication to trade clients, such as builders and contractors, for residential and commercial projects and also supplies area home improvement centers with more standard fare. About ten percent of its total business is retail, and, for these residential customers, the company will assist with installation instruction.

For uncomplicated jobs, Granitewerks prices by the square foot and has a published list of standard costs for different materials. Trade work is priced by the project and varies according to the cut and complexity of the design.

Hard Rock Fabricators ▭ ▭ ▭ ▭
20 North Skokie Highway, Lake Bluff, IL 60044
(847) 615 - 9300
Tile, marble and stone fabrication and installation

Hastings Tile & Il Bagno Collection ▭ ▭ ▭ ▭
1381 Merchandise Mart, Chicago, IL 60654
(312) 527 - 0565
Italian mosaics—marble and glass

Hispanic Designe 4 4 4 4
6125 North Cicero Avenue, Chicago, IL 60646
(773) 725 - 3100 www.hispanicdesigne.com
Tile sales and installation

International Marble & Granite Supply 4 3 5 4
2950 West Grand Avenue, Chicago, IL 60622
(773) 252 - 2550 www.internationalmarble.com
Tile, marble and stone sales, fabrication and installation

International carries more than 300 varieties of domestic and imported products, including marble, travertine, granite, limestone, slate and a sampling of ceramic tile designs from all the countries known for hand painting on tile. The company operates three fully automated shops with a substantial staff of sixty technicians. Four crews do on-site measuring, and seven crews are devoted to installation. A showroom contains examples of product and completed pieces.

"The company has quite a selection of marble." "I found the customer service to be good and the employees helpful."

Italdecor Inc.

1480 Landmeier Road, Elk Grove Village, IL 60007
(847) 290 - 0601 www.italdecor.com

Tile, marble and stone sales, fabrication and installation

K. Brothers Tile and Stone 4 3 4 5

816 Waukegan Road, Deerfield, IL 60015
(847) 945 - 1188

Tile and marble sales and installation

Stone work is a sought-after specialty of K. Brothers, which provides fabrication and also sells and custom installs ceramic, porcelain, marble and granite. Owner Stan Kawamoto manages six work crews from the company's combined showroom/warehouse, and clients tell us the crews are well trained and bring projects in on time and within budget. K. Brothers has been in operation for 43 years and works primarily on the North Shore, although it will accommodate clients in other outlying areas. The company provides a one-year guarantee, but clients say Kawamoto responds to any problems, regardless of when the project was completed.

"The quality of the work was unbelievable and the price was a bargain considering all of the time they put into my project." "The staff was well trained, polite and courteous."

Lodestar Statements In Stone 5 4.5 5 5

231 East 58th Street, New York, NY 10022
(212) 755 - 1818

Mosaic design, sales and fabrication

"Michelangelo of mosaics," Stewart Ritwo, owner and artist in residence, helps Lodestar Statements In Stone live up to its reputation. Since he opened his New York showroom in 1986, Ritwo has been dazzling the world's most discriminating residential and commercial clients with his designs. He and his select staff of artisans practice the centuries-old art of Byzantine and Florentine mosaic work, using a technique of composite patterning. What distinguishes Lodestar from other masters of mosaics, however, is Ritwo's incorporation of inlays of semi-precious stones, such as onyx, malachite, sodalite and quartzite. The designs include floor medallions, wall murals and tops for vanities and other surfaces.

Lodestar's commissions are found in some of the world's most elegant hotels, restaurants and residences. Designers say a visit to the New York showroom and gallery is worth the trip. Surprisingly, a typical Lodestar piece is completed within eight to twelve weeks. Prices are based on three variables: the stones that are used, the intricacy of the design and the size of the panel. While Lodestar's work is not within everyone's budget, many clients who've seen this star have been known to stretch.

"They have a design library and can help in the planning and execution of the entire project." "Stewart is a pleasure to work with."

Marion Restoration 4 4 4.5 5
3504 North Kostner, Chicago, IL 60641
(773) 286 - 4100 www.marioninc.com

Restoration of stonework, terra cotta and masonry

For restoration of brickwork and other masonry, Marion Restoration is peerless, we are told. The founder and president, Mario Machnicki, trained throughout Europe and the United States and is familiar with and experienced in all types and styles of masonry. Equipped with this knowledge, he and his team evaluate damage and determine how to render the line between intact and restored areas invisible and seamless. Utilizing photo-documentation and certified conservators, Marion restoration excels at restoring architectural details in stone. The company is equally adept at restoring stone and glass block. Marion has been operating throughout the Chicago area for 22 years. Clients say the quality is high, and so, they add, is the price.

"We are thrilled with our results and consider Marion to be an exceptional company." "They went to a great deal of trouble to educate us and get both of us comfortable with the process." "They did an excellent job and made repairs match our old, existing brickwork."

Poma Marble Inc. 3 3 4 4
9779 Berwyn Avenue, Rosemont, IL 60018
(847) 678 - 7662

Marble, stone and granite fabrication and installation

This is a small showroom with a growing following among Chicago-area interior decorators and architects. In six years, Poma Marble has gained a reputation for reliable workmanship in tile, marble, stone and even mosaics. The company imports tiles and natural stone, and professionals tell us they can depend on quality in product, design implementation and installation.

Roman Marble Company 4 4 4 4
120 West Kinzie Street, Chicago, IL 60610
(312) 337 - 3000 www.romanmarble.com

Marble, stone and granite sales, fabrication and installation

Carved marble mantelpieces, columns, pedestals and other architectural details are the specialty of Roman Marble and what give it high ranking among architects and interior designers, especially those who remodel older homes along the North Shore. For 30 years, the company has been serving this trade and also selling to private clients. Roman Marble also makes and installs kitchen and bath countertops. Samples of its work are on display in two showrooms, one at this location and another at 1650 West Kinzie.

Stone Fabrication Shop

1377 Merchandise Mart, Chicago, IL 60654
(312) 329 - 1295

Marble, granite and limestone sales, fabrication and installation

Principal Rick Doehler's early experience in construction, his clients tell us, serves him well in managing Stone Fabrication's installation crews. The company has 30 fabricators and installers who make marble and stone countertops and surfaces for residences and commercial installations in Chicago as well as Michigan and Wisconsin. The company's been in business for 20 years and offers a one-year guarantee on materials and labor.

Tithof Tile and Marble Inc. **5 4 4 5**

1657 Old Skokie Road, Highland Park, IL 60035
(847) 831 - 3444

Tile, marble and stone sales, fabrication and installation

Although this fabricator limits its customer base to Chicago's northern suburbs, its staff of more than 50 operates at high volume, specifying and then implementing designs by professional and private clients. We're told that principals John Tithof and Pat Jenkinson and the Tithof team are reliable and do quality work. The company presents a bid before work commences and offers a one-year guarantee once it's completed. While the company sticks to the bid, no matter what complications arise, it is more than liberal with the guarantee, we're told, and will respond to any problems that occur even after the first year.

"John and Pat went above and beyond the call of duty helping me with my kitchen countertops. They answered every question and returned every phone call."

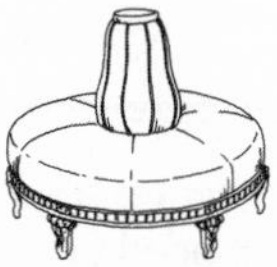

Hiring an Upholstery & Window Treatment Service Provider

Do the window treatments in your newly painted or designed living room need a makeover? Did you find a gorgeous set of Federal chairs at the flea market that need re-upholstering? Would you like to transform your aging—yet amazingly comfortable—armchair into a spectacular piece that matches your sofa and decor? Or are you ready to buy a complete set of custom-upholstered furniture for your living room? Whether you are thinking about the design and construction of your piece or which fabric to choose, upholstery and window treatment experts are the professionals to call.

Many high-end upholsterers who do specialized work deal exclusively with the trade (decorators and architects). We have clearly noted these professionals in our reviews. These service providers primarily focus on custom work—creating a piece from scratch rather than reupholstering. In the case of window treatments, high-end specialists do custom work rather than installing materials from retail stock.

What Type of Upholstery Service Do I Need?

Your three basic choices are custom upholstery fabrication, reupholstery and custom slipcovers. You may not need a completely new piece of furniture. Depending on the condition of your frame and webbing, you may choose to reupholster or have custom-made slipcovers as a less expensive alternative. A favorite decorator trick is to use a Crate & Barrel frame and upgrade the fillings to create a well-priced custom piece. An upholstery professional will be able to assist you in assessing the structure of your existing piece.

To help narrow down the service you need, determine how the furniture will be used. Is it a seating piece that is frequently used by the family and guests (and pets), or a more stylized piece that is located in a less frequently used space? If it will receive heavy use, you'll choose springs and cushioning that will stand up to this treatment as well as a fabric that is durable and easy to clean.

Know Your Upholstery Construction

Frames: The frame is the skeleton of your piece, determining the sturdiness as well as overall appearance of the object. The best frames are made of kiln-dried hardwood. Oak, maple and ash are the hardwoods of choice by professionals. Kiln drying removes moisture and sap from the wood which could cause the frame to warp or bend. When assembling the frame, the ideal method involves using dowels and cornerblocks. This is more costly than using nails and glue but will greatly increase the quality and add years to the life of your piece. Tacks are the preferred method for attaching fabric to the frame, although staple guns are sometimes used. Staple guns should never be used in constructing a quality frame, however.

Springs: The main function of springs is to support the furniture's cushioning. The two basic spring systems for upholstered furniture are round coil springs and flat, s-shaped "no-sag" coils. Most traditional pieces use hand-tied steel spring coils, in which coils are tied by hand in six or eight places around the diameter of the spring. S-shaped or zig-zag coils are sometimes used for contemporary pieces and do not provide the same support as spring coils. S-shaped springs can become lumpy or uneven over time.

CUSHIONS: These come in two types: attached and loose. In an attached construction, fiber-covered foam is placed over the spring system, then is covered with fabric. Loose cushions resemble big pillows that are easily fluffed, moved or turned over to prevent signs of wear. Some pieces may also include semi-attached cushions which look much like removable cushions but are actually part of the piece. Both types of cushions can be filled with a wide variety of filling, from luxurious pure down and down blends to synthetic foam fill.

Down is the ultimate cushion filling and comes at a premium price. The typical down-feather blend consists of 80 percent goose down and 20 percent duck feathers. The ultimate puff-look is 100 percent down, which offers almost no support. The biggest drawback of down or down-blend fill is the frequent need to fluff the cushions to keep the shape and comfort. Because of the high level of maintenance and cost required for down, many consumers prefer to go with a combination of down and foam/feather.

In very high-quality cushion construction, springs are individually wrapped, encased in foam, then covered in a down and feather mixture. This is all then encased in a muslin bag in order to contain the fluff before being covered with fabric. This combination provides firmness and helps to hold its shape.

FABRICS: The possibilities are endless when choosing upholstery fabric. With so many options, you can narrow your search by exploring a few basic issues. Prices vary widely, from $10 to well over $250 per yard. The most important issue is how the piece will be used. Do you need a super durable fabric that can withstand daily use? Or is it a not-to-be-touched showpiece that can be covered in a delicate silk? Some fabrics are simply stronger than others. Ease of cleaning should also be considered. Pieces in the TV room or children's bedroom may attract more dirt. Darker, more durable fabric that withstands frequent cleaning would be appropriate for this furniture. Upholsterers handle the issue of fabric in a variety of ways. Some have catalogs and swatches from which you can choose; others insist that you bring in your own fabric choices. This option is known in the trade as COM—customer's own material. If you do not have the time or inclination to shop for your own fabric, make sure you choose an upholsterer who provides this service. Keep in mind that the ease or difficulty of working with a particular fabric will affect the price of the job. You will need more yardage of patterned fabric so the upholsterer can match the pattern in visible areas.

WHAT TO LOOK FOR IN QUALITY UPHOLSTERY WORK

When viewing the work of an upholstery professional in the showroom or someone's home, keep the following points in mind:

- Fabric patterns should match at all seams and should be centered or balanced on any cushions or surfaces. This can be particularly important with more intricate patterns.
- Check to see if any of the seams pucker, such as those along the arm of a sofa or on the back of a club chair. Seams should be perfectly smooth.
- Are the sofa skirts lined? Is the cushion of the slipper chair invisibly secured with clips, and is the welt or trim tightly stitched?

ON COST

As with any specialized custom work, upholstery prices vary significantly. The more detailed and specialized, the more labor involved and the higher the price. To choose the appropriate expense level, you should assess the application. A chair in your four-year-old's room will probably not require the same quality of fabric or workmanship as a sofa in your living room where you entertain regularly. Most decorators view the "public" (living room, dining room) vs. "private" (bedrooms, playrooms) with two different price points. All the components discussed in the upholstery construction section above directly contribute to the cost. Knowing a little bit about the basic construction will help you understand the real difference between a $700 and $7,000 sofa and help you determine your specific needs.

WINDOW TREATMENTS

From a simple minimalist panel to a layer-upon-layer, elaborate design, many elements come together to make a window treatment. Carefully selected shades, sheers, curtains and valances may be held together with various trims, chords, brackets and hardware—and possibly finished off with decorative finials. Some upholstery and window treatment professionals also do hard window treatments, which include all types of shades, laminated shades (roller shades, covered in your choice of fabric) and blinds, custom made in your choice of materials to coordinate with your curtains.

WHERE DO I START?

To help you decide upon the perfect window treatment for your room, many shops can do miracles with photos and magazine clippings. Once you've settled on a basic design (perhaps with the help of your decorator or examples from your upholsterer), you need to take some measurements. Most service providers will come to your home and measure the window as part of their consultation. Some charge a fee to take measurements, others apply this charge once you place the actual order. Others do not charge at all. Ask the window treatment professional about his policy before setting up the in-home consultation.

It is highly recommended that you do not take the measurements—then you will not be responsible when they are twelve inches too short. Letting a professional do the measuring is preferred because there are many factors involved. Most treatments, for example, take up wall space as well as cover your window, and your window treatment specialist will know what to measure for in the entire room. Will you have finials that take up space on each side of the window? Will your drapes open from the center and be secured on each side with hardware? Be clear with your provider if you prefer just panels. All of these factors will need to be considered when measuring and developing the final plans for your window treatments.

WINDOW TREATMENT FABRIC AND CONSTRUCTION

As with custom furniture upholstery, fabric choices for window treatments are endless. As with upholsterers, some window treatment shops will provide you with a choice of fabrics and others will require you to provide your own. Ask how the service provider operates and if there will be any additional charges if you choose to provide your own fabric (usually there is not). In addition to selecting a fabric for color, texture and print, consider how easy it will be to clean. Curtains and window sills in the city are vulnerable to dust, dirt, grime and soot, whereas the elements are a bit more forgiving in the suburbs.

Most window treatments require more than one layer of fabric. For the most luxurious look, with excellent volume, curtains are lined and interlined. The interlining is commonly made of flannel, which not only provides heft and a bit of structure, but also a measure of soundproofing. This three-layer construction will provide you with material that will drape very nicely. If you are looking for something a bit more simple, a two-layer construction with a single lining will be sufficient.

ON COST

Your window treatment cost will be determined by some or all of the following: measurement fee, installation fee (will vary according to the complexity of the job), labor charges, fee for providing your own material or cost of fabric from the shop. Two of the most significant factors in the price will be the fabric, which varies widely in price, and the complexity of the construction of the draperies. A three-layer construction, with lining and interlining, will be significantly more expensive to produce than a single or two-layer construction.

TIPS ON CARING FOR UPHOLSTERED FURNITURE

GENERAL CARE

- Ask your upholsterer or fabric supplier exactly how to care for your new fabric.
- Vacuum often to get rid of dirt particles that cause abrasion and wear.
- Don't allow pets on fine fabrics—their body oils rub off on the fabric and are tough to remove.
- Protect fabric-covered pieces from the sun to avoid fading and deterioration, if not in use.
- Turn over loose cushions every week for even wear.
- Beware of sitting on upholstered furniture while wearing blue jeans or other fabric-dyed clothing—the color may "bleed" onto the fabric.
- Do not set newspapers or magazines onto upholstered furniture, as the ink may also bleed onto the fabric.
- Regular professional cleaning is ideal.

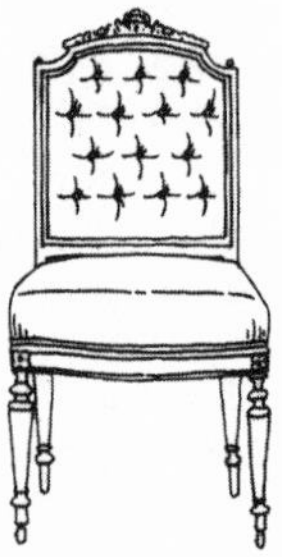

SPILLS

- Immediately after the spill, blot (don't rub) the area with a clean cloth. Dried spills are more difficult to remove.
- Carefully follow the instructions on the cleaning product (don't wing it).
- If you can use water for cleaning, be sure it is distilled.
- Choose a hidden area on the fabric to pretest the cleaner for color fastness before applying to the spill.
- Avoid making a small spill larger by working lightly, blotting out from the center. To avoid rings, "feather" the edges by dampening the edge of the spill irregularly and blotting quickly.
- Using a small fan or blow dryer (on low setting), quickly dry the cleaned area.

Upholstery & Window Treatments
Service Providers

Addison Interiors **4 3.5 3.5 4**
711 West Fullerton, Addison, IL 60101
(630) 628 - 1345
Trade only—custom upholstery

Clients say Addison is an ideal provider of custom upholstered pieces. Chicago decorators love to use this firm for high-quality work which it sometimes creates, guided only by a magazine. In addition, Addison has designs of its own and can handle reupholstering. It does not do window treatments. Servicing clients in Chicago and the suburbs for 20 years, this medium-sized firm seats a large number of satisfied clients on well-made, beautiful pieces.

"As high quality as one can get." "In the Rolodex of some of Chicago's finest decorators."

Alfred Cisneros and Sons ☐ ☐ ☐ ☐
4833 West Armitage Avenue, Chicago, IL 60639
(773) 237 - 9644
Retail and trade—custom upholstery

This upholstery firm works with both retail and trade clients and reportedly turns projects around quickly. Principal Carlos Cisneros and his crew build upholstered furniture, working from designers' specifications. It offers reupholstering and some furniture refinishing, but does not make window treatments. While clients tell us the company is both reliable and quick, they also report sometimes having difficulty reaching the firm.

Alistan Interior **3 3 5 4.5**
4019 West Irving Park Road, Chicago, IL 60641
(773) 282 - 5252
Retail and trade—custom upholstery and window treatments

This company gives and gets firm support. Residents of the North Shore and other upscale areas of Chicago, along with interior designers for the high-end market, have been relying on Alistan Interior for quality upholstery projects, window treatments and furniture refinishing and repair for the past 20 years. The company is known for its honesty, straightforwardness and good value for the dollar. The company is often entrusted with antiques and can ably apply gold and silver leaf. Clients say projects can take a long time, because the company is in high demand, but most consider the quality work worth both the wait and the price. Alistan Interior builds long-term relationships with its clients, many of whom have used the firm for years and describe the experience and the results in glowing terms.

"I'd give him anything and never question the quality of the service." "Guests have come into my house, admired my furniture and run home to hire Alistan themselves." "Stan is a really great guy—easy to deal with and truly honest." "The furniture is just beautiful." "They do everything."

Andrew Upholstery
2234 West Roscoe Street, Chicago, IL 60618
(773) 528 - 5599

Retail—upholstery and minor furniture repair

This one-man operation is a reliable source for smaller upholstery projects, slipcovers and furniture repair. However, he does not offer full reupholstering and works exclusively on residential projects. The business is built primarily on the recommendations of loyal clients.

Apex Interiors
7251 South Halsted Street, Chicago, IL 60621
(773) 846 - 2855

Retail—custom upholstery and window treatments

For the past 30 years, this company has been providing custom upholstered pieces—some from the firm's own designs—along with slipcovers and window treatments, including blinds and shades. Apex carries a selection of fabric and will also use the customers' own material. The company works strictly on residential projects and has a showroom with samples of its work. Apex also works with antiques and can do refinishing.

Atelier Gentry 4 4 5 5
708 Dobson Street, 1st Floor, Evanston, IL 60202
(847) 475 - 6274

Trade only—custom bedding, pillows, cushions and slipcovers

Linda Gentry is a true couturier of home fashion. She turned her talents toward home six years ago, following extensive training and experience in haute couture women's apparel. The move resulted in what Chicago interior designers agree are "extraordinary" custom duvets, comforters, bed skirts, pillows, slipcovers and other fabric accessories for their residential clients. Not surprisingly, she calls her work "couture sewing for the home," and clients note that it is replete with dress-maker detailing. She uses unusual and luxurious fabrics, such as silk, mohair and blends of metallic threads, in styles that range from sleek contemporary to ornate 19th-century designs.

Because she is the sole practitioner at Atelier Gentry, the volume is limited, although clients say she turns projects around in reasonable time. Designers tell us she keeps their most demanding clients happy and stands behind her work, and they credit her with a combination of artistry, dedicated craftsmanship and professionalism.

"Linda is so professional, she makes everything just right." "No matter who you talk to, they'll say she is wonderful." "The work is as good as anyone could do in America." "She's a one-person operation specializing in the finest detailing and she's fantastic."

B&D Custom Upholsterers 4 4 4 4
52 East 107th Street, Chicago, IL 60628
(773) 785 - 8766

Retail—custom upholstery

This is an easy-going, one-man operation that has been offering custom upholstery retail to both residential and commercial clients for the past 35 years. This professional works in all furniture styles, including antiques, and will also make slipcovers and upholstered headboards, walls and ceilings.

Quality	Cost	Value	Recommend?
	+	$	◆	★

Baird's Decorating Service 4 4 4 5

310 South Racine Avenue, Suite 500, Chicago, IL 60607
(312) 226 - 3300

Trade only—custom window treatments and upholstery

Recommended highly for its custom window treatments and cornices, this firm also provides excellent custom upholstery. Working exclusively with the trade, the workshop is able to draw up its own plans or follow those that the designers provide. With about 15 craftsmen working for this 45-year-old firm, all projects are handled in its own workroom. The company also reupholsters furniture.

"I cannot say enough about them—I use them all the time."

Brusic Rose 4.5 3.5 4.5 4.5

2201 South Union Street, 3rd Floor, Chicago, IL 60616
(312) 733 - 6868

Trade only—custom upholstery

Discerning Brusic Rose has one of the finest reputations in Chicago for offering exceptional quality and service, at a fair price. Now in its third generation of serving Chicago's interior design trade, the family-owned firm with 35 employees takes custom upholstery seriously. It makes custom pieces of its own design, ranging from traditional to contemporary, which are on display in its showroom. In addition, the company manufactures pieces according to a wide array of interior designers' specifications and even produces full lines for these clients. The staff draws on its long-time experience in seating to advise clients on comfort improvements. In return, clients praise Brusic Rose's attention to detail and ability to tackle anything that needs fixing. They also applaud the company's hands-on attention and friendliness.

"Very accommodating." "Their sofas are so lush, you just want to jump into them." "They do almost everything of ours—the product is great." "One of the absolute best."

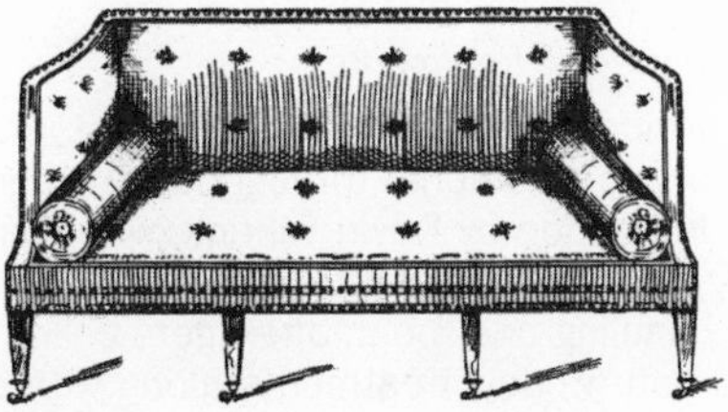

Cinematronix

424 North Oakley Boulevard, Chicago, IL 60612
(312) 243 - 2009 www.cinematronix.com

Trade only—custom upholstery and design of home theaters

See Cinematronix's full report under the heading Audio/Video Design & Installation

Dennis Drummer Drapery Service 3 2.5 4 4.5

1425 Lake Street, Evanston, IL 60201
(847) 869 - 8459

Retail and trade—custom window treatments and reupholstery

Over the past 27 years, the soft Louisiana drawl and good taste of Dennis Drummer have earned him recognition among interior designers and the occasional retail customer for technical expertise and craftsmanship with window

+	$	◆	★

treatments. He supplies the range of styles, from complicated draperies with fancy swags to shades and blinds, but is particularly strong, clients say, with straight draperies. They praise his versatility, attention to service and pleasant manner. Drummer also does reupholstering. He serves the North Shore and all of Chicago.

"I've never had a problem in 20 years of working with Dennis. He's incredibly reliable." "His draperies are wonderful—I use him all the time." "Better than most truly expensive people." "He can make exactly what you want." "He knows how to make people happy."

Drape Master 3.5 3.5 3.5 4
4518 North Kedzie Avenue, Chicago, IL 60625
(773) 539 - 8010
Retail and trade—custom window treatments

Drape Master offers the full range of soft window treatments and combines hard and soft elements, including valances. The company has a showroom, and its staff also travels to homes to measure and install. The family-owned business has been working with Chicago decorators and residents for the past 50 years and continues to get high marks and referrals from its customers.

Famous Home Furnishings Upholstery Co. 📁 📁 📁 📁
2913 North Cicero Avenue, Chicago, IL 60641
(773) 725 - 3900
Retail and trade—custom upholstery

With a network of 10 workrooms, this upholstery company's fame rests in its capacity for handling a wide range of custom projects. Its work encompasses all furniture styles, including antiques. The company also offers reupholstery and has been in business for 75 years.

G&W Window Treatments 3.5 3 4 5
167 North Racine Avenue, Suite L1C, Chicago, IL 60607
(312) 432 - 9380
Retail and trade—custom window treatments

Known for high-end window treatments and bedding, G&W has provided styles from contemporary to traditional throughout Chicago since the 1940s. The family-owned firm is headed by David Gibrick, who works with both retail trade and interior designers. He provides the former with fabric and color recommendations and, after handling one room, often gets called back for more. G&W handles both hard and soft window treatments along with combinations of both. Designers give the company good marks for service and describe Gibrick as reliable, reasonably fast and efficient.

"I was very pleased—people come into my house and notice the drapery right away." "They do all my clients' window treatments—bed linens, too." "One item was delayed and they called right away and kept me posted."

Guzman Upholstery and Repair 📁 📁 📁 📁
2451 North Pulaski Road, Chicago, IL 60639
(773) 278 - 9832
Retail and trade—reupholstery and repair

Hehn Custom Upholstery 3.5 2.5 4.5 5
2821 West Howard Street, Chicago, IL 60645
(773) 274 - 7665
Retail and trade—custom upholstery

Two generations of experience have made Hehn a staple resource for quality upholstering at reasonable prices throughout Chicago. We are told the workmanship is meticulous and that principal Guenther Hehn can handle any design or style. Turnaround time is considered reasonable. The company also upholsters headboards, and in addition, reupholsters and makes table skirts and pillows.

"As a designer in Chicago, I think they're wonderful. They do all my upholstering of furniture and I can rely on them." "Reliable—do whatever it takes to get it finished." "The nicest guys around."

Illinois Window Shade Company — 3.5 | 3.5 | 3.5 | 4

6250 North Broadway Street, Chicago, IL 60660
(773) 743 - 6025

Retail—custom window treatments

Indecor

5009 North Winthrop Avenue, Chicago, IL 60640
(773) 561 - 7670

Retail and trade—custom upholstery and window treatments

Interior Crafts — 4 | 3 | 4.5 | 4

222 Merchandise Mart, Suite 614, Chicago, IL 60654
(312) 943 - 3384

Trade only—custom upholstery, furniture and restoration

This company produces top quality in quantity. In addition to its custom upholstery for the upper end of the market, Interior Crafts makes furniture, including case goods, from its own designs and those of its interior designer clients. The company also makes antique French and Art Deco reproductions. The furniture frames are custom made of the highest quality materials. The company has 200 employees, multiple workrooms and more than 50 years of experience, all of which contribute to its reputation for reliable and consistent quality. Interior Crafts does not handle window treatments.

Interior Dynamics — 5 | 4.5 | 4.5 | 4

1802 South Canal Street, Chicago, IL 60616
(312) 243 - 4080

Trade only—custom upholstery and reupholstery

Among the top of its class, the reputation of this upholsterer is enough to recommend it to anyone who can afford its prices. The owner received his training at Parenteau Studios (see review), where he is said to have learned his craft superbly. Interior Dynamics's reputation and expertise result in a backlog of work, delays and a discriminating approach to clientele. While many interior designers consider it price-prohibitive for large projects, many use the firm for the public rooms. All agree, however, that the firm's work is of the highest quality and that its mastery of both upholstering and reupholstering is highly desirable.

"Amazing! It's the real thing—extremely breathtaking." "I do such volume in my projects, that it is not reasonable to use for everything." "You have to have a million dollars worth of patience to wait that long." "Meticulous work, and the attention to detail is astounding." "I would not consider anyone else for pieces with fine fabrics."

Jonas Upholstery — 5 | 5 | 4 | 4

44 West 18th Street, New York, NY 10011
(212) 691 - 2777

Trade only—custom upholstery and window treatments

Don't let the area code fool you. Although this upholsterer is based in New York, the trade-only firm, known for its high quality materials and careful craftsmanship, attracts business from interior designers throughout the country. Jonas is a favorite among many top interior designers who credit the firm with personalized service, a sophisticated approach and good timing in addition to outstanding quality. These clients consider the combination of quality and service worth the very high prices. While the vast majority of Chicagoans feel that it is unnecessary to go out of state, clients argue that, in some areas of expertise, the best can be found nowhere else.

"All it takes is three words and you are done." "You can't find quality like that anywhere else."

Kessler Drapery Studio **4** **2.5** **4.5** **5**
440 North Wells Street, Chicago, IL 60610
(312) 337 - 4198

Retail and trade—custom window treatments

This high-end custom drapery company is credited for its good value as well as its high quality craftsmanship. One client vouched for Ann Kessler's ability by reporting that all projects, even "bizarre" designs, are delivered in good time without a flaw. However, others say Kessler is strongest on smaller, less complicated projects. Kessler's reputation for soft window treatments and other work, such as pillows and bedding at good prices, keeps customers coming back and leads to referrals. Kessler, whose grandmother founded the business, also does some textile design, including painting on silk and fabric dying. We're told that many movie crews call on Kessler for their sets.

"There is no question of the quality." "Least expensive in the city for the quality that you get." "I always choose Ann; I've even used her in my own home." "Her great drapes are only matched by her great personality." "Good quality—had problems with installation but not anymore."

Les Tissus Colbert
207 West State Street, Geneva, IL 60134
(630) 232 - 9946 www.lestissuscolbert.com

Retail and trade—custom upholstery and window treatments

This eight-year-old transplant from Europe, where there are thirty Les Tissus Colbert home design stores, is the only one in the United States. Les Tissus Colbert specializes in European-style work, rendered in exclusive fabrics from France, Belgium and England. The company sells furniture, furnishings and fabric in addition to its upholstery service on new and antique pieces. In window treatments, Les Tissus Colbert is best known for an abundance of sashes, swags and looks with plenty of flair.

Ludwig Interiors **4** **3.5** **4.5** **4**
4634 North Lincoln Avenue, Chicago, IL 60625
(773) 989 - 1005

Retail and trade—custom window treatments

Owner Cornell Erdbeer has redirected the company that was founded by his father, primarily for upholstery, toward high-end custom window treatments. In the process, Ludwig Interiors gained a reputation for excellent quality among Chicago homeowners and interior designers. Ludwig offers complete service, including exclusive, custom drapery hardware, motorized window treatments and upholstered walls. References report that the firm is not always as fast as they would like, but agree that the high-end quality product is worth the wait.

Marshall Koral Pro Furniture Service
3148 A West Lake Avenue, Glen View, IL 60618
(847) 998 - 1355

Antique furniture restoration

See Marshall Koral Pro Furniture Service's full report under the heading Furniture Repair & Refinishing

Mastercraft Furniture Refinishing Co
3140 West Chicago Avenue, Chicago, IL 60622
(773) 722 - 5730

Retail and trade—furniture refinishing and custom upholstery

See Mastercraft Furniture Refinishing Co.'s full report under the heading Furniture Repair & Refinishing

O.G.Z. **4.5 3.5 5 5**
1313 West Randolph Street, Suite 322, Chicago, IL 60607
(312) 733 - 7476

Retail and trade—custom upholstery and furniture

Referred to as "our little secret" by a cadre of adoring clients, O.G.Z. specializes in creating high-end furniture from interior designers' sketches, including those scrawled on cocktail napkins. Principal Wiltold Zimmy, holder of a master's degree from the Technical University in Poland, drafts full-scale drawings and builds frames with dowels and counterblocks. Zimmy also has a reputation for decent pricing. The company has been in Chicago since 1993, and clients say, despite the firm's high level of craftsmanship, Zimmy keeps pricing within their preferred range.

"He can build anything." "Our design team is incredibly happy with them—they have saved us a few times." "Will do things quickly and on-site if necessary." "What a beautiful small shop. Wiltold's work is clean, simple and unbelievably reasonable."

Oakley Interiors **4.5 4 4.5 4.5**
424 North Oakley Boulevard, Chicago, IL 60612
(312) 243 - 4941

Trade only—custom upholstery and reupholstery of antiques

Oakley is a master of period work. The firm specializes in upholstering 18th- and 19th-century pieces using traditional techniques, such as eight-way, hand-tied coil springs, and materials, such as horsehair, down and jute webbing. The company will also restore and preserve old furniture frames and make furniture from interior designers' specifications. Some say, however, that they must provide very detailed drawings. Owner Jerry Chlopek was trained in Europe, and his excellent craftsmanship distinguishes Oakley from its Chicago-area competitors, according to many loyal clients.

Oakley shares a building with furniture restoration experts, Bernacki & Associates (see review), and with Cinematronix, which creates custom home theaters (see review). It often works with Cinematronix on seating for home theaters and antiques. Clients say Oakley is easy to work with and speedy in comparison with other firms.

"Their number is the first button on my speed dial." "Respectful and easy to work with." "Can create absolutely anything from a picture."

Parenteau Studios **5 4.5 3.5 4**
230 West Huron Street, Chicago, IL 60610
(312) 337 - 8015

Trade only—custom upholstery and window treatments

This company takes top-tier ranking. Many Chicago interior designers say this family-owned business sets the benchmark for quality upholstery in the area. It's not uncommon, for instance, for these discriminating clients to refer to other upholsterers as "not as good as Parenteau." The company's craftsmen are said to be very knowledgeable and detail-oriented. This trade-only firm offers high-end custom upholstery and window treatments, and also has expertise with antiques. Some designers who consider it the best also call it the most expensive. Despite a heavy workload which can lead to certain delays, many loyal customers continue to go back to Parenteau.

"The absolute best in Chicago, and as good as the finest worldwide." "Very easy to deal with—they understand what the finest means and all the details involved." "Slow—had to be on them constantly." "Their knowledge and expertise are unquestionably first rate." "The only ones I would trust with really fine antiques." "Best in Chicago." "They're incredible with window treatments. In an old, traditional estate, they can recreate draperies in their original grandeur—not a detail lost." "The Rolls Royce of upholstery."

Rosemark Designs **3** **3.5** **4** **4**
625 West University Drive, Arlington Heights, IL 60004
(847) 253 - 1106

Trade only—custom window treatments

Rosemark has made a mark with some nationally known high-end interior designers. The company specializes in custom soft window treatments in luxurious fabrics, offering "excellent detailing" that satisfies even the most demanding standards. The company's been in business for 30 years and has dressed the windows of many of Chicago's finest residences.

"Their work is gorgeous." "I can depend on it."

Steiger Custom Furniture Upholstery **4** **3** **4** **4.5**
2201 South Union Avenue, Chicago, IL 60616
(312) 738 - 1882

Retail and trade—custom upholstery and furniture finishing and repair

The strength of this mid-size shop is in the details. Since 1963, owner Emo Steiger has built and maintained a reputation for quality custom furniture and furniture restoration, including gold and silver leafing, as well as custom upholstery. We're told the firm excels on small projects and will increase its staff to manage larger ones, while still maintaining its high standards for quality. Steiger serves the North Shore and other Chicago neighborhoods, and customers say the staff is as easy to work with as it is talented.

"Their attention to detail is outstanding—Emo will do whatever is required to insure that a piece is well-done." "If there are any problems, they are right there to fix them." "Well worth the wait."

The Furniture Shop **4** **3** **4** **5**
1200 West 35th Street, Chicago, IL 60609
(773) 376 - 2525

Retail and trade—custom upholstery, furniture and restoration

References tell us The Furniture Shop offers an ideal match: craftsmanship plus reliability. The company makes custom furniture, including intricate pieces, from designers' specifications and will even produce prototypes. It's known for fair pricing and meeting deadlines in addition to good work. These characteristics, plus its experienced hand with high-end upholstery, led customers to tell us that Mark Roe and his staff always come through for them. While the firm works primarily with the trade and does not pursue private clients, it will work directly with individuals, and the crew is said to be very accommodating.

"Really easy to work with—Mark Roe is very serious about meeting deadlines." "They always come through for me." "They do all my custom work—you can give them a design and they can do it." "They go out into the field to see what's wrong and even occasionally help with delivery."

Vivo Upholstery **4.5** **4** **4.5** **5**
1528 West Adams Street, Chicago, IL 60607
(312) 226 - 7779

Trade only - custom upholstery and furniture

Viva la Vivo! Every decorator in Chicago seems to know that Al Vivo turns out great upholstered and reupholstered seating and creates top-notch custom designs. In addition to its work on antiques, the company also reupholsters modern pieces for clients such as Knoll and is recognized for its versatility. When people ask for a recommendation, the name Vivo is often at the top of the list.

Customers say they can expect a flawless result, even though they may have to wait for it. The company will take on projects of any size and complexity and it is always busy. For the past 20 years, the Vivo workmanship has won rave reviews from interior designers who serve the North Shore and all of Chicago. The company also has its own line of furniture on view in its showroom at the address above.

"Never ever have to send it back." "We use Vivo for everything—all other upholstery shops are headaches for us." "Needs a lot of time to complete, but only 10 minutes to look at and assess the job." "Vivo has the touch for down-filled cushions that look and feel luscious."

Weber Furniture Service
5915 North Ravenswood, Chicago, IL 60660
(773) 275 - 9061

Furniture repair, refinishing and custom upholstery

See Weber Furniture Service's full report under the heading Furniture Repair & Refinishing

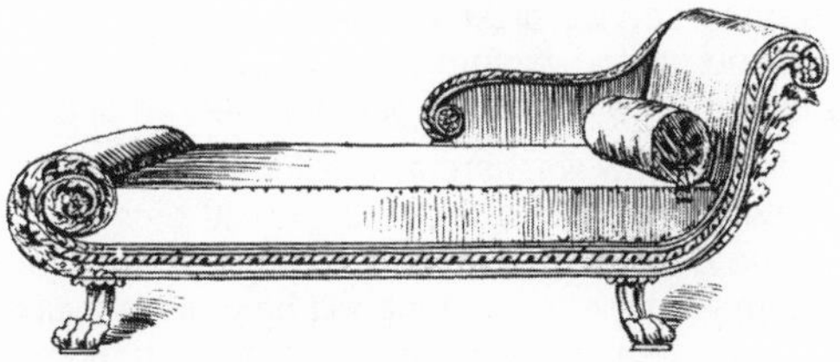

Workroom 2121 Inc.
2201 South Halsted Street, Chicago IL 60608
(312) 432 - 0737

Trade only—high-end custom upholstery

Zirlin Interiors 5 4 5 5
5540 North Broadway Street, Chicago, IL 60640
(773) 334 - 5530

Trade only—custom window treatments

Chicago's best dressed windows are draped by Zirlin. This is where many of the city's top interior designers go for stand-out custom window coverings. Known for highly decorative soft draperies and motorized window treatments, the expansive Zirlin workroom is always busy and in demand. While clients offer universal praise for its outstanding workmanship, some complain that the firm is too booked. After delivery, however, we understand that if any issues arise, Zirlin fixes it right away. Other references credit owners Ted, Paul and Glenn Zirlin for their vast experience, creative talents and thoughtful design suggestions. Zirlin Interiors has been in business here for 50 years.

"Zirlin is extraordinary with curtains." "Paul Zirlin is fabulous and easy, though not all clients understand the technical quality he brings to the job." "Zirlin is really responsive—probably less available than some, due to their huge popularity." "As a small decorator, I found them to be too busy so I stopped using them." "Paul is one of the sweetest men on earth and everything is so beautiful!" "He knows instinctively what I want."

Hiring a Window Washer

Everyone just adores a magnificent view, and keeping the sites crystal clear in the beautiful edifices in and around Chicago requires upkeep from professional window cleaners. Window washing may seem like a straightforward project, but because city buildings and suburban houses come in a variety of shapes, sizes and conditions, there are many variables for your service provider to deal with. You'll want to review your situation with the cleaning service before he or she shows up to do the actual cleaning.

Do Your Homework

Before contacting any window washers, you should note some facts about your windows. How many do you have? Are they storm windows or just regular ones? Do they have window guards? How many have grates? Are there panes? How many? Do the windows open in, slide up and down, tip out? Are they old or new? Are they dirty enough that they'll need to be power-washed or scraped? Does your building have hooks outside the window to which the washer can connect himself and his equipment? If so, are they all intact? Taking these factors into consideration, the service provider should give you a rough "guestimate" over the phone. If you omit any information, the work may end up costing more than the original quote once they come visit for the formal estimate.

It's customary for window washers to provide a free estimate, but you may want to confirm this on the phone with the service provider, too. Once they inspect the job to be done, they should be able to provide you with a written estimate. Getting the estimate in writing will help prevent unexpected charges later. For example, the service provider could claim that the job was more involved than expected, and try to charge a higher fee after the work is done.

What Should I Expect?

You'll also want to ask the service provider a few questions before signing any contracts. Inquire about the length of time they have been in business (the longer, the better), where most of their customers are located and whether they can provide references. The references will help you get an idea of how reliable they are: how long it takes to schedule an appointment, whether they get the work done on time and thoroughly, whether they clean up after themselves. We discovered that the window washers we listed didn't vary enormously; you might have to wait longer for an appointment with one company than another, but they all received good reviews from customers.

Be sure that your service provider is fully insured and can show proof of worker's compensation and liability insurance. If they do not have this coverage, you may be responsible for any accidents that happen on your property. There is no specific license or certification for window cleaning companies other than filing to operate as a business with the Department of Labor.

On Cost

There are three general methods of pricing: per window, per job or per hour with an estimate of the time necessary to complete the job. In addition, some companies have minimums and/or charge for estimates. The most common method of pricing is a basic rate per window that is usually based on window size. It is a good idea to inquire about a discount if you have a larger job (20 or more windows), as many vendors will negotiate a better price if there is a substantial amount of work to be done. For a basic 6-over-6 window (a window that has two frames that slide up or down, each with six separate panes) with no window guards, paint or unusual amounts of dirt, you can expect a price range from $4 to $15 per window, with the majority of vendors charging $8 to $10. Most of Chicago's homes have storm windows and a window washer may charge from $10 to 20 to clean a storm window inside and out.

Preparing for Window-Washing Day

Once you have set up an appointment, clear a path to the windows to prevent mishaps. Move that antique table with the priceless lamp. Clear objects that may obstruct access from sills and benches. Draw back your curtains and window treatments. Most service providers will show the utmost respect for your home and will protect your carpets and walls from drips and spills. If it makes you more comfortable, schedule free time for yourself on window-washing day so you can keep an eye on the process.

Cleaning Calendar

A professional window cleaning twice a year is usually sufficient, but if your residence is particularly exposed to the elements of city life you may need cleaning more often. Spring and fall are generally the busiest times of the year for this industry: an early spring cleaning will remove any dirt and grime left by winter rains, snow and frost, and a scrub in the fall will wash away spring and summer's pollen, bugs and dirt. Be sure to call well in advance if you want your windows cleaned at peak times.

Something Extra

Window cleaners often offer a variety of other services, from cleaning screens and blinds to waxing and sanding floors. They might pressure-wash canopies, awnings, sidewalks, garages and greenhouses; do heavy-duty cleaning of gutters, carpets, upholstery and appliances; some do basic handyman services, house painting, and clean-up after renovations. If you are pleased with the company, you may have another project for them to do. Now that you can see through your windows again, you might notice all kinds of things.

Tips for Washing Windows Between Professional Service Calls

- Never wash windows in the bright sunlight. They'll dry too fast and carry a streaky residue.
- Use a squeegee instead of paper towels.
- For best results, skip the store-bought spray cleaner and use a mixture of one cup white vinegar diluted in a gallon of warm water.
- Sponge the cleaning solution onto the window with a sponge, then drag the squeegee across the glass. Wipe the squeegee blade with a damp cloth after each swipe.
- For extra shine, rub window glass with a clean blackboard eraser after cleaning.
- If you absolutely *don't* do windows, share these tips with your housekeeper.

Window Washers

Ace Window Cleaning **3.5** **2.5** **4.5** **4.5**
3846 North Whipple, Chicago, IL 60618
(773) 478 - 0744

Residential and commercial window cleaning

Ace is trump with clients who appreciate efficient service and moderate pricing. It's a family-run business that has been serving the Chicago metropolitan area for three years. It does both residential and commercial work and also offers such additional services as power washing and gutter cleaning.

Active Window **4** **2** **4** **4**
5504 South Brainard Avenue, Countryside, IL 60525
(708) 352 - 9648

Residential and commercial window cleaning

Active Window, noted for its reasonable pricing, has been brightening the outlook at residences and commercial buildings throughout Chicago and the nearby suburbs since the 1930s. It has a loyal clientele of long-time users. Estimates are free, and Active charges by the job, not the window.

American Window Washing Company
5345 West Berteau, Chicago, IL 60641
(773) 282 - 3711

Residential and commercial window cleaning

Anchor Building Service Co.
3030 West Chicago Avenue, Chicago, IL 60622
(773) 533 - 3030

Residential and commercial window cleaning

Since it first set sail in 1922, Anchor's been polishing residential and commercial windows in downtown Chicago and the suburbs without dropping an oar. The company is also said to do an excellent job in power washing, carpet cleaning and lawn care. Anchor charges by the hour and gives free estimates.

Apollo Window Cleaning **4.5** **2.5** **5** **4.5**
3406 North Oleander Street, Chicago, IL 60634
(773) 637 - 0906

Residential and commercial window cleaning

After 43 years, Apollo continues to put its handsome shine on windows in the Chicago suburbs' residential and commercial buildings. It's also still a family-run business, and clients say reasonable, flat-rate pricing and efficient service account for Apollo's enduring success.

"They care, they clean with no fuss."

	Quality	Cost	Value	Recommend?
Avalon Window Cleaning and Building Maintenance	**3.5**	**2.5**	**4**	**5**

3115 North Kenmore Avenue, Chicago, IL 60657
(773) 281 - 1557

Residential and commercial window cleaning

The Avalon staff is known for its consideration of clients. We are told workers complete projects efficiently, clean up afterwards, then travel on. For 50 years Avalon has been washing windows at residences and commercial buildings in downtown Chicago. It also offers power washing and gutter cleaning, and customers appreciate its flat-rate pricing.

Azul Window Washing Corp.
4617 North Damen, Chicago, IL 60625
(888) 388 - 2985

Residential and commercial window cleaning

	Quality	Cost	Value	Recommend?
Campbell's Cleaning Service	**4**	**2.5**	**4**	**4**

4528 North Milwaukee, Chicago, IL 60641
(773) 282 - 4162

Residential and commercial window cleaning

Campbell's cleans windows at private homes and commercial buildings up to three stories high. It also offers gutter cleaning, power washing and janitorial services and has been in business since 1989.

	Quality	Cost	Value	Recommend?
CD City Cleaners	**4**	**2.5**	**5**	**4.5**

5707 West Windsor Avenue, Chicago, IL 60630
(847) 784 - 1000

Residential and commercial window cleaning

Clients enjoy much more than a new view from this small, young firm that is gaining a growing share of loyal clients. They say principal Robert Marzec gives personal attention to every job and are particularly pleased with the firm's efficiency, punctuality and very affordable rates. CD City works in residences and commercial buildings up to two stories, and also does power washing and gutter cleaning.

"They were great." "Love him. Recommended him to my neighbors, and they told me he didn't charge extra for additional work done on premises."

	Quality	Cost	Value	Recommend?
Central Greene Window Cleaning Company	**4**	**3**	**4.5**	**4.5**

P.O. Box 1442, Chicago, IL 60690
(773) 235 - 8039

Residential and commercial window cleaning

Over its 45 years of working for residential and commercial clients in Chicago's metropolitan and suburban neighborhoods, Central Greene has expanded by assuming the operation of additional window washing companies, including Associate and H & M (see review). References say the staff is punctual and does a good job, and the company has a healthy repeat business.

	Quality	Cost	Value	Recommend?
Dickerson Window Cleaning	**3**	**3**	**3**	**3**

1843 Bertau Avenue, Chicago, IL 60613
(773) 472 - 8455

Residential and commercial window cleaning

Gary Dickerson and his team work in the North Shore, downtown and Chicago suburbs, offering power washing and gutter cleaning in addition to window washing. The company has been in business for 18 years, and is open all year round.

H&M Window Cleaning and Building Maintenance **4** **3** **3** **5**

2430 West Augusta Boulevard, Chicago, IL 60622
(773) 486 - 8191

Residential and commercial window cleaning

Clients report that H&M is efficient, cooperative and quick to return phone calls. It has been serving metropolitan Chicago and the suburbs since 1976 and, although it was recently acquired by Central Greene (see review), the H&M staff and management will remain intact. The company also offers power washing, gutter cleaning and janitorial services. Estimates are provided for free.

Inviso Services **4.5** **2.5** **4.5** **5**

6N772 Tuscola Avenue, Saint Charles, IL 60174
(847) 695 - 5011 Inviso1@ameritech.net

Residential window cleaning, contracting and handyman services

Inviso outshines its competitors by tackling many troublesome tasks in addition to window washing. References cannot say enough good things about owners Judd and Dinna Nilles and their staff. Inviso's handyman services include power washing, gutter cleaning, plumbing and general contracting.

Clients praise the company's affordable prices and excellent service and say workers are punctual, "work like devils" and leave job sites clean. Inviso charges by the job and offers introductory discounts to new customers. Since 1986, it has expanded operations throughout The Loop, Chicago's upscale neighborhoods and suburbs and even into Wisconsin.

"A most enthusiastic couple!" "They do a wonderful job."

Morningstar Window Cleaning Company **4** **2** **5** **5**

P.O. Box 7076, Elgin, IL 60121-7076
(847) 750 - 1060

Residential and commercial window cleaning

For more than a decade, Morningstar has been improving the view for residential and commercial clients in metropolitan Chicago and nearby suburbs with what most say are moderate prices. It charges by the window and provides free estimates. It also does in-house screen repair, power washing and gutter cleaning. Clients give Morningstar good marks and the ultimate praise, repeat business.

Quality	Cost $	Value ◆	Recommend? ★

Mutual Window Cleaning Inc. 3 3 4.5 4.5
1722 West Grand Avenue, Chicago, IL 60622
(312) 243 - 4804 www.themutualcompanies.com
Residential and commercial window cleaning

Primarily a commercial window cleaning service that specializes in high-risk buildings, Mutual also serves some residential clients. It gives all clients free estimates and usually charges by the hour, adjusting estimates according to actual time spent. Our sources say Mutual's workers are punctual, polite and very thorough.

New City Window Cleaning 3 2.5 4 5
8130 Christeen Drive, Justice, IL 60458
(708) 594 - 1988
Residential and commercial window cleaning

Satisfied customers praise New City Window Cleaning's efficient and professional work and also appreciate its moderate pricing. The company works for residential and commercial clients and has been in business for 22 years.

"Clean. Professional. Efficient."

P&C Window Cleaning Services 4 2 5 5
3116 Elston Avenue, Chicago, IL 60618
(773) 463 - 3419
Residential window cleaning

Customers praise owners Phill and Carol Fastwolf for their efforts. After fifteen years as a professional window cleaner for other companies, Fastwolf enlisted his wife to form P&C, their own window cleaning business. The company serves both residential and commercial customers throughout the entire Chicago area. Clients say the Fastwolfs' team is punctual, neat and diligent, avoids disrupting clients while it works and cleans up after the job. We hear that this firm's rates are very reasonable.

"Does an excellent job."

Sidney's Services 5 2.5 5 5
725 North Skokie Highway, Lake Bluff, IL 60044
(847) 615 - 0800
Residential and commercial window cleaning

Sidney's Services was established by David "Sid" Gorter in 1980. Clients consistently credit the firm for window washers that are efficient, on time and very neat. Sidney's serves residential and commercial customers primarily around the North Shore area of Chicago. Window cleaning is charged by the job and no minimum is required. The company provides a free estimate.

Additional services from Sidney's include wallpaper installation and interior and exterior painting. It provides a free estimate that results in a flat fee which includes all prepwork.

The firm operates on a "one-stop shopping" principle, also offering landscaping, moving and hauling, snow plowing, valet service, hardwood flooring maintenance, handyman services, gutter cleaning, carpet cleaning and housekeeping services. In short, Sidney's lives up to this claim: It will do all the things around your home that you don't want to do, don't know how to do or don't have time to do. Clients extol the professionalism of the back office and the on-site workmen in all the service areas.

"I'd never expect such manners from my window washer." "These guys operate with the initiative of fine professionals." "They are a pleasure to work with." "They work like my dentist, calling in the spring for an annual window cleaning. I'm impressed."

Quality	Cost	Value	Recommend?
	✚	$	◆	★

Sparkling Window Cleaning Service

| | 4 | 2 | 5 | 5 |

6018 North Francisco Avenue, Chicago, IL 60659
(773) 973 - 1369

Residential and commercial window cleaning

The promise in Sparkling Window's name is fulfilled on the job, according to clients. Opened in 1999 by Robert Cummings, owner, it serves residential and commercial customers on Chicago's north side, downtown and in the western and northern suburbs. Estimates are free. Commercial jobs are charged by the hour and residential jobs, by the window. References say Cummings is personable, punctual and very efficient. The company is open year-round.

"Very thorough." "We will continue to use."

Sunshine Carpet and Window Cleaning Services

4 2.5 4.5 5

7655 West Ferragut Avenue, Chicago, IL 60656
(773) 594 - 1299

Residential and commercial window cleaning

Sunshine brings just that to the North Shore, Parkridge and other Chicago metropolitan and suburban areas. In addition to commercial and residential window cleaning, the company also cleans carpets and gutters. Estimates are free, and Sunshine usually charges by the window at rates that clients consider very reasonable. They also have high praise for owner, Paul Pistolarides, and say he is on time and efficient.

Taylor Window Cleaners

🗁 🗁 🗁 🗁

2421 West Pratt, Chicago, IL 60645
(773) 274 - 2689

Residential and commercial window cleaning

Taylor Window works primarily in Evanston and the north side. It has been in business for 30 years and serves commercial and residential customers. Estimates are free and charges are set per window. In addition to window cleaning, the company does power washing and cleans gutters and awnings.

A

B

C

M

N

O

P

R

THE FRANKLIN REPORT™

The Insider's Guide to Home Services

INSTRUCTIONS: To contribute to a service provider's review, fill out the form below and **fax** it back to us at **212-744-3546** or mail to 506 East 74th Street, Suite 1E, New York, NY 10021. Or you may complete a reference on our website, www.franklinreport.com. Please make sure that you give us a contact e-mail address and a phone number. While all information will remain anonymous, our editorial staff may need to reach you to confirm the information.

Thank you.

FILL-IN REFERENCE REPORT FORM

Client Name: ____________________

Client E-mail: ____________ Client Phone: ____________

Service Provider Company Name: ____________________

Company Contact: ____________ Company Phone: ____________

Service (i.e. plumbing): ____________________

Company Address: ____________________

PLEASE RATE THE PROVIDER ON EACH OF THE FOLLOWING:

QUALITY OF WORK: ❑ Highest Imaginable ❑ Outstanding ❑ High End ❑ Good ❑ Adequate ❑ Poor

COST: ❑ Over the Top ❑ Very Expensive ❑ Upper End ❑ Moderate ❑ Inexpensive ❑ Bargain

VALUE: ❑ Worth Every Penny ❑ Good Value ❑ Fair Deal ❑ Not Great ❑ Poor ❑ Unconscionable

RECOMMENDATION: ❑ My First and Only Choice ❑ On My Short List, Would Recommend to a Friend ❑ Very Satisfied, Might Hire Again ❑ Have Reservations ❑ Not Pleased, Would Not Hire Again ❑ Will Never Talk to Again

COMMENTS:

THE FRANKLIN REPORT™

The Insider's Guide to Home Services

INSTRUCTIONS: To contribute to a service provider's review, fill out the form below and **fax** it back to us at **212-744-3546** or mail to 506 East 74th Street, Suite 1E, New York, NY 10021. Or you may complete a reference on our website, www.franklinreport.com. Please make sure that you give us a contact e-mail address and a phone number. While all information will remain anonymous, our editorial staff may need to reach you to confirm the information.

Thank you.

FILL-IN REFERENCE REPORT FORM

Client Name: ____________________

Client E-mail: ____________________ Client Phone: ____________________

Service Provider Company Name: ____________________

Company Contact: ____________________ Company Phone: ____________________

Service (i.e. plumbing): ____________________

Company Address: ____________________

PLEASE RATE THE PROVIDER ON EACH OF THE FOLLOWING:

QUALITY OF WORK: ❑ Highest Imaginable ❑ Outstanding ❑ High End ❑ Good ❑ Adequate ❑ Poor

COST: ❑ Over the Top ❑ Very Expensive ❑ Upper End ❑ Moderate ❑ Inexpensive ❑ Bargain

VALUE: ❑ Worth Every Penny ❑ Good Value ❑ Fair Deal ❑ Not Great ❑ Poor ❑ Unconscionable

RECOMMENDATION: ❑ My First and Only Choice ❑ On My Short List, Would Recommend to a Friend ❑ Very Satisfied, Might Hire Again ❑ Have Reservations ❑ Not Pleased, Would Not Hire Again ❑ Will Never Talk to Again

COMMENTS:

____

____

____

____

____

____

____

____

____

THE FRANKLIN REPORT™

The Insider's Guide to Home Services

INSTRUCTIONS: To contribute to a service provider's review, fill out the form below and **fax** it back to us at **212-744-3546** or mail to 506 East 74th Street, Suite 1E, New York, NY 10021. Or you may complete a reference on our website, www.franklinreport.com. Please make sure that you give us a contact e-mail address and a phone number. While all information will remain anonymous, our editorial staff may need to reach you to confirm the information.

Thank you.

FILL-IN REFERENCE REPORT FORM

Client Name:

Client E-mail: Client Phone:

Service Provider Company Name:

Company Contact: Company Phone:

Service (i.e. plumbing):

Company Address:

PLEASE RATE THE PROVIDER ON EACH OF THE FOLLOWING:

QUALITY OF WORK: ❑ Highest Imaginable ❑ Outstanding ❑ High End ❑ Good ❑ Adequate ❑ Poor

COST: ❑ Over the Top ❑ Very Expensive ❑ Upper End ❑ Moderate ❑ Inexpensive ❑ Bargain

VALUE: ❑ Worth Every Penny ❑ Good Value ❑ Fair Deal ❑ Not Great ❑ Poor ❑ Unconscionable

RECOMMENDATION: ❑ My First and Only Choice ❑ On My Short List, Would Recommend to a Friend ❑ Very Satisfied, Might Hire Again ❑ Have Reservations ❑ Not Pleased, Would Not Hire Again ❑ Will Never Talk to Again

COMMENTS:

The Franklin Report™

The Insider's Guide to Home Services

INSTRUCTIONS: To contribute to a service provider's review, fill out the form below and **fax** it back to us at **212-744-3546** or mail to 506 East 74th Street, Suite 1E, New York, NY 10021. Or you may complete a reference on our website, www.franklinreport.com. Please make sure that you give us a contact e-mail address and a phone number. While all information will remain anonymous, our editorial staff may need to reach you to confirm the information.

Thank you.

Fill-in Reference Report Form

Client Name: ______________________________

Client E-mail: ______________ Client Phone: ______________

Service Provider Company Name: ______________________________

Company Contact: ______________ Company Phone: ______________

Service (i.e. plumbing): ______________________________

Company Address: ______________________________

Please Rate the Provider on Each of the Following:

QUALITY OF WORK: ❑ Highest Imaginable ❑ Outstanding ❑ High End ❑ Good ❑ Adequate ❑ Poor

COST: ❑ Over the Top ❑ Very Expensive ❑ Upper End ❑ Moderate ❑ Inexpensive ❑ Bargain

VALUE: ❑ Worth Every Penny ❑ Good Value ❑ Fair Deal ❑ Not Great ❑ Poor ❑ Unconscionable

RECOMMENDATION: ❑ My First and Only Choice ❑ On My Short List, Would Recommend to a Friend ❑ Very Satisfied, Might Hire Again ❑ Have Reservations ❑ Not Pleased, Would Not Hire Again ❑ Will Never Talk to Again

COMMENTS:

____

____

____

____

____

____

____

____

____

THE FRANKLIN REPORT™

The Insider's Guide to Home Services

INSTRUCTIONS: To contribute to a service provider's review, fill out the form below and **fax** it back to us at **212-744-3546** or mail to 506 East 74th Street, Suite 1E, New York, NY 10021. Or you may complete a reference on our website, www.franklinreport.com. Please make sure that you give us a contact e-mail address and a phone number. While all information will remain anonymous, our editorial staff may need to reach you to confirm the information.

Thank you.

FILL-IN REFERENCE REPORT FORM

Client Name: ____________________

Client E-mail: ____________________ Client Phone: ____________________

Service Provider Company Name: ____________________

Company Contact: ____________________ Company Phone: ____________________

Service (i.e. plumbing): ____________________

Company Address: ____________________

PLEASE RATE THE PROVIDER ON EACH OF THE FOLLOWING:

QUALITY OF WORK: ❑ Highest Imaginable ❑ Outstanding ❑ High End ❑ Good ❑ Adequate ❑ Poor

COST: ❑ Over the Top ❑ Very Expensive ❑ Upper End ❑ Moderate ❑ Inexpensive ❑ Bargain

VALUE: ❑ Worth Every Penny ❑ Good Value ❑ Fair Deal ❑ Not Great ❑ Poor ❑ Unconscionable

RECOMMENDATION: ❑ My First and Only Choice ❑ On My Short List, Would Recommend to a Friend ❑ Very Satisfied, Might Hire Again ❑ Have Reservations ❑ Not Pleased, Would Not Hire Again ❑ Will Never Talk to Again

COMMENTS:

Notes

Notes